CHIEFS, SCRIBES, AND ETHNOGRAPHERS

 THE WILLIAM & BETTYE NOWLIN SERIES
in Art, History, and Culture of the Western Hemisphere

CHIEFS, SCRIBES, AND ETHNOGRAPHERS
Kuna Culture from Inside and Out

JAMES HOWE

UNIVERSITY OF TEXAS PRESS, AUSTIN

COPYRIGHT © 2009 by the UNIVERSITY OF TEXAS PRESS

All rights reserved

Printed in the United States of America

First edition, 2009

Requests for permission to reproduce material from this work should be sent to:
 Permissions
 University of Texas Press
 P.O. Box 7819
 Austin, TX 78713-7819
 www.utexas.edu/utpress/about/bpermission.html

∞ The paper used in this book meets the minimum requirements of ANSI/NISO Z39.48-1992 (R1997) (Permanence of Paper).

LIBRARY OF CONGRESS CATALOGING-IN-PUBLICATION DATA

Howe, James, 1944–
 Chiefs, scribes, and ethnographers : Kuna culture from inside and out / James Howe. — 1st ed.
   p. cm. — (The William and Bettye Nowlin Series in Art, History, and Culture of the Western Hemisphere.)
 Includes bibliographical references and index.
 ISBN 978-0-292-72110-4 (cloth : alk. paper)
 1. Cuna Indians—Historiography. 2. Cuna Indians—Public opinion. 3. Cuna Indians—Social life and customs. 4. Ethnology—Panama—Authorship. 5. Indians in literature. 6. Indian anthropologists—Panama. 7. Participant observation—Panama. 8. Public opinion—Panama. I. Title.
 F1565.2.C8H688 2009
 305.897′83—dc22
                                                                2009013805

TO THE MEMORY OF:

RUBÉN PÉREZ KANTULE
AND
GUILLERMO HAYANS

CONTENTS

PREFACE ix

ACKNOWLEDGMENTS xiii

ONE   Introduction: Literacy, Representation, and Ethnography   1

TWO   A Flock of Birds: The Coming of Schools and Literacy   22

THREE   Letters of Complaint   45

FOUR   Representation and Reply   64

FIVE   North American Friends   88

SIX   The Swedish Partnership   117

SEVEN   Collaborative Ethnography   140

EIGHT	Post-Rebellion Ethnography, 1925–1950 164
NINE	The Ethnographic Boom, 1950– 190
TEN	Native Ethnography 214
ELEVEN	Chapin's Lament 245
NOTES	253
ABBREVIATIONS	279
BIBLIOGRAPHY	281
INDEX	321

PREFACE

Three episodes and three texts, all of them from past centuries, all precursors of the texts and events treated in this book: the first episode dates from the late seventeenth century, when British pirates were coming and going across the Darién, the easternmost and least settled region of Panama. In 1681, one of these adventurers, Lionel Wafer, was scorched by an accidental explosion, and his fellows, being pirates, left him behind to recuperate as best he could with their native guides. Before rejoining his vessel, Wafer spent four intense months with the Indians, and on returning to England, he wrote an absorbing account of his adventures (Wafer 1970), with vivid descriptions of the region and its native inhabitants, all of which received great attention even before the manuscript's publication in 1699.

A century and half later, in 1850, an American merchant captain named Jacob Dunham wrote a memoir of his trading voyages in Central America, which included several visits to the Coast of San Blas, the northern, Caribbean shore of the Darién. Some of the San Blas Indian "boys" were accustomed to shipping out on trading vessels, and on one voyage, Dunham took two men known to him as Billy and Campbell to New York. There a local doctor, whom Dunham had previously supplied with curiosities from his voyages, arranged for a public examination of the visitors, and after looking down their throats and examining their heads, the doctor opined that Billy and Campbell "belonged to the same species as those who inhabited the Sandwich Islands and a part of Asia" (Dunham 1850, 134–139). Afterwards, his students offered the boys a donation of eight dollars.

The third episode occurred two decades later. In July of 1870, the San Blas Indians, disturbed by recent incursions, dispatched a delegation to the capital of Colombia, which at the time governed Panama. Of the four delegates—who were named Yaginyanilele (also called José María), Balikwa (José Paulino), Guavia (Francisco), and Machigwa (Rosendo)[1]— Yaginyanilele died while on the journey in the city of Popoyán, and the other three did not reach Bogotá until the twenty-first of November, four months after setting out. On the twenty-second, however, they received an interview with the president of Colombia, and in short order the government drew up a comprehensive treaty establishing a native reserve called Tulenega, which means "Indian-land" in their own language. The agreement was set out in a publication entitled *Civilización de los indios Tules* (Estados Unidos 1871; see also Morales Gómez 1995), which also listed the Tule villages and their cash and subsistence crops, the eighteen chiefs who had sent off the delegation, and their grievances against outside intrusions.

The San Blas Indians, also known as Tule, also known as Kuna, inhabited a "contact zone" (Pratt 1992), a frontier area where multiple powers, interests, nations, and populations—Hispanic, Anglophone, and indigenous—met and interacted and struggled. It is clear from all three episodes that the zone's indigenous inhabitants held considerable fascination for Western outsiders. In the case of Campbell and Billy's New York adventure, nothing much seems to have come of the doctor's probing, but the other two encounters and the representations of the Indians that followed had serious repercussions. Lionel Wafer's account and its hopeful interpretations of Indian sovereignty and anti-Spanish sentiment encouraged Scotland to attempt a colony on the San Blas shore (Gallup-Díaz 2004, 77–116). The colony's almost instantaneous collapse in 1700–1701 had a shattering impact on the mother country, bringing on fiscal disaster, destruction of national hopes, the deaths of nearly two thousand colonists, and accelerated political union with England (Prebble 1968; Galbraith 2001). The Indians, too, drawn into confrontations between Scots and Spaniards and then caught up in regional turmoil and Spanish paranoia, suffered from the events set in motion by Wafer's account. Representations had consequences.

The 1870 encounter in Bogotá also suggests that the subjects of representation can, at least sometimes, anticipate those consequences and attempt to influence them. The Indian delegates obviously took pains to explain themselves—to name their leaders, villages, and crops, and to make sure their own names were written down and granted proper respect. Which, perhaps surprisingly, they were, to the extent that the territorial reserve received an indigenous name, and the document's title referred to Tule "Civilization," a word seldom accorded Indians in 1870. The subaltern, it seems, could speak.

Key elements from these episodes—mutually fascinated encounters between Westerners and Indians; the desire on one side to situate, record, and perhaps understand others, to reduce lives to text; and on the opposite side the insistence on making oneself understood and respected—all returned in force in the twentieth century, with the stakes raised even higher. The number of interested outsiders increased exponentially over the course of the century, including, eventually, professional outsiders, that is, anthropologists. The people being scrutinized, the Tule, or Kuna, of Panama, became aware of how often they were represented and misrepresented and how much images of Indians and discourses about civilization affected their treatment. The medium of representation, the written word, a white monopoly in 1900, gradually passed into the hands of the Indians, who used it to express their grievances, to answer scorn and mistreatment, and, within a few years, to record their own lives. The story, then, is of an extended ethnographic encounter, involving hundreds of active participants on both sides, an encounter still ongoing today as another century begins.

NOTES

1. I have changed some spellings to make names more compatible with the orthography used throughout this book.

ACKNOWLEDGMENTS

The people and institutions which at one time or another have supported the work published here cannot be encompassed in a few pages, not least because this book draws in considerable part on materials first collected for other purposes and other publications. Thus I can only say thank you, again, to everyone acknowledged more explicitly before (see Howe 1986, xv–xvi; 1998, vii–x), especially to the many colleagues and friends (epitomized by Mac Chapin, Olga Linares, and Joel Sherzer) whose friendship and support have spanned years and decades.

The research specific to this book was funded in part by small grants from the School of Humanities and Social Sciences at MIT, and by a grant (number GR6841) from the Wenner-Gren Foundation for Anthropological Research. Royalties from its publication will be divided between the Congreso General Kuna and the Congreso General de la Cultura Kuna.

As will become evident in Chapters 6 and 7, much here depends on research materials in Swedish, a language that at this stage in life I am entirely incapable of learning. Of necessity, I have depended completely on the helpful translations and paraphrases, intelligent explications, and unflagging patience offered by Karin Antoni and Tor Schoenmeyr in Cambridge, and by Bo Ernstson in Göteborg. My debt is especially deep to Bo Ernstson, who guided me through the collections at the Museum of World Culture (Världskulturmuseet) in Göteborg during a research visit in September 2002, and who generously shared some of the results of his own work on Erland Nordenskiöld. Thanks also to the directors and staff of the Museum, especially Magnus Dahlbring, for making my stay pleasant and productive.

In rendering sources from Spanish and French into English, I have relied for the most part on my own imperfect command of those languages. For more authoritative transcriptions and translations of some Spanish-language documents, however—in particular, several of the difficult unpublished letters excerpted in Chapters 2 and 3—I have called on the expert services of Ana Ríos Guardia.

For research since 1998, mostly in Panama, I am indebted in particular to the caciques and general secretaries of the Congreso General de la Cultura Kuna and the staff and researchers of the Congress's research arm, the Instituto Koskun Kalu; to the amiable archivists and other religious of the Claretian Order (in Vic, Spain, as well as in Panama); to directors and staff of the Archivos Ricardo J. Alfaro; to the descendants of Rubén Pérez Kantule; to friends and colleagues Jesús Alemancia, Cebaldo Inawinapi de León, Iguaniginape Kungiler, Arysteides Turpana Igwaigliginya, and Jorge Ventocilla; to Juana Carlota Cooke-Camargo for heroic struggles with the government bureaucracy; to colleagues and staff at the Smithsonian Tropical Research Institution; and to family and friends (especially Rodolfo Herrera, Ariel González, and Gonzalo Salcedo) in the village of Niatupu.

I owe most to three colleagues—Francisco Herrera, Mònica Martínez Mauri, and Bernal Kaibiler Castillo—who have offered unfailing encouragement, documents from their own collections, and most important, participation in a long-running and sometimes obsessive conversation about the manners and customs of Kuna scribes. In the case of Castillo, himself a leading scribe of his generation, the greatest part of our joint researches on his predecessors, which informs several chapters of the present work, is still to be published.

Over the last decade, many of the findings and arguments that have now reached their final home in this book were tried out first in a variety of fora, including the MIT Program in Science, Technology and Society (May 1996); the meetings of the American Anthropological Association, Washington, D.C. (November 1997); the National Museum of the American Indian, New York (March 1999); the conference of the Caribbean Studies Association, Panama (May 1999); el Congreso Centroamericano de Historia, Panamá (July 2002); the meetings of the American Society for Ethnohistory, Riverside, California (November 2003); two seminars at the University of Regina (March 2004); the International Congress of the

Latin American Studies Association, Las Vegas (October 2004); several presentations during a very pleasant week at la Universidad de Costa Rica (November 2005); the Museum of Man, San Diego (April 2006); and la Universidad Autónoma de Barcelona (October 2007).

The list of friends and colleagues cajoled into reading draft chapters or even the whole manuscript for this book has, I now see, grown alarmingly long. It includes Mac Chapin, Magnus Dahlbring, Bo Ernstson, Marta de Gerdes, Hugh Gusterson, Francisco Herrera, June Howe, Nicolas Howe, Judith Irvine, Jean Jackson, Olga Linares, Mònica Martínez Mauri, Lindsey Newbold, Joel Sherzer, Peter Wogan, and two anonymous readers for the University of Texas Press. There is little I can offer in my own defense for this imposition, except to note that, collectively and individually, these readers have greatly improved the final result, even when (as some may note with dismay) I have not always heeded their advice.

Last of all, and indeed long overdue, is an expression of gratitude and love for two Harvard University research institutions on which many non-Harvard scholars depend, Widener Library and the Tozzer Anthropological Library: I still feel the same awe on entering their stacks that I did more than forty-five years ago.

CHIEFS, SCRIBES, AND ETHNOGRAPHERS

Introduction

ONE *Literacy, Representation, and Ethnography*

The study offered here deals with one indigenous people, the San Blas Kuna of Panama, and in particular with three closely related aspects of Kuna engagement with the outside world: with writing and literacy; with representations of indigenous character and culture; and, most of all, with anthropology and its own characteristic form of textual representation, ethnography. Of necessity, I write as an outsider and an anthropologist, caught in the assumptions and practices of my discipline, and also as one of the book's subjects, one of many ethnographers who have written about the Kuna during the last century. I have tried, however, to position my listening post to narrate and make sense of this story as best I could from both inside and out: to treat writing as it was imposed, resisted, and ultimately accepted; to hear what outsiders had to say about the Kuna and what the Kuna had to say about themselves; and to situate writing and ethnography as both impositions and tools of self-knowledge and self-defense.

The Kuna, one of the most studied native societies of Latin America, have for centuries inhabited the Darién Isthmus, which today constitutes the eastern third of the Republic of Panama. Of the several regional Kuna populations, by far the largest, which has grown from roughly ten thousand at the beginning of the twentieth century to more than fifty thousand at its end, occupies four dozen villages scattered along the Caribbean shore on the Coast of San Blas (now officially known as Kuna Yala), most of those villages situated on small inshore coral islets. Supporting themselves with a mixture of subsistence agriculture, cash-cropping, wage labor, and artisanry, the Kuna have maintained an active village democracy, with elective chiefs and nightly council meetings (*onmaked*), which I call "gatherings," as well as an intense ritual life carried on by named specialists known collectively as "knowers of things" (*immar wisimalat*). At the same time that they have erected barriers between themselves and the world, the Kuna have crossed those barriers repeatedly to participate in the life of the country that claims them.

In November of 1903, when Panama gained its independence, the Kuna were finishing a century of benign inattention, an epoch of relative peace and isolation following two hundred years of war and struggle on the frontiers of the Spanish empire. As nominal citizens of Colombia, the Kuna engaged in cash-cropping and trade with merchant vessels but largely escaped effective national control. Subjects for centuries of commerce, diplomacy, war, missionization, and exploration, the Kuna of 1903 were still known to outsiders in terms of a few stereotyped words and traits, and no more than a handful of Indian men, all of them from a single village, could read or write.

All this changed drastically with Panamanian independence, beginning almost immediately. The struggles and convulsions that ensued, which reached a climax in 1925 with an uprising against Panama, formed the subject of my previous book, *A People Who Would Not Kneel* (Howe 1998, 2004b). The present study expands the temporal scope of that work to include the years after 1925, while at the same time narrowing its thematic range from indigenous-state politics in general to matters of discourse, representation, and media of communication—if indeed attention to such globally significant matters can be called narrowing.

In this book, the three topics of writing, representation, and ethnography overlap and interpenetrate, but in the world of theory they have generated large and only partly coterminous literatures notable for their contentiousness, which must be addressed. The reader should know what assumptions and studies have guided my work, why I fail to genuflect before certain altars, and how perhaps the Kuna case bears on the questions in play.

THE POLITICS OF LITERACY

The fundamental nature of writing, its relationship with oral communication, and its impact on thought and social life have engaged scholars across a broad range of disciplines. Recent work in anthropology and related fields has conventionally been sorted into two opposed camps or tendencies, both of which have their anthropological origin in an essay by Jack Goody and Ian Watt (1963), "The Consequences of Literacy," and in a volume edited by Goody, *Literacy in Traditional Societies* (1968). The so-called "autonomous model" (Street 1984; Collins and Blot 2003), or "literacy thesis" (Halverson 1991, 1992), associated with the work of David Olson (1994), Walter Ong (1982), and especially Goody (1986, 1987, 2000), treats the divide between orality and literacy in global terms, looking for the cognitive as well as organizational consequences of alphabetic writing. Proponents of the "situated," or "contextual," approach, often advanced in adamant opposition to the autonomous model, insist that writing and literacy, far from exerting universal effects, must always be understood in terms of their embedding in particular cultures and speech communities, each with its own complex mix of oral and written communication.

As much as I admire Goody's ambitious research program and regret the sometimes misguided criticism it has inspired, the present study belongs squarely in the contextualist camp. Like the contextualists (and like Goody in his own ethnographic explorations), I see writing as a social practice thoroughly enmeshed in webs of social and political relations. Like them, I will be concerned with the interplay between oral and written communication. And like them, I see writing as a practice and medium freighted with social meanings and implications for the identities of its users—and perhaps even more for its nonusers.

Writing and Struggle

Though many of the richest studies of schooling and literacy have been ethnographic, the present work follows another line of research from ethnohistory, one equally significant if so far less intensely theorized, which targets the role of writing in struggles between indigenous peoples and state and imperial powers. James Axtell's pathbreaking study, *The Invasion Within* (1985, 102–104), discussed the place of writing in the seventeenth-century evangelization of the Huron in New France largely in terms of Jesuit manipulation and Huron wonder and awe, an interpretation since critiqued by Peter Wogan (1994). More recent work has emphasized the extent to which colonized peoples have engaged with writing and attempted to neutralize or appropriate its power. James Merrell's fascinating study of eighteenth-century emissaries and mediators on the Pennsylvania frontier, for instance, describes extensive diplomatic use of letters by both colonists and Indians, often in conjunction with the beaded belts called wampum

(1999, 193–197, 215–221). Recognizing the power of the written word, Indians sometimes carried letters or decrees they could not read, but they were denied access to treaties and land titles, and when peace broke down irrevocably, few had yet learned to read or write.

A very different picture, of skillful, effective use of writing, emerges from Matthew Restall's study of the colonial Yucatec Maya (1997, 229–319). Village scribes produced documents in their own language, probably from public dictation and very likely drawing on preconquest scriptural traditions as well as a sixteenth-century Franciscan orthography. Among scribal documents, the most numerous were wills and other property records, which reveal a "masterful use of the Spanish legal system . . . to defend their lands" (1997, 234). Also significant were petitions combining professions of loyalty with complaints of suffering and expressions of "relentless hostility" against external authorities (1997, 266), and the books of Chilam Balam (1997, 276–292), mytho-historical histories validating land titles and the interests of indigenous elites.

The most dramatic and best-known story of indigenous success with writing is presented in William McLoughlin's magisterial *Cherokee Renascence in the New Republic* (1986). Early-nineteenth-century Cherokee leaders made unceasing use of letters, memorials, meeting records, and written laws to enlist white allies, denounce rivals and corrupt Indian agents, further indigenous nationalism, and counter proposals for dispossession and removal. Resisting encroachment in part by demonstrating the civilized nature of the Cherokee, a national council uniting conservative nativists with affluent progressives enacted a series of laws "that together constituted a political revolution" (1986, 284)—an example of what Philip Curtin (2000, 128–155) has called "defensive modernization"—and in the process its literate members perused national periodicals and state laws, published council legislation, and founded their own newspaper.

The modernizing program, in the few years before the Cherokee, however completely they had civilized themselves, were removed across the Mississippi, never resolved internal differences. Despite the extensive use of writing, all of it in English, bilinguals never constituted more than 15 percent of the population, literates 10 percent. In the early 1820s, however, after an illiterate man named George Gess, or Sequoyah, devised a syllabic writing system, "thousands of Cherokees were soon writing notes and letters to each other," helping them "tremendously in overcoming feelings of inferiority and self-doubt" (McLoughlin 1986, 351–352).

Elements from all three cases are readily apparent with the Kuna. Writing and schools initially provoked sharply mixed reactions: some illiterate but forward-looking parents embraced schooling for their children, while many conservatives objected strongly to the perceived threat to orality and gerontocracy. Among the handful of literates, some used their skills to gain power and displace their elders, while others were recruited and co-opted by illiterate chiefs. Kuna leaders bombarded the government with letters and petitions, and like the Cherokee, they eventually adopted written laws and meeting records, leading to a more formalized political system, a written constitution, and security for their lands. Most important in the present study, Kuna scribes recorded their own traditions, in an attempt to influence their representation to the outside world.

The Scriptural Economy

In indigenous-state struggles, writing is not just one more powerful technology like vulcanized rubber or repeating rifles, but a key medium, integral to state, colonial, and national systems, as well as to authoritative conceptions of civilization. Of all the different ways in which linguistic variation has been used to mark social difference,[1] the ability to communicate on paper or its lack has had special salience. Concerning Latin America, this understanding has been advanced most influentially by Angel Rama, who in *La ciudad letrada* (1996) argues that throughout the colonial era, literacy and its masters, the *letrados,* played a dominant role in the Spanish empire. "Servants of power, in one sense, the letrados became masters of power, in another" (1996, 24, 22). Just as literacy separated the urban minority from everyone else, mastery of elevated Spanish "crystallized a social hierarchy . . . marking a defensive perimeter between [elites and scribes] and the threatening lower classes" (1996, 33).

With independence from Spain, the "scriptural economy" (Collins and Blot 2003, 129), far from diminishing, grew in size and importance, as Latin American governments, like their counterparts elsewhere, called on schools and literacy to further nationalist sentiment and to create homogeneous populations speaking and writing the national language. If, as Hobsbawm argues, "the era from 1870 to 1914 was above all, in most European countries, the age of the primary school," Latin America was only a few years behind. As Hobsbawm also notes, however, state nationalism was "a double-edged strategy," alienating or rejecting "those who did not belong, or wish to belong, to the nation" (1987, 150). For marginal peoples like the Kuna, as the scriptural economy marked the external boundaries and internal hierarchies of the nation, language and literacy constituted not just "the means by which the battle is fought [but] the site of the battle itself" (Collins and Blot 2003, 131).

Writing and Mediation

Indigenous *letrados,* the first generations to read and write, have fascinated social scientists and historians, in part perhaps because they remind us of ourselves. The literature on these marginal actors does not always treat writing as a defining attribute of their practice, and literates and illiterates have sometimes played similar roles, but it is schooling that places most of them on the borders between social worlds. They have been categorized and conceptualized in a variety of ways—as go-betweens, cultural and political brokers, courtiers, *passeurs culturels,* or mediators, middlemen, new leaders, and intellectuals—each categorization promoting a different understanding of their nature and actions.

James Merrell's *Into the American Woods* (1999), mentioned above, shows that a motley collection of unlettered Indians and mostly literate colonists on the Pennsylvania frontier, recruited on an ad hoc basis and thrust into heated and sometimes intractable situations, succeeded nonetheless for years in keeping the frontier from erupting, typically while avidly pursuing their own private interests. F. G. Bailey's very different *Stratagems and Spoils* (1969, 167–182) analyzes "middlemen" as points of contact, not between clashing worlds, but between small encapsulated political units (in his examples, peasant villages in India) and the larger polities encompassing them. Like Merrell, Bailey emphasizes the moral ambiguity, deception, and difficult balancing acts inherent in the work of middlemen.

Between Worlds (1994), Frances Karttunen's absorbing portrait of nine indigenous "guides," "civil servants," and "native informants," while by no means neglecting politics or conquest, puts emphasis on translation and cultural mediation. Even more than Bailey and Merrell, Karttunen points to the marginalization and personal cost suffered by mediators, as well as the gratification and support some of them found in the wider world and the need some felt to explain themselves and their people in writing.

Concerning indigenous Latin American *letrados* of recent years, much recent work conceptualizes them as indigenous intellectuals and/or as a novel kind of leader in the "new politics of identity" (Brown 1993). As young literate men and women have attempted to create new movements and organizations, some of them specific to a particular ethnicity or region, others national or international in scope, anthropologists have watched closely, cheering on these new leaders but all too aware of their uncertain trajectory as they careen through an obstacle course set by multiple powers, constituencies, and discourses.[2]

Indigenous and subaltern *letrados,* when categorized as intellectuals, are most often analyzed from a perspective associated with Antonio Gramsci, concerned with the way in which so-called "organic intellectuals" produce the plans, demands, propaganda, and theory connected with political and social action, especially with nationalism and indigenous activism.[3] Despite an arguably superficial engagement on the part of his adherents with Gramsci's thought—few seem to have noticed or cared that he located organic intellectuals in the ranks of the Communist Party, or that he denied that peasants could analyze or critique their situation (Feierman 1990, 32, 18–19)—Gramscian perspectives and concerns have inspired notable work on subaltern intellectuals in Colombia (Rappaport 2005b), Guatemala (Warren 1998; Fischer 2001; and others), Mexico (Gutiérrez 1999; Lomnitz 2001), and elsewhere (Feierman 1990).

Throughout the present work, indigenous intellectuals, both literate scribes and the unlettered chiefs they served, are central characters (see also Martínez Mauri 2007). I am concerned with how the parties to this alliance represented themselves and their people in written communications with government functionaries; how, as mediators, culture brokers, and intellectuals, a number of them collaborated with foreign anthropologists; and how some came to write their own ethnography.

THE PROBLEMATICS OF CULTURAL REPRESENTATION

As a study of representation even more than of literacy, concerned with the ways in which insiders and outsiders have depicted the Kuna, this book enters a large and contentious field dominated by the figures of Said, Gramsci, and Foucault. These three preeminent theorists of our time, by focusing attention on the social and political work of discourse, the problematic nature of cultural representation, and the connections between power and knowledge, have effected a sea change in social thought. They have made it impossible to consider cultural discourses and representations divorced from either their political contexts or their impact on those they represent. Lamentably, they have also encouraged a monolithic, essentialized, and aprioristic understanding of discourse and ideology, in which questions about dominant ideologies and their effects are often prejudged rather than subjected to scrutiny.

Hegemony, Coherence, and Essentialism

One key question, concerning the degree to which dominant discourses are coherent, consistent, and unchallenged, was emphatically answered by Edward Said's epochal work, *Orientalism* (1978). More than sensitizing a whole generation of students and academics to the dangers and contradictions of alterity, to the ways in which Western discourses have essentialized and orientalized others, Said argued that a pervasive and comprehensive discourse about "The Orient" has proved so persistent and insidious, so invulnerable to experience or skepticism, that it governs "an entire field of study, imagination, and scholarly institutions—in such a way as to make its avoidance an intellectual and historical impossibility" (1978, 13–14, also 96). As numerous critics have pointed out, however, Said's claims for this discursive juggernaut, able to squash all doubt or contradiction in its path, could be maintained only through the same selectivity of which he accused others.

The essentialism, overgeneralization, and inattention to self-contradiction in *Orientalism* can also be found in many of the works using Gramsci's notion of hegemony—"the 'spontaneous' consent given by the great masses of the population to the general direction imposed on social life by the dominant fundamental group" (Gramsci 1971, 12)—a concept that comes to anthropology primarily through Raymond Williams (1977, 108–120) and John and Jean Comaroff (1991, 19–27). Although the content of hegemony—"signs and practices, relations and distinctions, images and epistemologies" (Comaroff and Comaroff 1991, 23)—is both broad and vague, there is general agreement, first, that, whatever it might consist of, hegemony is concerned with and constitutive of one group's domination of another, and second, that it is, by definition, naturalized, internalized, and taken for granted, even by the group it subordinates. According to the Comaroffs (1991, 24), ideology is voluble and noisy, while "hegemony, at its most effective, is mute," or as Sahlins (2002, 76) puts it less sympathetically, "Hegemony is supposed to determine not only what one thinks but also what one cannot think."

Despite Scott's powerful attack (1985, 1990) on the claim that subordinate groups accept their domination or that silence can be construed as consent, few enthusiasts of hegemony have faced up to the difficulty of demonstrating the universality and freedom from challenge or doubt that should characterize putatively hegemonic traits. The Comaroffs, to their credit, do recognize the problem, but their solution, that hegemony is "intrinsically unstable, always vulnerable" and that "the hegemonic portion of any dominant ideology may be greater or lesser" (1991, 27, 25), is a theoretical Band-Aid, which never makes clear how anything unstable, vulnerable, partial, challenged, and hard to locate can also be powerful and taken for granted.

The difficulties presented by notions like hegemony, orientalism, and "other terms from the same self-confident semantic family" (Burrow 2000, x) are empirical as well as theoretical, since they depend not just on tendentious text-reading but on spotty and selective sampling from whole universes of discourse—in Sahlins's pithy phrase, "hegemony is homogenizing" (Sahlins 2002, 20). Concerning the supposedly "'hegemonic voices of the West,'" J. H. Elliott notes (1995, 399), "in reality there are many voices, among the conquerors and conquered alike," while Sherry Smith (2000, 6), concerning early-twentieth-century popularizing authors, writes of "a cacophony of voices speaking about Indians."[4]

One might also wonder why more comment or concern has not been provoked by hegemony's family connections with false consciousness and delusion, or by its inherent condescension toward the poor and oppressed. As with false consciousness, part of hegemony's conceptual work is to explain why the revolution has not arrived, why subordinated groups fail to recognize their true interest in the way that we recognize it for them. As Kate Crehan makes clear, moreover, if Gramsci did not portray the consciousness of Italian peasants as absolutely false, he did find it incomplete, deficient, and badly in need of shaping by nonpeasant "organic" intellectuals like himself—an attitude understandable in a Marxist revolutionary in Fascist Italy, but much less so today (Crehan 2002; Feierman 1990, 18–20, 26).[5]

In the case considered in this book, I try to show that the dominant ideologies affecting the Kuna were sometimes stable and consistent (notably concerning the value of writing), but often displayed internal variation and disagreement and, over time, significant change. Higher and lower bureaucrats might agree on the inferiority of Indians but not on its implications; anti-indigenous polemics might be conditioned as much by the situation at hand as by enduring ideology; grudging admiration might sneak into philippics; subaltern groups might reject ideologies but not escape their pain; and what might seem like ineffectual gestures or imperial nostalgia could over time facilitate indigenous revindication.

Silenced Subalterns

The reverse side of hegemony is subaltern muting. A question posed by Gayatri Chakravorty Spivak (1988) in a famously opaque essay, "Can the Subaltern Speak?," was answered in a decisive negative—a denial not just of the presence but of the possibility of a subaltern counterdiscourse—which Spivak based almost entirely on theoretical grounds, through a critical reading of Foucault, Deleuze, Marx, and Derrida.[6] Her thesis, which, as Nicholas Thomas notes (1994, 56), reproduces "imperialism's own sense of its pervasive efficacy," has been emphatically and globally reasserted by John Beverley, a prominent member of the Latin American Subaltern Studies Group. "Spivak's notorious claim . . . is meant to underline the fact that if the subaltern could speak in a way that really *mattered* to us, that we would feel compelled to listen to, it would not be subaltern" (1999, 66), an argument whose circularity escapes him. For both Beverley and Spivak, the ultimate question is really whether a subaltern voice or consciousness can be identified or represented by the analyst, by the Spivaks and Beverleys of this world. A question about the subaltern, about "them," all too often ends up being about us.

The existence of subaltern voices and discourses, theorists to the contrary, is an empirical problem. Whether one hears them or finds them amenable to analysis does not affect whether words were uttered or written. A great deal of recent publication, brought out by subalterns as well as elites, shows that while Latin American peasants and Indians have regularly been silenced or denied access to schooling and the mass media, they have often had something to say, and that a surprising amount of subaltern discourse can be found if only one listens and looks (e.g., Rappaport 2005a, 2005b; Restall et al. 2005).[7]

Alterity, Othering, and Classification

One of Said's most influential ideas has it that orientalist discourses work by creating a spurious binary distinction between the Western self and a radically different and debased non-Western alter, a process now often referred to as "othering." This view, though no means universal (see Thomas 1994, 51–55), has been widely accepted (see Sax 1998; Rapport and Overing 2000). Cultural and ethnic distinctions are often treated as necessarily hierarchical and invidious, at least in the contemporary world. A related but much more nuanced position stresses distinctions, less between self and other than among non-Western others, a classificatory grid imposed on subject populations through such measures as maps, censuses, surveys, and reports.[8]

That colonial and orientalist discourses make invidious distinctions is in a rather obvious way undeniable. That colonial and national regimes control through classification is significant in nontrivial and suggestive ways. But cultural difference—between self and other, and between various sorts of other—is also real, in both superficial and fundamental senses, and its recognition is not in itself a crime (cf. Abu-Lughod 1991). The obvious objection is that the differences posited by ideology are often false, imaginary, or conducive to misinterpretation, exploitation, and abuse—all true. But no amount of guilty chest-beating or apriorist theory can prove that recognition of difference is by itself necessarily invidious, false, or controlling.

Exclusive emphasis on othering also obscures the complexity of national and colonial discourses and the extent to which they combine difference and similarity. Numerous writers have shown how Europeans contemplating New World peoples, while strongly asserting difference, also invoked resemblances with their own past and present (Elliott 1970; Grafton 1992; Pagden 1993): "their concern . . . was [often] directed to the finding not of otherness but of commonality" (Elliott 1995, 398). In a similar vein, Thomas Metcalf argues that in British colonial India there was "an enduring tension between two ideals, one of similarity and one of difference . . . At no time was the British vision of India ever formed by a single coherent set of ideas" (1995, x, 66). As later chapters will show, the same ambivalence and self-contradiction are evident in discourses about Kuna alterity.

It is also misleading to think that imperialism can only be constructed or rationalized on the basis of difference. Dominance and oppression, when they consist of making someone over—civilizing savages, reeducating the politically backward, turning heathens into Christians or Kulaks into collective farmers—depend on an assertion, explicit or implicit, of underlying similarity and mutability; an assertion, in effect, of the insubstantiality or ultimate irrelevance of difference.

In addition to alternate rationales, finally, colonization and domination can also have quite different styles, different culturally and situationally conditioned procedures and tendencies. The highly distinct style of the British Raj, as the very epitome of the classifying, bean-counting, distinction-making regime, had a great deal to do with the overwhelming ethnic and cultural complexity of nineteenth-century India, with the daunting task of dominating a subcontinent on the bureaucratic cheap, and with the "relentless need to count and classify everything . . . [that] defined much Victorian intellectual activity" (Metcalf 1995, 113). As we shall see, the Panamanian bureaucrats who tried to subdue and transform the Kuna, heirs to a radically different tradition, could not be bothered to study native customs, to count Indians accurately, or even to use their names: indigenous identities were to be blurred, ignored, muted, or suppressed rather than exhaustively studied and classified.

Power and Domination

Said insistently connects orientalist discourse to the exercise of power as precursor, rationalization, or constituent of imperialism, a manifestation of the West's sway over the Middle East. "Europe was always in a position of strength, not to say domination" (1978, 40, also 73)—a claim that blithely sweeps aside failed Western crusades, successful Ottoman conquests, and a seven-hundred-year Islamic occupation of Iberia. As Linda Colley points out, moreover (2002, 99–134), by locating the florescence of full-blown orientalism in the late eighteenth century, Said misses its development in the previous two hundred years during an era of Western fear and vulnerability.

Whether written from weakness or strength, comments on the Other, rather than unremittingly deprecatory, are surprisingly often mixed, ambivalent, and contradictory. Colley's close reading of a wide variety of British texts leads her to question "the extent to which Islam was regarded and treated as a uniquely different and degraded 'them', and also the degree to which Britons saw themselves as a unified, superior 'us'" (2002, 103). Karen Kupperman, similarly, finds in early British commentary on North America that "sometimes writers . . . [castigated] the Americans as primitive savages. But then again the very same writers turned and praised the Americans' vigor, simplicity, and primary virtue" (Kupperman 2000, 20; see also Pike 1992, 25–27, 31–34). Emma Teng (2004) finds the same mix of praise and criticism in Qing Chinese accounts of the aboriginal Taiwanese.

Some Westerners have gone beyond ambivalence to laud and defend subaltern peoples. As the example of several self-appointed friends of the Kuna will show, advocacy can be mixed with racism and condescension. As Thomas notes, moreover, "attractive and even sympathetic constructions of colonized peoples may admire or uphold them in a narrow or restrictive way" (1994, 54). But dismissing positive portrayals across the board as mere gestures or conceits—treating attacks as real and defense as illusory—obscures the sometimes positive effects of such representations over time. As Sherry Smith (2000, 14) argues concerning early-twentieth-century North American indigenist writers:

> To acknowledge that [popularizers] often failed to grasp the complexities of Indian peoples; that they often failed to transcend their own ethnocentric and even racist assumptions; and that . . . readers [today] might find their works sentimental, romantic, and simple-minded does nothing to negate their cultural power.

Some portrayals, moreover, have little to do with either domination or rescue, and everything to do with the situation of their authors. Philip Deloria's brilliant *Playing Indian* (1998) depicts generations of white North Americans dressing in feathers as a form of symbolic appropriation of perceived indigenous qualities such as freedom, authenticity, and a truly American identity. In the case of the Kuna, early-twentieth-century North American admirers, few of whom had ever visited San Blas, used them as abstract symbolic vehicles for their own preoccupations with racial boundaries, lost autonomy, and sexual threat.

Most generally, the notion of power itself, so widely invoked in contemporary social analysis as an all-purpose explanatory ether—or as Sahlins (2002, 20) puts it, "the intellectual black hole into which all kinds of cultural contents get sucked"—deserves more scrutiny than it receives. That some groups and individuals have vastly more power than others seems so blindingly obvious, and the concept of power so intuitively realistic and hardheaded, that we forget how theoretically and semantically complex power is (Pitkin 1972, 275–286) and how very difficult it can be to demonstrate its workings. Foucault's "poly-amorphous perverse" model (Sahlins 2002, 2) has in some ways usefully complicated understanding, but the neo-Foucauldian assumption that power and knowledge are so closely intertwined—indeed so nearly identical—that they can be routinely written as "power/knowledge" begs the questions it sets out to answer. We should be open to the possibility that not all of Foucault's epistemes are equally potent or monolithic, that power can be fractured, contradictory, and messy rather than smoothly controlling, and that even in the case of "great powers," you can't always get what you want.

Facts and Imaginaries

Another issue, closely related to those already discussed, concerns the role of "the imaginary," a term that has its origin in Benedict Anderson's *Imagined Communities* (1983), where it is integral to his argument that modern nationalism is based on units of such large scale that they can exist only as they are conceptualized or imagined by their members. The notion of the imaginary, influenced as much by Said (e.g., 1978, 71–72) as Anderson, has expanded and proliferated in works like Inden's *Imagining India* (1990) to suggest the creative power of the nationalist, racist, and colonialist imagination—its ability to conjure up and impose identities, essences, and fantasies regardless of uncomfortable or discordant facts, "to construct a world, geographic domain, or ethnic grouping in a comprehensive way, rather than merely express a particular perception of something that already existed" (Thomas 1994, 37). Studies of the eighteenth- and nineteenth-century Raj have in particular credited British colonial writers with imagining up a totalizing account of Indian society, a complete orientalist ethnography partly constituting the very institutions, such as caste and Hinduism, that it purported to discover (Inden 1990; Dirks 2001).

The notion of the imaginary has usefully focused attention on the often artificial and constructed nature of shared understandings about Others. But it can also obscure the extent to which ideologists begin and end with the known, with accepted "facts." Sati, foot-binding, the veil and the harem (and yes, the caste system and Hinduism) did not spring full-blown from the orientalist imagination: ideology did its work by interpreting and distorting these practices and inflating them with meaning, not by making them up out of whole cloth. In my own examination of the discourses articulated about the Kuna, I have been struck by how closely both friends and enemies usually stuck to the facts at hand, how much they imposed meanings on the Indians not through flights of fancy but through construal of such well-known characteristics as separatism and ethnic endogamy. Such interpretations can be just as biased, misleading, and mendacious as any fantasy, but they stay closer to the ground, and once elaborated, it is their alleged connections with experience and accepted knowledge that validate and reinvigorate them.

Ambivalence, Contradiction, and Mixed Messages

Social science, happily, is no more monolithic than what it studies. Ann Stoler and Frederick Cooper's influential introduction to *Tensions of Em-*

pire (1997) shook many prevailing "Manichean" colonial dichotomies, arguing that "the otherness of colonized persons was neither inherent nor stable" (1997, 7), and more generally, that "colonial states were often in the business of defining an order of things according to untenable principles that themselves undermined their ability to rule" (1997, 8). Nicholas Thomas, in the same vein, describes colonialism not as a "unitary project but a fractured one, riddled with contradictions and exhausted as much by its own internal debates as by the resistance of the colonized" (1994, 51). Such rifts and fractures are just as prevalent, moreover, in the programs and discourses of nationalism and internal colonialism in countries like Panama as they are in the high colonialism of the great nineteenth-century empires, and for that matter, in almost every cultural and social form.

THE REFLEXIVE STUDY OF ETHNOGRAPHY

Among different kinds of cultural representation, this book is concerned most of all with ethnography, sociocultural anthropology's endlessly problematic method of choice and, especially since the 1980s, the subject of its own agonized critical literature. I am concerned with ethnographic studies of a small-scale, non-Western society, a traditional, even old-fashioned, sort of subject population. At the turn of the twenty-first century, ethnographers are as likely to study financial traders, marine biologists, or drug dealers as they are peasants or indigenous peoples. Not so long ago, however, those peasants and "primitives" constituted anthropology's assigned subject matter, its raison d'être, and if we are to make sense of ethnography, whether as a process, a mode of inquiry, or a kind of social representation, we must attend to that past. Thus for the purposes of this book ethnography means accounts of the lifeways of non-Western peoples, mostly but not always written by Westerners, and the messy, problematic dialogues and collaborations from which they have emerged.

In terms of the scope of ethnography as written form, I have cast my net widely, drawing in travel books, magazine and newspaper articles, even letters, reports, fiction, poetry, and oral testimony—anything, so long as it attempts to portray a people's culture or character. The greatest attention goes to hard-core ethnography—professional and amateur nonfiction works based on co-residence, participant-observation, texts, conversations, and interviews—but I also attend to quasi-ethnographic forms of cultural representation at the borders of the genre, some of it by authors who never even saw their subjects.

Dialogue and Agency

Ethnography is in one way or another a collaborative enterprise, entirely dependent on conversations between investigator and investigated. The relationship between ethnographer and informant/consultant/assistant, typically extending across cultural and ethnic lines, has in recent years increasingly been seen as both significant and problematic (see, in particular, Roger Sanjek's fierce scolding of 1993). In response to such concerns, ethnographers have in recent decades searched for more overtly collaborative research practices and for new forms of writing aimed at preserving the dialogic or polyphonic nature of their research.

These laudable changes in the ethnographic present, which in a few short years have become the "disciplinary norm" (Spencer 2001, 450), have been paralleled by attempts, still incipient, to understand past ethnographic dialogues, with the goal not just of offering belated credit but of rethinking the whole enterprise. Some of the need is met by biographies of consultants and native intellectuals such as those by Karttunen mentioned above (1994),[9] but to my knowledge, the call for "a disciplinary history that paid . . . greater attention . . . to the role our informants play in the development of our ideas" (Herzfeld 2001, 9) has so far seldom been met (though see Darnell 2001).[10]

One reason these issues deserve attention is that "we begin to realize . . . that informants are engaged in theoretical practices" (Herzfeld 2001, 7; see also Clifford 1986, 117; Whiteley 1998, 13), that they bring their own perspectives, preoccupations, and agendas to the table, and that they join the ethnographic conversation in no small part because they understand "the connection between knowledge, ideas, and truth . . . and agency, power, and practice" (S. Smith 2000, 11). Here I examine one ethnographic tradition from two sides—assessing the agency and intellectual contribution of native informants and facilitators as well as their Western counterparts—and especially the articulation of the two.

Indeed, I argue that Kuna involvement in ethnography has been collective as well as individual, that in this case and probably others, communities, leadership networks, or whole polities can arrive at a rough consensus or even a conscious policy concerning ethnography and how to deal with it (see Murphy and Dingwall 2001, 344). Paul Sullivan's *Unfinished Conversations* (1989) recounts negotiations of Yucatec Maya with Sebastian Morley and Alfonso Villa Rojas concerning Villa's studies in their villages, though Maya leaders showed great interest in obtaining guns and next to none in revealing themselves to outsiders. At the opposite extreme, the Kwaio of Malaita long encouraged Roger Keesing's fieldwork in hopes that by recording their *kastom* he would bring them the power they perceived in writing and codified law (Keesing 1992). As Wellin and Fine put it (2001, 329), peoples like the Kwaio may "see the fieldworker as a tangible embodiment of the more abstract promise implicit in ethnography: that empathic understandings can matter in exposing and shaping realities." In the present day, indigenous groups in North and Latin America often have strong opinions and policies, positive and negative, about non-Indian scholars and their representations; quite a few, moreover, have embarked on their own ethnographic projects.

I am not the first, it should be said, to notice Kuna interest in their own representation. In *Mimesis and Alterity* (1993), a brilliant but exasperating work by Michael Taussig, he portrays the Kuna derisively as masterful colonial toadies, engaged in "a mimetic contract" with foreign explorers and anthropologists, "a set of largely unconscious complicities between the whites from the north and the Indians they are studying," and even more than that, "a positive connivance in Cuna men being mimetic with white men, and Cuna woman being alter" (1993, 162, 154). This characterization, strangely hostile as well as grossly unfair, nonetheless hits close to the mark: Kuna men and women have better things to do than connive at mimicry, and until the tourist boom of recent years, nothing they did could fairly be called self-marketing. But they have, for a much longer time, taken pains, not to sell but to represent themselves, mounting a sustained public-relations campaign to counter national anti-Indian prejudice. And the medium they seized on was ethnography.

Exclusion and Identification

Ethnographic representation, according to the politicized, reductionist claims that have taken hold in anthropology and critical theory, has throughout been an exercise in domination and deprecation, the creation of "a fantasized other easily digestible for Western colonialist and scientific consumption" (Rapport and Overing 2000, 10). As a key element in a general "process of exclusion" and a "strategy through which to disempower others" (2000, 13), ethnography has created its own object and placed it in an evolutionary past, thus denying the "coevality," modernity, and full humanity of non-Western others (Fabian 1983).

This widely accepted caricature, with just enough grounding in anthropology's colonial past to lend it superficial plausibility, depends on a relentless teleology and essentialism, and on an insistently ahistorical perspective from which no significant change is truly taken into account between the discipline's earliest beginnings and the moment (somewhere between the mid-1960s and the 1990s) when we all saw the light and repented. Like testimonials in an evangelical church, these confessions are filled with pride as well as guilt, and in their "wildly disproportionate sense of the efficacy" of theory and representation, such claims—characterized by Thomas (1997, 335) as "the megalomaniac pretensions of politicized scholarship and theory"—mask our deepest fear, which is not orientalism but irrelevance. The truth lies somewhere between our fears and hopes: ethnography can have real-world effects, some of them negative, but not all-powerful ones, and not necessarily those we predict or intend.

Among the ethnographic representations considered in this book, two of them do indeed place the Kuna in a retrograde barbaric past, but both were written by amateurs who took their cues from nineteenth-century diffusionism and evolutionism. Another set of representations attacked the Indians relentlessly and rationalized their domination, but these came from nonanthropologist bureaucrats with no interest in the lives of the dominated. Of the others, both amateur and professional, who wrote at length about the Kuna, almost all tried not just to describe their customs but to characterize them as a people in some fundamental way and to situate them in some larger narrative. These attempts inevitably reflected the dominant assumptions and ideas of their times, some of them racist, imperialist, assimilationist, ethnocentric, or naïvely romantic. But almost all of them showed sympathy and identification with their subjects, and far from remaining static, ethnographic narratives and portraits changed radically over the course of the twentieth century.

Indeed, I would argue that for many or most of the ethnographers considered here, like many others elsewhere, empathy, identification, and advocacy—in some cases a "possessive identification . . . analogous to the therapeutic relationship in psychoanalysis" (Wellin and Fine 2001, 326)— are more apparent than exclusion and othering. As Nicholas Thomas points out (1997, 334), the intimacy of fieldwork, the sense of indebtedness to those who help us, and a propensity to see oneself in others have "prompted ethnographers to adopt an affirmative attitude toward the people studied, even to write accounts of their culture . . . to some degree complicit in dominant local understandings."

For all the ethnographers, amateur and professional, considered in this book (myself included), their identification with the Kuna loomed large, not just in the field and, for the professionals, in their careers, but in the life histories and personae they presented to friends, family, and professional peers. They were not merely any old expatriate, priest, or academic, but Markham, our local expert on the San Blas; Gassó of the famous mission to the Caribe-Kunas; or Stout (Wassén, Sherzer, Howe), who wrote that book on those Indians in Panama. For all of them, "identity work and the (re)construction of the self [were] part and parcel of the ethnographic endeavour" (Atkinson et al. 2001, 324).

That being said, there can be no doubt that, here and elsewhere, the propensity to assume for oneself "the authority to define the essential elements and boundaries of [other] cultures" (S. Smith 2000, 9, 13), to characterize another in writing without chance of reply, necessarily creates a fundamental inequality. No matter the complicity in local understandings or the desire to present "the native point of view," it is an outsider's version of that point of view that is presented, and indeed, the more complete the attempt at ethnographic ventriloquism, the more problematic the representation. As Murphy and Dingwall note (2001, 341, 344), the greatest risk and the least power for those represented occur at the moment of publication, because whatever influence they can exert over the process, if any, has passed.

Here again, however, the story presented in this book is of change and indigenous agency, not stasis. As the Kuna recognized the potential impact of outsiders' characterizations, they latched onto friendly foreigners precisely to counter hostile misrepresentations already in circulation. Actively feeding material to visitors and anthropologists, and to the extent possible reviewing and correcting their work, when it came to publication they still had to trust to luck and their interlocutors' goodwill. Over time, however, they were able to control outsiders' access more systematically, to review what they had written, and by the end of the century to develop a cadre of their own anthropologists—one version of a story that has been repeated all over the world.

Single Subjects, Multiple Ethnographies

The present work follows in a short but useful analytical tradition devoted to the reflexive historical reexamination, not just of single classic ethnographies, but of a whole corpus of work on one society or region. This tradition, which can be traced back as far as James Boon's *Anthropological Romance of Bali* (1977), is as diverse as the scholars who have embraced it, though a strong tendency toward indicting as well as critiquing ethnographic predecessors is apparent (Gordon 1992; Apter 1999; Salemink 2003).

The approach adopted here has been shaped by several works in this tradition,[11] including, not least, Boon's supremely humanistic account and its dense, complex, sympathetic engagement with ethnographic texts and traditions, and by Jan Rus's "Rereading Tzotzil Ethnography" (2004), which deftly mixes appreciation for a collective ethnographic project with sharp criticism and close attention to the way the project was shaped and limited by its political context.

Also influential is the voluminous critical literature on the late-nineteenth- and early-twentieth-century ethnography of the North American Southwest and especially of the "Pueblo" Indians—archetypal primitives who were the destination and target for dozens of anthropologists and popularizers, the subject of every theoretical paradigm and every yearning for gender equality and communitarian wholeness (Bennett 1946; Hinsley 1989; Whiteley 1998; Dilworth 1996; S. Smith 2000; McFeely 2001; Jacobs 1999; Lavender 2006). Critical studies of Southwestern ethnography focus attention on amateur as well as professional work, and on the porous boundaries between the two. They show students of the Hopi and Zuni involved in complex cultural transfers and exchanges, in which ancient oral tradition was to be re-created in writing, indigenous identities could be transmitted to white audiences, and anthropologists and advocates could flirt with alterity in a liminal, intersocietal space, fashioning roles for themselves as feminists, anticonformist rebels, or heroic cultural mediators. Their writing about the Pueblos—self-referential, "drenched in antimodernism" (S. Smith 2000, 8), and pervaded by anxiety about industrialism, modernity, gender, and national identity—was also fractured by disagreement, self-contradiction, and a reluctance to acknowledge change or complexity. If San Blas and the Kuna never attracted quite such obsessive attention, many of the same themes and preoccupations reappear in the dozens of books and the hundreds of articles, poems, dramas, letters, reports, films, posters, museum exhibits, court documents, and advertisements dedicated to their representation.

CHAPTERS TO FOLLOW

In tracing the extended social and intellectual encounter between writing, anthropology, and the Kuna from the early 1900s to the present, this book begins in Chapter 2 with the first introduction of Western education, placing emphasis on the mixed feelings and conflicts schooling and writing inspired and the roles they promoted for young literate men. Chapter 3 considers the most important early use of writing, letters to government functionaries and other powerful outsiders. The considerable success indigenous writers enjoyed in conveying their grievances is contrasted with their failure to overcome stigmatized Indian identity.

Chapter 4 is concerned with representations and counterrepresentations of Indian identity and character in the early twentieth century. I argue that government functionaries could not be bothered to develop a systematic orientalist discourse, and that Kuna leaders, in answering attacks on their character, were limited by the dominant assumptions of the time. Chapter 5 deals with another and much friendlier sort of representation by Anglophone writers, who used Indians as symbolic vehicles for their own preoccupations concerning modernity and sexuality. As a loose alliance developed with sympathetic outsiders, and as government policies drove the Kuna to rebellion, two self-appointed advocates intervened on their behalf, in no small part through a kind of ethnography.

Chapter 6 is the first of two concerned with a remarkable collaboration between a Kuna chief and his secretaries and Swedish anthropologists led by Baron Erland Nordenskiöld. The narrative of a 1927 expedition to Panama and an extended trip to Sweden in 1931 by a young Kuna scribe focuses on the dialogue and symbiotic relationship that developed between Western and native partners. The second of the two chapters examines the published results of that collaboration, a massive ethnographic compendium and series of native-language sacred texts, showing how this corpus was shaped by the predispositions of the two sides, by their working methods, and by the largely textual nature of the material they generated.

Chapter 8 is devoted to other ethnography from the period 1925–1950, including a remarkable folkloric study situating Kuna culture in a national mosaic; Catholic ethnographies staking claims to wardship of the Indians; and popular works by Anglophone visitors carrying on a special relationship with the Kuna. Chapter 9 carries the story into the second half of the twentieth century, an era in which the growth of anthropology as a field and the increasing accessibility of the Kuna to both professional and amateur ethnographers led to proliferation of research and publication.

The tenth, penultimate chapter returns to the subject of auto-ethnography, work by the Kuna about themselves—first by a cohort of native scribes who worked as archivists, chroniclers, and ethnographers, and much later, by university-trained scholars and activists. I try to account for the shape of the corpus they generated and to come to terms with persistent questions about indigenous self-representation and ideology. A brief concluding chapter discusses questions raised by the book as a whole.

A Flock of Birds

TWO *The Coming of Schools and Literacy*

FIRST BEGINNINGS

During the nineteenth century or perhaps even earlier, a handful of Kuna men may have learned to read and write a little; certainly, a good many spoke some Spanish, English, or French.[1] But literate men, whatever their numbers, did not pass on their learning, and schooling only began in earnest at the turn of the twentieth century, with a number of Kuna boys who were sent away to live with non-Indian families, most often in Panama City. Under this arrangement, which was found in many Latin American countries, a young Indian or peasant boarder would be fostered or raised (*criado*) by an urban family, exchanging domestic labor for room and board and perhaps baptism and the chance to attend school. This practice, with deep roots in the colonial era, when Spanish American households would take in captive and ransomed Indian women and children, had its origin even earlier in efforts to convert captured Muslims during the reconquest of the Iberian peninsula (Weber 2005, 238–239). In early-twentieth-century Panama, unlucky boarders, or *criados* (the word can also mean servant), could be exploited unmercifully, but those fortunate enough to live with a benevolent family could receive baptism, some primary schooling, a little knowledge of the world, and perhaps even a lifelong patron.[2]

One of the earliest and by far the best known of such boys was Charles J. Robinson,[3] usually called Charly or Sali, who in the 1880s was taken at a young age by a sea captain of the same name to Providencia or San Andrés, English-speaking Protestant islands in the southern Caribbean. After spending several years living and studying in his mentor's household and several more as a sailor on vessels up and down the Atlantic coast, Charly returned as a young man in about 1902 to his natal village of Nargana.

Sometimes called Niga Gardaduled, "Young Writing Man" or "Letter-Man," Charly may for the moment have more or less monopolized literacy on Nargana, but he was only one among a number of returned sailors, the rest of them mostly unlettered but bi- or trilingual, and almost all open to some forms of change in their home village, including schooling for their children. Nargana, an island toward the western end of the San Blas coast, was a center of regional commerce, also the seat of Chief Abisua, one of the leaders of the coastal Kuna.[4] As later struggles would show, community members covered a wide spectrum of opinion, but overall, Nargana and its twin village Nusatupu, a few hundred yards away, were a good deal more open to change than any of the other thirty-odd Kuna communities on the coast.

For a year or so, Charly Robinson ran a tiny school in his home, in which he taught a few children and adult friends their ABCs in English, until it was closed down, reportedly at gunpoint, by irate conservatives from across the mountains in the Bayano Valley. With Panamanian independence from Colombia in 1903, a number of coastal Kuna leaders visited the new government the following year and received national flags, including Chief Abisua and Joe Harding, or Soowadin, of Nusatupu. Soon after his return home, Abisua died, in August of 1904, and his followers elected Charly Robinson to succeed him as first chief of Nargana.

As one of his initial acts as leader, Charly visited the government in late 1905, accompanied by the chiefs of three other progressive communities. During an interview at the presidential palace, Robinson and the country's first chief executive, Miguel Amador Guerrero, reached an agreement to bring children to the city to be educated. In October of the following year the chief returned to town with seventeen boys in tow, all but four from Nargana. The boarding annex set up for them at the newly established Normal School, which was financed by the government and run by the Christian Brothers, only lasted two years, but other boys from Nargana, and eventually girls as well, continued coming to the city in smaller numbers to be educated in religious and secular schools, sometimes on government scholarships.

Despite his Protestant upbringing, in March of 1907 Robinson welcomed a Spanish Jesuit, Father Leonardo Gassó, as representative of both the Church and the Panamanian government. An energetic, impatient, and highly combative veteran of mission struggles in Mexico and Ecuador, Gassó wasted no time in getting his foot in the doors of Nargana, Nusatupu (which he renamed Sagrado Corazón de Jesús), and soon thereafter, Tupile, or rather San Ignacio de Tupile. Within a few years he had brought in several more priests and brothers. In the process, he aroused tremendous antagonism and turmoil, stirring up factional struggles both within and without the mission communities and leading, in October of 1908, to an armed attack by pagan Kuna, which Robinson managed to repel with a display of guns supplied by the government.

Gassó did not stay the course. Reduced to poor health and discouraged by Kuna intransigence as well as waning government support and the death of his patron, the Bishop of Panama, in 1912 the disillusioned missionary returned for good to Spain. Other priests and brothers persevered for a few years, but the Catholic mission went into decline.

During his time on Nargana, Gassó tried to supervise the placement of Kuna children living in the city as *criados,* and on his own initiative he sent several more boys to urban schools. He also set up a small boarding establishment on Nargana and made tepid efforts to teach reading and writing to local children. But he relied much more on *oral* catechization, fearing that literate Indians would be exposed to such pernicious influences as newspapers and Protestant Bibles, and he took strong issue with the Catholic Church's reliance elsewhere on schools.[5] His halfhearted educational program sorely disappointed his followers, who badly wanted schooling for their children.

Gassó's Protestant successor, Miss Anna Coope, put schools at the center of her work. A middle-aged maiden lady and British citizen resident for many years in Rhode Island, Coope came to Nargana in 1913 at Charly Robinson's invitation. As brave and determined as Gassó (and as hostile toward rival missions), Coope took a good deal more flexible and patient line toward Kuna custom, except on the issue of alcohol. Although she initially provoked opposition and another unsuccessful attack on Nargana, as time went on she managed to silence or win over many of her opponents and to inspire personal devotion from her followers. Motivated by a characteristically Protestant commitment to Bible-reading as the key to true religion, Coope and a colleague named Martha Purdy promptly opened schools on Nargana and Nusatupu, where over the next few years they educated several dozen girls and boys. By 1916 they had also begun sending away several of their best male students to religious schools in the United States and Venezuela.

Coope's educational program, nonetheless, lasted little longer than Gassó's. Panamanian politicians and bureaucrats at first tolerated her mission, which enjoyed support from the Canal Zone and the U.S. Legation, but they were not happy that she taught children in English and that she seemed to encourage foreign loyalties. In 1915, President Belisario Porras, the leading politician of the age and a fervent proponent of Hispanic civilization for the Indians, made an official visit to San Blas, encouraged by both Charly Robinson and Cimral Colman, the latter the head of one of two village confederacies. After creating an administrative unit, the Circumscription of San Blas, with its headquarters on an island renamed El Porvenir, "The Future," at the far western end of the coast, Porras went on to establish public schools and police posts on Nargana, Nusatupu/Corazón, Tupile, and Playón Chico. Intrusive Black turtlers and forest workers, who had already clashed repeatedly with the Kuna, renewed their efforts, this time with official support and supervision, and a North American concern with a government contract established manganese mines and a banana plantation at the foot of Mandinga Bay, the deep-water gulf in western San Blas.

The four new schools, humble as they were, formed part of a broad effort to modernize and unify Panama through education.[6] In addition to two national secondary schools established soon after independence—the Escuela de Artes y Oficios, dedicated to practical arts, and the more academic Instituto Nacional—primary schools were opened or expanded all across the country. Education received special emphasis during the administrations of Belisario Porras (1912–1916, 1918–1919, 1920–1924): in the first two years of Porras's presidency, school enrollments in the Republic jumped from sixteen to twenty-two thousand (Pizzurno Gelós and Araúz 1996, 83). Porras and others hoped that schooling, in addition to fomenting literacy and a host of improvements to the moral, social, and political character of the Panamanian populace, would unify the nation: "Never will be considered excessive the role of highest transcendence that in a democracy corresponds to the public schools, whose teaching is the basis of all education: that is the place where all the inequalities of caste, fortune, and others that have given birth to social prejudices will disappear" (in Sisnett 1956, 252).

Prominent among those prejudices, as Porras saw it, was the refusal to join the nation so prominently displayed by the Kuna. In San Blas, schools first and foremost were supposed to *civilize* and *conquer* the Indians—in the words of one local official, "to obtain the inculcation and deep-rooting of modern ideas and civilization,"[7] thus erasing the differences that separated them from the national population. However benign education might be considered as an instrument for changing and winning over the Indians, the announced goal was nonetheless *conquest*. As one official report put it: "We the [police and administrators] are the sappers who clear the terrain . . . but the employees [of the Department] of Public Instruction are those who will establish themselves in the conquered position and hold it" (Howe 1998, 181–182).

On Nargana and Nusatupu/Corazón, competition between government schools and their Protestant counterparts soon led to antagonism and conflict, pitting schoolteachers, policemen, and local supporters against Coope and Purdy and their adherents. In 1919 the administration forced Coope to sign a contract forgoing all of her activities other than mission services. Two or three years later, the head of the local police detachment effectively closed her down altogether by punishing anyone who even visited her house, and after the Kuna rebellion of 1925, the government bought out her establishment and passed a law banning non-Catholic foreign missionaries.

SCHOOLING AND KUNA SOCIETY

Even before the return of Charly Robinson and the arrival of Coope and Gassó, the nineteenth-century Kuna had begun to engage with the issues of writing and schools. They used the word *garda* (or *karta*), which obviously derives from the Spanish *carta*, or letter, to refer to any piece of writing, and by extension, any news or message, written or oral—an indication that they had been thinking about writing and its functions even before they learned how to do it themselves.[8]

During the first decades of the century, schools aroused passionate disagreement on Nargana and throughout San Blas, appealing to different and contradictory aspects of indigenous culture. The Kuna, first of all, had no difficulty perceiving the practical advantages of keeping their own written records or being able to review someone else's, especially in their commercial dealings. During the nineteenth century, some Kuna men had acted as agents for foreign merchants, and all of them sold coconuts and bought manufactured goods (Olien 1988). Unlike Indians and peasants in much of Latin America, held in perpetual servitude by debts owed for goods advanced to them, the Kuna avoided entanglement by stringently limiting coasting merchants' access and by carrying some of their coconut harvest in sailing dugouts to sell in Colón or a coastal town. Merchants still inspired unease and accusations of sharp practice, however, against which literacy seemed to offer some protection. In general, the Kuna readily understood not only that writing could be used against them, but that they too might exploit it on their own behalf.

Beyond its practical effects, writing brought into play questions of respect and self-worth, heavily conditioned by the dominance of "the lettered city" in Latin America (Rama 1996) and the social and political value of schooling in nineteenth- and twentieth-century Panama. The Kuna were aware that Latin Panamanians looked down on them as uncivilized semi-savages, in no small part because of their illiteracy, and that the indigenous language was called a dialect (*dialecto*), as it still is today. As Cimral Colman wrote in a letter to the president of Panama (quoted more fully below), "You all say that we are brute and savages that they do not know the law of God because they do not want to learn to read and write thus say you." Schooling, it was hoped, would counter this prejudice.

Writing also had implications for rank *within* Kuna society, tapping into the system by which Kuna men competed for prestige and recognition by filling positions in ritual and politics. Among the wide array of ritualists called *immar wisid,* or "knower of things,"[9] an *inaduled,* "medicine-person," cured through physical substances prepared as baths and infusions, an *igar wisid,* or "chant knower," through one of a great number of texts, most of them performed at the end of a patient's hammock. One such specialist, the knower of Muu Igar, chanted to alleviate difficult childbirth; another, who knew Masar Igar, guided dead souls to heaven; and the *absogedi,* or "converser," rid whole villages of dangerous spirits. A *gandule,* or "flute man," performed a chant cycle lasting several days at rituals marking the maturation of adolescent girls, and *sailas,* or chiefs (of which each village had several), learned "Father's Way" (Bab igar), a body of tradition composed of metaphor, cosmology, conventional wisdom, and, especially, Kuna sacred history. Except for one role, that of seer, or *nele,* which was restricted to individuals born with an innate ability to look into the invisible spirit world, every pursuit was open to any adult male with the interest and energy to apprentice himself with a teacher, and in the case of the more demanding practices, with the stamina to persevere over the years and decades required for mastery. Many ambitious men acquired multiple roles, for instance as chief, medicinalist, and puberty chanter.

Men gained stature by learning, practicing, and finally teaching these ritual specialties, as well as by filling village offices, of which the most important were chief, or *saila,* chief's spokesman (*argar*), and town constable (*sualibed*). Most men acquired enough knowledge and acted in village politics sufficiently to at least establish a position of respect in their own community, while the leading chiefs, exorcists, seers, and medicinalists made names for themselves known up and down the coast, attracting students even from distant villages.

Arcane knowledge and mastery of esoteric languages were important throughout the system. Every pursuit had its secrets, while chant cures, the puberty cycle, and chiefly chanting each had its special language: the first two were spirit tongues largely unintelligible to laymen, and the third, belonging to chiefs and their spokesmen, was mostly intelligible but full of special vocabulary and stylistic conventions. By extension, knowledge of human but foreign languages and of distant places also brought some prestige, and leading chiefs, in particular, worked hard to supplement Father's Way with useful knowledge of the outside world. Writing, as an esoteric technique with its own associated knowledge and, since the Kuna did not write in their own language, a foreign tongue as well, could be taken as the equivalent of or even replacement for traditional chants and ritual.

Kuna ritual, it should be noted parenthetically, had its own form of written record, a kind of picture-writing that accompanied some chants and medicinal cures. Tiny drawings representing the beings and objects used in cures were drawn on boards or into school notebooks. Each ritualist who used picture-writing (some did not) devised his own idiosyncratic set of elements, which evoked or enumerated key features of his practice but did not directly represent the words of chants or any other elements of spoken language. Although picture-writing soon attracted great interest from outside observers, who tended to see it as a survival of some ancient and perhaps more developed system of hieroglyphs (see Chapters 6 and 7), it is much more likely, given its elaboration in cheap mass-produced notebooks, that it had developed quite recently. Confined entirely to the field of ritual, it played no part in the struggles over literacy.

Some Kuna, finally, began to realize that writing offered a path to material reward in the form of salaried employment. Over the next several decades, a number of families from Nargana and Corazón went on to place successive generations of children and grandchildren as teachers, policemen, government functionaries, and political operatives, more than fulfilling the ambitions of their unlettered but forward-looking forebears.

But writing and literacy could also arouse highly negative feelings. Traditional ritual and politics depended on the assumption that men would acquire mastery only gradually, reaching their peak of influence and respect in late middle age, and many such men were dismayed by the possibility of literate youths using new skills to contend with and even supplant their elders. The obvious equivalence between modern education and traditional apprenticeship (even today Kuna medicine-men say that *their* school is the forest) implied rivalry between the two. It soon became evident, finally, that all the outside powers promoting schools, secular and religious, were intent on using them to indoctrinate and make over students, and eventually, to replace traditional lifeways altogether.[10]

On Nargana in the late 1910s, literacy and writing also involved controversial choices between languages and cultural traditions, since Kuna schoolchildren always learned to read and write in Spanish or English. Strategic ties with English-speakers went back to the seventeenth century, when the Kuna had guided buccaneers across the Isthmus, provisioned their ships, and joined them in raiding Spanish gold mines. At the end of that century, at least some of the Kuna had welcomed a colony of Scots during a brief, disastrous stay in San Blas, and for much of a long eighteenth-century struggle against the Spanish, the Indians received arms, canes of office, and other encouragement from the British government. Even under the more peaceful conditions of the nineteenth century, English-speaking traders continued to visit the coast regularly.

The imprint of this centuries-long Anglophone association can be heard in the Kuna language, which is peppered with English loan words. Money in Kuna is *mani*, an old man is called *orman*, time is counted in hourly units, or *wachi*, and several marine fish sport borrowed names such as *orwaib* (old wife) and *yaladela* (yellowtail). In addition to long indigenous names like Olobilibilele or Igwa-aliginya, in daily life many Kuna men went by Charly, William, Henry, or Joe.

But the Kuna had been dealing with Hispanic powers for just as long. Mission *reducciones* had been established in the seventeenth and eighteenth centuries; colonial authorities and middlemen kept chiefs as clients through gifts and payments (Gallup-Díaz 2004); and both the pirate Wafer and the Scots found that quite a few Kuna spoke at least a little Spanish. By the twentieth century, Hispanic names and Spanish loan words were also pervasive in the Kuna language, the most important of them in this context being the one noted above, *garda*.

Villagers on Nargana and Corazón de Jesús, confronted by a choice between rival languages and schools, made their decisions on the basis of strategic choice and dispositions toward change, as well as tradition and sentiment. Public schooling in Spanish often implied hope for greater commercial ties and paid jobs in the Isthmian economy, as well as acceptance of rapid cultural change and assimilation into national society, and perhaps most important, acquiescence to Panamanian nationality and state control. Those who embraced English accepted change but usually at a slower pace, with acculturation to North American as well as Hispanic models, and they sought to preserve as much as possible of their present autonomy, accepting nominal allegiance to Panama and active participation in trade but avoiding all but a minimum of state control. With the suppression of Protestant schools in 1919, all pupils henceforth learned Spanish, but a few continued to cultivate the knowledge of English they had already acquired (Howe 1990, 1991a, 1992).

While Nargana and Nusatupu families were steering their courses through the local minefields of school choice, regional Kuna leaders were trying to come to terms with the issue on a wider scale. The conservative Inabaginya of Sasardi, who until 1919 continued to give his allegiance to Colombia, would not allow schools into any of the villages in his confederacy. His rival and leader of the other confederacy, Cimral Colman of Ailigandi, rejected schools for his own island, at least for the moment, but he sent his son Ceferino away to be educated. In the period from 1912 to 1915, moreover, when Colman was committed to cooperating with the government, he encouraged officials (without success) to revive the special boarding school in the city. As he wrote in a letter to President Porras:

> When the beginning of the world God left you that you should seek money in order to eat and in order to put Stores and thus you go on gaining and growing stature and you have gotten rich and you have left your Teachers here in the land since in that time there were my Fathers and they were afraid [of] money and Now I am [here] I am not afraid [of] money and I would like it that all my children knew how to speak each languages to write it and read it and you all say that we are brute and savages that do not know the law of God because they do not want to learn to read and write thus say you what I want [is] to place or that you place for me a school there in Panama so that you/he teaches me it and civilizes me it and then I can send you the little indians (*indiesitos*) as did Dr. Amador.[11]

After Colman, the two leading men of his confederacy were Olonibiginya of Carti in the West, and Nele Wardada, or Nele Kantule, of Portogandi, or Ustupu, in the East. Nele's solution was to exclude government schools altogether and instead to invite two young Nargana students of Anna Coope named Fred Philips and Samuel Morris to open a modest educational plant in 1918 in a little thatched house on his island. The two boys had between them only thirty or forty students, male and female, and though years later the village offered Samuel a small ex gratia payment for his pioneering contribution, during their three years there the pair received only room and board. The intendente of the time approved of Nele's school, thinking it a good deal better than nothing, and when the original two moved on to finish their own educations, he arranged to have their successor, a youth named Juan Pérez, put on the government payroll as a nominal indigenous policeman.[12]

CLAUDIO IGLESIAS: SCHOOLING AND AMBITION

Coming after Charly Robinson, by far the most famous literate Kuna man of the early twentieth century was Claudio Iglesias, who showed the same devotion to change and to his own political advancement as had Robinson before him, and who, when he returned to Nargana from school, entered into an intensely oedipal, winner-take-all struggle with his by-then middle-aged predecessor.

Claudio, the son of a medicinalist named Alicio, or Eliseo, Iglesias, was baptized in 1907 by Father Gassó. In 1910 he went with a cohort of boys from Nargana and Nusatupu/Corazón to the orphan's Hospice of Don Bosco run by the Salesian Order, where he studied carpentry. Graduating in 1917, the only one of his group to finish his studies, he returned to Nargana the same or the following year. As tensions between the public and Protestant mission schools ratcheted up during 1918, his friends invited him to take the leadership of the young men's group being organized to support the public schools and promote modernization.

Many histories attribute the changes that occurred on Nargana and Corazón over the next few years—especially the defeat of Coope and Robinson, the suppression of puberty ceremonies and traditional women's dress, and the imposition of Western dancing—directly to Claudio and his followers. The documentary evidence, however, shows that on the dress issue the young turks followed the lead of President Belisario Porras, and that the idea for social dancing first came from a teacher, Ana de James (Howe 1998, 121–129). The young men's faction, nonetheless, fought ruthlessly to promote these changes and to increase its own power at the expense of Charly Robinson.

Conflict broke out in early January 1919. In the aftermath of an evening of Christmas entertainments in the government school, including a Panamanian folkloric dance, the police arrested a follower of Charly Robinson's for denouncing the dancing as immoral, and when Charly's group tried to break the dance critic out of jail, a riot ensued, followed by further skirmishes and turmoil. In April President Porras sent orders that schoolgirls must not wear noserings or limb bindings, and Coope's school was closed down permanently. Weeks of maneuvering culminated at the end of June in an uprising by Robinson's faction, put down a few days later by police reinforcements. The ringleaders were fined, Claudio Iglesias was appointed honorary police chief, and though Charly Robinson clung to his chiefship, power on the island shifted decisively to the radical youths and their police allies (Howe 1998, 121–129).

Claudio personally had only a year and a half in which to enjoy his victory. In April of 1921, as the government extended the nosering ban to include adult women, further turmoil erupted on Nargana, and one woman fled to her brother on nearby Kwebdi, or Río Azúcar, a dissident named Charlie Nelson. That night a police detachment, including Claudio Iglesias, was dispatched to arrest the pair, and in the ensuing skirmish, Claudio and another indigenous policeman were killed, along with four Río Azúcar men. The government made Claudio into a martyr for civilization, erecting a memorial on Nargana and lending his name to a government launch, a village park, and young men's clubs on other pacified islands. Leadership passed to another young man, Estanislao López, who continued the campaign for civilization and against Coope and Robinson.

LITERACY AND MEDIATION

The intendente and the police badly needed the services of young literate Kuna men.[13] The most fervent, dedicated, and accomplished among them, like Claudio and Estanislao, were expected to lead the campaign to civilize and hispanicize the Kuna and to convert other young men to the cause. But even lesser men and boys might play important roles. In formal talks with outsiders, Kuna chiefs often insisted on having their own people translate, and officials objected to ceding control or initiative for want of a native speaker of their own. In 1921, the intendente urged his superiors to hire an official interpreter:

> The greatest part of the times that I have had to conduct an interview with a saguila [chief], there have served as interpreter one

or another Indian who manages our language with difficulty....
Moreover ... the interpretations made by those indians are completely unreliable. (Intendente to SecretaryJ 4/18/21,[14] AI)

But officials had few options, at least among non-Indians, very few of whom spoke Kuna, except for a pair of brothers, Narciso and Eduardo Navas, who for reasons now unknown had mastered the language. Narciso had translated for two presidential visits to the coast in 1910 and 1915, and in 1909 Eduardo headed a new police post on the border at Puerto Obaldía. When the government was elaborating its plans for colonization in 1912–1913, the brothers offered written suggestions, and in 1918–1919, Narciso was made a sublieutenant on the police force, though he lasted only a few months. Thereafter, the brothers' services were apparently not used again until 1925.

Kuna speakers were also rare among the Colonial Police. The only unambiguous exception was Guillermo Denis, a mulatto policeman with a surname suggesting West Indian origin who spoke some Kuna and fathered a child with a local woman (see Howe 1998, 186). But few police agents other than Denis showed a willingness to learn more than a few words and phrases in the Indian "dialect."

Thus from the beginning the administration recruited quite a few young literate, bilingual Kuna youths as *policía indígena,* paying them a fraction of the salary of their non-Indian colleagues. Apart from increasing the total number of agents—always a pressing concern for an understaffed, underpaid, and lightly armed force facing a perpetual threat of rebellion or attack—indigenous policemen acted as cultural and political mediators in the villages under government control, transmitting orders, organizing, interrogating, listening, spying, informing, and encouraging unofficial collaborators. They also supplied local skills in short supply on the regular force, especially paddling and sailing dugout canoes.

But literacy did not lead inevitably to collaboration. In Claudio's case, he came home a proponent of Hispanic, Catholic civilization and radical modernizing change because his Salesian teachers had taught him a good deal more than writing and woodworking, and he carried on the fight in Nargana and Corazón with the active encouragement of police colleagues, teachers, and higher officials. Many of the boys inspired by his example, moreover, embraced the cause *before* rather than after learning to read and write. Without denying the capacity for action and purpose—the agency—demonstrated by Claudio and his followers, one cannot help noticing that they accepted models of literacy and of the role of literate men fostered by their Panamanian sponsors and allies, and that for all their ambition and ferocity, they acted as cultural brokers strictly within the limits of those expectations.

Other young men, actively recruited by Kuna chiefs, took the other side, in effect overturning Panamanian notions about the effects of literacy and turning them back against themselves (Pitcock 2000). Whereas Claudio sought power as *jefe* of his community, but at the cost of subordinating himself to outsiders, these other young men overtly deferred to native chiefs, but with the tacit advantage of gaining influence and prominence unusual for their age.

Native leaders needed literate youths as much as the police did. Except for Charly Robinson, Kuna leaders of the day were all unlettered, and those active in regional politics—which meant the heads of the two confederacies, Inabaginya and Cimral Colman, as well as quite a few of the more ambitious and energetic village chiefs—required helpers to write letters for them and to translate in face-to-face encounters. Even chiefs dead-set against schools, as was Inabaginya, found they could not do without at least one literate assistant. The men and boys they recruited, often fresh out of primary school, were called *secretario* in Spanish and *sikkwi*, or bird, in Kuna, after the marks made by their pens on the page. By extension, the name *sikkwi* came to encompass not just scribes in particular but young literate men as a class.

By recruiting scribes and giving them important but dependent positions in village and regional politics, chiefs gained some control over a potent new technology, one they themselves had no chance of mastering, as well as control over the technology's practitioners; co-opting young potential rivals, they forestalled the kind of intergenerational conflict that had broken out between Charly and Claudio. Age did not thereby come to trust youth entirely: stories circulate even today of deliberate mistranslation by secretaries and of embezzlement or deception of monolingual chiefs in the city. Nele Kantule is often quoted as having sung that *sikkwis* would materialize a devil in the gathering house. Even when secretaries served faithfully, they often saw things differently than chiefs. But many of them developed strong loyalties to the leaders for whom they worked, to the cause of Kuna autonomy, and even in some complex way to traditional culture. As the struggle against police tyranny intensified in the early 1920s, several of them ended up playing active, even indispensable parts in the drama of resistance. And in the long run, quite a few of them became chiefs themselves.

Even those young men who signed up on the Panamanian side did not always stay there. Officials complained of indigenous agents on Nargana and Playón Chico who sometimes protected their compatriots and subverted official aims. By the time the Kuna rebelled in 1925, quite a few native policemen and other collaborators had been alienated by the oppression they were expected to further.

FOUR BIRDS

The paths open to literate men, the various roles they played as teachers and scribes on one side or as government collaborators and native policemen on the other, can best be seen in the lives of four representative figures, Manuel González and Benito Guillén of Playón Chico, or Ukkup Senni, and Mateo Brenes and Pilip Thompson of Niatupu, or Tigantiki.

Manuel González

Manuel González was brought to Colón at about the age of nine by Benito Guillén (see below), who arranged for him to be taken into the Panama City household of a policeman named Anibal Lindo. Manuel spent seven years with the Lindo family, reaching the fifth grade in local elementary schools and receiving baptism, with Sr. Lindo standing as godfather. He then worked for a year or two in and around Colón. When President Belisario Porras made an official visit to San Blas in 1915, González was one of the secondary interpreters. At about this time he returned to Playón Chico, married, and assisted the carpenter building the first school on his island.

In 1917 or 1918, a chief from the Bayano region across the cordillera visited Playón Chico and arranged with the government teacher, Manuela Frago, to bring González back with him to act as his secretary and to run a small village school. In about 1919 González returned to San Blas, where he was recruited as a secretary to Cimral Colman, though another young *sikkwi* of Playón Chico, Manuel Hernandez, seems to have played a much more active and aggressive role in Colman's campaign of resistance. In 1920 or 1921 González accompanied Colman and his lawyer, José de la Rosa, to what proved to be a heated meeting with Belisario Porras at the presidential palace, and in the aftermath, fearing arrest by the intendente and Colonial Police, he fled back to the Bayano, where he stayed four years.

Although González missed the Kuna rebellion in February of 1925, he returned shortly afterwards to Playón Chico, where for fear of police reprisals the village lived for a few years in a single large communal house on the mainland. González, by then in his late twenties, was chosen as a secondary chief of the village. Over the next few years, he mastered Father's Way, the stuff of chiefly learning, as well as a curing chant called Sia Igar (the Cacao Way), and he became a puberty ceremony chanter, or *gandule*.

In 1931, after the death of a daughter, González returned once again to the Bayano, to the village of Pirya, where he was soon chosen as chief. He stayed in Pirya until 1946, at which point he returned to San Blas. Elected first chief of Playón Chico, he presided over village affairs for twenty-one years until retiring in 1970. I interviewed Manuel González and copied a short written biography of his career in 1975.

Mateo Brenes

As a small boy on Nusatupu/Corazón de Jesús, Mateo Brenes was baptized a Catholic, and according to his own account, Father Gassó wanted to send him to Spain for schooling, but his parents refused permission. Later, while a student in Martha Purdy's Protestant school, he was dispatched with several other boys to be educated in Venezuela, where he stayed two or three years. On his return, he moved from Nusatupu to join kin on Niatupu a few miles to the east.

Brenes, who spoke both Spanish and English, worked for about a year as secretary to Colman, assisting at the same contentious meeting in 1920 or 1921 with President Porras as Manuel González. When González fled over the mountains, Brenes hid for about a year in the eastern shore village of Magemmulu, or Caledonia. After his return to Niatupu, the police established a post there in 1924, imposing the same program of forced culture change already perfected on Nargana and several other islands. Young Brenes headed the local club where men and women were forced to dance to the music of a wind-up Victrola. In late February of 1925, as local dissidents prepared an uprising, he and his followers were given the chance to redeem themselves by keeping up carnival festivities as a cover for the men who ambushed and killed the three policemen on the island.

After the Kuna rebellion, Brenes followed a quite traditional life path as an agriculturalist, medicinal curer, and *argar* in the local political hierarchy. In the 1970s and 1980s I knew Mateo well as a good friend and one of the most kind and helpful consultants in my research.

Pilip Thompson

Philip, Pilip, or Felipe Thompson (Tansan) was a grandson of the well-known chief of Nusatupu, Joe Harding, or Soowadin, who was later baptized by Father Gassó as Francisco Soo. According to what Pilip told his son long afterwards (OH Ricardo Thompson 4/14/85), he accompanied his grandfather as a young boy to the city to receive flags following Panama's independence from Colombia, and he was among a group of five boys who were taken to Panama City for schooling even before the larger cohort sent by Charly Robinson in 1906. Left in the household of a prominent Panamanian, Francisco de la Ossa, Pilip soon traveled to Washington, D.C., with a kinsman of de la Ossa's, Juan Ehrmann, who was named to the Panamanian consulate or legation. In Washington the young boy was enrolled in about 1907 in a charity school, apparently run by the Jesuit Order, remembered in the family as "The Children's Association."[15]

In 1914, upon receiving a message from his grandfather that his father had died, Pilip returned to Panama. After more schooling in Panama, he returned to Nusatupu/Corazón, married, and settled down as an agriculturalist. As the situation on the twin islands heated up, Pilip took the side of those opposed to Claudio Iglesias and the police. A letter from June of 1919 written by the detachment head denounced Pilip as a ringleader in the defense of women's dress (Garrido to Intendente 6/06/19, AI). According to his son Ricardo, Pilip was subjected to so much pressure by the police and modernists, first to conform to their program and later to become an indigenous policeman himself, that he fled to Niatupu, which in those years received a number of dissidents from Nargana and Corazón:

> "Then when things began to happen like that," truly, he said, "they began to persecute me too. Why? I was on the elders' side. I didn't want to harass the elders. I began to be persecuted too, the *guardia* seized me too. For me, well, twice they locked me up, well, in the stocks. I was punished. Then with that, it really hurt my heart, see. They took me off to Porvenir. They gave me a uniform. But, that uniform, I fled to Niatupu, and I threw it in the water," he said. "I couldn't do that." (OH Ricardo Thompson 4/14/85)

Later that year, another letter by the Nargana detachment head (Garrido to Intendente 11/30/19, AI) named Thompson as one of the Niatupu men who had violently resisted the police as they tried to arrest his kinsman, which led to the torching of the whole village (see Howe 1998, 140–142). In 1924 he was chosen as an interpreter and political agent for the delegation that accompanied Richard Marsh to the United States (see Howe 1998, 239–253). In February 1925, Pilip helped lead the uprising on Niatupu, though without participating in the killing or allowing hotheads to murder Kuna collaborators.

In 1930, Pilip accompanied a delegation led by Nele Kantule that negotiated an end to the antagonism between Panama and the rebel Kuna, though he apparently disapproved of the agreement's terms. Over the years he secured educations for his children, two of whom worked as teachers and one of whom, Ricardo, served for many years as the first Kuna judge for San Blas.

Benito Guillén

Perhaps most intriguing of all the birds was Benito Guillén, whose complex and contradictory life can only be glimpsed at scattered points in the historical record. Evidently schooled as a *criado* in the city at the turn of the century, he first surfaces in Father Gassó's account of an attempt in 1909 to found a missionary outpost on the island of Tupile (Gassó 1910), which recorded the young man's hostile encounter with the missionary near Playón Chico. Four years later in 1913, Guillén's name appears in a letter from Chief Cimral Colman to President Porras in which Colman mentions that Guillén was coming to Panama to bring the letter and act as Colman's emissary. The letter also identifies Guillén as an *alcalde,* or *argar,* that is, a senior leader in his home community, and another man as village secretary. Two or three years after that, when the government set up a school and police post on Playón Chico, Guillén was named as an official Indigenous Policeman.

In January 1919, now estranged from Colman, Guillén wrote Humberto Vaglio, the recently named intendente, to denounce the chief as a fraud.

> With all due respect I direct myself before you to inform you of the following once is confided in me as an ajent of the Police of the republic my duty is to inform my *jefe* of everything that happens.
> It happens that *Saguila* [chief] Conma, what he gives as an impression to the Government is a Sham because when he is here

he always continues with his backward ideas that in blace of advancing all comes in backwardness and because I don'tfollow his ydeas he is upset with me he doesn't want school nor in any way in benifit of pro gress (*a de lanto*).

Saguila Olopanique of Playon Chico now he is in agreement witheverything he sez that he is in agreement with what the Government orders and to respect everything. (Guillén to Vaglio 1/03/19, AI)

Later that year, after Vaglio and President Porras had forced the schoolgirls on Playón Chico and several other islands to give up their noserings and leg bindings, Guillén took down a letter dictated by the island chief, Olopanique, protesting the imposition and threatening to remove the children from school—which suggests some disaffection from the government program on the part of Guillén as well as the chief (Olopanique to President 7/01/19, AI):

Plallon Chico July 1 of 1919
Señor
    President of the Republic of
Panama mi dear sir with due rrespect we Inform you the following, that the Village was veri inspired with the school but now the fathers of the children are upset with wanting to suppress their customs such as the Use of [?] beads., the yuse of their noserings (*arsamuros*), we bulieve that in dis way instead of hattracting, everything advanced will be in vain, So we are deciding not to send our children toschool: after the girls are sibilized thei themselves without forcing her would have chaged Customs; withnothing further, I sign myself:
    saguila
        Olopanique

In late 1924, as the situation in San Blas came to a crisis, the head of the detachment that encompassed Tupile and Playón Chico, Miguel Gordón, wrote to condemn Guillén for condoning villagers' offenses and the flight of dissidents to rebel islands in the East.

Yesterday morning at 8 A.M., the Agent Benito Guillen, their ringleader fled on him, one Iguapicnique, all the reports obtained say that Agent Guillen abetted the flight. Agent Benito Guillen is, if you will, the worst enemy that the Government and the Police in this region have, this indian is the greatest one for covering up the misdeeds that the indians commit on a daily basis, for which reason in a separate communication that I am sending you will see the punishment that I am requesting for him. (Gordón to Mojica 10/25/24, AI)

In the end, however, Guillén's leniency did not save him. Early on the morning of February 22, 1925, when the Kuna rose up against Panama, the rebels on Playón Chico seemed ready to let him live, but their allies from Ustupu and Ailigandi burst onto the scene and clubbed Guillén to death.

THE TRIUMPH OF SCHOOLING

Even before the rebellion, by the late 1910s and early 1920s, a surprising number of graduates of Coope's establishment and of the four government schools were continuing on for secondary education in the city, most of them at the Instituto Nacional and the national trade school, the Escuela de Artes y Oficios. The family of Claudio Iglesias and other modernists actively sought scholarships, and according to a biography of Claudio's brother Alcibiades (M. Iglesias 1958, 36), no less than seven Iglesias siblings studied at one time or another in Panama City. A striking photograph at the Instituto Nacional taken in 1923 shows thirty-seven Kuna boys and nineteen girls, many or most of them apparently from Nargana and Corazón de Jesús.

After the uprising of 1925, however, Western education made a slow recovery. The Catholic Church applied successfully to oversee government schools in San Blas, and in 1928 missionaries returned to Nargana.[16] The Nargana/Corazón school, whose grades were soon increased from four to six, was staffed by Franciscan nuns, and Claretian priests oversaw the whole district. As numerous passages in the Claretian reports make clear,[17] they saw their involvement in schooling as a vehicle for conversion and a base from which to reassert missionary control of all the Indians. The government, for its part, assigned Indian education to the Secretariat of Government and Justice, indicating the continuing importance of schools in pacifying and assimilating the Kuna (V. Smith 1982, 296).

Only two schools functioned that first year, on Nargana and nearby Río Azúcar, with nine teachers and 284 students between them. Though

FIGURE 2.1 Kuna students photographed at the Instituto Nacional, Panama, 1923. Rubén Pérez Kantule is in the second row, ninth from the left.

others were added one by one, as of 1937–1938 only six villages had accepted schools, and except for Nargana, all of them had only one or at most two grades: teachers totaled thirteen and students 627. Four years later, numbers had jumped to thirteen schools (representing about a third of the roughly forty villages then on the coast), thirty teachers, and 1,192 students. Parents from elsewhere who wanted their children educated further than was possible on their own islands boarded them on Nargana, either with a local family or in a church-run *internado* opened in 1934.[18]

In addition to government schools, a number of islands sponsored small private elementary schools, and in 1933, a revived and indigenized Protestant mission opened a school on Ailigandi. For some years government and private schools competed on Ailigandi and Ustupu. The regional leader, Nele Kantule, and other Kuna activists repeatedly lobbied the government for scholarships to urban secondary schools, though the number provided was always disappointing. The Catholic Church and Protestant mission also facilitated studies in Panama and abroad, and Nele tried unsuccessfully to send boys to study in the United States.[19]

In 1945, San Blas schools were transferred from the Ministry of Government to the Ministry of Education (Calvo Población 2000, 447), and in 1950 public schools were returned to secular control, though nuns continued teaching on Nargana and Ustupu for many years (Holloman 1969, 350). In 1955 the private schools had 218 students, public schools 1,391 (Peña 1959, 71).

Some parents continued sending children to the city to board with Latin Panamanian families. In 1955 a study found 46 Kuna boys and 56 girls in Panama City elementary schools, with another 26 children in the schools of Colón (Peña 1959, 71). Many of the students, according to the study's worried author, were so overworked by their host families that their studies suffered. She estimated that another 125 Kuna were studying at secondary and private schools in Panama, and that an equal number were working in Colón as domestic servants without access to schooling.[20] Much later in the century, many Indian families moved to the terminal cities, often remaining there at least until their children's education was complete.

Throughout the twentieth century, Nargana/Corazón continued to lead the way, sending many of its children to urban secondary schools or even establishing city homes. In 1956 the first regional secondary school was established on Nargana (followed later by several more on other islands). According to Holloman (1969, 193), in the late 1960s just about every Nargana household boarded at least one student from another community and fed itself in considerable part on food sent by boarders' fathers. Graduates from Nargana, Corazón, and Río Azúcar were also the first to seize the opportunities for salaried employment. From the early 1930s on, members of several interrelated families spread out across the region, snatching up jobs as they were created, and it was not until much later that their dominance began to be challenged by graduates from other large islands (see Holloman 1969, 346). For fiscal year 1967, Holloman (1969, 132–133) counted eighty-three teachers, an estimated thirty National Guardsmen, and ninety-seven other functionaries and laborers, plus forty-one employees of the Protestant mission—the great majority in all categories Kuna.

Outside of Nargana and the other two islands in its cluster, Western education made much slower progress. Although Inabaginya reportedly recognized the inevitability of schools, he kept them out of his sector throughout his lifetime. After his death in 1939, the chief's home island, Mulatupu, began very tentatively to accept schooling, but others yielded more reluctantly, some as late as the 1960s. As recently as 1970, one or two islands out of a regional total of about fifty still lacked a school, and two-thirds of the Kuna population was illiterate.

A sense of the accelerating pace of change in the latter part of the century can be gleaned from figures in the decennial national census. In 1960, out of thirteen thousand people in San Blas aged ten and older, only 26 percent were literate. By 1970, the percentage had risen to 34 percent. Of 5,796 children aged seven to fifteen in that year, slightly more than half, 3,243, were in school.[21]

By the year 2000, the Kuna had at last shed their collective ambivalence about education. The Kuna population aged four and older in the whole country numbered just under fifty-five thousand, of which only fifteen thousand, or 27 percent, had never attended school. Twenty-two thousand, evenly divided between males and females, had completed some primary school, eight thousand of them reaching the sixth grade. Another thirteen and a half thousand (eight men for every five women) had gone on to secondary school. Increases were most dramatic for higher education, as was the gender imbalance: a thousand men, but only five hundred women, had studied at the university level. The census recorded twenty-five Kuna with master's degrees and two, both males, with doctorates.[22]

THE IMPACT OF SCHOOLS AND LITERACY

Learning to read and write did not immediately destroy traditional beliefs and practice. Like Manual González and Mateo Brenes, literate males could follow graduation and a few years as secretary with careers in agriculture, ritual, and village leadership. During my own fieldwork in the 1970s and 1980s, I was repeatedly struck by the ability of educated Kuna friends to balance seemingly incompatible interests and pursuits: reading newspapers, voting, sending their children to school, but also practicing as medicinalists and performing as chiefs and interpreters.

But schools and literacy have indeed effected great changes in Kuna life, some of them just the ones that early opponents anticipated. The balance of power between the generations has shifted, though perhaps not so much as once feared, especially now that parents as well as children can read and write. Boys unsocialized to forest work increasingly choose wage labor or salaried jobs or diving for lobsters over agriculture. Adolescent students fall in love and get married (or make babies before marrying), decisively ending the old system of parental control. Indigenous curers, with many clients but few apprentices, take their knowledge with them to the grave. And as has happened around the world, schooling itself eats up family resources.

Few of these changes follow from schooling or literacy alone, and the simple ability to read and write has probably exerted less influence by itself than the reallocation of children's time, the nonindigenous language of instruction, and the nationalist and progressivist content of teaching. Despite periodic agitation for bilingual education, serious efforts did not begin until the twenty-first century, and if most Kuna still speak their own language, almost none of them write it.

These changes, however, as significant as they have proved for Kuna lives, will not be discussed again in this book, which is concerned, not with the global impact of literacy and schooling on Kuna society, but with writing as a tool of cultural representation and self-representation, and the engagement of Kuna scribes and leaders with anthropology and the demands of the nation-state. As will become evident, much of what happened and much of what these scribes accomplished occurred when they still constituted a small fraction of the population, working with unlettered chiefs and a proudly illiterate majority.

Letters of Complaint

THREE

THE USES OF WRITING

Over the course of the twentieth century, the Kuna turned writing to a variety of ends, public and private, from enforcing communal labor to codifying customary law (see Howe 1979, 1986). Most of these practices, however, took years or decades to develop fully. It was chiefs who first exploited the new technology, and then almost entirely for external communication. They wrote occasionally to the press, to lawyers, or to private parties, but most of all they sent letters to government functionaries with authority or influence over Indian affairs and the San Blas coast. Of these officials, those closest at hand were the heads of three local police detachments at Corazón de Jesús, San Ignacio de Tupile, and Puerto Obaldía; and above them, a police lieutenant and the governor, or intendente, who from 1915 on headed the special administrative unit called the Circumscription of San Blas. Next was the intendente's immediate superior, the Secretary of Government and Justice; and at the top of the ladder, the President of the Republic. In the highly personalistic politics of the tiny nation, even Indians and campesinos sometimes went right to the top, and heads of government received a stream of letters and petitioners at the presidential residence, called the Palace of the Herons. Belisario Porras, in particular, who was chief executive for most of the years between 1912 and 1924, and who took great interest in civilizing the Kuna, kept his door and his mailbox open wide.

Of the letters sent to officials by Kuna leaders up to 1925, several dozen have survived in private collections and in theses and publications (especially Castillo and Méndez 1962); also in the presidential archives of Belisario Porras at the University of Panama, the files of the U.S. Legation and Canal administration; and most of all in the records of the Intendencia in El Porvenir. Along with face-to-face interviews, such letters constituted the principal medium, the primary form of social action, through which Kuna leaders confronted and presented themselves to the outside world.

TRANSLATION AND DICTATION

Letters, according to Charles Bazerman (1999), offer one of the most basic, universal forms of written text, the generic type out of which many more specialized forms have developed. Linking specified senders and receivers, letters are supremely social, and in their plasticity and flexibility, they are strongly marked by social tasks and social contexts: "We can see how the letter, once invented to mediate the distance between two parties, provides an open-ended transactional space that can be specified, defined, and regularized in many different ways" (Bazerman 1999, 18; see also Barton and Hall 2000). The political missives sent by early-twentieth-century Kuna chiefs show the strong imprint of the bureaucratic communications that young secretaries tried to emulate, and even more of Kuna oral discourse and the social situation of the letters' creation.

Writing and translation were for the Kuna closely bound together. Except for a handful who penned their own letters—Charly Robinson and Claudio Iglesias on Nargana, and Inabaginya's secretary, Samuel Guerrero, who occasionally wrote over his own signature—Kuna leaders dictated in their own language, and their words were taken down by someone else in Spanish or English. Letters, moreover, fulfilled the same functions and had much the same content as did oral interviews with outsiders.

Although I have not found descriptions of translation practice in the 1910s and 1920s, it undoubtedly followed much the same patterns I observed in my own fieldwork, which began a half-century later (Howe 1974, 199; 1986, 112–113). In my experience, if a non-Indian speaks today in a gathering or congress, or if a Kuna speaker addresses an audience made up at least partly of non-Indians, he stops every minute or so for a secretary to translate.[1] When a letter arrives in a village gathering house or a session of the Kuna General Congress (since 1945, the governing body of the Kuna reserve), a secretary reads the Spanish or English original and then immediately translates extempore (even though today most of his audience understands Spanish quite well). When a chief sends a letter, he dictates, usually in Kuna, and a secretary writes the document down in Spanish or (much less often) in English. Although, regrettably, I did not pursue the point closely in my fieldwork, in the instances I observed in the 1970s and 1980s secretaries sometimes wrote a second draft for a letter but more often sent their first draft, with perhaps a few corrections. Certainly the letters from early in the century show numerous signs of being first, and largely uncorrected, drafts.

WHAT LETTERS COMMUNICATED

The forms and goals of chiefly letters are best presented through a brief series of examples. In the excerpts that follow, most of them translated from Spanish, I have tried to approximate the form and style of the originals, breaking lines at the same places, indicating crossed-out words where they can be read, superscripting interlinear corrections, and attempting English equivalents for errors in Spanish spelling and grammar. Such things do not translate readily, however, and the English rendering of the letters in Spanish is at best an approximation. Bracketed question marks follow doubtful readings, and empty brackets indicate words that were illegible or cut off in microfilm or photocopies.

The range of functions in such letters was fairly narrow. In a few the sender tried to ingratiate himself with the recipient, to signal recognition of the recipient's social status, or otherwise to devote significant space to the social amenities, as is certainly the case in the short letter excerpted immediately below, sent to the intendente by Inabaginya in late 1919, soon after the chief had been induced to change his allegiance from Colombia to Panama (Inabaginya to Vaglio 10/28/19, AI).

Señor Don
    Humberto Vaglio M.
        Porvenir
Dear friend

      I greet you cordially in the union
of your esteemed family, and I wish for you every kind of
Happinesses, I arrived here without problem, all
the villages are very happy with my trip to

> Panama, the only one who is not in agreement
> with me is Sancurman [i.e., Colman].[2]
>
> The little bird that in entrance
> requested from me I haven't gotten it, but I am sending you
> a little dove.
>
> Without anything else to say to you my
> regard to your family.
>
> Your affct. friend,
> Inapaginya

Most of the time, however, except for sketchy attempts at formal salutations and closings and mostly unconvincing protestations of friendship, chiefs and their secretaries devoted relatively little space or effort to cultivating either the social graces or their correspondents.

Chiefs also asked for things in letters, though again, not that often. In one letter from 1913, for instance, Cimral Colman noted that his followers had complained about a coat—probably a uniform—that President Porras had given him and suggested that he should receive a more suitable replacement. Much more frequently, letter writers reported on recent events or their own actions, especially on meetings held and steps they had taken to fulfill agreements made with government officials. Two examples follow, the first written by Cimral Colman to President Porras in 1913, the second, from 1919, by Colman's rival Inabaginya to the head of the police detachment in Corazón de Jesús. Colman's letter reported on a meeting held by the villages under his leadership to discuss a visit to the president he had made the previous year (Colman to Porras 1/31/13, ANP, courtesy of Francisco Herrera).

> *Muy Señor mio:*
> I take up the pen to greet and to say the following.
> When I went to Visit in the days of Easter
> and as I ad said you that I was going to mak
> a meeting like a congress to tell him
> How the Trip had gone for me.
> And they came to visit in the days 28-29-30 of
> January of 1913. and they came and I am goin to name for you
> those who

have come to Visit.
Village Quepti[3] Chief Olo Wintitiler—Secretary Olo aviguiña,
Policeman Antonio Vasquez—Watchman Seakk.
Village Ticandiquí.[4] Chief Olo Wiliguiña Alcalde Igua Soguiguiña—secretary Igua tiniguiña—and a policeman.
Village irgandi. chief, Pepé. and a policeman.
Village Playon chico, chief Olo Vaniquilele—Secretary Olo in quique—Alcalde Benito Guillen.[5]
Village Tupile. Chief Luis Ami—secretary Igua aliguiña Alcalde Ina Soba—Watchman Oleliguiña.
these are the chiefs that came to mak the
meeting, to know how the trip had gone for me
and I have said everything all those I said to you. and they
were very pleased with my trip.
I told him ᵗʰᵃᵗ I arrived on the 25th at 1 am and on the following day we got the Pass[6] and in the afternoon
we went away to Panama and we arrived at 7 P.M. and immediately they found a hotel for us, and
they sent us im mediately to lodge us
there in that hotel, and on the following day we went
tosee Dr. B. Porras. and he received ᵘˢ with much
affection. I spok of everything what we spok
there in Panamá. and they were very content with my trip.

Inabaginya's much shorter letter also reported on a regional meeting, this one a rump session in which he tried—unsuccessfully, as it turned out—to supplant Charly Robinson and Colman with men of his own choosing and to proclaim himself chief of all the Kuna (Inabaginya to Garrido 11/08/19, AI).

Dear Carrido
I make this letter to say the following.
we metthe fifth of november of 1919~~18~~
The Narganaand tigri and the other village had
here. I want you to recognize
Charlie Lewis as Jefe of the indians in Narganá.[7] Elimin
ated the indians of ᴺᵃʳᵍᵃⁿᵃ[?] left Charles Rovinson, alone.
Now they friends of ours. When you arrive this letter

and answer me ~~nele~~ I compel ^{all} chiefs
I want them to treat the indians of naragana well
now I am Jefe of the indians. also I ~~remove~~
in Aglicanti I have they change Colman cannot be
Chef of Aglicandi any more.

I am yours attentively,
Inapaquiña

These accounts of recent meetings undoubtedly addressed concerns felt by their non-Indian recipients, who knew that the Kuna were divided, that different collections of villages followed Colman and Inabaginya, and that Nargana and Corazón de Jesús stood apart from both confederacies. Presidents, government secretaries, and intendentes certainly wanted to know that agreements made with Kuna leaders would hold and that they enjoyed grassroots support. But the reports also followed models from Kuna oral discourse: chiefs and delegates returning from regional convocations invariably deliver long verbal reports to their followers at home, offering detailed remarks on who attended, what was discussed, who said what, and what if anything was decided. If the meetings include chanting, a returning chief will sing to his village on his return, summarizing and repeating the performances he has heard. Such debriefing, an overt acknowledgment that chiefly power derives from popular consent, signals the importance in Kuna politics of consultation, information sharing, and the collective building of consensus (Howe 1986). It is not surprising that such concerns loomed large in external letters, or that later on, as procedures were formalized for regional meetings—or general congresses, as they came to be called—Kuna secretaries began writing up detailed minutes, or *actas*, of all the principal speeches and decisions.

More generally, Kuna political rhetoric makes heavy use of reported speech (see Sherzer 1983, 201–207). Orators often quote others at length, passing on something said by someone else (a friend met on the trail, a witness to a quarrel, a spirit apparition, a speaker at a regional meeting, Great Father as he created the world) and sometimes embedding one quote within another within another like a Russian egg or Chinese box. Colman, in his 1913 letter excerpted above, reported to President Porras not only on the meeting he had held with his principal followers but also on what he himself told his followers about his visit to Porras the year before—a rhetorical flourish that cannot have meant much to the president.

The list of names in Colman's letter—the chiefs, village constables, and *argars,* or chiefs' spokesmen (called *alcaldes* in the letter), who attended the meeting—also shows the imprint of Kuna discourse and social structure. Kuna villages are in many respects best seen as collections of named individuals (or at least of named males): both men and women traditionally receive unique Kuna names, and even with the Spanish and Anglophone names that have dominated in recent decades, overlap is minimized, as parents attempt to give each child a name otherwise absent in their village. In the councils or talking gatherings that occur several nights a week (Howe 1986), men participate, by and large, as individuals and not as representatives of kin groups, and in the sacred gatherings in which chiefs sing to their followers, they often begin by enumerating all the classes of leader and ritual adept present in the hall, thus emphasizing the wholeness and organic integration of the community (for examples, see Howe 1986, 37; Sherzer 1990, 52–53). And as later chapters will show, this profusion of named individuals and roles even characterizes cosmology and mythology, or sacred history, which enumerates not just the dozens of heroes sent from heaven to put things right on earth, but all the village elders who received them.

In the case of Colman's letter, the names and the form in which he listed them cannot have meant much to President Porras. Like the embedding of one narrative within another mentioned above, this feature of Kuna discourse lacked what Blommaert (2005, 69) calls semiotic mobility, the capacity to cross social and discursive space, not because individuals bored Porras (who was said to have stood as godfather to several hundred children), but because the individuals named by Colman were not ones who mattered to the president.

As is evident in all the letters reproduced above, Kuna leaders also devoted a great deal of space to attacking each other. Inabaginya, in particular, after giving up on Colombia in 1919 and pledging allegiance to Panama, wrote frequently to denounce Colman and inform the government of what his enemy was supposedly doing. Such rivalrous sniping formed one subset of a larger class of letters in which the writer attempted to bring something deplorable to the attention of authorities, or else, if the events or actions in question were already known, to influence how they would be interpreted. In effect, the archetypal form of communication was the denunciation, complaint, or counterargument, one move in a contentious politics of information.

In the pair of letters offered below, the opponents, Charly Robinson and Cimral (or Sam) Colman, change places, one as author and the other as target of attack. (For other examples, see Chapter 2 and Howe 1998, 20, 138, 171, 283.) In the first letter, from early 1913, Robinson was writing the government to defend Anna Coope, the Protestant missionary then newly arrived on his island, countering denunciations by Catholic priests, a neighbor chief, and especially Colman. The letter, written by Robinson himself rather than a secretary, is in English, and since the first page has been lost, the version given here starts *in medias res*. Elaborating on his insistence that Coope not be sent back to Colón, Robinson represented his goals through the metaphor of forward movement (Robinson to Porras 3/n.d./13, ANP).

Children like her very
much Dear sir lady going
with school very fast and
all my People like her but
san Colman he dont wanted
schooling in san Blas coast
and he dont wandet theire children
to Know anything and he
wandet Just like himself
I am well wandet schooling
in my Velices [i.e., villages] and all People
wandet in his velices Dear sir
it is Time to Indians learn
something other chief he dont
have nothing to do with me
I am trying my children to

Go a head and not go
back behind but
san Colman he Trying
to sent lady backe to Colon
we not senting lady back
to Colon we want lady
to go a head with schooling
if San Colman are [i.e., or] Joe Herdin
tell you anything you can
tell him to go to Chief

> Robinson in san Jose
> Nargana Dear sir you can
> tell him you dont heave
> nothing to do with lady
>
> General Charles Robinson

The second, very brief excerpt comes from a much longer letter sent by Colman to Intendente Humberto Vaglio in early 1919, during the brief period in which Colman was actively cooperating with a program to consolidate Panamanian sovereignty on the coast. After reporting on efforts he had been making on the government's behalf, Colman complained of reports that noserings were being suppressed on Nargana, which, as he would soon learn, signaled the beginning of an official campaign to suppress Kuna custom and the end of his partnership with Vaglio (Colman to Vaglio 2/01/19, ANP).

> I have had notice, and at the same time
> I inform you that the *poli-*
> *cial*[8] established in San José de Nar-
> ganá I don't know if with an order from Cha-
> rles Rabenson, it is said that he jailed
> an *indio,* and an *india* for rea-
> sons of having put a nosering
> on their little daughter, all this is
> a most ancient custom

THE POLITICS OF INFORMATION

For Kuna leaders, letters like these constituted a key mode of social action (Barton and Hall 1999), one they used, however, more effectively in some ways than others. Along with personal interviews, letters of complaint provided the primary vehicle for a politics of information and interpretation (discussed at length in Howe 1998, 119–149) through which different political actors tried to get their version of local events out to the press, to private parties, or most often to higher government officials. A letter or emissary or delegation sent to the city from San Blas could take anywhere from twenty-four hours to a week to reach the port of Colón on the Atlantic side, depending on weather, luck, and transport, and then at least several hours more to cross the isthmus by the only means possible, the Panama Railroad. (Government functionaries encouraged those they wished their superiors to hear by providing free rail passes.) San Blas was in effect isolated enough so that information did not flow readily into Panama City, but near enough (much closer, say, than the upper Amazon was to Andean capitals) to make it possible to push that information along with a reasonable chance of success.

Pitted against each other in this epistolary combat were rival chiefs, rival missionaries with their supporters, and especially Indian leaders in conflict with policemen and bureaucrats. With one notable exception—a petition from 1893 appealing to Queen Victoria against U.S. and Panamanian encroachments (see Howe 1998, 20; Salvador 1997, 91)—few contentious letters antedate the appearance of native scribes in the second decade of the century.[9] The first burst of polemic dates from 1913, when Charly Robinson brought Anna Coope to Nargana, and then when President Belisario Porras initiated a program to colonize and pacify the coast (Howe 1998, 85–86, 98–101). Letters really began to flow in 1919, when Porras appointed a fierce new governor, or intendente, Humberto Vaglio, who began actively suppressing Kuna culture. During the struggles that ensued on Nargana between Charly Robinson and Claudio Iglesias, the two sides bombarded officials with missives, petitions, and delegations. Colman, for his part, began the year with friendly letters to the new intendente (including the one excerpted above), but as both men came to appreciate the radical incompatibility of their goals and outlook, they began making numerous complaints against each other. Vaglio's successor, Andrés Mojica, noted with great irritation that Colman:

> would embark frequently for Colón and there he would relate, in his way, the events from the Coast of San Blas, and with ideas put in his head by external influences, he would opt to direct himself in person to the President of the Republic and the Secretary of Government to inform him that the Indians were outraged and mistreated.[10]

The "external influences," who are discussed below in Chapter 4, were headed by a lawyer from Colón named José de la Rosa, who for three years worked with Colman in a fruitless scheme to purchase titles for Kuna lands, provoking even more vitriolic letters from intendentes and their assistants, until October of 1922, when President Porras banned de la Rosa from San Blas (Howe 1998, 121–149, 188–191). Thereafter, Colman and his followers continued sending complaints, though perhaps less effectively than before.[11]

Overall, Kuna dissidents did a good job communicating their discontents. Unlettered and largely monolingual chiefs, assisted by youths with at best a few years of grade-school education, managed to convey crucial information and opinion to distant bureaucrats and newspapers. Their complaints, moreover, were heard and, sometimes at least, partly heeded. Official files include numerous queries from the Secretary of Government and Justice to the effect that an Indian leader or group had complained of one thing or another and would the intendente please respond or investigate and report on the truth of the matter (see Howe 1998, 130–176). Most of these demands were shrugged off, either summarily or after a perfunctory inquiry, but over time they contributed to a growing impression that something was wrong. In late 1920, during a few months in which Belisario Porras stepped down, the acting president, Ernesto Lefevre, eased Humberto Vaglio out of office, though Vaglio was probably most hurt by his own intemperance (Howe 1998, 145–146). In 1924, further allegations of abuse, combined with a critical letter by a visitor to the region (see Chapter 5), provoked another crisis of confidence. Although President Porras did not fulfill a promise to go investigate personally, the frosty tone of letters to Vaglio's successor, Andrés Mojica, indicates that he, too, had lost the confidence of his superiors (Howe 1998, 197–198). The Kuna never succeeded in stopping the police and intendente altogether, but overall, in their tenacious resistance, they did surprisingly well.

THE PRESENTATION OF INDIAN SELVES

In another respect, however, namely, presenting themselves as individuals and as a people through their letters and personal interviews, the Kuna were much less successful. What I have in mind here is not self-conscious defense of indigenous culture and ethnic identity, which is discussed in Chapter 4, but rather the arts of impression management in communication.

Laura Graham, in an essay entitled "How Should an Indian Speak?" (2002), has written insightfully on the dilemma of self-presentation as it affects Indian leaders today in making their case to external audiences. Graham suggests that a Catch-22, or double bind, confronts native representatives: if they speak their own language, whether from choice or necessity, they may be accepted as "real" Indians and thus tap into the authenticity of Indian identity, an association that may be further strengthened by native dress and other displays (see also Conklin 1997). But they also lose some control of their message and its interpretation. If, on the other hand, Indian representatives use a national language like English or Portuguese, they maximize control but endanger their authenticity. As Graham and Alcida Ramos (1998) have shown for Brazil, enemies of native organizing may seize on just such putative inauthenticity to attack Indian activists or even deny them legal rights reserved for indigenous peoples.

Nonetheless, native peoples of today at least enjoy the resources of positive symbolic associations and sometimes-friendly audiences, resources the Kuna and other Latin American Indians in the 1910s and 1920s mostly lacked. As Chapter 5 will show, some romantic ideas about Indians as a noble but vanishing race could be found among North Americans of the Canal Zone, and pro-indigenous rhetoric was beginning, very tentatively, to reappear in Latin America (see also Chapter 8), but such discourses had so far made only a slight impact on Panama outside the Zone. There was thus no significant reservoir of positive ideas on which the Kuna could draw. Latin Panamanians, who referred to indigenous peoples politely as *naturales,* or *indígenas,* more slightingly as *indios,* or with scorn as *cholos,* invoked a proverb (still heard occasionally today) that there are three ungrateful animals, the cat, the dove, and the Indian. Educated people, for their part, fully embraced evolutionary schemes that relegated aboriginal peoples to the levels of savagery and barbarism.

Within the larger category of *indio,* the Kuna occupied a marginal and partially favorable position. Unlike the Emberá, or Chocó, of the Darién, the Kuna went around fully clothed except for their bare feet, and though Kuna women's dress struck many Panamanians as garishly and offensively exotic, at least their men wore recognizable pants, shirts, and hats. Known to be monogamous, to engage in trade, to live in fixed communities, and to be organized politically, the Kuna were sometimes credited with being no worse than *semi-salvajes.* If government officials and others would not accept Kuna claims to being fully civilized already, they did grant them the possibility of becoming so fairly soon if they would just abandon noserings and chichas. Less positively, Kuna assertiveness, their lack of the humility expected of Indians, grated on Panamanian nerves.

Thus Indian leaders, in their letters and meetings with outsiders, faced a difficult version of the task most famously analyzed by Erving Goffman in *The Presentation of Self in Everyday Life,* with the important difference that Goffman was interested mostly in face-to-face interaction, while for the Kuna such encounters were often mediated in writing. Native leaders, who wanted respect and acceptance rather than the scorn they clearly recognized, attempted to present themselves as worthy individuals (while running down their rivals and enemies as lying no-goods), and by implication, to present their people as a whole in the same positive light. In Goffman's terminology, a chief and secretary constituted a team, and the "on-stage" region was found on paper and in the consulting rooms of government secretariats and the *presidencia*.

Also apposite is Goffman's *Stigma*, because chiefs were attempting to manage a spoiled or stigmatized identity, one very like those considered by Goffman himself. The stigma of being Indian was in one sense non-negotiable (and *passing* as non-Indian was in this case not contemplated). From another perspective, however, the assumptions and associations of Indian identity might be challenged or renegotiated. In Europe and the Americas, the seemingly fixed distinctions of ethnicity, race, and class were interwoven with a set of assumptions about education and breeding. Worthy, elevated people could be recognized not just by their physiognomy and ancestry but also by the level of formal education they had attained (Hobsbawm 1987, 174–179), and by the way they dressed, walked, ate, spoke, and wrote letters. These distinctions of manner and taste helped maintain, structure, and legitimize, but also unsettle, class hierarchies, as they still do today (Bourdieu 1984; Lamont 1992),[12] while providing opportunities (illustrated by dozens of novels) for occasional individuals or groups to raise themselves up. In the quite fluid society of late-nineteenth- and early-twentieth-century Panama, cultural capital allowed for considerable mobility, as was illustrated by the career of Belisario Porras himself (or rather, *Doctor* Belisario Porras), who had risen to national leadership from illegitimate birth and a middling provincial background by way of university studies in Bogotá and Belgium (see Szok 2004).

While every aspect of lifestyle and demeanor counted, those based on language probably counted most. In all societies, communication involves what sociolinguists call indexical meaning, marking aspects of the social context of communication, and "through indexicality, every utterance tells something about the person who utters it" (Blommaert 2005, 11). In all societies, especially all stratified societies, linguistic resources are unequally distributed: "speakers can/cannot speak varieties of languages, they can/cannot read and write, and they can/cannot mobilize specific resources for performing specific actions" (2005, 11). Linguistic varieties are also judged unequally, even invidiously (Irvine and Gal 2000; Blommaert

2005, 58, 61). And in complex, multiethnic societies, the daunting task that confronts many speakers and writers, including Kuna scribes, is to use linguistic resources not just on their home ground but "translocally," across boundaries of culture and ethnicity (Blommaert 2005, 69).[13]

In the long-established "scriptural economy" of Latin America (Collins and Blot 2003, 129; Rama 1996), literacy, measured in levels of written fluency as well as the absolute distinction between literate and illiterate, mattered as much as oral mastery of the national language. As social index and form of cultural capital (Barton and Hall 1999, 11), letter writing may in past centuries have mattered most for elites,[14] but by the nineteenth century, striving literate members of the middle and working classes in Europe and the Americas were busy writing letters of all sorts (Dierks 1999; Schultz 1999).

Although Kuna chiefs and scribes could certainly not expect, especially in the short term, to overturn or significantly alter long-established class and ethnic hierarchies, they could influence the judgments of powerful others by conforming to the distinctions of style and taste embodied in written communication, and these judgments, in turn, could influence the actions and general dispositions of those men. These distinctions were set out, for those who did not absorb them in school or at home, in handbooks of correspondence (e.g., Diez de le Cortina 1915; Fuentes and Elías 1918; López Paniagua 1943), which made it clear that through a letter one projected a self, a self that, if perhaps not gentlemanly, might seem sufficiently serious and respectable to persuade its recipient to interact and to grant at least provisional social acceptance. In her study (1996, 1999) of streetside scribes in Mexico City, Judy Kalman shows that clients (most of whom can read and write) resort to professional letter writers precisely because they recognize the importance of projecting "seriousness" through letterhead paper, typewriting, and conformity to literary and bureaucratic convention. Both clients and scribes assume that the letters will be judged, and that "by extension, any judgment about a text might be carried over to its bearer" (1999, 141).

> Written documents are one of the many ways that image is projected in societies with complex administrative and political bureaucracies. Our uses of writing ... are part of the social semiotic ... multiple identification cards we carry around with us and when interpreted by others reveal who we are. ... Both the scribes and their clients recognize the authority of writing as a means to legitimize social

action. . . . Written language is exposed to both moral and political judgments and its use has social consequences for the user. (Kalman 1999, 49, 113, 137, 141–142)

Unfortunately, Kuna scribes, most of them teenagers fresh out of primary school, were by and large not yet up to this demanding social task: in sociolinguistic terms, they had not yet mastered the repertoires of bureaucratic communication. Although their letters varied widely in polish and grammatical correctness, on the whole they fell well below what recipients would have considered minimum standards, and the worst were close to incoherent. The grammatical and stylistic lapses were numerous. Kuna secretaries often omitted H's in their writing, as in *agame,* for *hágame,* or else they added them where they were not needed, as in *hasí,* for *así.* The letters B and V were often mixed as well, for instance in *bendido,* for *vendido,* or *barios,* for *varios,* as were initial Y's, I's, and LL's. Punctuation and accenting were erratic at best, as was use of the formal conventions of letter writing: most scribes made stabs at standard greetings and, less consistently, at *despedidas,* or closings, but did much less well with the self-consciously elevated vocabulary and hypercorrect diction of bureaucratic communication.

Linguistic interference between Kuna and Spanish caused other problems, especially concerning the pairs of consonants or stops represented in Spanish by the letters T/D, P/B, and Qu, C, or K/G, and their closest but distinctly different equivalents in Kuna, which sometimes led scribes to write *greo* in place of *creo,* or *basa* or *vasa* instead of *pasa.*[15] More generally, the Kuna language makes no grammatical distinctions by gender, verb forms do not change by person, and plurality is not always overtly marked. Thus (as I have learned the hard way myself) someone accustomed to Kuna may not always make proper distinctions of person, gender, and number in speaking or writing Spanish.

Secretaries were in fact inconsistent on quite a few points—they omitted accents and punctuation or misspelled words in one place but not another—suggesting that at some level they knew better, and that many of their mistakes resulted from haste and insufficiently internalized norms. This inconsistency, along with the many run-on sentences, some of which begin with one subject and end with another, leaves the distinct impression of someone struggling to keep up as best he could with chiefly dictation. The letters, in other words, were heavily and negatively marked by the circumstances of their production, as well as by the limited skills of their producers.[16] Perhaps most important, they reflected the great value placed in Kuna oratory on the ability to respond to the situation at hand, to stand and speak with no advance preparation—and in this case to write without drafts or revision.

Just what most letters lacked can be seen clearly by contrast with a much more polished missive—a petition by Claudio Iglesias and his followers against Charly Robinson (1/30/21, AI)—in which the writers obviously benefited from coaching and editorial help from their allies among the police and teachers. The letter, which, unlike almost any of the other documents in the sample, was typewritten, began as follows:

> Señor Secretary of Government and Justice,
> PANAMA
> Most honorable and respected sir:
>
> We the undersigned, who compose the majority of the wholesome and responsible element of the islands of Narganá and Corazón de Jesús, protest in our own name and in [that] of the above-mentioned tribes before his Excellency the Sr. President of the Republic through the worthy channel of yourself, of the bad, reprehensible, and unbearable conduct that for some time the Ságuila [i.e., Chief] Charles Robinson has been observing.
>
> To give you an idea of who Charles Robinson is and of the way that he has treated and mistreated all the indians of our villages, allow us to point out to you various of his actions: . . .

The petition, though it displayed a few minor infelicities of its own, projected just the image of seriousness and progressive civilization that chiefs' letters lacked.[17]

It was not just form but content that put Kuna writers in a bad light. Chiefs and others asked for things, sometimes in ways that could make them appear grasping or wheedling or childish. Much of what they asked for, moreover, consisted of symbolic acknowledgments of their status, like the uniform coat given Colman in 1913, and the titles affected by Kuna leaders. At one time or another, Charly Robinson, Colman, and Inabaginya all styled themselves "General" (Inabaginya more precisely as Brigadier

General), and one of the inducements offered the latter in 1919 to persuade him to abandon Colombia was that he could retain his honorary title (Howe 1998, 132).

The barely hidden scorn with which Panamanian officials held these gifts and affectations came out clearly in one of Humberto Vaglio's tirades: "General Colman would like to cover his body with a brilliant uniform and burden it with a multitude of decorations, even though these are of copper and have no value."[18] As I have argued in a different context (Howe 1998, 215–216), gifts to indigenous recipients often tacitly dishonor them. Even with less tainted goods, Kuna leaders, by relying on national authorities to grant or ratify their status, appeared at their most dependent, belying the cultural and political autonomy on which they otherwise insisted.

Kuna leaders also made themselves look bad through their mutual hostility, ultimately besmirching themselves with the same accusations of duplicity and dishonesty they threw at each other. Colman may possibly have learned this lesson, if one can make valid inferences from an apparent absence of written polemics in later years, but Inabaginya, who in 1930 was still fulminating in print against Colman's successor Nele Kantule (Howe 1998, 295), certainly never did. Again, the outspoken Humberto Vaglio undoubtedly voiced what other officials thought: "It is true that lies are innate in Indians, just as it pleases them to be the carrier of everything bad and uproarious" (Howe 1998, 134).[19]

The irony is that the Panamanian recipients of Kuna letters indulged in just the same vices. The letters of bureaucrats and politicians are full of requests to patrons and superiors for largesse, both material and symbolic, not to mention slander and invective. Belisario Porras spiced his letters with attacks and cutting remarks against his many enemies, some of them previously his friends.[20] But personal attacks have their own rules and procedures, as Joanne Freeman, in *Affairs of Honor,* has brilliantly shown for North American political feuding at the end of the eighteenth century (2002, 105–158); though similar studies have yet to be written for Panama, one may be sure that the clumsy broadsides Kuna chiefs leveled against each other did them little good.

If criticism by their recipients of specific letters has not come to light, broader criticism of Indian character and practice certainly has. The two men who probably received the most Kuna letters and who in their different ways were most receptive to the Indians and their discontents, President Belisario Porras and his cabinet secretary, Ricardo Alfaro, both expressed harsh global judgments of Indian immaturity. Porras urged on his subordinates "soft and convincing measures, which demonstrate that we are civilized men, because in no other way will we justify ourselves in aiming to carry civilization to . . . an inferior race" (Howe 1998, 131), sentiments echoed in a scornful letter written by Alfaro following the Kuna rebellion of 1925 (see Chapter 5 below).[21] The biased judgments articulated by the two leaders—the persistent anti-Indian prejudices, however *superior* they might have considered them—undoubtedly preceded their correspondence with Kuna leaders, but at best the letters did nothing to dispel them.

WRITING AND CIVILIZATION

If there is a personal, reflexive element in my arguments, it is certainly not that I look down on these chiefs and early scribes in the supremely difficult task they undertook. On the contrary, I find it all too easy to empathize and identify with them. Although I came to Panama in 1970 enjoying vastly more privilege than the Kuna, I failed then, and to a slightly lesser extent I still fail today, to project myself in Spanish as I would wish. My problems are most acute in spoken rather than written language, in particular the rapid-fire speech of urban Panama; but otherwise I feel great kinship with those adolescent boys of 1915 and 1920.

It may seem to some readers that I ask too much of the early secretaries, or that failure to write correct letters is trivial in comparison with all the economic, legal, social, and political handicaps suffered by native peoples. But writing, or its absence, has played important parts in the struggles of many indigenous Americans (see the discussion in Chapter 1), and the difficulties experienced by unschooled Indians in making their way in the world of lawyers, bureaucrats, and company ledgers have perpetuated their exploitation and suffering nearly as much as have guns, hunger, and disease. Today at the beginning of the twenty-first century, educated Kuna, by now in the majority, speak and write a Spanish vastly better than that of either the early *sikkwis* or my own, but even sympathetic Panamanians have commented to me repeatedly on the Kuna tendency to pronounce *peso* and *beso* alike, and as recently as 2003, an academic at the University of Panama, Professor Milciades Ortiz, provoked a small uproar (as well as outraged but highly literate and polished replies from contemporary Kuna intellectuals) with an anti-Indian polemic that concluded: "Personally, it bothers me to see an indian who doesn't know how to speak Spanish well because he has the privilege of being an 'autochthonous Panamanian.' I have nothing against our indians, but one must tell the truth."[22]

Native peoples struggle for dignity and respect as well as land and food. If we listen to the indigenous rights movement of today, we hear peoples and organizations engaging in a contentious dialogue with national and international society about what it means to be an Indian. The precocious Kuna entered into that dialogue sixty or seventy years early, and if in 1915 or 1920 their self-presentation lacked polish, later chapters will show that they were just beginning to find their voice.

Representation and Reply

FOUR

In the previous two chapters, emphasis fell on the active roles played by the Kuna, first in grasping or rejecting the opportunities presented by schools and writing, and second in turning literacy to political ends. The present chapter takes up the topic, central to the work as a whole, of writing as a tool of cultural representation. After briefly surveying the state of ethnographic knowledge of the Kuna at the beginning of the twentieth century, I consider the paradoxical ethnocidal program imposed on them between 1919 and 1925, paradoxical because government functionaries, rather than developing a systematic orientalist portrait of their target, effectively ignored and obscured indigenous identity and culture. To the extent that they did focus their gaze on the Kuna, officials directed angry words at the situation immediately at hand, denouncing and assigning blame for Kuna separatism and resistance to national authority. Their attacks inspired Indian replies, including two failed but significant attempts to answer their detractors. The chapter—and the book—are thus concerned with a long-running and often contentious dialogue, with both representation and counterrepresentation, and with the close connection between representation and action.

EARLY ETHNOGRAPHIC KNOWLEDGE

Given the tenacity with which the Kuna had resisted foreign rule and the frequency with which they had consorted with Spain's enemies, it is perhaps surprising just how little anyone recorded about their lives before the twentieth century. Buccaneers, missionaries, and colonial officials in some cases offered vivid if naïve and fragmentary impressions of Indian life. The best known of those accounts—from the pirate Lionel Wafer, a frustrated Jesuit named Jacobo Balburger, and a late-eighteenth-century governor, Andrés de Ariza—indicated that the Kuna practiced matrilocal residence and bride service, that albinos were common among them, and that the most prominent figures were the chief or captain, the *lele*, or sorcerer, a performer Ariza called *camoturo*,[1] and a martial figure called the *urunia*, but on many other questions they were silent.[2] The most frequently cited nineteenth-century source, the Frenchman Armand Reclus (1881), plagiarized much of his ethnographic sketch from Governor Ariza's report of a hundred years before,[3] while a compendium assembled by a Colombian scholar, Vicente Restrepo (1888, 55–63, 77–88), served mainly to show how often observers repeated each other and how little was known on even the most basic points.[4]

Toward the end of the nineteenth century, at a moment when the Colombian government was imposing control over coastal trade with the Indians, the port inspector of Colón dedicated a few pages of a report to San Blas, based apparently on a visit in 1890 or 1891.[5] A few small errors crept into his account, particularly when he wrote that diviners, or seers (properly *nele*, or *lele*), were called *mila*, a word that actually means tarpon. But he correctly recorded the most salient facts not just of indigenous governance (village chiefs, a paramount leader at Sasardi, annual regional gatherings, the prominence of Nargana), but of domestic life (bride service) and collective rituals for females at birth, puberty, and marriage. If he dwelt unpleasantly on supposed threats to kill women and children in the event of outside invasion, and on the immolation of an insane woman on Nargana, he also credited the Indians with religious beliefs, careful burial customs, and even with keeping peace during their drinking bouts.

Serious ethnography began with Leonardo Gassó, the missionary who worked on Nargana from 1907 to 1912. Father Gassó, steeped in the Jesuit tradition of scholarship, published the diaries from his first two years with the Indians (Gassó 1911–1914), as well as a native-language catechism (1908a), a grammar (1908b), and a series of letters that took up where the diaries left off—all of it in Spanish religious journals.[6] In addition to the vivid, if quite biased, portrait of Indian life and politics that emerges from Gassó's narratives (see Howe 1998, 35–63), two diary chapters (X and XI) were devoted to an extended ethnographic sketch, which increased what was known about the Kuna by a whole order of magnitude.

Gassó provided a fairly complete and more or less accurate account of matrilocal residence, marriage by capture, bride service, and other key elements in Kuna domestic organization. His remarks on native leadership and law were heavily colored by his disappointment with Charly Robinson's limited power and by his shocked fascination with the lynching of the mission's greatest opponent. Despite Gassó's vehement opposition to "gentile" religion, he was the first to give any sense of the abundance and nature of Kuna ritual specialists. His account, very much within the mold of missionary ethnography, returned repeatedly to the character and moral qualities of the Indians, and to whatever advanced or impeded his own work, particularly Kuna aversion to the outside world, which seemed to echo his own loathing for the corruptions of modernity. He kept finding parallels between indigenous practice and its Catholic and Spanish equivalents—and especially between himself and his perceived archenemies, the senior village ritualists—while at the same time insisting on their radical alterity (Howe 1998, 7–8, 49–50). Ambivalent throughout, he often lauded the Indians for industry, piety, modesty, intelligence, and domestic harmony, though he undercut his praise by crediting their virtues to his eighteenth-century predecessor, Father Jacobo Balburger.[7] When crossed or frustrated, he blasted the Kuna as children, savages, madmen, or beasts.

Gassó's account, it must be said, is seriously flawed by careless, slapdash linguistics and ethnography, and his grammar (Gassó 1908b), based on the dogmatic assumption that the Kuna tongue is a combination of several others, is a complete disaster. Despite these flaws, his writings provided the first usable, comprehensive, and mostly trustworthy account of Kuna lifeways—though not one that many people read other than prospective Spanish missionaries and a handful of European scholars.[8]

Few Panamanians, in any case, learned about Indians from foreign books or obscure government documents. Afro-Hispanic *costeños* who inhabited the coast between San Blas and Colón knew the Kuna from both peaceful trade and conflict over natural resources. In Colón, ideas and information came from Kuna visitors and migrant laborers, and from opinions on the Indians offered by the captains and crews of trading vessels. Many on the north coast learned two indigenous words, *ságuila* (*saila*), or chief, and *machigua*, "boy"—the latter a label applied to all Kuna regardless of age or sex. Recognized for chiefs and monogamy, for clothes, commerce, and fixed villages, Kuna society was otherwise hardly known at all.

CULTURAL POLITICS AND ETHNOCIDE

Despite the ignorance of indigenous life pervasive in Panama, cultural questions dominated the struggle between the Kuna and the Republic during the first quarter of the twentieth century. Leonardo Gassó, who worked in San Blas as an agent of the government as well as of the Church, professed a willingness to tolerate Indian custom but ended up campaigning relentlessly against puberty ceremonies and their associated heavy drinking, and even more against the Kuna sacred gathering, which he correctly perceived as his mission's principal competition. By the time he departed in 1912, Gassó left the Kuna very much on the defensive concerning their way of life.

Anna Coope, the Protestant missionary who succeeded Gassó in 1913, was much more tolerant and patient, and except concerning alcohol, which she, too, opposed with all her might, she was willing to work slowly through quiet persuasion, even against customs she abhorred, such as piercing the noses of female babies. Two years later, when the government first imposed schools and police posts on Nargana and three other villages, its employees also refrained at first from interfering much in Indian life.

This tolerance ended abruptly, however, at the beginning of 1919, as the administration of Belisario Porras moved first to suppress the noserings and leg bindings worn by Kuna women, and soon thereafter, all of indigenous culture. As I have previously argued at greater length (Howe 1991a; 1998, 177–178), Porras and other nationalist officials, oppressed by the infant republic's weakness and its domination by the United States, responded to the task of nation-building with a program of cultural homogenization. Forced to accept the presence of one foreign, non-Hispanic enclave in the very heart of the country, they could not tolerate another among the nation's Indians.

The government's civilizing campaign was undoubtedly influenced by very sketchy information about the Indians from a variety of reports and memoranda.[9] These written sources were overshadowed, however, by two successive visits to San Blas by Presidents Carlos Mendoza and Belisario Porras in 1910 and 1915.[10] Warmly welcomed at some islands, both presidential parties were defiantly rebuffed at others displaying Colombian flags. At Sasardi in eastern San Blas, an angry mob confronted Mendoza's vessel, announcing that Chief Inabaginya was at that moment in Bogotá. At the same place five years later, Inabaginya personally rejected Panamanian claims to sovereignty and proclaimed his equality with President Porras. Both encounters dramatized the separatism and subversive loyalties of the Indians, as well as the state's inability to control them. On Nargana, where both parties were well received, the visitors could not help contrasting the progress of civilization under Charly Robinson with the remnants of native barbarity, evident most of all in the costume of Kuna women. In this instance, ethnographic and quasi-ethnographic writing (what little there was of it) yielded to dramatic firsthand experience.

Given the prominence of ethnocide among the government's goals, one might have expected its officials and apologists to have developed a systematic discourse about the Indians, an authoritative representation of their character and customs. Theorists of orientalism and colonial discourse, whatever their many differences on other points, almost all agree on the scope and reach and power of such discourses. Orientalist discourses are seen, not just as supports or rationalizations for Western domination, but as an integral part of the colonial project.[11]

In this light, it is striking how very little Panamanian officials knew or cared about native *usos y costumbres:* an official discourse was in fact notable, if not for its complete absence, at least for its very sparse, patchy, desultory nature.[12] Although a newspaper writer for the *Diario de Panamá* (8/18/1910) who covered the 1910 presidential visit called for anthropological studies as a sound basis for civilizing the region, government functionaries could not be bothered to pay much attention to the customs they wished to extirpate, except for a few key traits taken as indices of Indian barbarism, notably the supposed lack of hygiene in their island villages and the noserings and limb bindings worn by Kuna women (and even women's dress attracted no serious attention). Characteristically, in 1919 the administration suppressed the consumption of alcohol as a cause of disorder, taking hardly any note, positive or negative, of the elaborate rituals in which drinking was embedded (Howe 1998, 133–134, 180–181). The Indians, though scorned, were not orientalized except in the most minimal, offhand fashion.

The only aspect of native practice that gained the complete and undivided attention of government officials was the one they hated most: resistance to national control.[13] In effect, they defined and understood indigenous society negatively, according to what the Indians missed or rejected—a lack of civilization, an absence of loyalty, an unwillingness to join the nation, an inability to resist outside influences, and an anarchic refusal to submit.[14] Some of this intensely negative opinion made its way into print, mostly in intendentes' reports published in the biennial *Memorias de Gobierno y Justicia;* the greatest part, however, was conveyed in letters from lower-level officials to their superiors, the Secretary of Government and Justice and the President of the Republic.

It should be acknowledged that in at least two cases, both of them antedating the period of most active conflict from 1919 to 1925, Kuna separatism and resistance inspired ambivalent, half-positive characterizations. The memorial that introduced the 1912 legislation authorizing colonization of San Blas alluded to the coast's unnamed inhabitants as "the indomitable race that bore without yielding the fire and iron of the Conquistadores." Otherwise, however, the memorial depicted them as irrational holdouts from a great national project, who had caused "notable damage to the tranquility of the country and the exchequer" through their independence and their dealings with pirates and *contrabandistas*. It would thus be wrong "to preserve, plunged in barbarism, with a mockery of civilization and humanity, no less than twelve thousand individuals belonging to the Panamanian nation" (*Gaceta Oficial* 1912, 3848–3849; Howe 1998, 98).

Similarly, in his initial report, Enrique Hurtado, the first intendente, appointed in 1915 to head the newly created Circunscripción de San Blas, analyzed Kuna resistance in his biennial report in a way that mixed praise and criticism.

> Colonization cannot be improvised, nor can the nature of a race be changed just by coming closer to it, and if this race is like the indian, a race completely pure, which has lived completely free from all foreign power, the work is much more difficult. Their own customs are an obstacle to imposing on them the obligations of our laws. Their form of government in which authority is relative and no one holds it except when it is conceded by the whole people for each special case, makes them reject all other authority, which in their primitive minds will appear absurd, since one exercises it only without having adopted its trappings.
>
> Slave peoples are easy to dominate, a little kindness or rigor is sufficient to make of them what might be wanted; free peoples are indomitable and the methodological attraction, the slow evolution on the course that the superior will has predetermined is the only means of exercising its fusion with the race. The Indians of San Blas are free men.[15]

These early and partial concessions to native independence, however, were not repeated, and the unusually tolerant Hurtado resigned as intendente in 1917 after only two years. During the period of active struggle from 1919 to 1925, Kuna resistance was depicted as an unmitigated evil by his successors, Humberto Vaglio (1919–1920) and Andrés Mojica (1921–1925), as well as by the teachers and police agents under their command.

VEXATIOUS MEDDLERS

In explaining Indian separatism, police and intendentes first of all blamed third parties—interfering, seditious outsiders who egged the Indians on and intruded into situations that did not concern them.[16] This mindset, already evident in the memorial attached to the 1912 legislation and reinforced by the two presidential visits, was invoked repeatedly in the late 1910s and early 1920s.

> One cannot describe . . . just how difficult the work is made for us here when there are in the midst of those same Indians individuals who consciously work to instill in the Indians all the hostility and rebelliousness that are set against the advancement and subjugation of the tribes. Therefore, I regard as the most effective measure the expulsion of every pernicious element existing on this Coast. (Intendente Humberto Vaglio to President Belisario Porras 12/16/19, ABP)

Official writers typically focused their invective against the individual or group who had most recently thwarted them, beginning with the *contrabandistas* and others who were thought to be encouraging the Kuna in old nineteenth-century loyalties to Colombia.

> Compounding the intrigues of [Chief] Inabaginya are those of the Colombian traders who come there and in turn exploit the ignorance of the Indians. . . . To gain the Indians' friendship they speak to them against Panama, telling them that Panama belongs to the Yankees and that the Yankees will come to San Blas and expel them from there—while Colombia, on the other hand, would oust the Yankees and Panamanians from their waters, leaving them in the isolation they long for. (Enrique Hurtado to Secretary 8/15/13, ANP)

As Colombian interest in San Blas faded in the decades after Panamanian independence, fears of eastern sedition waned, and bureaucrats complained more often of noxious influences from the West, in particular, the masters and crews, many of them of Antillean origin, of coasting merchant vessels based in Colón, who were suspected of selling arms and liquor to the Indians, of carrying unfortunate news back to the city, and in the case of itinerant goldsmiths, of encouraging Indian women to hold on to their gold noserings.

> ... I firmly believe that the general tendency on the Coast on the part of almost every one of its exploiters, most of them foreigners, is to create difficulties for the Government of the Republic ... sowing among the Indians mistrust of the Government and instilling in them disobedience to the Government and its authorities. ... And all this is nothing other than the consequence of the selfishness of commerce: that thirst for gain and the innate desire of the merchants to make a fortune on this Coast, no matter what it takes, as the goal of their exploitation. (Intendente Vaglio to President Belisario Porras 12/01/19, ABP)[17]

Merchants, however, inspired official invective less frequently than did the missionaries Anna Coope and Martha Purdy. Suspicions about the Protestant mission, and more generally about North American influence on the coast, intensified during struggles that wracked Nargana during 1919, and especially after June of that year, when Charly Robinson, hard-pressed by Claudio Iglesias and his police allies—and, it was assumed, egged on by Coope—mounted a brief, unsuccessful uprising (Howe 1998, 121–129). Thereafter Coope was blamed for any and all troubles in Nargana or Corazón de Jesús—and often beyond.[18]

> [from a letter addressed to Coope herself:] There is little else I could say to make you desist, as is my wish, from interfering with the Nargana authorities, constantly advising Ságuila Charles Robinson as to how to act against our laws and precepts. (Intendente Vaglio to Anna Coope, in Intendente to Secretary 4/04/19, AI)

> Since it could be that the already frequent uprisings by the Indians may be primarily the work of a few individuals in their midst or some outsider, it would be advisable for you [to deal with them]. This office has reasons in this case to suspect a North American missionary. The current purpose of her mission seems to be to make the Indians regard Panamanian things as devoid of any use

or value. (Sub-secretary of Government and Justice to Intendente 6/30/23, AI)

Antagonism against third parties was by no means confined to foreigners. As scapegoat, even Anna Coope yielded to José de la Rosa, the lawyer from Colón who cooperated with Cimral Colman from 1919 to 1922 (see Howe 1998, 136–191). Anger at the meddling lawyer knew no bounds.

> ... De la Rosa, that man without scruples who only wants to exploit the rich mother lode of the Indians' credulity. (Intendente Vaglio to Secretary 12/01/19, ABP)
>
> This petition could not be any more slanderous or implausible, written as it is by José de la Rosa, whose malignancy of spirit and hatred toward us are apparent in all his actions. ... I tell you again that de la Rosa together with Colman are the ones responsible for the terrible events that take place on this Coast and who damage and obstruct the good wishes that the Government yearns to establish in this region, and that the great leniency shown towards them up to now has given rise to the constant interruptions suffered in the discharge of our official functions. (Police Lieutenant Antonio Linares to Secretary 10/06/20, AI)

There can be little doubt that police and bureaucrats did indeed have much to complain about. Before his expulsion from the region in 1922, de la Rosa skillfully thwarted the administration at every turn while egging on Kuna dissidents. Anna Coope, though she plausibly insisted on her devotion to the precept of rendering unto Caesar, did foment dissension at least indirectly by teaching a foreign religion and foreign loyalties. A Mexican vagabond, Olivo Olivares, who passed down the coast in 1922 fulfilled bureaucratic fears with a vengeance, actively stirring the Indians up against the government (Howe 1998, 188–190; Herrera 1984, 181–188).

Blaming third parties, however realistic on occasion, became fixed in official discourse as an all-purpose explanation and justification for failure—its status as ideology, in other words, does not stand or fall on its occasional truth value. The category of seditious meddler expanded freely, to include Indians from unpacified villages who influenced or even communicated with communities under police control, followers who supported resistance by their own leaders, and even, implicitly, higher-ups in the government who restrained the police and intendente or listened to Indian complaints (see Chapter 3; also Howe 1998, 137–139). In the last analysis, anyone who came between officials and the Indians they expected to dominate was a third party.

Such attitudes, far from unique, turn up regularly wherever multiple powers impinge on subaltern peoples. In seventeenth-century New England, Puritans of the Plymouth and Massachusetts Bay colonies were preoccupied with the influence on the Indians of their rivals and enemies, as were the British, French, and Spanish throughout the colonial era.[19] Much more recently, alliances between Indians and foreign NGOs in Brazil have provoked a nationalist backlash and accusations of subversion (Conklin and Graham 1995; Ramos 1998). Given the heterogeneous collection of interests and ethnicities on the San Blas coast in the early twentieth century, the massive U.S. presence on the isthmus, and the Panamanian government's insistence on making the Kuna over forthwith, blaming third parties was probably inevitable.

INCORRIGIBLE MALCONTENTS

Diatribes against meddling outsiders in no way absolved the Kuna they were accused of leading astray—indeed Indian character came to be defined partly in terms of its alleged susceptibility to such influence. Blame fell most of all on village and regional chiefs, who were called *saila*, or *sagla*, or in the spelling most common in the documents, *ságuila*.[20] For most of the period in question, the government lacked the personnel and resources to rule the Indians without using *sailas* as intermediaries;[21] it was only in the latter stages of pacification that chieftainship was suppressed altogether, and then only on the islands most firmly under police domination. For most of this period, authorities depended heavily on the support or acquiescence of a handful of compliant chiefs. But they never envisioned indirect rule as more than a temporary expedient, and over time, they increasingly took native chiefs as the source of their troubles.

On occasion they railed against ordinary village-level *sailas* who proved troublesome or resistant.[22] They reserved their most heated invective, however, for chiefs with regional authority or influence, among them Nele Wardada of Ustupu, or Portogandi, later known, much more famously, as Nele Kantule.

> I have just this moment been informed by Captain Scott of the schooner Marcella that Saguila Nele Guartata of Portogandi had threatened to kill him if he sought to catch turtles in this area.

I believe this man needs to be given an exemplary punishment, since he is the most insolent Saguila to be found anywhere in the Circumscription. (Santiago Castillo, Head of 2d Police Detachment, to Intendente 5/31/21, AI)

After 1915, the errant chiefs also included Charly Robinson of Nargana, who had once been the government's great hope for civilizing the Indians.

That everything that happened is purely and simply the work of the cunning Saguila Charles Robinson, who, egged on by his coterie of old, obstinate, and treacherous men, came to harbor the lofty ambition of becoming the Saguila General of the coast, and for that reason he rebelled against the Government . . . (Intendente Vaglio to Secretary 6/11/19, ABP)[23]

Inabaginya of Sasardi, seen as the government's greatest enemy until his conversion from Colombia to Panama in 1919, was cultivated thereafter for his willingness to inform on his rival leaders, which, as it turned out, did not shield him from further criticism.

Inabaginya is deceitful like the rest of the Indians, and his deceitful and hypocritical conduct is well known to us, tired as we are of seeing him promise one thing to us and turn around and do something else, or to incite the other Indians to proceed to counter the legal and appropriate dispositions issued by the Government. (Intendente Vaglio to Secretary 1/20/20, ABP)[24]

It was Cimral Colman, however, the most dogged, persistent opponent of government domination, who came in for the most impassioned attacks. Colman, his enemies claimed, was a fount of vice and malignity, the source of every problem, every failure on the Coast of San Blas.

Colman does not just exploit the Indians but also looks everywhere for the way to obstruct the path of advancement and civilization on this Coast, earning the friendship of all the Saguilas and Indians who, like him, intend to live out their lives as savages and are always prepared to counter all the good done to them. (Intendente Vaglio to Secretary 5/14/20, AI)

Second of all, we have the undeniable[25] truth that Colman . . . resorts to tales, lies, imaginary deeds, false accusations and disparaging statements that are always directed at the long-suffering local police force. . . . On a great many occasions Colman has been the instigator of discord among Indians. (Lt. Linares to Secretary 11/27/20, AI)[26]

However much bureaucrats and police agents were moved to write by their consuming hate for Colman and by their frustrations of the moment with any other enemy, by implication their philippics encompassed *all* native leaders. Taken together, their attacks created a collective (and self-contradictory) portrait of Kuna *ságuilas* as obstructive and power-hungry opportunists—two-faced, ignorant, lazy, anarchic, simultaneously vacillating and stubborn, both clever and stupid, opportunistic but set in outmoded ways, dictatorial but dominated by their followers, opposed to everything progressive and uplifting. Once in a while, bureaucrats brought these individual polemics together into a collective indictment:

Chiefs like Colman, Charles Robinson and the rest have absolutely no interest in the advancement of the work of civilization, since the ignorance of their peoples is the source of their well-being. In general none of the Saguilas governs his people, they lack authority, since they hold on to their positions only by the fact that they know how to toady to the Indians without in the slightest discouraging them in their usages and customs. (Intendente Vaglio to Secretary 6/04/19, ABP)

. . . when one believes that this or that Indian Chief is an efficacious collaborator with the Government it turns out that he is an apostle of opposition. (Report by Intendente Mojica, 1921)[27]

. . . since the ones giving orders and commands [in Kuna villages] are the Ságuilas, most of them old reactionaries who do not want schools, and if they do accept them is due to the presence of the Police. (Intendente Mojica to Secretary 11/14/23, AI)

Ultimately, of course, Kuna chiefs, with their many vices and failings, merely embodied the character faults of all the Indians, who were constitutionally incapable of recognizing the benefits of civilization and order. On *this* aspect of Indian essence at least, officials had a great deal to say.

It is no less true that the Government must prevail upon them with a firm character and no hesitations of any kind, since the Indian tribes are by nature indolent, with little love for work and highly attached to ancient traditions that enable them to live in a poor and small-minded manner, with very little thought for the future well-being of their children. (Intendente Vaglio to Secretary 6/04/19, ABP)

I do not want it forgotten that all Indians are the same, deceitful, talkative, and they forget tomorrow what they promised today with the same ease with which they promise friendship and loyalty. (Intendente Vaglio to Secretary 6/07/19, ABP)

The idle talk of the Indians, who like phonographs, repeat everything Miss Coope tells them against the Government. (Intendente Vaglio to President Porras 12/02/19, ABP)

Since it is a matter of reducing to civilized life a retrograde element, opposed even to the slightest suggestion . . . to improve or change their customs . . . when it is a matter of correcting their faults . . . it is not possible to enforce the laws because . . . they will not let themselves be treated in the same manner as civilized people. (Report by Intendente Mojica, 6/30/21)[28]

Nothing is more pleasing to Indians than the love of dissent; it is inborn in them, just as it is in us. (Intendente Mojica to Secretary 6/30/22, ABP)[29]

The Indian is always rebellious, and if he does accept civilization it is because he recognizes his weakness, yet in his heart he harbors hatred, resentment against those of us who seek to reform them. (Intendente Mojica to Secretary 10/04/23, AI)[30]

IDEOLOGY AND THE IMAGINARY

These sweeping attacks, taking in all Indians as a class, indicate clearly that government officials were going beyond merely venting their frustration to articulate a generalized discourse about the Indians, a highly negative collective portrait. As noted in Chapter 1, the scholarly literature on such discourses has increasingly used the notion of "the imaginary" to suggest their ability to create a comprehensive and largely fictitious set of ideas and images about a population or domain through which it is to be understood. In this context, it is notable that Panamanian official discourse, however biased, one-sided, unfair, and even mendacious, did not create a Kuna imaginary. Complaints against native leaders and followers, like those against third parties, held a large grain of truth. Rebels and dissidents did reject "civilization"; they did hate their oppressors; they did deny the legitimacy of official rules and punishments; they did undercut government initiatives; and they did lie to the enemy without compunction.

This is not to say that official letters and reports, by denying any legitimacy or sense to indigenous actions and by distorting the motives behind them, did not misrepresent the situation and slander the Kuna. Intendentes never acknowledged that prevarication, inconstancy, and deceit had been forced on the Indians, that native leaders who seemingly accepted schools at one moment and fought them at another, or followers who retracted testimony previously extracted from them, had been left no alternative other than complete surrender or outright rebellion. Panamanian officials, it was clear, could recognize no form of order except the one they wished to impose. Resistance to pacification and ethnocide could be attributed to a variety of character faults but never to the clash of two civilizations or two polities. Still less could it be acknowledged that many of the traits they attacked and distorted—elected chiefs who encouraged resistance but could not compel obedience; local and regional conclaves prone to endless discussion; a political culture firmly grounded in religion and tradition; villagers who resisted punishment, disobeyed orders, and vocally opposed anything they suspected or disliked—were all signs of a vibrant native democracy (Howe 1986). Officials might themselves belong to a democratic regime chosen through a particularly messy and tumultuous electoral process, but they could not recognize or tolerate its equivalent in the people they wished to subdue.

Even at its most unfair, however, official discourse did not pluck fantasies out of the air. Representation of the Kuna, rather than constructing imaginaries, worked by distorting and imposing meaning on the situation at hand, the all-too-real struggle in which the two sides were locked—the essence of ideology was interpretation, not imagination.

AUDIENCE RECEPTION

Intendentes, police lieutenants, and others who commented on Indian character and actions wanted most of all to convince the President of the

Republic, who through most of these years was Belisario Porras, and the Secretary of Government and Justice, until 1924 the very moderate Ricardo Alfaro. One might well wonder how much this intended audience accepted what it was told, or, put differently, the extent to which high officials already shared with their subordinates an unvarying, hegemonic ideology about the Indians.

Alfaro, for his part, was obviously swayed at times by Kuna complaints *against* the local administration, and when Humberto Vaglio was eased out in late 1920 during a brief period in which Porras was out of office, the intendente was undone in no small part by the intemperance of his attacks against Indian enemies. Porras, though more intent on subduing the Kuna than Alfaro, had by 1924 also reluctantly concluded that something had gone wrong in San Blas (Howe 1998, 146, 198). Indeed, all the successes enjoyed by Kuna leaders in their informational campaigns depended on exploiting fundamental differences between local officials and their superiors in attitudes toward Indians and change. If one can give credence to a later account by Narciso Garay (see Chapter 8), who claimed that as a member of Porras's cabinet he argued for greater respect and patience vis-à-vis the Kuna, then cracks had already begun appearing in the dominant ideology, even among high functionaries.

But Porras, whose outlook was indelibly stamped by late-nineteenth-century Liberalism, joined wholeheartedly in scapegoating third parties in San Blas, especially José de la Rosa, and both he and Alfaro accepted the negative labeling of indigenous leaders. When the head of a police detachment condemned Nele Wardada as a rebel (see above), Porras responded in the way hoped for: "Well informed by the note . . . concerning the hostility of the Záguila of Portogandi—I am going to consider the measures that will be needed to take to subdue to the point of complete submission the aforementioned Záguila" (Porras to Intendente 7/23/21, AI).

Neither man took much persuading, moreover, concerning the bad character of the Indians and its negative influence on the civilizing process (see Howe 1998, 131). Alfaro, in a letter to his brother following the rebellion of 1925, a letter in which he frankly admitted that the Indians had been mistreated, wrote: "With these ignorant and superstitious beings, full of infantile prejudices, one must have the tact and patience that one has with children" (R. J. Alfaro to Horacio Alfaro 3/13/25, ARJA). Porras and Alfaro, their attitudes polarized between sympathy and intolerance, could simultaneously condemn police mistreatment and Indian resistance without recognizing any self-contradiction.

COUNTING, NAMING, AND IGNORING

Bureaucratic prose is by no means the only medium by which subaltern peoples can be characterized and classified. In recent years historians and social scientists have demonstrated the power of routine documentation in the form of maps, registries, lists, and especially censuses to control people by shaping the ways in which they are typified and understood. Censuses and their ilk have been called "an exercise in social naming, in nominating into existence" (Goldberg 1997, 29), "the state's attempt to make a society legible" (Scott 1998, 2), and devices by which to impose a "totalizing, classificatory grid" on territory and population (Anderson 1983, 184). The categories into which such bureaucratic forms divide people, whether established by administrative fiat or arrived at through bargaining or political conflict, impose "an authoritative tune to which most of the population must dance" (Scott 1998, 83; see also Kertzer and Arel 2002). If so, it seems the Panamanian state either couldn't think of a tune or couldn't be bothered to whistle.

To be sure, in San Blas the police and administration used documents to control the Indians, recording punishments, imposing travel passes, and noting down births and deaths on official forms. As I have argued before (1998, 180), they also seem to have interpreted such documentation as a kind of symbolic claim-making, an interpretation confirmed by the indignant reaction to what they took as a rival registry of births and deaths kept by the Protestant mission on Nargana: to count and record was to incorporate and appropriate. But the national census, to the extent that it influenced Indian identity, did so by ignoring rather than recording.

The government, though unable to include the Indians in the first census of 1911 (the headquarters at El Porvenir was not established until four years later), counted them twice in 1920, first in an enumeration sponsored by the intendente, and then in the decennial national census, which gave a roughly plausible figure of 17,716 (Howe 1998, 130, 321n. 5). Curiously, when the census was published two years later, the San Blas count was reported in only the most truncated and confusing form.[31] With the total population of the coast given as barely 500, the predominant race was identified as *Negra*, with 55 percent of the total, followed by *Mestiza*, with 20 percent, White with 16, and only then Indian, with 9 percent (República de Panamá, Dirección General del Censo 1922, 15, 17). The strange results, it turns out, derived from only fourteen sites, of which five non-Indian camps and villages accounted for 80 percent of the total (República de Panamá, Dirección General del Censo 1922, 74–75).[32] Only seven Kuna sites were listed, with a supposed aggregate population of just 92.[33]

The published census offered no explanation for the reduced figures, nor even the slightest indication that all but a small portion of the coast's population had been excluded. A commercial yearbook for the City of Panama published a few years later (Andreve 1926, 23) lists under the heading of "Indigenous Population not Enumerated" 17,044 Indians in San Blas and 33,358 for the country as a whole, but the official census publication gave no indication that the indigenous population had been excluded or why, nonetheless, a few Indians *had* been counted.

Whatever their immediate causes,[34] the truncated results for San Blas seem of a piece with the pervasive inattention to indigenous custom and practice discussed above. They suggest that bureaucracies may sometimes control by ignoring or blurring or slighting difference rather than by the relentless counting, classifying, and differentiating that the literature on colonialism—especially British and Dutch colonialism in Asia—takes as standard operating procedure. Although it seems unlikely that Panamanian officials were actively trying to exclude or hide indigenous citizens, especially in light of their determined efforts to incorporate and assimilate the Kuna, they were not eager to recognize them as a distinct population, still less as a people (*pueblo*). What mattered was the national identity toward which they were being precipitously impelled, not their absurd claims to have a civilization or identity of their own.

This interpretation finds support in a recent volume on censuses and identity formation edited by Kertzer and Arel (2002), in which it is argued that for differing reasons, in places as diverse as Macedonia, Burundi, Israel, and France, the Holmesian dog that did not bark in the night, meaning in this case a refusal or failure to count or to name, may be as politically significant as an insistence on doing so.[35] Certainly, the Panamanian government's lack of interest in the Indians or willingness to name them went well beyond the census. The designation Cuna, or Cuna-Cuna, was becoming widely recognized as an ethnic name in this era—Father Gassó called them the Caribe-Kunas. The Colombian government as early as 1871 had identified them as the Tule, which is what the Kuna call themselves in their own language. Even the more commonly used terms Samblaseños, Sanblasinos, or San Blas Indians clearly referred to an ethnic and cultural unit, as well as a regional population. But in thousands of pages of official documents from 1919 to 1925, I have almost never seen them referred to in any way more specific than *indígenas* or *indios*. As in the cases discussed by Kertzer and Arel (2002), silence spoke volumes.

UNCOMFORTABLE METAPHOR

The schizophrenic quality of bureaucratic discourse and government programs targeting the Indians should do away with the idea that such discourses always "other," that is, that they inevitably create or reinforce difference, distinction, and social distance—or indeed that the play of mimesis and alterity is anything but mixed, complex, and ambivalent. The program of cultural transformation imposed on the Kuna followed from the premise that the Indians differed from everyone else in fundamental and unacceptable ways, and indeed that Kuna difference had to be suppressed almost overnight. In seeming anticipation of that result, however, official action and inaction—not counting, not naming, not studying, not paying close attention even to the diacritics of difference—tended to minimize or even implicitly to deny a separate identity for the Indians. Indeed, the ethnocidal program itself, with its avowed goal of rapidly making Spanish-speaking citizens out of the Indians, assumed that difference was mutable and temporary.

In the course of the struggle, however, difference was strongly reasserted in explaining why the Kuna resisted so tenaciously. Chiefs and followers refused to submit, it was alleged, not for reasons to be found in human or Panamanian nature but because of character flaws peculiar to Indians. In the catalogues of vice conveyed in anti-Kuna diatribes, I have found only one instance ("Nothing is more pleasing to Indians than the love of dissent; it is inborn in them, just as it is in us")[36] in which polemicists conceded, even in passing, any resemblance to their own behavior. Still less could they admit any analogy between Kuna resistance and Panama's struggles against U.S. domination.

The irony is obvious. It was precisely bureaucrats' own experience with the turmoil, intrigue, power-seeking, clientelism, and verbal warfare of bureaucratic and electoral politics that made the charges against Indian leaders so subjectively plausible and that provided the models for their own diatribes against indigenous enemies. In effect, an overt insistence on difference, on the singularity of Indian misdeeds, depended on a tacit and unacknowledged perception of similarity and a displacement of uncomfortable facts about the self onto the other.

DEFENSIVE ETHNOGRAPHY

Colman and his fellow chiefs may not have seen the invective published about them in the *Memorias de Gobierno y Justicia,* certainly not more than a few of the attacks contained in unpublished official correspondence. But they had no difficulty recognizing either the scorn of the police and bureaucrats, or the threat posed by the government's program of pacification and ethnocide and the insult it offered to them as a people, not to mention the specific dangers it posed to noserings and chichas and chiefly power.

They resisted in two ways. On the local level, in the partly pacified villages, people attempted to subvert or go around or defy police prohibitions (Howe 1998, 167–176). At a higher level, Kuna leaders, most often Cimral Colman, tried to support indigenous practices verbally, to argue in letters and interviews for the value or at least the harmlessness of custom, and by extension to convince Panamanian officials of the worth of the Kuna as a people. Most of Colman's arguments have unfortunately been lost, leaving only scattered fragments. On one occasion (noted in Chapter 3) he invoked the virtues of antiquity and continuity by describing women's ornaments as "a most ancient custom" (Colman to Porras 2/01/19, AI). On another, he was reported to have urged "that the indians be permitted the use of *chicha fuerte* at *determinadas fiestas* (particular/defined/determinate celebrations)," a phrase that associated chicha ceremonies with tradition and order rather than drunken chaos.[37] Like the Latin goldworkers who on one occasion spoke out in defense of the women to whom they sold noserings, Colman probably argued that Indian women had as much freedom to dress as they pleased as other *panameñas,* and like Gassó's opponents, he pointed to analogies between native and national society.[38]

Two fuller examples of Colman's defense of native custom have survived, each in its own way highly revealing.[39] The first dates from 1913, when Colman first began dealing actively with the government. On January 31st, the chief wrote Belisario Porras to follow up on a trip the previous year to Panama to meet with the then newly elected president (see the excerpt in Chapter 3 above). After two pages devoted to other questions, the letter turned to a report that on Nargana, Charly Robinson and a Catholic priest—probably Benito Pérez, successor to Leonardo Gassó—had burned or planned to burn wooden curing figures, which the Kuna call *nuchu* or *sualluchu,* but which Colman referred to by analogy as *santos* (saints). According to the letter, the priest had dismissed Kuna use of the figures as idolatry, the foolish worship of a bit of inanimate wood.

> Now in these days charles wanted to make a new fable (*invencion*), since the priest had said to him, that all the *santos* that we had he wanted to burn them it [sic], because the priest was saying that why do we adore them that that was a bit of pole, but now we say that

since God has left us in a place alone and God not left said that all kinds of tree and plants so that we make medicine and thus God has left us alone there is one of you also believe that we do not have a doctor (*medico*) that he does not gather the medicine. and you [singular] do not believe that a person or a chief (*cacique*) can tell lies. and God has not left said here on earth, that do not tell lies.[40] (Colman to Porras 1/31/13, ANP, courtesy of Francisco Herrera)

The thrust of Colman's answer to the priest's accusation was that the Kuna did not worship the wooden figures but rather made use of them as was intended by God, who had placed humans on earth with the great resource of trees and plants from which to make medicine and curing figures.[41] He added that some Panamanians doubted Kuna curing; and that they also might not believe that a chief, meaning Charly Robinson, could tell lies.

If Porras or a subordinate read this far into the letter, he may have caught its gist, but only at the cost of considerable difficulty and confusion, as Chapter 3 shows was often the case with Kuna letters of the period. As Colman dictated the letter in his own language, he probably used a standard phrase, *we namneki an obesmala*, "he left us here in this earth-place," earth-place (*namnega*) being a ceremonial name for the terrestrial world. Colman's secretary, however, rendered the phrase in Spanish much more ambiguously as "in a place" (*en una parte*).[42] More confusing yet, the letter writer twice used a mysterious phrase concerning God's actions, *no [a] dejado dicho*,[43] literally "[has] not left/let said." "No" here, rather than a negative, is almost certainly a contraction of *nos* "us," and "left said" is probably the secretary's attempt to render into Spanish a special Kuna-language construction used to describe actions taken or words said on the point of departure, in this case at the moment that Great Father returned to heaven after animating the world. What made perfect sense in spoken Kuna—"Father said as he left us here"—ended up as bewildering nonsense. Here again, Kuna self-presentation did not cross the boundaries between indigenous oral discourse and its written Panamanian equivalent.

The letter went on to list, first the major political leaders of Colman's community, Ailigandi, and then its major ritualists, for most of whom he used the honorific Spanish title *Doctor*. The specialties listed ranged from that of mass exorcist or "converser" (*absogedi*) to medicinalist (*inaduledi*), puberty ceremony chanter (*gandule*), pepper chanter (*gaburduled*), death chanter (*masarduled, Masar Igar wisid*), and chanter for difficult childbirth (*Muu Igar wisid*).

1st Dr Ina Teguiña—Absoguedi. he says that one they called him if something [bad] happens or if the village there are many people sick, he can take away the fever. and to see everything that happens in the village, that one we call him absoguedi He is named Olo niguipilele.—D^r of medicine Olo Wigueguiña. there is another D^r who is 100 years old who is the Father of Chief Colman, he is named Machus.—there is another who is also 100 years old also he is a D^r he is named Tiguiña. *Cantule niga pippi*[44] (they say in Indian [language] Wigutur Calla) that means in Indian, a dog of the star.—there is another who is called Caburtule) this they call him. so that he prays for him that prayer the fever is taken off him right away on the next day. Ina tisualiler there is another prayer in order that headache. Antonio. there is also another who prays with the cane. He is called in Indian masar tuledi, this prayer is when someone dies, to rise up his soul to heaven. he is named. Tibiguí.—Muy igar knower, he is called in Indian. when a woman gives birth. that is a prayer. José Maria. . . . [etc.] (Colman to Porras 1/31/13, ANP)

Like the written reports on regional meetings discussed in Chapter 3, Colman's list of the major ritual specialists and their functions followed traditional patterns in oral discourse, with their emphasis on named roles and individuals. More generally, it made sense that Colman would base his claim to respect from the outside world on the prowess of Kuna ritualists, given that within their own society men gained prestige and recognition largely by filling political offices and ritual roles. Colman's use of the title *Doctor*, moreover, with its implicit claim to parity with holders of the Latin American honorific, again invoked equivalences with Panamanian institutions.

The list of curers undoubtedly caused as much confusion as the rest of the letter, and the appropriation of the title *Doctor*, if the recipients noticed it, could only have provoked scorn.[45] Porras, by no means persuaded of the value of Indian culture, initiated an accelerated program of ethnocide only a few years later. Despite the letter's failure to sway the president, it nonetheless represents a decisive step in Kuna thinking and resistance strategies. It shows Colman not only recognizing Panamanian skepticism and scorn toward his people's beliefs and practices, but trying to counter those attitudes systematically, not just piecemeal, and to defend his people in a global sense by presenting beliefs and practices so they could be understood and appreciated. It was, in effect, a first attempt at ethnography as cultural self-defense, a strategy Kuna leaders would use in later years to much greater effect.

THE LIMITS TO INDIGENIST RHETORIC

The other example of cultural defense occurred eight years later, in September of 1921, at a moment when conflict between Colman's group and the intendente's minions had sharply escalated. Earlier the same year a police raid on the village of Río Azúcar near Nargana had ended in the death of four villagers and two policemen, one of them the leading modernist collaborator, Claudio Iglesias.[46] A statement attributed to Colman appeared in *La Estrella de Panamá* later that year, just a week after a Colón court acquitted five Río Azúcar men of murder (Howe 1998, 153–159).

> We don't know what the cause of this hate is on the part of certain authorities towards the genuine sons of the Circumscription. We accept establishment of schools in the villages, as well as other measures of civilization that are carried out in a peaceful manner. What is not pleasant to us is the violence that certain authorities exercise to tear off their *guines* [bead wrappings] and *alzamuros* [noserings] from the mature and elderly indian women.
>
> As we see it, the school is the center in which civilization should begin. There future generations become accustomed to the disuse of those irritating adornments, and in a very short time they will be extinguished. Later on the mature women and the elderly will make comparisons, and they themselves will understand the ease that the civilized life offers over the primitive and uncultured, and they will not only leave off wearing such adornments but also they will imitate the way of life of the educated generation that is arising.
>
> Another measure of civilization that our government should carry into effect in those villages is sending missionaries, who with religious and soft words do a hundred times more than certain present authorities with arms, fines, and jails.[47]

The statement attributed to Colman, with its apparent endorsement of schools and missionaries, its apologetic discussion of women's dress, and its use of the master notion of civilization, might be taken as a confirmation of a line of argument emphasizing the *reactive* nature of anticolonial discourses. The stronger and more problematic version of this form of interpretation suggests that subaltern groups cannot resist on their own terms, or worse, that a particularly insidious form of hegemonic control renders them able to resist but only in ways that ultimately reinstate the dominant ideology and their own subordination.[48] In this case, if the statement did come from Colman, it may indeed reflect Kuna doubts about their place in the world, and in particular about their poverty and illiteracy. Otherwise, however, the statement showed a *tactical* decision to use arguments with some hope of success, not Colman's core beliefs. He did not see noserings and bead bindings as "irritating adornments," still less concede that his people and their lifeways were uncivilized. He did not want schools in his villages—at least not government schools and not for the moment—any more than he wanted a return of missionaries.[49] The only assertion that rings true was that he wanted an end to violence and forced change.

The text, whether or not Colman had a chance to approve it, was almost certainly drawn up by his lawyer, José de la Rosa. De la Rosa, who had sat in on meetings in which Colman and his followers railed against the suppression of Kuna custom, thus knew perfectly that he was putting words in the chief's mouth. He, and probably Colman as well, made the strategic decision *not* to make any claims for the worth of indigenous practices, but rather to rest their case on the virtues of moderation, restraint, and patience. By now, they undoubtedly knew their audience, knew that almost no one in power, least of all Belisario Porras, saw anything worthwhile in Indian culture, but that Secretary Alfaro and for the most part Porras himself favored persuasion over coercion, and that Intendente Vaglio's intemperance had led to his removal the previous year. The judge whose court had just ruled in favor of Kuna defendants, moreover, clearly thought they should enjoy the same rights to due process as other citizens.

The newspaper statement, nonetheless, cannot have had much effect on President Porras except to add to his already growing anger against de la Rosa, which led to a presidential order the following year expelling the exasperating lawyer from the region. More fundamentally, the statement highlights a dilemma faced by Colman and other defenders of Kuna culture, the lack of a favorable national discourse or set of values that they could invoke, and in particular, none that attributed any special virtues to indigenous identity or indigenous rights. Indeed, postindependence Liberal governments of Latin America had adopted as fundamental a discourse of *universal* rights and the rejection of categorical distinctions among different segments of the national population (De la Peña 2005, 719–720).

In the United States and Europe, even before the era of Indian wars had ended, many people were ready to romanticize and idealize Native Americans, at least in the abstract, but as indicated in Chapter 3, such sentiments were only occasionally voiced in early-twentieth-century Panama. As I suggest in Chapter 8 below, signs were just beginning to emerge that leaders like Porras might be willing to adopt long-dead Indian leaders as national symbols, and that elites might be willing to consider embracing their mixed, *mestizo* heritage. But very few were ready as yet to argue publicly either that indigenous lifeways deserved preservation, or that Indians were owed special entitlements. All of de la Rosa's considerable success as Colman's legal advocate he achieved by arguing that they deserved the same rights to due process as other Panamanians, and even his failed land scheme was not based on the idea that indigenous peoples had a special moral or legal claim to their ancestral territories.[50]

To the extent that Indians *were* seen as essentially different from other Panamanians, difference implied inferiority or subordination. Acting President Ernesto Lefevre, when he began the process of removing Humberto Vaglio from office in 1920, wrote: "If the authorities of that circumscription keep in mind that those poor peoples cannot change customs in a day, things will proceed better."[51] In other words, it was the backwardness of those poor peoples that called for special patience, an attitude also evident in Secretary Alfaro's exhortations to moderation. For their part, intendentes argued that the Indians *were* a special case: they were uncivilized, politically immature, and resistant to either change or control, and thus they should be governed by special rules and powers,[52] an argument that resembles in spirit the nineteenth-century laws of Latin American countries dominated by Conservatives (Carmack, Gasco, and Gossen 1996, 217–219), and more recently, Brazilian constitutional law, which has treated Indians as jural minors and wards of the state (Ramos 1998).

The Kuna, in short, were preaching to the deaf, trying to make an argument their audience could not hear, and the more they struggled and argued, the more they confirmed their reputation for recalcitrance and backwardness. To pitch their case successfully would require a sea change in the national consciousness, the appearance of ideas or values with which their claims could resonate, so they could persuade or at least gain acceptance as part of an ongoing debate. In 1920 or 1921, that debate had barely begun. In the meanwhile, Kuna leaders could carry on complaining and defending, hoping to win a few contests and perhaps contribute to larger changes in public opinion. They could turn to advocates more attuned to their point of view than de la Rosa. Or they could seek out a different audience. As later chapters will show, they did all three.

North American Friends

FIVE

The hostile depictions of the Kuna discussed in the last chapter had a much friendlier counterpart in English-language accounts of the Indians. This popular ethnographic literature, though it drew on some of the same sources as writings in Spanish, and though it, too, zeroed in on Kuna separatism and resistance to domination, differed radically in its sympathies and tone, as well as its implications for its subjects. Turn-of-the-century Anglophone writers, very few of whom had actually seen San Blas, treated the Indians first of all as objects of contemplation, metaphorical foils or parallels bearing on strongly felt questions in their own lives. Detached admiration could grow into empathy and concern, however, especially among those who made the effort to visit the Indians on their home ground, and as the Kuna increasingly sought an external audience and source of support, a few North Americans appointed themselves advocates for their Indian friends, attempting to defend the Kuna by shaping how they were perceived. When in desperation the Kuna resorted to armed rebellion and a pair of North Americans signed on to their cause, representation and struggle became one.

The expatriate community with which this popular ethnography was associated had its origins in the mid-nineteenth century with the building of the Panama Railroad and the establishment of a terminal city on the north coast, first called Aspinwall and then renamed Colón after Christopher Columbus. Although the vast majority of foreigners crossed on the railroad and continued on to California or some other destination as fast as they possibly could, a few stayed on, including a small colony of North Americans, with their own English-language newspaper, the *Panama Star and Herald*. In the 1880s, a French attempt to build an interoceanic canal brought a huge influx of laborers and officials, and though most departed when the French effort collapsed, even more foreigners came a few years later when Panama gained its independence and the United States took up the construction work. After the canal opened in 1914, several thousand English-speaking Whites and Blacks stayed on to sustain the operation, and many thousand U.S. soldiers served terms of duty on military bases, creating a large North American enclave. During the construction era and for years afterwards, many tourists and journalists came to see the engineering marvel and token of hemispheric dominance, some of them to also offer a few choice remarks on the locals, including the Indians.

Tourists and Zonians learned about the San Blas Indians, as they were mostly known, from the reports of coastal merchants and contacts with Kuna laborers in Colón, just as Latin Panamanians did. Some also had access to information less readily available in the Republic, from U.S. military surveying parties, employees of companies setting up mines and plantations on the north coast, Protestant missionaries, and a series of adventurers and journalists intrepid enough to venture into Indian territory. By the late 1910s (and perhaps earlier), Zonians were organizing excursions to San Blas on rented coasting boats.[1] A set of popular understandings developed about the Indians, and with them, a good deal of interest and sympathy.

The Zone, whose economic and political edifice rested on a foundation of institutional racism, was by no means a hotbed of progressives and bleeding hearts. But distaste for Blacks and Latins could combine easily with positive, if sometimes unrealistic and patronizing, attitudes toward Indians. Some, at least, felt guilt about the mistreatment of Native Americans at home, and they shared in the romantic revival of interest in the continent's aboriginal inhabitants, closely connected with antimodernist doubts about the trajectory of contemporary civilization (Lears 1981; Dilworth 1996; P. Deloria 1998, 95–127; S. Smith 2000). Among the fraternal organizations established in the Zone, the Improved Order of Red Men sprouted seven local lodges, including a "San Blas Tribe."[2] However silly they may now seem, these middle-aged white men dressed up in robes and addressing each other as sachems and sagamores, and however contradictory and compromised the Indian identity they tried to appropriate

(P. Deloria 1998, 38–94; Pike 1992, 31–34), they undoubtedly looked on indigenous peoples more favorably than did most Latin Panamanians. Local aficionados, apart from commenting on the Kuna themselves, provided a reservoir of Indian lore on which visiting journalists and travelers could draw.[3]

LAND OF THE CACIQUE

Out of this expatriate community appeared one of the earliest and most remarkable examples of Anglophone writing on the Kuna, authored by James S. Gilbert, a local poet sometimes called the Kipling of the Isthmus. Gilbert, who lived in Panama from 1886 until his death from malaria in 1906, worked first as an employee of the railroad and later as partner in a shipping agency, writing poems on the side for publication in the *Panama Star and Herald*. He brought out his first book of verse locally in 1891, and another in 1894. Then in 1901, Gilbert produced a larger volume called *Panama Patchwork*—encompassing several dozen romantic, comic, and satiric poems, which went through a number of editions, both in Panama and the United States. The Kuna appear in a poem entitled "The Land of

FIGURE 5.1 "The Cacique or San Blas Indians," from James Gilbert, *Panama Patchwork*

the Cacique," *cacique* being a Spanish-language term for Indian chiefs going back to Columbus's era (Gilbert 1905, 162–167).[4]

> 'Tis a lyric of these people,
> Of their customs quaint and curious,
> Of the rites to them peculiar,
> That the bard would strive to sing:
> Sing in humble words and simple
> To a harp uncouth and awkward,
> As befits the modest minstrel
> Of a lowly race of men.
> Lowly? Yea, but lowly only
> As retired from observation—
> As without the pale of notice
> Of the nations of the world
> For within his own dominion
> The Cacique and his subjects
> Are as dignified and haughty
> As the proudest of mankind.
> In their veins no mixed blood courseth,
> In their land no stranger dwelleth,
> For this simple child of nature
> Guards his country with his life.
> Guards his race from all admixture,
> Guards his ancient superstitions,
> His religion and his customs,
> Zealously and jealously.
> For a solemn oath doth bind him—
> Sworn above his father's body—
> To kill wife and son and daughter
> Should an enemy approach
> To obtain his fair possessions
> Or to other laws subdue him
> Ere he marches to the battle
> That can end but with his life.

Gilbert's poem, first published in the 1894 volume, left the distinct impression that he knew the Kuna personally—that he had gone perhaps to Sasardi to visit the high chief, who in that era would have been

Inanaginya (uncle of Inabaginya), and that he had conversed with native curers.

> Every hamlet hath its chieftain,
> Subject still to the Cacique—
> The Cacique of Sasardi—
> Who is ruler over all.
> Every village hath its Mila,
> Arzoguete and Tulete[5]
> (Priest and teacher and physician,
> Councillor and wisest men).

In point of fact, many of these little ethnographic touches (including the confusion of *mila* for *nele*) came, not from experience, but directly from the port captain's report discussed in Chapter 4, which had been published just a year or two before. Other Kuna words and ethnographic snippets not found in that report may have been taken from some other written source, now lost, but it seems more likely, given the poet's admiration for the Kuna, that they derived from conversations with men who had come to Colón to trade or work, or even perhaps from a trip down the coast to see the Indians.

Gilbert went on to recount the rituals for piercing the noses of Kuna girls, celebrating their puberty, and finding them husbands.

> Let us visit the Fiestas:
> Three days since unto an Ohme
> A Punagua child was born;
> And with shouts of great rejoicing
> And libations of the Chicha,
> They will pierce the tiny nostril
> For the hoop of yellow gold.
> Haste we quickly to another—
> To a festival more joyful:
> For in turn the shy Punagua
> Hath an Ohme now become.
> Oh, the drinking! Oh, the dancing!
> As they cut the maiden's tresses;
> In her father's house immure her
> Till her husband shall be found[6]

The poem continued on at length, describing Kuna marriage practices, for the most part correctly, as no one other than the port captain had done since the eighteenth-century Father Balburger.

> With rejoicing comes Machua[7]
> Comes and claims his promised wife.
> To her father's house he bears her,
> There to serve their daughter's parents
> Till to him is born a daughter
> And his freedom thus is gained

The poet concluded with an admonition to his readers to leave the couple, and their people, in peace:

> Let them live in their seclusion,
> Let them keep their fair possessions,
> Let them rule themselves unaided,
> O ye nations of the earth!
> Let them practice their religion,
> And observe their rites and customs
> O ye pushing missionaries
> Of accepted creed and sect!
> Trouble not this gentle people—
> Leave them to their peace and quiet—
> Nor disturb this tropic Eden
> Of the red men of San Blas!

INDEPENDENCE AND RACIAL PURITY

In its length, detail, and emotional involvement with its subjects, "The Land of the Cacique" stood apart from other English-language writing of that era on the Kuna, in which the norm was a brief and highly stereotyped passage in an article or book devoted to the Isthmus and the canal. Long or short, however, almost every mention of the Indians foregrounded the same themes dramatized by Gilbert. Of all the qualities for which primitives have at one time or another been praised, North Americans focused on precisely those for which the Kuna would soon be excoriated by Panamanian officials: their independence and stubborn resistance to domination.

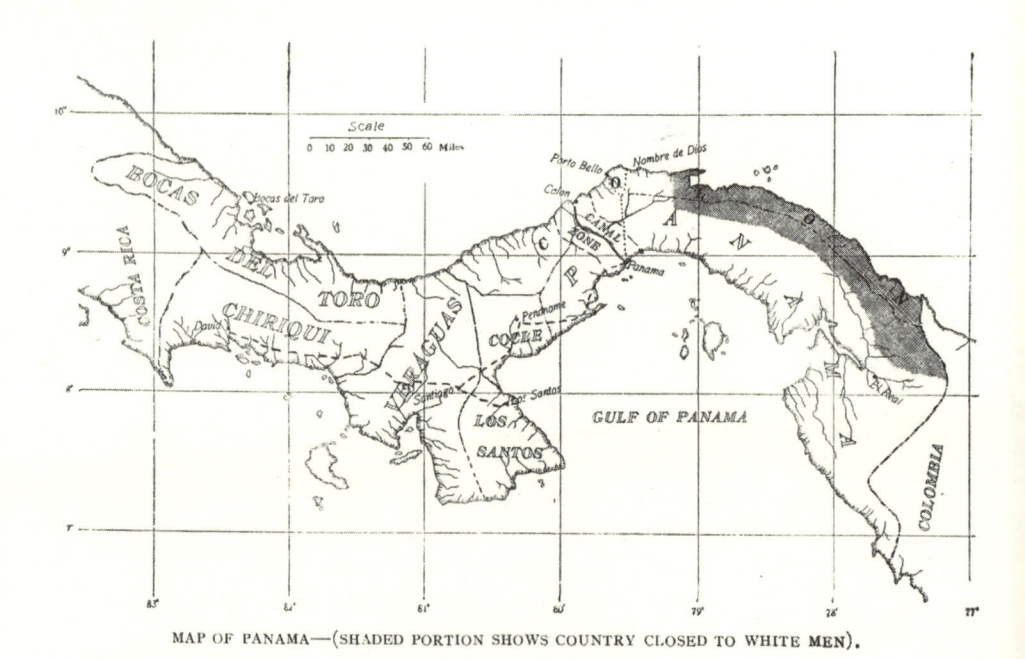

MAP OF PANAMA—(SHADED PORTION SHOWS COUNTRY CLOSED TO WHITE MEN).

FIGURE 5.2   Map of Panama from *Panama Guide*, 1912.

> Behind its frowning tree-belt dwell the famous and infamous Indians who have made the name of San Blas blood-red in Isthmian history. . . . The San Blas natives are the only unconquered tribe of red men in modern history. Never have they bent the knee of homage to a foe. Only a dozen miles from civilization, never have they acknowledged the yoke of the white man, maintaining always a bullet-emphasized defiance. . . . It is a tradition of the Isthmus that a white man has never remained alive in the San Blas territory without an Indian escort. (*The Conquest of the Isthmus*, Weir 1909, 45–46)

> Among the San Blas Indians . . . the exclusion of aliens is the result of well-founded political reasons. Their respected traditions are a long record of proud independence; they have maintained the purity of their race and enjoyed freely for hundreds of years every inch of their territory. They feel that the day the negro or the white man acquires a foothold in their midst these privileges will become a thing of the past. This is why, without undue hostility to strangers,

they discourage their incursions. ("Little-Known Parts of Panama," Pittier 1912, 649)

The territories of the Cuna-Cuna and the Chucunaque have long been nearly a sealed book to the outsider, and until recently it has been a tribal law with the San Blas that no stranger should be permitted to remain after nightfall, due, it is said, out of fear for their women. (from *The Panama Canal and Golden Gate Exposition,* Avery 1915, 299)[8]

Writers returned repeatedly to a few key signs of Kuna independence: the seclusion of Indian women, seen only occasionally in San Blas and virtually never in the city; the refusal to allow merchants ashore or outsiders of any sort into their forests; the threat to kill women and children sooner than surrender, mentioned by the port captain and dramatized in Gilbert's poem (Nicholas 1903, 232; Bell 1910, 629–630; Minter 1948, 30); and an encounter in which Kuna had, it was said, refused to sell sand for canal construction.[9]

During the early days of the Canal project it was desired to dig sand from a beach in the San Blas Country. A small United States man-of-war was sent thither to broach the subject to the Indians, and the captain held parlay with the chief. . . . The old Indian courteously refused the privilege: "He who made this land," said he, "made it for Cuna-Cuna who live no longer, for those who are here today and also for the ones to come. So it is not ours only and we could not sell it." (*Panama and the Canal in Picture and Prose,* Abbott 1913, 313)

Though few writers dwelled on these themes at the same length as Gilbert, it is clear that he was not the only expatriate or visitor for whom Kuna separatism struck a chord.

The second great theme for Anglophone writers, closely linked with but not identical to the first, was sexual and racial exclusion. The Kuna were a people in whose "veins no mixed blood courseth," a people who, as other writers put it, "from early days . . . have been able to keep their women free from contamination" (Collins 1912, 138); who "have preserved their racial integrity to such a degree that their blood is now as pure as it was in the days when discovered by the early Spanish explorers" (Oliver n.d. [1916]).[10]

Their color is dark olive, with no trace of the negro apparent, for it has been their unceasing study for centuries to retain their racial purity.... So determined are the men of this tribe to maintain its blood untarnished by any admixture whatsoever, that they long made it an invariable rule to expel every white man from their territory at nightfall. (*Panama and the Canal in Picture and Prose*, Abbot 1913, 310–311)

They have never been conquered and have not allowed intermarriage. They boast that "no San Blas woman has borne a half-breed, that no San Blas man has fathered a mongrel." (*Panama, the Canal, the Country and the People*, Bullard 1918, 85)

The question of colonial and national imaginaries, raised in previous chapters, is also relevant here, since Anglophone writers did not imagine Kuna attitudes or practices into being. The episode in which the Indians had supposedly turned away canal engineers, plausible on its face, may well have occurred, and the threat of collective suicide, though never implemented (nor, I suspect, seriously contemplated), could have been uttered by a Kuna orator or spokesman. Certainly the seclusion and protection of Kuna women, the refusal of sexual relations with outsiders, the reluctance to allow merchants ashore, and the struggles to keep miners, turtlers, and forest workers out of Indian territory were daily realities. Writers constituted the Kuna "imaginary" less through unbounded fantasy than through selection and interpretation, by choosing, foregrounding, exaggerating, and reinterpreting elements of indigenous practice that fit their own ideological requirements.

The theme of resistance, especially resistance to encroachment, conquest, or unjust domination, which readers of academic books and journals today may associate with the political Left, in fact appeared across a broad spectrum of romantic writing—poems, novels, dramas, histories, tracts—of every political and ideological position, associated with such diverse heroes as Horatio at the Bridge, Vercingetorix, Roland, Robin Hood, Rob Roy, Prince Charles Edward Stuart, and Robert E. Lee. A widely read Victorian novel by Charles Kingsley (1866) glorified Hereward the Wake, a Saxon holdout against William the Conqueror. The more specific notion of mass suicide in the face of defeat turned up again in the late-twentieth-century Masada myth (Ben-Yehuda 1995).

The writers who celebrated Kuna independence were heirs to a North American variant of this romantic tradition, one that eulogized defeated indigenous leaders. Histories, biographies, and especially numerous popular dramas staged during the 1830s treated chiefs such as Metacom, Pontiac, and Tecumseh as tragic heroes. Gordon Sayre (2005) argues that this tradition, while by no means free of "colonial nostalgia" (Rosaldo 1989) or superficial regret for the vanishing Indian, was ultimately more complex. Indian leaders impressed many Whites as truly tragic figures, and while such dramas could function to appropriate indigenous virtues for the dominant society (see also P. Deloria 1998) or to symbolically resolve the dilemmas of westward expansion, they could also function as critiques or expressions of deep ambivalence about white imperialism. For their part, patrician European visitors like Tocqueville identified strongly with Indian resistance and defeat, treating their own interethnic encounters as "symbolic quests for contact with a primitive aristocracy [putting them] in touch with their innermost selves" (Liebersohn 1998, 166).

Despite the thematic plasticity of heroic resistance—its potential connection with any number of ethnic, nationalist, and regionalist causes, as well as its ability to stand alone, to evoke sublime sentiments without necessary reference to any particular cause or event—Zonians and visiting North Americans undoubtedly connected the Kuna with their own lives. They may have seen themselves as joined with the Indians in opposition to Panama, construing native separatism as metaphor for the Zone's protected enclave. But for early-twentieth-century expatriates, like European admirers of the Mandan and the Natchez in the previous century, the Kuna seem to have had the greatest emotional resonance not as simple analogues of the self but as exemplars of what the self had lost in the modern age: courage, autonomy, and resistance to domination. Somewhere in the world, the Kuna example said, lived an indomitable people who, like Hereward or Horatio or Tecumseh, still shouted defiance at their enemies, a people who would rather die than submit.

Kuna ethnic endogamy, construed in terms of racial antagonism and separation, connected in a direct way with what Joane Nagel (2003) has called "ethnosexual politics," specifically the fears widespread in North America during that era of sexual permissiveness and racial threat. Anglo-Saxons could be distinguished from degraded Blacks and Latins by their sexual restraint and decency (however tenuous and threatened), while *mestizaje*, one of the most objectionable characteristics of Latin America, was seen as an obvious cause of the region's backwardness (Stoddard 1920; Harris 1922; Williamson 1984; Pike 1992). In every way, the Kuna offered an object lesson, a shining example of "race-consciousness" and "racial hygiene."

In regard to both separatism and sexuality, the Kuna were apt subjects for metaphorical projection and contemplation because it was someone else's national control and someone else's national project that the Indians were rejecting. Too little was known about the Kuna, moreover, to complicate or qualify their idealization as models of independence and racial hygiene, and Kuna women were too isolated and too undesirable by Western standards ever to become the object of interethnic longing, taboos, or boundary-marking (Nagel 2003; Stoler 1989, 1992, 2002a). Instead, North Americans admired Kuna husbands and fathers, very much in the abstract, for preserving female virtue.

In this context, one obvious question is whether white authors correctly perceived Indian attitudes and practices—whether the Kuna really were the racists they were made out to be—and whether Indian and white attitudes shared a common origin. The well-known theorist and Latin Americanist Michael Taussig, who has written at length on the Kuna, argues strongly in the affirmative, claiming a close causal connection, even an indigenous "connivance," with white racism. Perceiving "an uncanny coincidence, a veritable mimesis," between Cuna fears and North American prejudices (1993, 149), Taussig derives one from the other: "It is difficult to believe that [the] minutely orchestrated color-line [of Zonians and other Americans] . . . could not have had an effect on the reckoning of blacks and whites held by Cuna people" (1993, 148).

Kuna antipathies, however, dated back at least to the eighteenth century and followed in obvious ways from a long history of intrusion, violence, and economic competition from Black frontiersmen. If their attitudes were reinforced by the attitudes of influential outsiders, moreover, the process is more likely to have occurred in Panamanian national society (whose racial stratification Taussig ignores almost entirely)[11] and not the Canal Zone, where the Kuna did not begin to work in really significant numbers until the 1930s, well after publication of most of the texts considered here.

Kuna ethnic endogamy, which barred relations with any outsider, not just Blacks, had obvious historic roots in the early eighteenth century, when they rose up against high-handed French pirates who had taken Indian wives (Severino de Santa Teresa 1956, 256, 301–306; Castillero Calvo 1995, 205–206). In the light of subsequent events, moreover, Kuna sexual fears seem prescient rather than excessive: in the early 1920s, mestizo police agents in pacified villages established obligatory social dances and, over strong local objections, seduced, appropriated, married, and, in at least a few cases, raped indigenous women (Howe 1998, 182–187).

It should not be assumed, finally, even that Anglophone writers were quite so fixated on Blacks as Taussig suggests: the texts I have found, when they specify the race against whom the Kuna were on guard, mention Whites more often than Blacks, which can be taken to suggest, first, that writers identified the threat to the Indians generically as Western civilization as a whole, and not just a particular segment of it, and further, that they felt the same uncertainty and ambivalence about modernity and Western expansion that characterized antimodernists and self-appointed friends of the Indians in other places (Lears 1981; Dilworth 1996; P. Deloria 1998, 95–127; S. Smith 2000). Implicitly at least, they were pointing to themselves as part of the problem, as soldiers in the enemy horde. Mentions of Kuna separatism, however brief and stereotyped, thus involved complex identifications connecting Western readers with both the threatened and the threat.

VISITORS AND ADVOCATES

In the second and third decades of the century, residents of the Canal Zone began to make contact with Indians in situ, as well as with the idea of Indians. At least as early as the late 1910s, groups began taking overnight boat excursions to western San Blas, mostly to Nargana, where the presence of Anna Coope and Charly Robinson assured them a friendly welcome, and the more daring even flew out in seaplanes.[12] Among repeat visitors, at least a few undertook amateur studies of native culture: one manuscript, written by a Zonian named Rene Reynolds, offered extended observations on marriage by capture, bride service, funerals, puberty ritual, naming, women's dress, albinos, justice, and even conflict over alcohol and nose-rings.[13] Though direct experience led to more complex and sometimes critical attitudes toward the Indians, the time-honored themes of separatism, racial purity, and sexual exclusion persisted. Despite some backward traits, Reynolds judged, the Kuna were "a cleaner and a better class of people than the natives[14] who are mixed with the negroes and whites," and he concluded by quoting the final lines of Gilbert's poem warning against disturbing the Kuna's tropic Eden.

Zonian friends, with their racist admiration and sentimental preference for Indians, offered an important strategic resource. Indigenous peoples like the Kuna, caught in regions where multiple powers contend, buffeted by conflicting forces and demands, have often allied themselves with one nation or empire or sought its help against another, as the Kuna themselves had in previous centuries with the French, English, Scots, and Spanish in the Darién. In early-twentieth-century Panama, the Kuna could not expect

North American authorities to intervene directly on their behalf—or at least so it seemed for a long time. But they could look to the Zone and to visitors, both for friends who might offer unofficial help of one sort or another, and for an audience sympathetic to their plight.

In this respect, the foreign community in Panama formed a small-scale precursor of the worldwide constituency for indigenous causes that would develop decades later. Today a group that wishes to make its case to the world can count on a wide range of environmental and human-rights organizations, as well as a network of professionals, activists, and sympathizers, which was definitely not the case in the early twentieth century. Despite remarkable campaigns against the slave trade and the brutalization of the Congo and the Amazon (Hochschild 1999, 2005), international communications and international consciousness had not developed to the point at which peoples whose suffering was less egregious could routinely expect such support. The Zone and its aficionados of Indian life were the best approximation available then in Panama. The difficulty with such friends was of course that, seen from a Panamanian perspective as meddling gringo outsiders, they were themselves part of the problem.

If the Kuna turned to English-speaking sympathizers in the years between the publication of J. S. Gilbert's poem of 1894 and the beginning of the government's campaign to civilize them in 1919, they left few traces, and any active support Zonians might have offered between 1913 and 1920 undoubtedly went mostly to Anna Coope's Protestant mission. From 1919 on, however, as government demands escalated, Indian leaders increasingly turned to outsiders, both Latin and North American. In addition to the lawyer José de la Rosa, a Mexican vagabond named Olivo Olivares thoroughly stirred up San Blas in 1922 (Howe 1998, 188–190; Herrera 1984, 181–188). A few months later the Kuna found their most effective foreign advocate, an employee of the Panama Railroad named William Markham, who visited San Blas at the invitation of some Kuna friends for a few weeks in 1923. His hosts on Nargana seem to have been covert dissidents, and the last stop on his tour was Carti Suitupu, whose chief, Olonibiginya, was Colman's chief lieutenant in western San Blas. The adventurous traveler returned home a committed advocate of the Kuna.

Markham, whose visit I have described previously (1998, 193–198), wrote a carefully noncontroversial account of his experiences, which he evidently hoped to publish or at least circulate among friends. The narrative reveals ambivalent attitudes toward cultural difference, tradition, and change. In some passages Markham dwelt on the craftsmanship of

Kuna houses and canoes, the morality and harmony of their lives, and the freedom from such defects of civilization as war, prison, and strikes; in others, he took for granted the inevitability and superiority of modernizing change.

Markham's ambivalence was particularly evident concerning women and their dress. He called their short haircuts hideous, noted outsiders' objections to limb binding, and on the whole trip found only one woman he could call attractive. He even asked Kuna men why chiefs did not force women to change their costume. But he also collected molas enthusiastically and worked hard to get permission to photograph women. On one occasion he caused offense by asking in jest which Indian girl he would get, and throughout the manuscript he returned obsessively to questions of dress and difference.

Markham saved his criticisms of the situation in San Blas for a long letter to President Porras written early in 1924. His characteristically simple, direct note, rewritten by someone else in a much more formal style, was sent in early February, along with a copy of Markham's manuscript, and on the tenth he and a friend had an interview with the president.[15]

To make his case for the Kuna, Markham had to craft his remarks carefully, skirting a number of issues and couching his argument in a form he thought his audience would accept. Portraying himself as a supporter and friendly critic of the government's civilizing program, he tactfully conceded the bad record of the United States in dealing with Indians, praised the government school on Nargana, and told Porras that the Kuna were personally devoted to him. He criticized Anna Coope for introducing a foreign religion and language, thus distancing himself from the Anglophone threat perceived by Panamanian nationalists. But he also insisted that Coope's adherents were arbitrarily punished, and he severely criticized police agents on Río Sidra for an incident in which "to my amazement [they] proceeded to forcibly drag the Indians from their houses . . . as unwilling subjects for my photography." In a rhetorical move in two directions, he repeatedly depicted police abuse as the acts of individuals subverting good government policy, while treating the moral and commonsense norms in question as universally applicable: "The requirements for administering to the Indian both in the United States and in Panama are parallel."

Kuna difference was praised, somewhat obliquely, at the beginning of the letter: "It should be a matter of pride to the citizens of this Republic that a race of beings unique in so many ways reside within the borders of their country." Markham did not argue, however, that traditional practices should persist, nor did he discount the value of civilization and Isthmian patriotism, but rather urged Porras to proceed with less haste and coercion. In enumerating Indian fears—of land loss, obligatory dances, intrusive outsiders, and police lechery—Markham characterized their worries less as justified in fact than as understandable under the circumstances and thus as something the government could put to rest by such measures as issuing land titles and making dances optional. Without overtly endorsing Kuna racial attitudes, he presented them sympathetically. "It is a matter of wide spread knowledge that this race regard their traditional purity of stock as an article of religious faith."

Controversies over culture change were placed in the framework of generational succession—"The elders regard these dances identically in the same light as elders have done so the world over"—a move that simultaneously domesticated and universalized the issue. Throughout, Markham rhetorically detached undesirable practice from the Kuna by anticipating its disappearance. Condescending in places (the original manuscript letter notes, "Of course your agent will have to take into consideration that he is dealing with children"), Markham portrayed the Indians as a worthy, if tradition-bound, people fully capable of joining the nation.

The letter and interview had some effect. Porras, who for the most part really hoped that the Indians could be transformed through kind persuasion, was already disturbed by recent developments in San Blas—not by the suppression of Indian custom, which he had himself ordered, but the abuse of their civil rights. He wrote Markham on March tenth promising to begin straightening things out within a few days.[16] As it turned out, he never acted. Later that year, another petition alleging mistreatment was sent by a women's club in the Canal Zone, undoubtedly at Markham's behest.[17] But the intendente, Andrés Mojica, though he lost Porras's confidence, held on to his post even under a new president, and conditions on the coast continued as before.

THE TULE DECLARATION

As the situation continued to worsen through 1924, another potential ally appeared. Richard Marsh, an engineer and adventurer, had visited the Darién in 1923, and having convinced himself that he had met white Indians outside the town of Yaviza, he returned to Panama early the next year with an expedition dedicated to various scientific and commercial goals, but especially to discovering the lost white tribe he was sure lurked in the forest. By the time his party had ascended the Chucunaque River and crossed over the mountains into San Blas, almost everyone in it had fallen ill and two men had died, but Marsh had so far seen only one white Indian.[18]

Marsh's self-deluded quest did have a core of reality, because (as others had already told him) there were a great many albinos among the Kuna. When Marsh finally encountered white Indians, he conceived a plan to present them to the world and at the same time to publicize Kuna sufferings. At the first tour stop at the island of Ustupu, or Portogandi, Marsh was taken in hand by Chief Nele, Colman's second-in-command. Expressions of interest in native material culture as well as white Indians inspired villagers to produce five albinos and great quantities of artifacts, in the process demonstrating to Nele the political value of his culture. By early July Marsh was in New York, with a party of three young albinos and five nonalbino adults.

The party's highly publicized visit reinforced the connection between native culture and external alliance: delegates could see that North American scholars were eager to study Kuna language, music, and material culture, as well as the now-famous white Indians (Densmore 1926; Krieger 1926). In January 1925, Marsh took the party back to Panama and on to Ailigandi, where he wrote and circulated a "Declaration of Independence and Human Rights of San Blas and Darien,"[19] and at the end of February, Colman's group rebelled against Panama, killing a number of policemen and putting the rest to flight.

The Declaration, the last of a series of attempts on Marsh's part to represent the Indians and the culmination of Anglophone popular discourse about Kuna political, sexual, and racial exclusionism, was sent to Panamanian as well as U.S. authorities and printed in its entirety on February 27 in the *Panama Star and Herald*. Supposedly dictated to Marsh, the text assumed the voice of the Tule, the name the Kuna use among themselves, identifying them as "the last remnants of a once great and highly developed people," who were none other than the ancient Maya.

The document heaped praise on Tule democracy and morality, especially "the precepts of personal chastity and conjugal fidelity." Marsh claimed that the Tule deity and hero, named "A-oba," was white, that native white races had intermingled with brown, and that the Tule, until they realized their mistake, had revered the first Europeans as God-men. Afterwards, to maintain their racial purity, "we killed our women who had been violated by the Spaniards, and destroyed their children." Over the following centuries, the Tule maintained their isolation, saved from disease by "our strict habits of personal chastity."

The twentieth century, however, brought intrusions by unemployed

FIGURE 5.3 Kuna delegates working with linguist J. P. Harrington in Washington, D.C., 1924

Black workers and subjugation by "negroid" policemen and teachers, who stripped islands bare of vegetation, extorted illegal taxes, abused women and girls (who were deprived of their "gay colored, modest native dresses"), and taught impressionable Tule youth "to be idle, to steal, to betray their people . . . in short . . . to be 'Panama citizens'!" Very recently, however, a group taken to America learned of their Maya ancestry, as well as the U.S. right to intervene in Panamanian affairs, while scientists concluded that "our race should not be permitted to be exterminated or mongrelized by negro infusion," if for no reason other than its scientific interest. The Declaration, which called for a U.S. protectorate, was unanimously approved by "the national congress of the Tule race" on February 12, 1925, which, it noted, fell in the year 5,825 since their migration from the ancestral home of Tulan.

Marsh's Declaration was a pastiche or bricolage, an assemblage of bits and pieces of heterogeneous origin. Some of these bits—such as elected chiefs or the arrival of teachers and police—obviously reflect Kuna input, though Marsh got many of the details wrong. ("A-oba," for instance, is merely the Kuna pronunciation of Jehovah.) Other elements follow the tradition of local Anglophone writings. Still others, such as lost races of pyramid builders, fair-skinned culture heroes, Mexican homelands, and invaders mistaken for gods, derived from Marsh's reading in popular history and social theory. A few last notions he collected during the Kuna visit to the United States, when Aleš Hrdlička (1926) noted a physical resemblance to the Maya.[20]

However heterogeneous in origin, the bits and pieces in this pastiche were actively shaped by Marsh, fitted to the presumed mindset of his intended audience of North American diplomats and military men. Aware that Kuna women's dress, which Panamanian authorities had worked so hard to suppress, offended many outsiders,[21] he took pains to praise "the gay-colored, intricately designed and embroidered garments which long custom has led us to consider the most beautiful, most healthful and most suitable to [the] environment"—remarks representative of a more general strategy, to reverse the values of selves and alters by situating the Indians on the rhetorical baseline and treating Panama as the intrusive and offensive other. The document was also shaped and filtered, perhaps less consciously, by Marsh's preoccupations and prejudices, most apparent among them his intense antipathy to Blacks and his fixation on sex and its control. Although the policemen were in fact mostly mestizo and the politicians responsible for civilizing the Kuna almost all white, Marsh saw Blacks everywhere. Kuna husbands and fathers worried about consensual as well as coerced sex—Marsh was fixated on rape.

As obvious as are the gendering and sexualizing of Marsh's account, they must be interpreted with caution. Michael Taussig, in an extended discussion of Marsh and his fantasies (1993, 156–187), argues that in tropological or ideological terms, Marsh depicted the Kuna and the land as essentially female, in Taussig's vivid phrase, as "the Great White Cunt" (1993, 171), and that the search for the white Indians was a form of symbolic penetration. There is some basis for reading Marsh's advance up the Chucunaque as a kind of penetration, though by no means the wildly orgasmic "performances of civilized power ejaculating multicolored magic against the dark backdrop of the jungle" of Taussig's hyperbolic interpretation (1993, 164). It is also true that in a few passages in the book Marsh later wrote (1934, 110, 121–123), he expressed a longing (if a rather tepid one) for liaisons with Indian women. What Taussig misses is that Marsh depicted himself mastering those impulses, just as in the Declaration he harped on Kuna morality and restraint. Unbridled licentiousness in the form of Panamanian lechery was seen as a threat, indeed as *the* threat, and the key to proper sexuality, both for the Indians and oneself, was control (cf. Pike 1992, 52).

Marsh was an ardent Social Darwinist, and as such he had difficulty accepting the humble status of Kuna tribal society. Not only did he link the Indians to past Mayan glories, but he attempted to compensate for the inadequacies of their public works and technology with domestic virtue. On the question of whether grandeur or modest integrity was ultimately more to be desired, he waffled:

> The vainglory of a complicated, artificial, material civilization, huge cities, stone temples and edifices, leading in turn only to dissolution, passed from our minds as the fancies of a child fade before the realities of age and experience. Perhaps the pendulum of our fate swung back too far. (Marsh n.d. [1925])

Despite this ambivalence, and despite the assemblage's heterogeneous elements, it creates a consistent picture. As I have argued elsewhere at greater length (Howe 1991a; 1998, 262–263), by putting his case in terms that he hoped would move his intended audience as well as himself, Marsh gave free rein to his own identification with the Kuna. As he portrayed them, they resembled the self-image of old-line WASP "native Americans" in the 1920s, especially those who embraced eugenicist and nativist ideology, people who felt their racial purity and social dominance threatened by pushy newcomers and newly mobile Blacks (Grant 1916; Stoddard 1920; Higham 1966). In effect, Marsh projected the fears of Anglo-Saxon America onto the San Blas coast.

For all the effort Marsh put into the Declaration, it had at best mixed success. His catalogue of suffering was later confirmed by other sources and thus belatedly may have helped make the case for Kuna rebellion (see below).[22] But the many extraneous details such as migrations from Tulan and white god-men merely cast doubt on its indigenous authorship. The claims to nationhood, today a staple of Native American indigenous rhetoric, in that era sounded foolish and grandiose. Marsh had already made himself notorious in Panama the previous year with speculative theorizing and public controversies about the Indians.[23] Although some recent sources have, quite surprisingly, accepted the Declaration as authentically Kuna, at the time it was widely recognized as Marsh's handiwork. Ultimately, it focused attention on his own character and culpability—he was called a "faker" (*farsante*) as well as a "bandit"—and it detracted from respect and recognition for the Kuna.[24]

GOOD REBELS

Despite the failure of Marsh's literary efforts, the involvement of a notorious North American adventurer in domestic unrest did arouse great concern. Panama in the 1920s was still a U.S. protectorate. The United States, though by no means as eager to get embroiled in local affairs as Marsh supposed, did retain the right to intervene in civil disturbances, and Panama, which lacked an army or well-armed police force, was sometimes forced to ask for help. In this instance, two vessels set out for San Blas on February 26, one a borrowed launch filled with a hastily recruited collection of Panamanian policemen, and the other a cruiser, the U.S.S. *Cleveland*, with the minister to Panama, John Glover South, and a number of officials from both governments on board. The instructions cabled to South from the State Department urged a hard line, encouraging him to take Marsh into custody for punishment by Panamanian authorities, and if possible, to have the cruiser overawe the Indians into submission (Howe 1998, 281). Also along but with a different outcome in mind was William Markham, whose weeks in San Blas had qualified him as the leading expert on the Indians.

On the morning of the twenty-seventh, the two vessels reached the island of El Porvenir, government headquarters for the Indian area, where the police disembarked. The *Cleveland* continued on across the Gulf of San Blas to anchor near the island of Carti Suitupu, where Marsh was holed up with one rebel force. Markham went ashore to confer with Marsh, after which he brought him out for a long talk with Minister South, in which Marsh managed to break down some of the minister's preconceptions with a recital of Indian grievances and a not entirely truthful account of his own activities. At a subsequent meeting arranged by Markham on Suitupu, South listened to translations of impassioned Kuna speeches. It seems clear, even at this early stage, that the rebels had been coached by their American friends on which claims would get the best reception. Though Markham was working indirectly through the words of others, he was in effect offering a kind of dramatic ethnography, an account of Indian character and experience that might justify their rebellion. According to his narrative:

> One chief told of the way the San Blas Indian had kept his blood pure, how the policemen had taken the Indian girls, raped and insulted them and if the father or mother protested they were thrown in jail and fined from five to twenty five dollars gold. Another chief told how one Indian was hung by his hands for seven days without food or water. Another chief told how the Panamanian police cut down their cocoanuts, and that they had gone to Panama to see the President. He had promised them relief, but it did not come, only more policemen. Another chief told how they pulled the nose and ear rings out of the girls nose and ears and kept them and did not give back anything in return only abuse and insult. At last the head chief got up and in a clear even voice told us that they did not object to education but not in the way that the Panamanians wanted them to have it, which meant a policeman with a 44 on his hip and the authority of the government behind them.
>
> Also their land was being taken away from them, the turtles were being taken from them and there was no hope for them in the future but starvation and ruin.[25]

South listened sympathetically and offered to mediate the crisis. On the twenty-eighth he received a cable from Washington approving his proposal to facilitate a negotiated settlement by removing Marsh from Panama without a trial. That afternoon he informed Markham that a government representative would arrive next day to conduct an investigation. Dispatched in a ship's boat to recruit Kuna witnesses, Markham called at nearby islands and sent off sailing canoes as far as thirty miles east. On the afternoon of the twenty-ninth, a party of Kuna came aboard and presented testimony to South and a justice of the Panamanian Supreme Court, Francisco de la Ossa (see Howe 1998, 283–286).

South, now firmly convinced that Kuna actions were "just and reasonable and inevitable,"[26] took a seaplane back to the city, and after persuading the Panamanian foreign minister, Horacio Alfaro, to his point of view, he flew back with Alfaro to Carti. On March fourth, officials of both countries met on El Porvenir with regional Kuna leaders in protracted negotiations (at which neither Marsh nor Markham was present): after several hours the Kuna grudgingly exchanged a renewed pledge of allegiance to Panama for guarantees of cultural and legal rights. On the fifth, South took the document to Colman on Ailigandi, and again with great difficulty, elicited the chief's consent. By the sixth the cruiser was back in the city, and a week later Marsh was shipped out to the United States. Tensions between the Panamanian government and the Indians persisted for years, but to everyone's surprise, the agreement held.

The Kuna and their advisors, more than anything else, had to convince others of the legitimacy of rebellion, and in this respect, the American minister seems to have been more receptive than some of his colleagues.[27] But South by no means sympathized with all rebels. During an urban rent strike later the same year, he readily supplied troops to be used against rioters.[28] Throughout the Caribbean and Central America, the United States came down most often on the side of order and the status quo (Healy 1988). Thus Marsh, Markham, and the Kuna had their work cut out for them in persuading South that this particular rebellion was justified.

In some respects the audience of Panamanian officials was of secondary importance, since the Kuna reached them most effectively through South. But South, rather than insisting, pressured and exhorted his Panamanian colleagues to follow his lead, so in one way or another they, too, had to be convinced. In the case of de la Ossa, South and Markham's accounts leave the impression that the justice was so fixated on Marsh's guilt that he paid little heed to other issues: Markham's efforts as stage manager and director on board the *Cleveland* seem to have been aimed more at wringing public admissions out of the justice than convincing him.[29] But the crucial players on the Panamanian side all reached the conclusion that the Indians had indeed been mistreated, though not necessarily that they were thereby justified in killing policemen. As Horacio Alfaro wrote his brother Ricardo, "Marsh was undoubtedly the spark that provoked the fire; but the fuel was there long before, since it cannot be doubted that the Indians had profound motives for resentment and for hate because of the inhumane treatment that was afforded them."[30] Ultimately, Markham, South, and the Kuna pushed the Panamanians, if not all the way to their own point of view, far enough to get the job done.

If one considers the media of communication and persuasion used in the affair, it is clear that the Kuna did much better in open meetings than they had done so far either in writing or in private interviews at government offices. Avoiding the grammatical and stylistic lapses characteristic of their letters, they exposed their listeners to the force and passion of their grievances even if their words were unintelligible, which is exactly what Markham intended. In addition to shaping the content and rhetoric of Kuna complaints, Markham seems to have chosen witnesses for maximum impact, including the outspoken daughter of Chief Olonibiginya.

> A girl or young woman came to me and started to point at me with her finger. She talked fast and furious with fire in her eyes. . . . She was the chiefs daughter, eighteen years old. . . . Next I told the chief that I wanted three girls around fourteen years old, also his daughter Se a be be.[31] He looked at me and thought a bit then says "yes" turned and called for the girls of that age. I picked three out of perhaps fifty. . . . I wanted to take them face to face with the Chief Justice of Panama and point out to him the type of girls his negro police were raping and insulting. The chief's daughter I thought that if she could tell them just hundredth part as much as she told me it would be a plenty to win their cause.[32]

The translation of Kuna speeches, provided by the same imperfect secretaries who had written the letters, probably left much to be desired.[33] But the basic message of abuse made it through. Equally important, unlike the letters, which afforded no glimpse of their writers, the speech-making and speech-makers were immediately at hand. My own field experience convinces me that indigenous eloquence can register even without translation, just as Gordon Sayre (2005, 14–15) argues it did on the North American frontier. Treaty negotiations, according to Sayre, "were less diplomatic conversations than a series of performances" by Indian orators, which for white listeners resembled "watching an opera without subtitles." In the case of Minister South, "I was greatly impressed by the intelligence, forcefulness, sincerity, and honesty displayed by the Indian leaders during my talk with them."[34]

In the final negotiations, two translators worked, an Indian named

Charlie Penn, or Bean, interpreting between Kuna and English, and a Latin Panamanian, Narciso Navas, between Kuna and Spanish. Navas was one of two brothers (discussed in Chapter 2), Kuna-speaking Latins who had assisted the government a number of times over the years. Unlike most native scribes, Navas was apparently fairly fluent in both languages, and he seems to have been trusted by both sides. He took an active role in the give-and-take of the interchange, for which Horacio Alfaro gave him great credit: "Sr. Navas was a most efficacious assistant in our work in San Blas, and I am convinced that a great part of the favorable result that we reached is due to him."[35]

Through their successive presentations in the three meetings, the efforts of Kuna leaders to make real to their listeners the abuses they had suffered undoubtedly benefited from North American readiness to believe the worst of Latin Americans, and even more from corroborative testimony collected in the city from Reginald Harris, a biologist who had accompanied Marsh, and from Colman and Nele, who were interviewed by U.S. officials sent down the coast on a tug. Markham also gave South a copy of his letter to President Porras, and Marsh's Declaration undoubtedly now seemed in some respects more creditworthy than before.

Justification of rebellion could not be separated completely from the question of Marsh's guilt. If the Kuna had been duped by Marsh (which many Panamanians have since assumed), then their uprising lost legitimacy. Conversely, if circumstances at least partly excused rebellion, then perhaps Marsh deserved less blame, which was what South ultimately concluded. Kuna sufferings were also tied inextricably to their identity as a people. It was crucial that they be seen not just as victims of tyranny, but as patient, long-suffering, *worthy* victims. The question of who and what they were as a people, their essence and identity, was still crucial, and the successive verbal presentations, as they were shaped by Markham, represented that essence as much as any of the written documents considered in the last three chapters.

What the Kuna were, first and foremost, was different, and the most obvious sign of that difference, as always, was women's dress. In the hearing on board the *Cleveland*, Markham confronted the issue head-on.

> The chief sat down then I went and got his daughter Seabebe by the arm and placed her before him. I asked him "Mr DeLaOssa what objection do you have to this ladies dress.["] Taking off her head dress "what is wrong with the nose and earrings has not she the same right to wear ornaments as your wife or mine?"

He says sure. "Look at her dress it is modest neat and respectable also adapted to their way of living and if they think it is pretty you and I ought to be satisfied.["] He got a little bit excited and says we have no objection to their dress. "Yes but you did". Turning to the interpreter I told him to tell her troubles to this man and she did better than I thought she would. To think she is the first woman of her tribe that has been allowed to plead their cause and if womens rights are ever obtained in San Blas it will be Se abbe that has set the ball rolling she did not use the fire in her voice that she used with me but she told how the negro police had torn the rings from the nose and ears and had never given them a cent in return. How they had stopped them wearing their pretty little NooLa [sic] or dress and compelled them to wear a dress that was long and in the way, would always get wet when getting in the cayuca how it took so much time to put on and take off, told how the negro police caught the little girls and took them away. Then I called Mr DeLaOssa's attention to the three little girls sitting in the chairs.[36]

Thus, according to Markham, the costume of Kuna women, rather than bizarre and unhealthful, was practical, modest, and pretty, and far from being a sign of essential difference, it was just one more variation on the fashions to which women in all societies were prone. Difference, such as it was, was temporary and unimportant.

Another issue, significant though not so intuitively obvious, was how to place the Indians in terms of social class, a question that might seem nonsensical applied to an egalitarian society, but one that European and Euro-American observers often asked.[37] The earliest colonists in North America looked for familiar signs of status difference: "Reports from every region echoed the language of English aristocratic self-presentation" (Kupperman 1997, 220). As attitudes in Puritan New England hardened, colonists took particular offense at the long hair and dedication to deer hunting of Indian men, both traits characteristic of the English aristocracy (Axtell 1985, 157–158, 174–178; Cronon 1983, 56). In the nineteenth century, the popular dramas mentioned above portrayed native chiefs as elevated, quasi-royal figures (Sayre 2005), while French and German visitors identified with the Indians as native aristocrats devoted to the chase, war, and freedom (Liebersohn 1998).

Less friendly observers took it for granted that native peoples, if they survived, would end up at the bottom of the social ladder, and they found it disconcerting when people like the Kuna disagreed. Father Benito Pérez, after years in San Blas, complained bitterly of the "proverbial haughtiness" of the Indians and the "innermost scorn (as incredible as it seems!)" with which they viewed outsiders like himself (Howe 1998, 86). Both poles of the dialectic were obvious in Gilbert's poem, which first called the Kuna "lowly" and then "dignified and haughty as the proudest of mankind."

Marsh and Markham gave different answers to the class question. As the son of a congressman, nephew of a Supreme Court justice, son-in-law of a nationally prominent engineer, educated at private schools, MIT, and the University of Lausanne, Marsh thought the Kuna, if he was to support them, should be superior beings: he imagined them as Maya aristocrats, fallen from past glories perhaps, but still retaining elevated moral and intellectual qualities. Markham, a solidly lower-middle-class employee of the railroad, though less explicit on the question than Marsh, portrayed the Kuna as simple but worthy folks, democratic, honest, and straightforward. Minister South, as a prominent doctor married into one of the leading political families of Kentucky, may have been closer to Marsh's background, but he came from the American heartland, and it was Markham's portrayal, which raised the Kuna up but not too high, that he accepted.

None of the sources on the days after the Kuna rebellion says so explicitly, but it seems likely that, consciously or unconsciously, Markham had a key image or metaphor in mind. There were, after all, so many examples of bad rebellion that might offend a conservative Kentucky Republican, from France in 1789 to Russia in 1914 or last week's *golpe* in Latin America, but good rebels worthy of wholehearted admiration were scarce. The analogy with the greatest power and positive resonance was, of course, 1776. The Kuna, portrayed as yeoman agriculturalists—democratic, eloquent, long-suffering, slow to act but strong and righteous when aroused—sounded just like the embattled farmers of Concord and Lexington, who demonstrated the possibility of good rebellions and good rebels.

Marsh and Markham, however much they differed in their aims, methods, and results, both subscribed to what has been called imperial liberalism, the certainty that Americans had the right and duty to save the world by improving the deficient morality of other nations (Pike 1992). Practitioners of imperial liberalism, in imposing what they saw as universal standards, mostly exported the usages and customs of their own country, and it was in large part through projections, inversions, and reversals of the North American self that they understood both Indian and Latin others. Later chapters will show that Marsh and Markham, though the last to intervene so dramatically, were by no means the last to adopt the Kuna cause or to appoint themselves advocates for the Indians. The difficulty with such allies was, as always, that in Panamanian eyes they were easily recognized as the nosy foreign meddlers prone to subverting *nuestros indios*.

INTERPRETING REBELLION

Post-rebellion commentary followed well-worn ideological paths. Andrés Mojica, now removed as intendente, gave a long newspaper statement blaming Marsh—the ultimate subversive third party—and summoning up dark visions of an ongoing capitalist conspiracy to take over the coast, a line adopted by a number of officials.[38] Even more implausibly, Anna Coope also came in for blame as a supposed éminence grise of rebellion.

On the other side, Indian sympathizers returned to well-worn tropes and images. *La Estrella de Panamá/Panama Star and Herald*, the bilingual paper owned by the Cuban-Panamanian Duque family, took a fairly sympathetic position, one that seemed to reflect the sensibility of its cosmopolitan and partly North American staff. Editorials and columns mocked and condemned Richard Marsh but also called for investigation of Kuna grievances, praised the negotiated settlement, and lamented government vindictiveness in the weeks afterwards.[39] On February twenty-seventh, soon after the uprising, an English-language columnist on the *Star and Herald* signing himself J.K.B. came to the defense of the Indians, noting ironically that Panamanian forces could benefit from his own country's experience in genocide: "a few bombs dropped from the air and the San Blas will be with the Mohawks and the Mohicans." Despairing of Kuna survival, J.K.B. suggested they might have done better by resorting to mass suicide, as some Amazonian tribes supposedly had, but added that it was "impossible to withhold ... sympathy from an Indian Horatius inciting his people to a last stand":

> But how could man die better
> Than facing fearful odds
> For the ashes of his fathers
> And the temples of his gods?[40]

A few days later J.K.B. returned to his theme, specifically to the complaint that the Kuna had always rejected the civilization kindly offered them by the government. He noted that while modern civilization "has enormously increased the wealth and power" of Western nations,

> Whether it has added to the sum total of human happiness is open to question. . . . No single instance can be cited where contact with civilization has brought to the Indians anything but loss and degradation. . . . Ultimately, I suppose, they will have to swallow the dose, but let us not be so hypocritical as to pretend they ought to like it. (Star & Herald 3/02/25)

Finally, in August, about six months after the rebellion, a Spanish-language editorial in *La Estrella* revived the old story of the attempted sand purchase, which put Kuna separatism in a much kinder light than killing policemen or consorting with subversive explorers.[41] Following a long tradition going back to Montaigne and Las Casas, the editorialist found in Indian virtue a reproach to the ills of his own society.

> We were reading yesterday an anecdote that . . . deserves to be inscribed in the spirit of every Panamanian. . . . The Canal builders . . . needed sand one day for concrete to build the Gatun locks. To the southeast of this Zone . . . there is a tribe of Indians. It is the tribe of the "Cuna," haughty Indians, protective of what is theirs, worthy heirs of that race that defended their land with arrows during the unforgettable blood-thirsty conquests carried out by the civilized world. It was to this people that the builders went, offering them gold for the sand that was needed; and then, in the face of this proposal, in the face of the prospect of trading that unproductive matter for glittering money, in spite of everything, the poor and half-naked Indian replies with the following words: "HE WHO CREATED SAND MADE IT FOR THE CUNA WHO EXISTED BEFORE, FOR THOSE WHO EXIST TODAY, AND FOR THOSE WHO WILL EXIST TOMORROW, AND SO IT DOES NOT BELONG TO US AND WE CANNOT SELL IT".
>
> Whoever reads the lines as they were transcribed, whoever weighs the savage's odd reply, will he not find there . . . cause for profound reflection? Where can one find an attitude that is nobler, more upright, more worthy of praise and perpetual imitation? If every ambitious, selfish leader who looks upon the *patria* as a

fiefdom, who regards the national wealth as his own, could read the anecdote of the Isthmian Indian and understand . . . that nothing that he administers belongs to him . . .

How happy our fatherland would be if one were to hear every so often that virile and noble phrase . . . that synthesis of a whole moral code, that pulse of sincere patriotism, that magnificent lesson that the savage, without realizing it himself, provides to these peoples so proud of their civilization!

The Swedish Partnership

SIX

In early 1927 the secretaries of Chief Nele of Ustupu received a newspaper clipping about a party of Swedish scientists who were in Panama to study the country's Indians.[1] In late May or early June friends passed on word that the vessel carrying the Swedes had entered San Blas and was calling at the village of Kwebdi, or Río Azúcar, well to the west. A subsequent report advised them of the boat's progress down the coast, and by June eighth it was at Ustupu itself.

In this period, two years after the great uprising, the rebel Kuna had yet to clarify their relationship with the government or the nation. The administration had imposed an embargo cutting off their islands from trading boats, and the insurrectionists, for their part, continued to fly the Tule flag devised during the rebellion and to insist on their independence. Both sides avoided forcing the issue through armed confrontation, but relations remained tense and fundamentally ambiguous. Cimral Colman, by now gravely ill, seems to have continued as titular leader of the rebel group until his death in 1929, but Nele of Ustupu was taking over as effective alliance head, while Inabaginya continued to lead the villages that had remained loyal to Panama.

The foreigners coming to Ustupu were led by a well-known Swedish anthropologist and nobleman, Friherre, or Baron, Erland Nordenskiöld, who had inherited the title from his father, a famous polar explorer of the nineteenth century.[2] Nordenskiöld, like many of his academic generation, lacked formal training and had ended up as an anthropologist after beginning in other fields, in his case zoology and paleontology. He had participated in one expedition to the southern cone of South America and led five more, the first to Patagonia in 1899 and the others, in 1901–1902, 1904–1905, 1908–1909, and 1913–1914, to the borderlands where the Andes meet the Gran Chaco thorn desert.

When he began his Panama travels in early 1927 Nordenskiöld was forty-nine, the head of a small but respected anthropological museum in Göteborg, or Gothenburg, a port city on the west coast of Sweden. Fourteen years previously he had taken over what was then one part of a general museum, a nondescript section dedicated to exotic curiosities brought back from other continents by mariners and travelers. He built up the South American collections with material gathered on his own expeditions and those of colleagues such as Curt Nimuendajú, Alfred Metraux, Rafael Karsten, Max Uhle, and Gustav Bolinder, in the process establishing the Göteborg Ethnographic Museum as an internationally recognized research institution.

For most of his career Nordenskiöld specialized in the study of technology and material culture. He was best known internationally for dry, technical analyses mapping out culture elements in South America, distribution studies that were characteristic of an era in which modern archaeology was just getting underway and some scholars still hoped to reconstruct culture history from contemporary trait distribution.[3] One of the biggest questions addressed by such work was the relative weight to be given diffusion and independent invention. Although Nordenskiöld, like a majority of scholars, envisioned a balance of the two factors, he also argued strongly for panhuman creative capacities and thus for multiple centers of civilization (Nordenskiöld 1999).

To reach a wide international audience, Nordenskiöld published most of his scholarly articles and books in languages other than Swedish, quite a few of them in the largely English-language monograph series put out by his museum. There was another and much more lively side of his work, however, published in his own language. He reported on his expeditions in engaging travelogues, *Indian Life in the Chaco, Indians and Whites in Northeast Bolivia,* and *Researches and Adventures in South America 1913–14,* which introduced South America and indigenous ways of life to a Swedish popular audience.[4] (Two books were subsequently translated into German and one into French.) His commitment to popular education was also evident in numerous newspaper and magazine articles and in the design of museum exhibits.

Nordenskiöld, despite his title, did not descend from the old aristocracy, and though affluent enough to own a summer cottage as well as keep a substantial home in the city, he could by no means finance his expeditions and publications without the backing of wealthy patrons. Resentful against the Stockholm establishment for having rejected him as director of a national museum and sharing the provincial defensiveness of the elite of Sweden's second city, he also scandalized polite society by marrying the daughter of a carpenter, while insisting throughout on being addressed as Friherre. Characterized as "a remarkable combination of a radical and a reactionary,"[5] thoroughly ambivalent about modernism and progress, the scientific establishment, and his own class background, Nordenskiöld espoused progressive social views, lifelong atheism, unusually tolerant and admiring views of Indians and sharp criticism of their exploiters, combined with deeply ingrained racism against Blacks, whom he encountered in Latin America but not Sweden.[6]

NEW RESEARCH

The Panama trip represented a major departure for Nordenskiöld, according to Bo Ernstson, who has been studying the episode intensively. Nordenskiöld had absorbed the new models for ethnographic fieldwork emanating from Franz Boas and his students in the United States and from Bronislaw Malinowski in Britain. Boas, with close connections to Scandinavian anthropology, had visited Göteborg in 1924 while preparing a book on non-Western art, and his text-based ethnographic writing may have provided a model for Nordenskiöld. As for Malinowski, when Curt Nimuendajú wrote Nordenskiöld to ask for advice on fieldwork and analysis, he sent him a copy of *The Sexual Life of Savages* (1929).[7] Although Nordenskiöld did not settle down in Panama for the sort of long-term participant-observation advocated by Malinowski, he did begin to think in more complex and holistic ways about culture.

Nordenskiöld was also increasingly drawn to questions concerning the thought processes of so-called primitives as they had been discussed by Malinowski, Lucien Lévy-Bruhl, Wilhelm Schmidt, and others. Thus, although the announced goal of the research in Panama was to trace the distribution of indigenous cultures across northern South America (Lindberg 1996, 374), Nordenskiöld was ready to move on to new questions.

In 1924 Göteborg cohosted the International Congress of Americanists, and during the sessions, Nordenskiöld interacted with Robert Lowie, which led to an invitation to teach at Berkeley as visiting professor in the fall of 1926. Alfred Kroeber, some of whose work had a good deal in common with Nordenskiöld's distributional studies, was unfortunately away, but Nordenskiöld did see Lowie again, as well as the South Americanist Julian Steward, then an advanced graduate student. He also visited Franz Boas, Clark Wissler, and others in New York and Washington on his way west. While Nordenskiöld depended on his established methods and results for his California lectures, he was exposed to work from different perspectives by Lowie, Edward Sapir, Paul Radin, and others.[8]

At the beginning of 1927, Nordenskiöld traveled by ship from San Francisco to Panama, where he linked up with his wife Olga, an adult son Erik, and a young researcher, Sigvald Linné, who was to carry out an archaeological reconnaissance. During a visit to Colón, Nordenskiöld encountered Kuna men, but he was put off by their clothes, the pomade on their hair, and what he took as their rude, snobbish attitudes (1928b, 14). By no means the naked, unspoiled Indians he was seeking, they were, he concluded, uninteresting subjects for anthropological study. Instead, he proposed to proceed along the Pacific side of the Isthmus to the Darién and on down the west coast of Colombia, traveling on a thirty-six-foot coasting vessel named after his wife, which had been donated by Swedish backers.

The party set out in mid-January.[9] After a brief stop at the Pearl Islands in Panama Bay, they continued on to the Río Sambú in the southeastern Darién, where they were pleased to encounter "real Indians" *(riktiga indianer)*, the Emberá Chocó, who lived in homesteads scattered up and down the rivers of the region (1928b, 37). Nordenskiöld went up the Sambú as far as the home of a prominent shaman, Selimo Huacoriso, with whom the anthropologist, in a marked departure from his previous field methods, rapidly established a strong working relationship. Although Selimo never shared his beliefs or curing chants to the extent Nordenskiöld hoped, he acted as sponsor, guide, facilitator, translator, and principal subject throughout much of the rest of the trip.

Members of the group interacted closely with the Emberá, eating their food and sleeping in their houses, and for an expedition of that era, Nordenskiöld and the others dealt with the Indians in an unusually egalitarian manner. While traveling with them on the *Olga,* they slept as well as ate with their Indian companions, as many as ten people lying on the deck of the small vessel, and when the nights grew chill, the Emberá ended up under the blankets cuddled with the Swedes. Despite frictions with Selimo and others (as well as tensions within the European party, particularly between Olga and Linné),[10] Nordenskiöld liked and admired the Emberá and rejoiced in the preservation of their culture.

Much less ready to find virtue in the Afro-Panamanian population of the Darién, Nordenskiöld peppered his travelogue with unfavorable comparisons and intensely hostile criticism.[11] More than that, he doubted the value of what any group in the modern world had to offer the Indians, predicting facetiously that the day might come when they would announce that they were ready to become Christians because they had learned to steal (1928b, 79).

In late February the party made a brief return trip to Panama City to restock and then set off again down the coast into Colombia to visit both Emberá and the closely related Noanama, or Wounán, Chocó, many people from both groups friends, kin, and wives of the polygynous Selimo. Despite taking precautions, by this point almost everyone in the expedition had come down with malaria or other fevers. They returned briefly to the Sambú and then continued back to the city, taking Selimo with them to get his reactions and comments on Western civilization and other Indian peoples. Crossing the Isthmus on the canal and sailing west along the northern coast (in the opposite direction from San Blas), they went ashore to see the local Indians (a branch of the Guaymí, or Ngöbe) but had little success, since their guides sent out warnings ahead of the party.

TO SAN BLAS

Largely as an afterthought, Nordenskiöld decided to visit the Kuna, though he later wrote that his hopes for them were still modest (1928b, 192). He had read Father Gassó's memoirs, the pirate Wafer's account, and other sources, as well as newspaper reports from a few years before on the controversies over Richard Marsh and the supposed white Indians, but so far the Kuna had not excited much curiosity, in large part because they struck him as much more acculturated than the Emberá. However limited Nordenskiöld's expectations, he strongly sympathized with Kuna separatist tendencies, in part because he assumed, incorrectly, that the policemen who had oppressed them were Black, but mostly because the Kuna had fought to preserve their traditions (1928b, 197; Nordenskiöld et al. 1938, 7). So strongly did he feel on the issue that at one point in his travelogue he referred to police confiscations of native medicines as "sacrilege" (1928b, 221).

The party set out from Colón on May twenty-seventh. After presenting their papers to authorities at the government headquarters on El Porvenir, they proceeded to Kwebdi, or Río Azúcar, a few miles short of Nargana. There they signed on as interpreter a young educated man named Roberto Pérez, who in turn introduced them to a local medicinalist, Charlie Nelson. Nelson, who had been one of the toughest local opponents of Panamanian control and the target of the 1921 police raid that had led to the death of Claudio Iglesias (Howe 1998, 153–159, 171), was happy to work with the Baron and to sell him some of his medicines and paraphernalia. Especially intriguing to Nordenskiöld was the picture-writing that Nelson drew for him (1928b, 208–210), along with the elaborate cosmology and mythology that emerged from his explication of the pictures. Nelson and others, Nordenskiöld felt, were much more ready to reveal secrets than Selimo had ever been, at the same time that the Swedes, who slept on board each night, were never able to interact with the Kuna as freely and intimately as they had with the Emberá (1928b, 197–198).

The party stayed at Río Azúcar only a few days, until June third. Though Nordenskiöld bypassed nearby Nargana, where he anticipated his work would be impeded by "pushy, self-important blacks" (1928b, 214), he was eager to press on, and in particular to meet Nele Wardada, or Nele Kantule, of Ustupu. In addition to Nele's prominence as leader of the rebel Kuna, he was also the best-known *nele*, or seer, in San Blas and a leading teacher of almost every branch of ritual, and Nelson had urged Nordenskiöld to seek him out.

CONVERGING ETHNOGRAPHIES

The party made brief and not very satisfactory stops at Tupile and Kainora[12] and then reached Ustupu on June 8, where a great many men and boys came aboard the *Olga* as soon as it was anchored. When the party went ashore, Nordenskiöld wrote, they were nervous about entering the village only two years after the rebellion. Several gifts to the chief, however, including whiskey and an alarm clock, followed by a speech in which Nordenskiöld praised Nele and explained their purposes there, yielded an appointment to begin collaboration next morning (1928b, 226).

Nordenskiöld, as he soon discovered, had hit the ethnographic jackpot, because the Kuna were as ready to impart information about themselves as he was to gather it.[13]

> Nele is very concerned that I accept the idea that the Cunas are a civilized people with an old culture. He hopes that I, someone he

FIGURE 6.1   Erland Nordenskiöld on board the *Olga* at Ustupu, 1927

thinks is an important person, will be a favorable witness for the
Cunas when I return to my own country. (1928b, 242)

The free Cunas are now trying by every means possible to reinforce
their position. They are very eager to be regarded as civilized,
and they are very interested in other countries. That we . . . were
so very well treated by them, and that they even assisted us in our
work in every way, was in part probably because they wanted us to
spread propaganda for their cause. (1928b, 197)

Nordenskiöld encountered the Kuna at an important transitional moment. Colman and Nele's group had won their brief rebellion, and though local Panamanian administrators and policemen were sometimes vindictive and punitive, higher functionaries, recognizing the error of their previous impatience, embarked on a much more gradual campaign to win over and assimilate the Indians. Though Nele and his principal followers were devising strategies to preserve and strengthen Kuna autonomy, they also recognized the impossibility of maintaining complete independence and thus the need to come to terms with Panama, in no small part through a public relations campaign.

Not only had the six years of ethnocidal attacks from 1919 to 1925 reinforced Kuna self-consciousness and protectiveness toward their way of life, but the attentions of visitors such as William Markham and Lady Richmond Brown (the latter an English visitor to the coast who in 1922 had bought hundreds of molas and other artifacts) showed the Kuna that many foreigners found their culture fascinating. This lesson was strongly reinforced by Richard Marsh's expeditions in 1924 and 1925 and the studies carried out in Washington of Kuna language, music, and technology. By 1927 the Kuna were ready to talk about their culture and even to enter into the job first initiated by Cimral Colman in 1913 of recording it themselves. They had in effect become their own ethnographers.

Nordenskiöld's interest in ritual and belief does not seem to have surprised or fazed the Kuna. As Colman's letter from 1913 had shown, they found it natural that outsiders should be concerned, either negatively or positively, with what they themselves considered the most prestigious and important part of their own culture. It is still striking, however, that they entrusted Nordenskiöld with the sort of esoteric knowledge denied him by his Emberá consultant Selimo. The Kuna did not take such arcana lightly. Contact with the invisible world is *islikwagwa*—dangerous, taboo, unpredictable. Young men were supposed to begin their apprenticeships with lesser chants and safer medicines, saving the great cures and their inner secrets for later. Overly ambitious or undisciplined practitioners were likely to damage their souls or even to die early. That Nele and his followers would let the Swedes copy picture-writing and immerse themselves in cosmological questions is a measure of their commitment to the rapidly developing alliance and to ethnography as an adaptive strategy.

Undoubtedly much of the impetus for the project, which had begun before the Swedes appeared, came from Nele himself, but it was his secretaries, Rubén Pérez Kantule and Guillermo Haya, or Hayans,[14] who carried out the work and kept the project going. Both young men were natives of Nargana/Corazón; both had gained their primary education at home, first with Protestant missionaries and then in local government schools; and both had moved on in the early 1920s to urban secondary schools, Hayans to the Escuela de Artes y Oficios, Pérez Kantule to the Instituto Nacional. While in the city, Pérez was by his own account strongly influenced by a Canal Zone employee named Robert Hall whom he met in 1922. Hall took the young man under his wing, improving his English, encouraging him to learn typewriting, talking about Indian reservations in the United States and possible reserves for the Kuna, and generally exhorting Pérez to take an activist role in defense of his people. Pérez's consciousness was raised further on his return to Nargana in 1924 by a shocking encounter in which he met a strange woman with Panamanian clothes and long Western-style hair who turned out to be his own mother.[15]

After the 1925 rebellion, Pérez and Hayans found themselves out of sympathy with the police and modernists, who regained control of Nargana and Corazón within a few months. Along with several other young men, they moved east to Ailigandi, seat of Chief Cimral Colman, where Pérez and Hayans began to study Kuna traditional knowledge. Since Colman's health was rapidly declining, both soon transferred to Ustupu, where they became first and second secretaries to Nele and taught in the village-controlled school.

As best one can tell many years later, the goals of the ethnographic project were both internal and external: Nele and his secretaries set out to record Kuna tradition to preserve it for themselves as well as to make it available to sympathetic outsiders. In both respects, the work was informed and motivated by the prestige accorded literacy in national society and the use of writing and schooling to mark the boundary between civilization and barbarism: Nele and his secretaries, much like the Latin American scholars who were busy across the continent writing down the customs and expressive culture of their rural countrymen (see Chapter 8), were converting oral tradition into written form that could command respect, as well as protect it against change and decay.

As for the two young secretaries, it is clear that they set out to *acquire* as well as record Kuna lore—in other words, to create for themselves some new, literate version of the prestigious role of "knower of things" *(immar wisid)*, thus mediating or bridging the gap between traditional and modern forms of wisdom. By his own account, Pérez Kantule defined his goal as learning "all the knowledge that the old men possessed about our cuna race."[16] On Ailigandi, he studied curing with local ritualists and Father's Way with Cimral Colman, who, though palsied and confined to his hammock, continued to teach until close to death. On Ustupu, Pérez Kantule worked with Nele, and by his own account, he wrote down what the two chiefs taught others, as well as what they dictated directly to him.

In his work with Nordenskiöld, however, Rubén often found himself in the secondary role of intermediary or guide, helping the anthropologist to work through texts credited to Nele and others. Nordenskiöld was grateful

FIGURE 6.2 Erland Nordenskiöld and Nele Kantule, Ustupu, 1927

to Pérez Kantule and interested in him, especially as an ardent Kuna nativist despite his schooling. He never obscured or minimized Rubén's role in the research. But it was Nele, not Pérez, who epitomized for him the intellectual richness of Kuna culture (1928b, 224; Estrella 8/07/27). Surprisingly, despite the chief's barrel chest and imposing manner, Nordenskiöld found him physically unprepossessing (1928b, 225), and he was bemused to encounter the great man sitting alone one day outside his house making a shirt on a sewing machine (1928b, 230). In intellectual terms, however, Nele fascinated Nordenskiöld, as preeminent teacher, repository of lore, superior individual—and implicitly, as the Baron's own native alter ego. The obvious strength of indigenous thought in Nele and others helped Nordenskiöld reconcile his conflicted feelings about Kuna use of Western dress and technology by underlining the distinction between the tainted material realm and the still-vibrant mental world of the Indians.[17]

USTUPU AND BEYOND

The work was as much textual as ethnographic, since Nordenskiöld spent the time not taken up with acquiring material objects in copying and going over the documents that Pérez and Hayans had already created, both in pictographs and Western writing. One of his greatest finds was a long text dictated by Nele tracing Kuna history from the time of legendary culture heroes (1928b, 232, 248–249; 1929, 147). He was most excited about acquiring picture-writing,[18] which gave him something concrete and substantial to study. His notebooks indicate that by going over pictures, first with Charlie Nelson and later with Rubén, he was able to elicit a great deal of information about, for instance, the ship on which the sun circles the heavens and its demon passengers.[19]

Even more importantly, picture-writing, through its associations with hieroglyphics and high civilizations, confirmed the worthiness of Kuna culture as an object of study. Nordenskiöld, it must be noted, had never shown himself an ethnographic snob. In his previous fieldwork he had dealt with humble and often truly downtrodden Indians in the Andes and Gran Chaco in a direct and unassuming way, and his popular books and articles were meant to convince his readers of the worthiness of aboriginal lives. Nonetheless, his pleasure was obvious at having found a culture as elevated as that of the Kuna, one intellectually complex and apparently linked to high civilizations.[20] After all these years, he had found his true subjects.

In the travelogue he published a year after his return, Nordenskiöld, like Gilbert, Marsh, Markham, and others, focused on questions of sexuality and restraint. He insisted repeatedly on the chaste habits of the Emberá, despite obvious contradictory evidence from the behavior of his Indian companions (1928b, 43–44, 75; Lindberg 1996, 452–453), and his lengthy, almost obsessive, remarks on Kuna sexual morality hit the same note, harping on their supposed puritanism and "racial hygiene," just as numerous North American writers had before him (1928b, 233–238). Factually correct on the question of sexual relations with non-Indians, which both Kuna and Emberá strongly discouraged, he erred seriously concerning their private lives, which are far from staid. Like Marsh, he let his own observations be overridden by racist ideology, which identified Africans with libidinous urges and sexual aggression and the better sort of Indians and whites with self-control and racial exclusion.[21]

The party spent only a couple of days on Ustupu.[22] Having found the ethnographic mother lode, Nordenskiöld might have been expected to settle in and dig out as much as possible, but he could not break the pattern set on his previous expeditions, in which he had moved frequently from one place to the next. In this instance, he was eager enough to continue the work begun on Ustupu to bring Pérez with him on the *Olga* as far as Tuppak, or Isla Pino, a few miles to the east, and while Linné and others went ashore, Nordenskiöld (who was also dealing with a seriously infected cut on his leg) spent his time on board copying Nele's historical document (1928b, 248–249).

After Isla Pino, the boat continued on to the border post of Puerto Obaldía. There the travelers were confronted by antagonistic police agents, who refused them permission to continue on until a ruling arrived from superiors in the city. Police suspicions, already aroused by Nordenskiöld's visit with the rebel Kuna on Ustupu, were exaggerated by negative reports on the expedition from followers of Nele's rival Inabaginya, in which Nordenskiöld's gift of an alarm clock turned into a gold watch.[23] Fortunately for the Swedes, Puerto Obaldía was the site of a U.S. military radio station, and after a day and a half, government orders came freeing the party, so they were able to cross the border into Colombia. There, in addition to looking up a Carmelite priest, Padre Severino de Santa Teresa, author in later years of notable ethnographic and ethnohistorical works, they briefly visited the Kuna of Río Caimán Nuevo and investigated the site of the first mainland colony in the New World, Sta. Maria la Antigua del Darién (1928b, 249–263).

On their return to Ustupu, where their police troubles gained them sympathy and solidarity, the Swedes were encouraged to stay on and given letters of introduction to other islands. The condition of Nordenskiöld's leg had worsened, however, forcing him to return immediately to Colón for treatment. Even in his hospital bed he continued working on texts, now with another scribe, Samuel Morris, a young man who had been one of the first teachers on Ustupu.

As soon as he was able, Nordenskiöld sold the *Olga* and returned to Sweden, scrapping plans for further travels in Colombia and Venezuela. Before leaving, he made an extended statement to *La Estrella de Panamá* (8/07/27). Concerning the Kuna, whom he tactlessly introduced as "the famous Republic of Tule," he praised their elevated culture and morality. "In order not to offend Panamanians I will say to you that [they are] more moral than Swedes or other Europeans." While commending the government for dealing gingerly with the Kuna in recent years, he offered advice on how to improve relations. On "the delicate question" of literate youth, he doubted whether any of them other than Nele's secretaries found much outlet for their talents. Overall, Nordenskiöld's impolitic comments and open connection with the rebel Kuna seem to have caused considerable offense (Garay 1930, 16–19).

FIRST RESULTS

Back in Sweden, Nordenskiöld rapidly produced a number of publications, including several popular articles and a book-length narrative of his travels, all written in Swedish (Lindberg 1996, 505–506, 515–516). By the end of the decade he had also brought out a number of scholarly articles and two English-language monographs in the series published by his museum: *Picture-Writings and Other Documents by Néle, Paramount Chief of the Cuna Indians, and Rubén Pérez Kantule, His Secretary* (Nele and Pérez Kantule 1928) and *Picture-Writings and Other Documents by Néle, Charles Slater, Charlie Nelson and Other Cuna Indians* (Nele et al. 1930). These years represented the culmination of Nordenskiöld's career: offered the directorship of the ethnographic museum in Stockholm for which he had previously been passed over, he also received the Frazer Medal, the highest honor in British anthropology, as well as several honorary doctorates and a gold medal for his own work during the commemoration of his father's nineteenth-century explorations (Lindberg 1996, 507–511).

Nordenskiöld nursed the hope of returning to San Blas for further fieldwork, but his teaching and administrative duties kept him close to home. He did correspond with Rubén and Nele and sent copies of his publications, encouraging them to keep up their work and to send criticisms: "[I] will be *extremely interested* to receive anything that you wish to send me concerning your traditions past and present. It is in my opinion of great importance to record all this before it is lost."[24] The criticisms were according to Pérez pretty harsh: "I found many errors in the books, and then

I sent a letter telling him that the books would not serve in any way for the studies of the real Cuna race for the scientists."[25] Nele and Pérez, for their part, asked Nordenskiöld for copies of books and articles cited in his publications, and the latter said he would do the best he could given the volumes' scarcity.

On February ninth of 1931, Rubén asked in one of his letters:

> Look, is it true that you said to Sr. Storm [Carl Ström, the Swedish owner of two restaurants in the Canal Zone] that you wanted me to come to your country? That would be something enormous for us, in that way we could write strictly the traditions of cuna. I am going to study deeply right now; if you say you want me for the journey, with great pleasure I will be at your command.[26]

Two months later in early April, Nordenskiöld communicated a plan by which his friend Ström would make arrangements for the young man to take passage on a Swedish freighter.[27] Rubén received the invitation when he came to town later that month with Nele, who was on his way to make a complaint to the government. Recognizing the opportunity presented by the invitation, Nele hired a seaplane to take them back posthaste to Ustupu. Rubén spent only a few minutes collecting notebooks and personal effects before climbing back aboard the plane for the return flight to the city. On the second of May he embarked in Colón harbor on the *Margaret Johnson,* a cargo vessel also fitted out for passengers that was bound that day for Göteborg.

THE GREAT TRIP

With a strong sense of the historic significance of his voyage, Rubén kept a detailed diary throughout.[28] In a methodical and mostly unemotional fashion, he recorded each day his activities, changes in the weather, and on board ship, its latitude and longitude. Writing things down seems to have come naturally: he even recorded verbatim letters connected with the trip such as Nordenskiöld's invitation, plus several of the letters received from home while in Sweden. Despite the restrained tone of most of the writing, Rubén's pleasure and excitement at seeing the ocean and the *Margaret Johnson*'s ports of call come through clearly, as does his enjoyment of the shipboard dancing and other festivities and the two evenings he went to bed feeling the effects of aquavit.

Nordenskiöld met Pérez Kantule at the dock in Göteborg on May twentieth. The next morning the young traveler was awakened early by the northern sun but returned to sleep when he saw that the streets were still empty. Later that day, when a reporter asked him what he hoped to do in Sweden, "I replied that I came with the object of writing some books about our tribe and to assist Professor Erland Nordenskiöld."

Pérez Kantule spent almost exactly six months in Sweden. Following an initial ten days in the city, he went with Nordenskiöld, his wife Olga, and a young assistant named Henry Wassén to the Baron's summer home in the village of Dalbyö on the Baltic coast southwest of Stockholm. They stayed until the very end of August, then returned to Göteborg, where Pérez Kantule continued until the end of November.

During his half-year in Sweden, Rubén divided his hours of work among several tasks. In Göteborg, especially during his second period in the city, he devoted attention to preparing catalogue cards for the Kuna artifacts collected in 1927, with native names and descriptive and explanatory remarks. Beginning in August, he also worked with a young researcher named Karl-Gustav Izikowitz on Kuna linguistics. Izikowitz was to improve the phonetic transcription of Kuna words and to accumulate material for a grammar; Pérez, to judge by his diary entries, saw their task as primarily lexicographic, and at one time he and Nordenskiöld planned to publish a dictionary (Lindberg 1996, 516–520; Wassén 1938a, xxii–xxiii).

Many hours were devoted to editing texts (Wassén 1938a, xxi), including those collected in 1927 as well as new texts Pérez brought with him, and even a few sent by Guillermo Hayans while his friend was in Sweden. He also dictated a number of tales and histories to Wassén, which were later published (1934, 1937). Rubén's diary suggests that he spent a great deal of time working on his own, especially in Göteborg, while Nordenskiöld attended to teaching and administration. In Dalbyö the two held formal interview sessions, for some of which Henry Wassén acted as secretary, but the diary suggests that many of their talks were more casual, seated at the table after dinner, and in Göteborg, while walking to and from the museum. They also went over Father Gassó's linguistic writings and the ethnographic chapters of his published diary: Nordenskiöld's copy contains critical marginal notes in his hand but Pérez Kantule's words.

In everything he did, Pérez demonstrated discipline, a retentive memory, and a concern for detail and accuracy—qualities as appropriate to scribes as to traditional Kuna "knowers of things." Wassén, who commented several times on the visit over the years, wrote that "the indian Pérez worked

FIGURE 6.3 Rubén Pérez Kantule working at the Ethnographic Museum, Göteborg, 1931

with zeal and determination," and he credited him with a passion for his people's history and a scrupulous insistence on sticking to what he knew. In less kindly fashion, Wassén depicted Rubén as unimaginative, impassive, and incurious: "It was characteristic of Pérez that he never asked about anything."[29] Though Wassén pointed to Rubén's diary as evidence for this supposed indifference, the text in fact displays an avid interest in science, industry, new places, city life, and the families of his Swedish colleagues. Correct to the extent that care and retentiveness outweighed creativity in Rubén's mindset, Wassén's slighting remarks misinterpreted Pérez's reserved nature, his fear of social missteps, and his unwillingness to display ignorance through naïve questions—none of which is surprising in a youth of twenty-four on his own in a foreign land.

The research was broken by numerous outings: to the zoo, botanic gardens, concerts, several museums, an amusement park, and factories; shopping in Göteborg and trips for provisions from Dalbyö; as well as a physics experiment and two excursions to Stockholm (where Rubén found the noise and crowds almost overwhelming); and even to the cemetery to put flowers on the grave of a Nordenskiöld son. The factory visits and science experiments, in particular, seem to have had a didactic tinge, exposing Pérez Kantule to the positive aspects of modern civilization, to which he responded enthusiastically.

Rubén, it was clear, had come to Sweden to absorb such experiences and to acquire knowledge as well as to help produce it. Nordenskiöld's large research library was put at his disposal, and evening hours not devoted to his diary were spent laboriously typewriting copies of works devoted to Panama, the Darién, San Blas, and his own people, including the complete text of Gassó's diaries. He also collected dozens of books to take back with him. Once again, Pérez Kantule was adapting the role of traditional apprentice in ritual and esoteric lore to modern conditions. Like Kuna ritualists who traveled to other coastal villages or over the mountains into the Darién; like Kuna chiefs, such as Colman and Nele, who acquired knowledge of the outside world as well as indigenous tradition (see Howe 1998, 64–70); and like the ancient shaman culture-heroes who had traveled to other realms of the universe, Pérez Kantule was going to come home from far places loaded down with rare knowledge.

Mary Helms, in ethnohistorical and comparative studies inspired in part by Kuna ethnography (1979, 1988), suggests that distant knowledge and foreign goods have been accorded symbolic value and prestige particularly in archaic civilizations—in tribal societies and even more in ranked chiefdoms and early states. This mindset, however, is just as prevalent in the modern world: James Buzard's analysis of the literature of the European Grand Tour (1993) and Harry Liebersohn's account of nineteenth-century aristocratic visits to North America (1998, 64–65, 133–135, 166–167) show travelers in self-conscious pursuit of elevating and individuating experience. In his own European tour, Rubén Pérez had gone farther off the beaten track than any previous Kuna voyager, leaving in his dust the knowers and scribes who had gotten no farther from home than Panama or the United States.

Nordenskiöld paid Rubén in money as well as prestige, the amounts carefully recorded in the latter's diary. He also received gifts and supplies, including a double-barreled shotgun, an axe, a globe, a small microscope, books, and a variety of souvenirs, some of this largesse, it was hoped, to be used in further field studies on his return home. Despite the generosity of the gifts, they underscored the obvious inequality of the relationship: although Pérez Kantule held a great resource—his knowledge of Kuna language and culture—it was only through the Baron's wealth, position, social status, and knowledge of the world that an Indian was able to come to Sweden or to use that knowledge.

More than that, the visits of aboriginals to European capitals as curiosities and objects of study, which had been going on since the fifteenth century, were freighted with colonial relations and attitudes, as was blatantly obvious in a living exhibit of Africans from Senegal located across the way from Nordenskiöld's residence. "From there in the distance they are seen ... dancing, playing drums, and other musical instruments brought from their African land." Although the diarist did not compare himself with the Africans or comment explicitly on their situation, he included four different photographs with X's marking the exhibit's location. Noting the birth of a child to one of the Senegalese women, he also wrote that Swedish children always asked their parents whether the Africans' dark skin was painted on.

Concerning his own situation, there is no doubt that the reporters who several times interviewed him and his hosts treated him as a curiosity (as one headline put it, "The Indian at the museum was a find in himself")[30] and that the Baron allowed selected members of local society and a number of his colleagues from Sweden and elsewhere access to his guest, who was widely known as "Erland's Indian" (Lindberg 1996, 516–518). That being said, however, Nordenskiöld and his colleagues seem to have treated Pérez at all times with respect. Rubén remarked on the pleasure of comparing notes with the missionary-ethnologist Father Guisinde, and on the books and letter with which the Danish anthropologist Kai Birket-Smith followed up on his meeting with Pérez. Living in Nordenskiöld's household and eating with the family, Rubén shared in their activities, such as seining schools of fish on an annual run in early June. On the twenty-second of that month, in the long northern evening, the family played the Swedish equivalents of hide-and-seek and prisoner's base on the lawn in Dalbyö, and on the twenty-third they danced in a circle to celebrate St. John's Day, the midpoint of the short Swedish summer.

Photos show Rubén dressed formally and very well, and when he was

FIGURE 6.4 Magazine cartoon of Rubén Pérez Kantule speaking to reporters, Sweden, 1931

presented to the Baron's friends and colleagues, he was able to converse with them in English. His cool poise and sense of his own dignity undoubtedly served him well. To judge by remarks made by Wassén and others, and by my own brief encounter with Rubén a half-century later in the Nargana library, he had a reserved manner, though not so much as to prevent him from establishing strong ties with his hosts. By the middle of his two months in the countryside he was referring to Nordenskiöld in his diary as Erland, and he recorded a conversation that occurred as they left Dalbyö in which he expressed how much the time there had meant to him. Closer to the end of his stay, on the tenth of November, he wrote with emotion that the Baroness told him that her husband talked about him constantly to his friends, which, she said, gave her great pleasure. "I said to the *señora* that I have much *kurguin* [*gurgin,* or aptitude] that the Great God gave me at birth and therefore I have an extraordinary memory to recall the knowledge acquired during my studies. I have never [previously] spoken of my person, but she got me to say the truth, and I believe that she will remember this until her death."

The sometimes leisurely quality of the work in Dalbyö gave way back in Göteborg to increased pressure to finish the project. Nordenskiöld had concluded that the northern winter would impose a great burden on Rubén, and oral tradition among the latter's descendants suggests he worried about spending time away from events in San Blas and from his base with Nele in Ustupu (Martínez Mauri 2007, 321). It was decided that he would go home at about the same time that Nordenskiöld himself went on tour to present the results of his new research. In particular, he planned to discuss the concepts he saw as crucial to Kuna religion: *gurgin,* "aptitude, destiny," *niga,* "vital force," and *burba (purba),* "soul or spirit."

WRAPPING UP

During their final weeks the anthropologist tried out his ideas on Rubén and pressed him for clarifications and corrections. "We continued with more warmth our conversations concerning the customs of my Cuna race; and more questions difficult to answer rained down, and I continued answering. . . . At times we remained for an hour on the sidewalk of the avenue, talking of our subject, and thus we sometimes arrived very late at the house." During these weeks Rubén also struggled with the impossible task of putting in order all the accumulated texts.

On November 13, the day before Nordenskiöld and his wife were to start his tour, Rubén had serious talks with them at the table. Nordenskiöld expressed an intention to return to San Blas. Pérez Kantule says he told him that the Kuna believed that when two persons had discussed hidden knowledge about the origins of things, one of them always died, and that in their own case they did not know which it would be. The next day, husband and wife departed separately, Nordenskiöld in the morning and Olga in the evening, and Rubén saw each of them off at the train station. In his notes, he referred to "my mamá Olga," and to the profound sadness he felt at their parting.

Pérez Kantule and Nordenskiöld had in effect exchanged symbolic goods. Each had acquired knowledge from the other, and through their work together, each had received confirmation of his own intellectual mastery, reinforcing one man's position in the anthropological world and the other's in indigenous society. A photo of the two in Rubén's diary has the caption: "The Indian Rubén Pérez Kantule with his great teacher, the Swedish sage Professor Erland Nordenskiöld, Director of the Ethnographic Museum of Göteborg." In a similar vein, after intensive conversations on November eleventh, Pérez Kantule noted that the anthropologist could speak confidently on his tour, "since he has much knowledge [based] on my explanations given to him. He was my great teacher and I too was his teacher."

For the rest of his life, Rubén's place, among his own people, as well as in urban Panama and elsewhere, was set by his European trip and his association with foreign savants. Much the same was true for Nordenskiöld. Although, as a museum director and internationally recognized ethnologist, he was greatly senior to Pérez Kantule, to date he was chiefly known outside Sweden for technical distribution studies, serious and weighty but unlikely to set scholarly pulses pounding. With his Kuna investigations, Nordenskiöld was poised to step out, to make his mark in the developing field of modern ethnography, with results that he knew would attract attention. On the European tour on which he embarked as Pérez was getting ready to return home, he delivered a radio talk in Vienna and at least three lectures in Paris. (At one lecture, introductory remarks were offered by the poet and essayist Paul Valery, who concluded that "all primitive life is poetry.") The talks attracted attention from artists and intellectuals as well as academics, all of them as interested in the novel experiment of bringing an Indian to Sweden as they were in Nordenskiöld's findings.[31]

The exchange had its problematic aspects, notably concerning the respective roles of the two men and the question of publication. It was ambiguous whether Pérez Kantule was co-investigator or assistant, a conduit or a source of knowledge in his own right. Concerning the end results of their endeavors, Pérez Kantule alluded in his diary to "our book," as did Nordenskiöld in a letter the following year. But Rubén also mentioned in more than one place his intention to produce a book or books of his own, and he called his word list "my dictionary."

As Chapter 7 will show, when Nordenskiöld's magnum opus finally emerged in 1938, Rubén received considerable credit, though not for the active and creative role he believed he had played. (In the end, neither man determined the final shape of the work.) Both Rubén Pérez and Guillermo Hayans kept writing and studying Kuna custom for years, and Rubén at least received wide recognition, being named as the first and only indig-

FIGURE 6.5 Rubén Pérez Kantule at a meeting of the Panamanian Academy of History (year unknown)

enous member of both the Society of Americanists in Paris and the Panamanian Academy of History. But neither Pérez nor Hayans ever had the resources to publish a book on his own, nor (with one marginal exception) was either one granted the title of author by anyone other than Nordenskiöld himself.

On November twenty-fourth, two days before his departure, Rubén was still struggling to finish the interlinear paraphrases. Later that day his companions at the museum took him for a valedictory dinner. Izikowitz delivered an affectionate farewell speech into which many Kuna words and phrases were inserted, with praise for Rubén's *niga* and *gurgin* and a flattering comparison with the greatest of culture heroes: "You are the new Ibeorgun of the Cuna."[32] Pérez, who replied at length, was deeply touched.

The diary conscientiously records the four boxes and the iron trunk taken aboard ship, the titles of all seventy-two books and pamphlets accumulated, and the eighteen sections of document copies made in

Nordenskiöld's library. Rubén noted that it was precisely at 6:15 on the evening of the twenty-sixth that he went aboard the *Axel Johnson,* and that he was so overcome that he could only make his farewells through his handkerchief.

AFTERMATH

In the following months, Nordenskiöld pushed ahead with publication plans. He also expressed a desire to return to San Blas and to visit the sacred mountain Dagargunyala. Not long after Pérez's departure, however, the dire prediction about the results of studying secrets came true. Nordenskiöld was hospitalized for an operation in March of 1932. Suffering from multiple conditions, including a return of malaria, he succumbed on July fifth, just short of his fifty-fifth birthday.

Pérez Kantule, though he outlived Nordenskiöld by many years, was besieged by troubles on his return to Panama. He lost a dispute with Nele and Ustupu concerning possession of the books and copies he had brought back from Europe. He also lost a child to illness, and his marriage on Ustupu, already strained, soon ended, sending him back to Nargana. Worst of all, in 1933, a scandal erupted concerning five thousand dollars missing from tribal funds.

The problem arose from political and economic reforms promoted by Nele in the post-rebellion years. One measure, first adopted by Colman, was an alliance war chest, to be used for major expenses such as lobbying the government, engaging lawyers, and hiring launches and seaplanes. In 1930, the year before the Swedish trip, a delegation had opened a savings account in the amount of ten thousand dollars. In 1933 five thousand dollars was noted as missing, withdrawn, according to the bank, by Pérez Kantule, who for his part claimed he was being framed to cover up embezzlement. Nele and other Kuna rallied to his cause, and a prominent lawyer and a pro-Indian newspaper, the *Panamá América,* undertook Rubén's defense, but he was convicted and served a year in prison.[33] The evidence, as discussed in contemporary newspaper accounts, seems contradictory and confused. Nothing suggests Rubén ever enjoyed extra funds—a few years later a columnist found him sweeping the floor in a Panama bar—and skepticism increased when a bank manager disappeared, leaving twenty-seven thousand dollars in debts. On Pérez's release he was taken back into the fold and the matter laid to rest, though it was never entirely forgotten (see also Martínez Mauri 2007, 321–322; Wassén 1987–1988, 41–42).

Collaborative Ethnography

SEVEN

A NOTABLE PARTNERSHIP

The alliance between the Swedes and the Kuna produced, in the words of Alfred Metraux (in Nordenskiöld 1932, 460), "material of a prodigious richness." Before his death, Nordenskiöld published a travel narrative (1928b), two short monographs (Nele and Pérez Kantule 1928; Nele et al. 1930), several scholarly articles (1928a, 1929, 1932a, 1932b), and a number of popular sketches and articles. His successor, S. Henry Wassén, published two Kuna monographs (1938b, 1949) and a series of articles (1934, 1937, 1952). The linguistic material collected by Izikowitz and others was eventually turned over to a linguist, Nils Holmer, who published two grammars and a dictionary of Kuna (1947, 1951, 1952a). Between the late 1940s and the early 1960s, Holmer and Wassén published a number of long chants with Spanish and English translations (1947, 1953, 1958, 1963; Holmer 1952b). Among all the publications, by far the weightiest was a massive compendium of texts and essays totaling more than seven hundred pages (Nordenskiöld et al. 1938), which was compiled and edited by Karl-Gustav Izikowitz and Henry Wassén in the years following Nordenskiöld's death.[1] Within the space of a few decades, the collaborators published a small scholarly library, making the Kuna one of the most thoroughly studied peoples of Latin America.

With a few exceptions, moreover, the results were much more reliable and credible than many previous ethnographies, thanks in large part to

Pérez Kantule's disciplined insistence on getting things right and his refusal to go beyond what he knew. Naturally, the heavy dependence on a single informant led to some idiosyncratic or aberrant results—a confused drawing by Pérez of the Kuna cosmos (Nordenskiöld et al. 1938, 357), for instance, has misled later scholars (Helms 1979, 118; Taussig 1993, 117)—but overall readers could count on what they read.

The Swedes also distinguished themselves by their readiness to acknowledge their indigenous partners, as a matter of principle as well as a guarantee of authenticity. The two monographs published by Nordenskiöld mentioned every native author and collaborator prominently, not only at the head of each text but even in the volume titles (Nele and Pérez Kantule 1928; Nele et al. 1930). For both volumes, Nordenskiöld's name appeared on the title page only as publisher, and the second of the two was dedicated to Nele and Rubén.

Henry Wassén was less generous. His first two Kuna articles, collections of narratives dictated by Pérez Kantule (1934, 1937), acknowledged the latter as source but not as author. The title page for the magnum opus of 1938 listed Wassén as editor and Nordenskiöld as author, with the words "in collaboration with the Cuna Indian, Rubén Pérez Kantule" in minuscule type. Wassén's remarks on Rubén and his role in the project, moreover, were condescending, even a touch dismissive (1938, xiii–xviii, xx–xxii). In the chant texts published from the 1940s through the 1960s, the collector—who in every case was Guillermo Hayans—and the chanter from whom he gathered the text were on some title pages acknowledged handsomely (Holmer and Wassén 1958) and on others less so (e.g., Holmer and Wassén 1953). Despite his lapses, however, even Wassén gave more credit than have most anthropologists, then or now.

In this chapter I look critically at this ethnographic corpus, attempting to show how the directions taken and the conclusions reached were guided by indigenous text production, by Swedish research methods, and above all by the agendas and outlooks the two sides brought to their partnership. I leave the task of placing Nordenskiöld's work definitively within his intellectual milieu and changing anthropological theory to the anthropologist and historian Bo Ernstson's ongoing investigations. What I try to do is account for the shape and direction of a research project, to understand how certain conclusions were reached and how one portrait of a culture among many possible came to seem inevitable.

TEXT-BASED ETHNOGRAPHY

The 1938 compendium (which Nordenskiöld seems to have intended publishing as two or three separate monographs) is a miscellaneous and sometimes overwhelming collection of disparate elements. Wassén and Izikowitz struggled to work it into some kind of order, though with mixed success. Roughly one-quarter of the total consists of ethnographic essays and essay fragments written by Nordenskiöld, with a few later additions and changes.[2] At the very end of the volume are fifteen color plates of picture-writing.[3] The rest consists almost entirely of texts produced by the Kuna and edited by the Swedes.

The texts are a mixed bag. One set consists of three kinds of spoken or sung esoterica—chants, short incantations by which the soul of medicines is "admonished" and brought to life, and the inner secrets, or *burba (purba)*, of chant cures—all of which were dictated by ritualists and taken down in Kuna using Spanish orthography by Pérez Kantule.[4] Another set (1938, 510–544) consists of medicinal recipes, some with associated admonishments. For all these texts, the researchers worked hard to clarify and standardize transcriptions, and Pérez Kantule produced interlinear glosses for Kuna words. Only a few, however, have even the sketchiest of translations, which severely limits their usefulness.[5] (The texts published through the 1940s and 1950s almost invariably include translations, though of mixed quality.)

A third class encompasses didactic texts on biographical, ethnographic, geographic, and historic subjects dictated in Kuna and taken down in Spanish and English, ranging from a fragmentary two-page biography of Nele (pp. 89–91) to very long mytho-historical narratives.[6] A final miscellaneous class consists of Spanish versions of speeches by Chief Cimral Colman (pp. 91–104).

It would be unfair to apply to the compendium the methodological standards of the late twentieth century, especially those that can only be met by heavy use of tape and video recorders, and allowance must be made for the repercussions of Nordenskiöld's death before completion of the project. Nonetheless, the Swedes would have done well to have published fewer texts and edited them further, and in particular they could have done more to make the key texts accessible to their readers. There was no way that Nele and Pérez could be expected to appreciate just what was needed to reach a foreign audience, and it was up to the Swedes to bridge that gap and not to assume that the texts would speak for themselves. One might also expect them to have been less complacent about the complex, problematic nature of written documents derived from a predominantly oral culture. Nordenskiöld was so pleased, perhaps even relieved, to have the texts that he never seriously questioned them, never scrutinized their special nature as hybrid forms produced in an intersocietal context. Rather, he took them as natural and unproblematic, which did both the Kuna and his readers a disservice.

NATIVE HISTORIOGRAPHY

From his first day on Ustupu in 1927, Nordenskiöld took great satisfaction from the opportunity to copy a long historical document dictated by Nele (Nordenskiöld 1928b, 232, 248–249; 1932a, 6). An article from the following year (1929, 147) calls the text "this precious document," and a brief communication entitled "Panama Chief Writes History" (Anonymous 1927) characterizes it as "one of the rare trophies" of the expedition. Published in 1928 (Nele and Pérez Kantule 1928, 5, 79–93), the text was supplemented by several more histories that Pérez Kantule brought to Sweden in 1931.

Nordenskiöld thought that Nele's chronicles showed an unusual degree of historical consciousness, qualifying the chief as "an historian of a sort" (1929, 149; Estrella 8/07/27). The new texts, even longer and more intriguing than the first one, included events from previous centuries that had apparently been preserved in native oral tradition, and they spanned the whole of Kuna history, from the creation to the present. According to Wassén, Nordenskiöld planned a monograph entitled "The History of an Indian Tribe over a Period of 400 Years," in which he would match up Nele's oral account with written sources.

> His intention was, as he pointed out in several lectures . . . to follow the Cunas' history from their discovery to our own time and to place the facts brought out in relation to the Cunas' own traditions, this to be done through studies of actual sources. This historical section was, however, never written. (Wassén 1938a, xxiii)

Despite Nordenskiöld's untimely death, Nele's chronicles received pride of place in the great compendium. The entry entitled "History of the Cuna Indians from the Great Flood up to our Time" takes up one hundred pages (1938, 125–224), more than was allocated to anything else in the book.

Although Wassén as editor wrote of a single text, the original of which consisted of twenty-one pages of typescript, the entry in fact encompasses two separate texts with overlapping content, both taken down from dictation in Kuna by Nele, one in Spanish, the other in English. A third long narrative, also written in Spanish from Nele's dictation (1938, 228–267), covers some of the same events and characters.[7] Taken together, the texts constitute a remarkable project in native historiography.

Unfortunately, much of their potential was vitiated for non-Kuna readers. Despite being typed out, which would suggest that they were first taken down by hand and then copied on the typewriter, the texts display the same grammatical and stylistic defects as early secretaries' letters, with run-on sentences, minimal punctuation, and cryptic or garbled phrasing. Pérez Kantule and Hayans showed elsewhere that they were capable of writing much more lucid historical texts, but they had not apparently developed a method for processing dictation, especially not at this great length, and Nele had not worked out how to communicate complicated information to a nonindigenous audience.

Nordenskiöld was certainly aware of the problems. He went over a great many confusing passages with Rubén, incorporating clarifications within brackets. He also wrote a corrected version of the primary texts, and he or his editors hit on the solution of matching up the original and corrected texts on facing pages. The arrangement is hard to follow, however, especially when the pages get out of synch, and the "improved" version does not invariably interpret the intent of the original correctly.

The texts are further complicated by long ethnographic digressions, especially concerning the teachings of the great founding culture hero, Ibeorgun. Here Nele was clearly building on a traditional model, in that a chief chanting about Ibeorgun or another hero will typically mention what he or she taught the ancestors of the Kuna or the vices the hero corrected. But Nele carried things to an extreme, embedding exhaustively detailed descriptions of ceremonies within his historical narrative (1938, 132–137, 238–256) and listing and glossing almost every kin term, current and archaic (1938, 128–129, 236–237).[8] A similar problem arises from the great profusion of long Kuna names for historical figures, a difficulty alleviated only in part by a helpful glossary (1938, 323–332).

Most of all, the narrative itself is convoluted and bewildering. Each of the three texts begins abruptly, without introduction or lead-in, and each starts, not at the opening of Kuna history, but somewhere in the middle. The second text, the one taken down in English (1938, 172–224), begins with the struggles of the great solar hero called Dad Ibe, or Machi Olowaibipiler, and then continues in a linear progression up to the present. The other two texts begin in a relatively straightforward way (pp. 126, 228), but at a certain point in the narrative they abruptly jump backwards in time (pp. 148, 256), after which they again move forward to the end of the narrative.

The flashbacks make no sense unless one knows that one of the most common rhetorical devices in Kuna public speech is the embedding or nesting of one quote within another: a speaker will quote another speaker, who will quote another, who will quote another, and so forth (Sherzer 1983, 201–207; 1990, 30, 76, 124–126; see also Chapter 2). Chiefs chanting to their followers in the gathering house will sometimes use the same stylistic flourish by singing about one historical figure, such as Ibeorgun, who will be described singing in turn about one of *his* predecessors, in effect nesting one narrative and one chant within another (Howe 1980, 22). In the first historical text published by Nordenskiöld et al., the flashback (p. 148) is not signaled at all, but in the third text there is an ambiguous hint in one sentence (p. 256): "*Ibeorgun* preached once again for the people about what [had] happened [to] *Dad* [i.e., Grandfather] *Carban, Calib,* and *Acban*" (leaders of a previous era). Although Wassén would continue publishing Kuna narratives of various sorts (1934, 1937, 1938b, 1949, 1952), it would be more than thirty years before the mysteries of their sacred history, both its component narratives and its complete span, were clarified in a booklet authored by a Peace Corps volunteer, Mac Chapin (1970) (see Chapter 9).[9]

GRANDFATHER FRANSOA AND HISTORICAL TRUTH

It mattered a good deal to Nordenskiöld not only that Kuna history formed an unbroken temporal chain but also that it included accounts of past events known from written sources to be true. Nele's texts mentioned leaders and actions from the nineteenth century, but only one identifiable episode from the colonial period, the sojourn of French pirates with the Kuna, which lasted from the late seventeenth to the mid-eighteenth century (Nordenskiöld et al. 1938, 193–201). The French narrative thus provided Nordenskiöld's most important evidence for the historicity of Kuna oral tradition.

> We know, among other things, what the Cuna still know of the Spanish conquest of their land, and of the French colonization of

their territory at the beginning of the eighteenth century. The comparison of these oral traditions with what we read in the chronicle made in the same epoch by some Europeans is of great interest. We have thus an *apercu* on the value of oral tradition as an historic document. (1932a, 6; see also Nordenskiöld et al. 1938, xiv)[10]

Among other things, the question mattered because such historical consciousness confirmed for Nordenskiöld the uniqueness and superiority of the Kuna as a subject of investigation. Tribal peoples were thought to have myth instead of history, and indeed an awareness of the "real" past, which the Kuna seemed to possess in some measure, was taken as a diagnostic sign of literate civilization. If the Kuna were now a tribal people, their complex culture showed that "we can consider these Indians as constituting the relic of one of the great civilizations of Central America" (Nordenskiöld 1932a, 29). In some way the Kuna seemed to bridge the great divide between oral and literate culture.

It was not that Nordenskiöld insisted on the literal reality of all Kuna beliefs. Like many anthropologists since his time, he was ready to embrace notions he was far from believing himself, such as evil spirits who caused illness by kidnapping souls—ready, that is, to take them as fascinating and praiseworthy examples of human creativity. So long as the Kuna worldview was complex and absorbing, he did not demand that it be literally true.[11] Nonetheless, the seeming facticity of Nele's history was for Nordenskiöld a point of great interest and significance.

As early as his 1927 field trip, Nordenskiöld was preoccupied with the French pirates and colonists, whom he believed to be Huguenots, in large part because he saw them as the most likely source of Kuna moralism and of other aspects of their religion that reminded him of Christianity.[12] The Calvinism of the French colonists turns out to be an illusion, however: documentary material published in the 1950s by Severino de Santa Teresa (whom Nordenskiöld met in the field in 1927) shows that many or most of the Frenchmen were Catholics or quite willing to become Catholics (1956, 197–310). Whatever the religious persuasion of these French settlers, one may doubt whether a hard-bitten set of ex-pirates scattered along the Caribbean shore would have put theological concerns first in their relations with the Indians.[13]

Seen from an alternative perspective, what is most striking about Nele's narrative of the French sojourn is how much it reflects conditions in the villages pacified by the police in the early 1920s just a few years before the narrative was collected (Nordenskiöld et al. 1938, 192–201). According to Nele's account, Dada (Grandfather) Fransoa and other complacent Indian leaders accepted French interlopers, who established jails and dance clubs, fathered children on Indian women, and tyrannized Indian men, until a "civil war" erupted and the French and their collaborators were overcome. Despite the scholars who have naïvely accepted this tale as a trustworthy account of eighteenth-century events, it is much more plausible that the interest in the French question shown by Nordenskiöld in his days on Ustupu in 1927 prompted Nele to create a narrative combining material from the Swede's questions on the subject with recent oppression by the Panamanian police. Such a narrative would, moreover, have fit with a key assumption of chiefly tradition, namely, that people today often carry or revive the spirit, or soul *(burba,* or *purba),* of past eras. The same readiness to work popular Latin American history and figures such as Christopher Columbus and Bartolomé de Las Casas into Kuna accounts has also turned up in more recent ethnography (Sherzer 1994; S. Herrera n.d. [2003]).

It should also be noted that although the Kuna sometimes tie their historical narratives together into a single sequence as Nele did, the parts are not commensurate. The greatest number of narratives, and the ones that are regularly performed in the gathering house, resemble European ideas of myth, in that they depict early historical eras in which spirits, animals, and humans interacted, and in which the foundations of society and the natural world were established. At the near end of the sequence, the Kuna preserve vivid memories of mundane events and actors from the last few generations (today with special emphasis on the 1925 rebellion). The middle period covering events from roughly 1500 to 1800 or 1900 is underpopulated and hazy. Father's Way describes in a very general manner the coming of the Spaniards and their oppression of the Indians, but it has nothing to say about Scots colonists, Dominican or Jesuit missions, English buccaneers, or (except in Nele's text, which has since been forgotten) French pirates.[14]

Nele's grand narrative was, in effect, a stretch, an effort to reach back, extending the limits and filling in the blank spaces of oral history. Among all the many facts and ideas about the wider world that Nele avidly collected throughout his adult life (Howe 1998, 64–70), no one knows precisely what it was that inspired his chronicle, possibly a model of history brought back from school by Pérez or Hayans or the example of one of the books collected for the Ustupu library. His creative historiographic effort was, in any case, more noteworthy and, I would insist, much more deserving of admiration than mere historical retentiveness or recall.

TEXT AND CONTEXT: KUNA RELIGION

Text-based ethnography can offer ethnographic richness, depth, and access to indigenous ideas, but it also sets traps for the unwary. The key documents in the 1938 magnum opus, the long histories dictated by Nele, appeared on the page *only* in contact languages, either English or Spanish, while other texts taken down in Kuna were translated in the most sketchy fashion or not at all. Equally important, the texts by themselves, absent contextual information from other sources, could say little about their articulation with performance, practice, and daily life. In the case of the Swedes, this neglect of context was taken to an extreme, limiting and distorting understanding even of the texts themselves. During the month he spent in San Blas and Urabá, Nordenskiöld devoted only a few days to research on Kwebdi and Ustupu, much of it with his nose in school notebooks (Nordenskiöld 1928b).[15] When Henry Wassén made his own field trip in 1935, he allotted only ten days to San Blas, nine of them to working on texts with Pérez Kantule and Hayans in Nargana (Wassén 1938b, 1–10). As frank as Nordenskiöld and Wassén were about the brevity of their fieldwork and their near-exclusive focus on texts, apparently neither one found those limitations worrisome.

Nordenskiöld did supplement the texts with extended interviews during Pérez's stay in Sweden, in which he concentrated on the spirit world, human spiritual capacities, and interaction between the two. The essays based on those interviews (1932a; 1932b; Nordenskiöld et al. 1938, 333–373) have robustly withstood the tests of time and later research, constituting some of the most useful results of the whole collaboration, and indeed one of the most important explorations of indigenous cosmology of the era. Nordenskiöld's remarks on politics, kinship, and social usages (1938, 28–54, 79–80) are quite a bit sketchier, and about the economy the compendium only offers a page and a half of random fragmentary notes (1938, 55–56).

Even for religion—or ideology, as Nordenskiöld called it—inattention to context and practice had negative consequences. Concerning curing, death rites, and puberty ceremonies, Nordenskiöld did give some sense of what people did and what they believed (1928b, 276–282; Nordenskiöld et al. 1938, 56–78, 134–137, 238–256, 445–611). On the other hand, the central religious rite of the Kuna, the *onmaket,* or gathering, seems to have escaped serious attention. A single paragraph (1938, 53) alludes vaguely to meetings, held on "no definite days," in which the first village chief might sing and in which "Nele is apt to narrate stories about the tribe's history and tell legends," though only as diversions from debate and discussion. There is not a hint that all chiefs sang, that they performed the histories recorded by Nele's secretaries, that speakers interpreted the chants as moral lessons, and that frequent meetings drew the community together as a congregation (Sherzer 1983; Howe 1986). It was as if someone tried to describe Protestant Christianity in terms of Bible stories without noting their use in religious services—or for that matter, without wondering where people disappeared to on Sunday morning and the function of those white buildings with steeples scattered around town.

It is puzzling how Nordenskiöld could have slighted the sacred gathering, given that Gassó, whose diary he read and used, fulminated obsessively against what the priest dubbed "the house of errors" and the rites carried out within it.[16] Some of the reasons for the neglect may have been practical. Pérez and Hayans (both of whom came from the only community that had abandoned gatherings) were undoubtedly guided by their own biases, and even more by Nordenskiöld's professed interests. Gatherings, unlike curing and puberty ceremonies, have little associated paraphernalia to catch the ethnographer's eye, and though Nordenskiöld did not directly observe rituals of any sort, he did view Charlie Nelson's pharmacopoeia and the remains of recent puberty ceremonies (1928b, 215–221; Nordenskiöld et al. 1938, 68).

The more important causes for the neglect were probably personal (Nordenskiöld's atheism) and intellectual. If Nordenskiöld had been reading Émile Durkheim, he would have been thinking about religion in terms of sentiments, rites, and social solidarity. Instead, he was concerned with the workings of the supposedly primitive mind, following writers like Father Schmidt and Lucien Lévy-Bruhl, to whom he dedicated his essay on Kuna conceptions of the soul (1932b). However, Nordenskiöld's attention, in contrast with Lévy-Bruhl's, was most attracted by minds that were singular rather than collective, and at the time of his death, he was sketching out an essay on the cultural importance of individuals.[17] By the individual, Nordenskiöld particularly had in mind superior people like Nele and himself. Guided by his personal identification with the great chief, and by his conception of them both as scholars, he treated religious knowledge as the possession of a skeptical elite:

> When we study the Cuna Indians' concepts we must distinguish between the great mass of beliefs and what the Great Seer Nele

and the thinking people believe. . . . [Concerning arcanae about the creation of the world:] here we have wisdom which is concealed from most of the Indians, wisdom which is only possessed by the few. . . . I have only wished to point out the difference between the ideas of those initiated in religious wisdom and the ideas of the great masses, between those who think and those who simply do what everyone else does. (Nordenskiöld et al. 1938, xviii–xx, 81; Nordenskiöld 1932a, 11, 22)[18]

This interpretation, which located knowledge in the minds of superior men rather than in collective representations or institutions, harmonized with a self-image that competitive Kuna ritualists often articulate, but it blinded Nordenskiöld to another, more inclusive native theory of knowledge characteristic of the gathering house, which treats history and cosmology as a shared patrimony and the basis for *collective* action.

The distorting effects of a largely text-based approach extended even to the names and attributes of the deities, who are always spoken of, both in daily life and in the gathering house, as Great Mother (Nan Dummad) and Great Father (Bab Dummad), or simply as Mother (Nana) and Father (Baba). Nordenskiöld, however, relied almost exclusively on curing chants in which God was called Diolele (Nordenskiöld 1928b, 221; Nele and Pérez Kantule 1928, 8; Nele et al. 1930, 8), and he and his successors Nils Holmer (1953) and Henry Wassén (1989/90, 20) jumped through linguistic hoops to analyze and etymologize that name,[19] despite recognition elsewhere in the compendium (Nordenskiöld et al. 1938, 378–379) that the vocabulary of the curing chants consists in large part of *substitutions* or *alternatives* for everyday names and words.[20] It was as if a theologian inferred from gospel fragments that there was a Christian deity or hero alluded to as "The Son of Man" without realizing that his name was Jesus.

Because the Kuna do not as individuals call on God to cure illness, Nordenskiöld jumped to the conclusion that Father keeps little contact with humanity except in punishing individual misdeeds after death (1938, 432–433). Here again, he might have paid more heed to Gassó, who took offense at the Kuna tendency to attribute recent events to Father's intervention, and who despite his missionary prejudices recognized the communal nature of his native opponents' religion.[21] Nordenskiöld should also have noted the many punishments of humanity described in his own texts, which might have suggested, correctly, that he was dealing with a moralistic and millenarian creed (see Howe 1974; Moeller 1997). And if he had stayed ashore during his visit to Ustupu for even an evening or two, he would have heard Nele and other chiefs chant to their assembled followers, reminding them of God's goodness to his chosen people, and of his anger if they neglected the gathering house.

As a pair, Father and Mother are very much like Kuna parents—Father is more powerful, Mother more beloved—and they work together in partnership. Nordenskiöld felt confident, however, that he could separate aboriginal aspects of Father's role (i.e., world-creation) from those acquired from Christianity (morality) (Nordenskiöld et al. 1938, 432–444), no doubt following theorists like Tylor, who saw morality as a late arrival in religious evolution (Tylor 1958 [1871], 445–447).[22] In a further imposition of antiquated anthropological theory, Nordenskiöld wrote that the whole notion of a male deity had in post-Columbian times been grafted onto a cosmos previously credited to an "original mother" (Nordenskiöld et al. 1938, 439)—an argument elaborated in later years by Henry Wassén (1959, 1989/90). Like Father Gassó when he corrected Kuna grammar based on his experience of other languages, Wassén and Nordenskiöld filled in the gaps in their local knowledge with material from elsewhere, and like Gassó, they were sure they knew better than the people whose beliefs they were studying.

TEXT AND CONTEXT: MUU IGAR

One of the greatest successes of the Swedish-Kuna collaboration, certainly the greatest after the 1938 magnum opus, was the series of long chant texts, most of them used in curing, painstakingly transcribed and translated by Guillermo Hayans and sent to Sweden, where a number of them were edited and published by Holmer and Wassén (1947, 1953, 1958, 1963; Holmer 1952b). The greatest prize was Muu-Igala, or Muu igar, "Grandmother's Way," a chant used to intervene in cases of difficult childbirth, which Nordenskiöld had longed to acquire (Nordenskiöld et al. 1938, 368–373)[23] for its "old and aboriginal ideas" on childbirth and conception. Holmer and Wassén answered the call by publishing the text twice, first in 1947, and then again in 1953 after Hayans sent them a final section of the chant, along with a complete set of picture-writing to accompany it.

Muu igar is what Mac Chapin, who has written the definitive study of Kuna curing, calls an expedition chant, a text whose knower dispatches his invisible familiar helpers to the abode of a spirit held responsible for a medical condition, either freeing a sequestered soul or seizing a threatening devil (Chapin 1983, 311–318). In this instance, the familiars journey to the celestial home of the great birth-spirit Muu (whose name means both grandmother and midwife), where she and her daughters and granddaughters nourish and mold fetuses before sending them to earth to be born. Sometimes a human mother breaks a taboo, or Muu and her helpers cannot bear to give up a fetus-soul, in which case spirit expeditionaries must be sent to liberate it.

Muu igar gained fame in anthropology through a brilliant and highly influential essay by Claude Lévi-Strauss entitled "L'Efficacité Symbolique," first published in 1949 and then reprinted in 1958 and 1963 in his collection *Structural Anthropology*. Following Holmer and Wassén, Lévi-Strauss argued that the Kuna chanter (whom he mistakenly thought was a *nele*) dispatched his spirit familiars through the underworld in what he was sure was really a metaphorical representation of the patient's uterus and birth canal. He suggested that the chant "seems to have as its principal aim the [metaphorical] description of these pains to the sick woman and the naming of them" (1963, 195). Much like psychoanalysis, the chant cured by offering a persuasive mythic drama with which the listening patient could identify and thus work through her problems. Lévi-Strauss's essay has been widely read and admired, for its uncharacteristic clarity and simplicity, for the acuity of its close reading of the text (some though not all of which has withstood restudy), most of all for the great appeal of its solution to the problem of symbolic curing, which he located in the manipulation of persuasive metaphors and narratives.

What Lévi-Strauss did not know was that his answer could not work, at least not for Muu igar. As Mac Chapin later demonstrated in a succinct but devastating reanalysis (1976), a Muu igar–knower, who is only consulted if delivery has been delayed for many hours, never enters the birth hut. Instead, he chants on the other side of a partition or in a separate building. Even if the suffering woman could hear the chant, and even if she were in a condition to listen, she could not follow along and identify her plight with its narrative, because the text is composed in the language of the spirits, which is largely unintelligible to ordinary Kuna.[24] Dazzling as it was, Lévi-Strauss's reanalysis was a failed guess, because Holmer and Wassén had no firsthand information to offer on the use, performance, and context of Muu igar. In the complete absence of case histories, Lévi-Strauss could not really know *whether* the chant cured, let alone how.

DOES PICTURE-WRITING EXIST?

From the beginning of his investigations in San Blas, Kuna picture-writing seized Nordenskiöld's imagination, and it was one of the first topics on which he published after his return from the field (1927; 1928b, 230, 276–282; 1929; Nele and Pérez Kantule 1928; Nele et al. 1930). Picture-writing seemed to offer data of special significance through which to "study primitive methods of thinking" (Nele and Pérez Kantule 1928, 12), as well as the nature of memory in tribal society, since it was, he asserted, used predominantly "as an *aide-mémoire* during a conjuring ceremony" (1929, 152–153). Picture-writing also confirmed the antiquity of Kuna culture and its links with high civilization. "What it most resembles is possibly the picture-writing of ancient Mexico, and I incline to the opinion that it constitutes a degenerated form of it" (in Nele and Pérez Kantule 1928, 21–22). If attention to the topic has faded somewhat since Nordenskiöld's time, the elegant structural and semiological analyses of Carlo Severi (1982b, 1985, 1996, 1997; Severi and Gómez 1983) have in recent years revived interest.

Doubts, however, might be raised about picture-writing, in particular about its supposed function as a kind of script or score for long curing chants. Mac Chapin, the anthropologist who has studied Kuna curing in the greatest depth, carried out research on several different islands in the 1970s, notably Ustupu, which was where Nordenskiöld had worked with Pérez Kantule and Nele, and where Guillermo Hayans lived for most of his adult life. As Chapin began to learn the curing chants, he asked to see the picture-writing, only to hear that it did not exist.

> When I asked Kilu [Chapin's teacher on another island] about the picture writing for his Muu chant, he rather derisively said there wasn't any, and that none of the chants had them. When I got to Ustupu I asked chanters about it, and they said no, nothing like that. I have since gone through dozens of books in which specialists have transcribed their own chants [in Spanish orthography] or have had their literate sons transcribe them, and I have never, ever, seen any pictographs. (personal communication; also Chapin 1983, 212–215)

How in the light of this denial is one to interpret the picture-writing supplied to Nordenskiöld for curing chants, in particular the complete pictographic text sent by Guillermo Hayans to accompany Muu igar

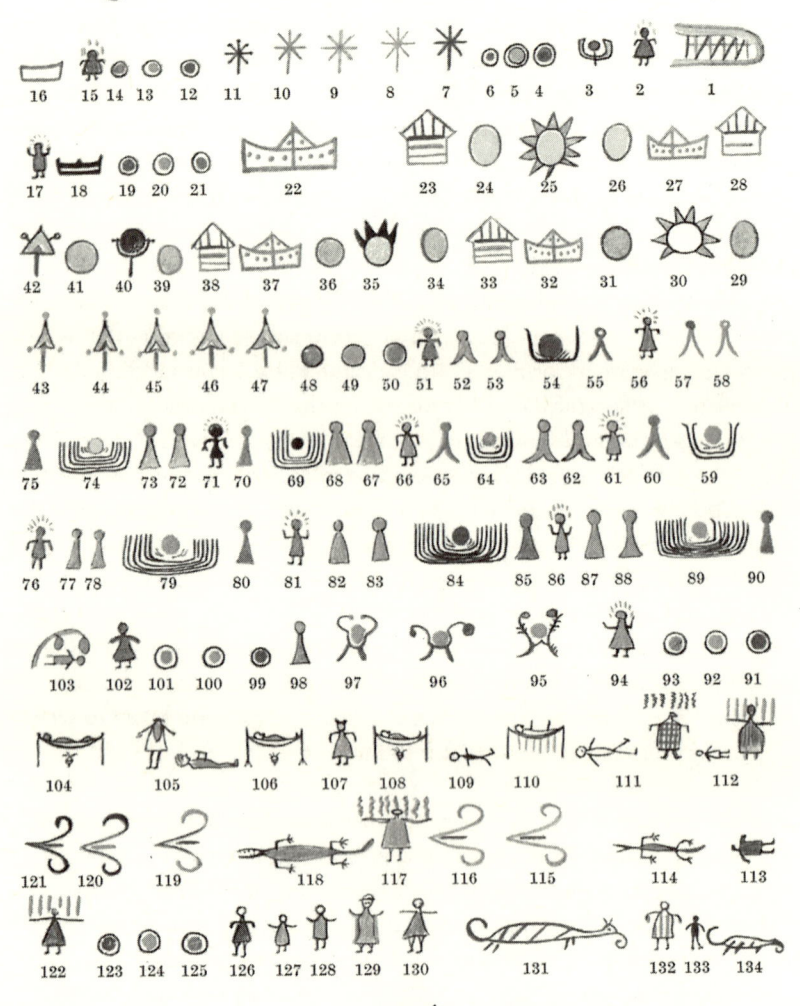

Picture-writing for the Song of *ákŭaléle*. Original in *GM.27.27.1444*.
Scale, 2/3.

FIGURE 7.1 Kuna picture-writing, from *An Historical and Ethnological Survey of the Kuna Indians*, 1938, plate VII

(Holmer and Wassén 1953), the very chant for which Chapin's teacher denied its existence? In retrospect, it stands out, not only that a great part of the picture-writing collected by Nordenskiöld came from only three men, Hayans, Pérez Kantule, and Charlie Nelson (Nele et al. 1930, 19), but also that they produced quite a lot of it more or less on demand, as Nordenskiöld freely admitted.[25] In the three monographs with examples published by Nordenskiöld,[26] not only did Pérez Kantule provide by far the largest number, but he also furnished almost all the ones in which picture-writing follows a chant verse by verse.[27] In the case of Muu igar, Holmer and Wassén noted with precision that Hayans—not the knower from whom Hayans acquired the chant—drew the pictographs over a three-month period from July 13 to October 12 of 1949 (Holmer and Wassén 1953, 7).

As Nordenskiöld pointed out, each ritualist had his own idiosyncratic set of pictographic symbols, and Pérez Kantule wrote his lines in a different direction than his teacher, left-to-right and top-to-bottom rather than the opposite (Nele and Pérez Kantule 1928, 18). As for Hayans's picture-writing, Holmer and Wassén (1953, 17) noted that Pérez Kantule had severely criticized his work "as creations of non-Indian origin, and as imitations of the illustration technique practiced in books by white people." None of this shook the Swedes' faith in the authenticity of either man's designs.

From the evidence, it seems clear that picture-writing is associated with aspects of Kuna ritual *other than chants*—with medicinal curing; with cosmology, especially beliefs concerning spirit strongholds *(galu, kalu)* (see Severi 1997); and with the inner secrets, or *burba,* of various cures, which typically consist of brief accounts of the origin of a spirit or ritually potent object (Chapin 1983, 212–216; Nordenskiöld et al. 1938, plate XII; Holmer and Wassén 1958, 16–37; 1963, 82–85). Pictographic symbols are also painted on boards displayed during puberty ceremonies. Picture-writing that functions as a script for a chant, following it verse by verse, is, to say the least, rare, and neither Chapin nor Sherzer nor I have ever seen a specialist consult picture-writing while performing any sort of chant.

It is hard to avoid the conclusion that Pérez Kantule and Hayans created picture-writing scripts for chants *de novo* in response to the interest shown by the Swedes. The two native ethnographers almost certainly did not believe that they were practicing deception, merely extending the scope of picture-writing or recreating a form that they assumed had lapsed. Certainly, someone with as strong a design sense as both men showed, especially Hayans, could have composed the pictography fairly easily, even for a long chant, simply by writing one symbol for each verse. In effect, once Hayans was done, picture-writing *did* exist for chants, and as one can readily see in the 1953 publication, he did a beautiful job. Other ritualists may have independently done the same for their chants.

Doubts on one point breed doubt on others. Nordenskiöld and his successors, who badly wanted to minimize the distance between Kuna pictographs and more developed forms of writing, consistently wrote that the visual symbols represented or corresponded to words or sentences (Nordenskiöld 1928b, 276–282; Nele and Pérez Kantule 1928, 18–19; Holmer and Wassén 1953, 18–19). But if Kuna picture-writing is used most often for information that is *not* embedded in texts, then one must conclude that the individual pictographs necessarily correspond to entities or concepts, such as kinds of medicine, not to spoken linguistic units. A sign depicting a certain spirit stronghold stands for that stronghold, for its identity as a unit in a series of strongholds, not for the words *Galu Dwibis*.

It is probably a mistake, moreover, to think of picture-writing exclusively in terms of mnemonics. Certainly the pictographs help medicinalists keep in mind elements of their pharmacopoeia and practice, as Chapin demonstrates for a page of picture-writing for snakebite cures (1983, 213–215). Cosmological pictographs, similarly, may help knowers recall the great profusion of spirit strongholds and other features of the invisible world. But from my limited experience,[28] the drawings associated with the inner secret, or *burba,* of a chant cure, like the books of Renaissance magi, should be seen less as *aides-mémoire* and more as repositories of arcane power.[29]

Even the age of Kuna pictography is open to serious question. Nordenskiöld himself wrote: "The remarkable thing is that, apart from Gassó and Harris [a biologist who accompanied Richard Marsh in 1925], not one of the numerous writers who have written on the Cunas since the beginning of the 16th century has mentioned this picture-writing" (in Nele and Pérez Kantule 1928, 16). Nordenskiöld blamed this lacuna on his predecessors' superficial knowledge of the Indians, taking heart from chronicles mentioning pictography in other parts of the region, and from Nele's insistence that Kuna pictography had been established by Ibeorgun: "These traditions referring to the great antiquity of picture-writing go to prove its being a genuinely Indian culture element" (Nele and Pérez Kantule 1928, 17).

How likely is it, however, that a form of writing that is today entirely dependent on the availability of cheap, mass-produced notebooks really stretches back to antiquity? Nordenskiöld implicitly got around this problem with the claim that writing on wooden boards came first. One of "the most valuable things of our collection" consisted of several painted boards that did not come from the puberty ceremonies but instead accompanied a chant about the snake hawk (Nele and Pérez Kantule 1928, 16; Nele et al. 1930, 64–67, plates VI, VII). However, those boards, which merely represent a series of spirit strongholds and not verses from the chant, cannot prove either the priority of boards over paper or the antiquity of picture-writing.[30]

It seems much more plausible that during the period of rapid change and cultural ferment through the mid- to late nineteenth century, Kuna knowers would have begun recording or representing aspects of their ritual practice and learning, perhaps borrowing some of the iconography of the painted boards from the puberty ceremonies. As with molas, picture-writing probably developed in a period when the Kuna were dealing actively with non-Indians, and as happened with the famous nineteenth-century Cherokee syllabary (see Chapter 1), the idea of writing was very likely borrowed even if its execution was indigenous. That this innovation was ultimately not carried further, that experiments like those of Hayans and Pérez Kantule did not evolve into something much closer to a true writing system, is undoubtedly due to the twentieth-century spread of literacy in Spanish, which allowed hundreds of ritualists or their sons to take down their chants and medicine recipes phonetically in those same school and record notebooks (see Chapter 10).

NAMES AND FACTS

No one can spend more than a few minutes perusing the great compendium without being struck by its profusion of events and facts, and even more, of names and identifying characteristics for people, spirits, animals, and places. This typological and nomenclatural abundance was certainly furthered by the interests and working methods of the Swedes, with their voracious, omnivorous, and uncritical consumption of almost every text fed to them. Its origins, however, lie with the Kuna.

In this respect, an early and unassuming section of the great book, entitled "Geography and Population Statistics" (Nordenskiöld et al. 1938, 8–28), offers a key to the whole. It includes a (highly unreliable) census of San Blas prepared by Pérez Kantule in his capacity as Nele's secretary,[31] along with a map of one section of the coast, two separate lists of geographical features, and profiles of six communities. The profiles, which were specially sent to Göteborg by Guillermo Hayans while Pérez was working there in 1931, include population figures and more lists of geographic features and, for four of the villages, sketches of local history. Both the census and the gazetteer are obviously based on borrowed models. The lists of mountains, rivers, and so forth are patterned after a published geographic survey probably owned or read by Hayans, *Geografía de Panamá* (1905), which was produced for the public schools by Ramón Valdés, President of the Republic from 1916 to 1918.[32]

In recent years a number of authors have analyzed censuses, maps, social and geographic surveys, and other forms of official documentation as instruments of national and imperial power, as was discussed in Chapters 1 and 4.[33] If one accepts this analysis, the obvious question is why Nele and his secretaries would offer up such material to readers. Why would they divulge information that peasants and indigenous peoples around the world have fiercely resisted giving up? I doubt that the Kuna failed to recognize the power of documentation. They had just come through a period in which the police controlled pacified islands through written decrees, travel passes, birth and death registers, standardized records of investigations, and lists of offenses and punishments; and they themselves later adopted the travel passes as a tool of internal social control.[34] A few years later, when Nele and his secretaries produced their own censuses, maps, and gazetteers, it was precisely because they *did* recognize such documents as aspects of state power, which they wished to appropriate for themselves. Even after giving up on the dream of complete independence a year or two before Pérez's trip to Sweden, Kuna leaders were still eager to assert their autonomy, in this case through self-documentation. Thinking like a state, they claimed territory and population by recording them.

The documents have another and equally significant dimension. The second of the two lists of geographic features covers hills or mountains *(cerros)* that a curer "ought to know, since . . . illnesses can come from all of these places," as well as named reefs and whirlpools. Whirlpools *(biryagan)* are not material aquatic dangers, but rather the underwater abodes of spirits and animals that ritualists had stilled and rendered invisible as the Kuna moved out onto the coast. The second list, in other words, covers topographical features of the unseen *spiritual* environment.

Extended descriptions of the invisible world turn up in other places as well. Nordenskiöld devotes a whole chapter of the popular book on his Panama researches to a highly detailed account of the journey a soul makes after death through the levels of the universe, proceeding from one named river, path, and spirit village to the next (1928b, 268–275). Similar celestial travelogues appear in several other places in his publications (Nele et al. 1930, 36–47; Nordenskiöld et al. 1938, 291–320, 450–451).

Even the curing chants seem to favor description over action, as Lévi-Strauss discovered in his analysis of Muu igar (see also Chapin 1983, 198–204; Taussig 1993, 108–109).

> We are surprised to find that the song, whose subject is a dramatic struggle between helpful and malevolent spirits . . . devotes very little attention to action proper. In eighteen pages of text the contest occupies less than one page. . . . The preliminaries, on the other hand, are highly developed and the preparations, the outfitting of the [familiars], the itinerary, and the sites are described with a great wealth of detail. (Lévi-Strauss 1963, 192)

This wealth of detail extends to nongeographic subjects in the compendium. In the second volume of texts published by Nordenskiöld, two sections are dedicated to his notes on interviews conducted with Charlie Nelson concerning the dozens of spirits who accompany the Sun and the Moon on their celestial ships (Nele et al. 1930, 48–53, plate IV, fig. 13) and to all the different illness spirits associated with the color red (Nele et al. 1930, 57–59). Similarly, the 130-odd pages devoted to illness and curing (Nordenskiöld et al. 1938, 479–611) give at least an impression of the tremendous multiplication of medicines, spirits, whirlpools, and spirit strongholds, while the historical texts, however confusing, suggest the high population density of Kuna history, with its abundance of named heroes, shamans, villagers, and spirits.

Why the profusion of description and naming? Chapin, in his study of Kuna curing, sees it as a way to gain control of the spirits.[35]

> The Kuna believe that in order to control the course of events in the world of spirit—and consequently, in the world of substance—one must be able to tell the spirits about themselves. A specialist must demonstrate to the spirits that he knows who they are, how they came into being, what their physical and behavioral characteristics are, where they live, and what their names are. (1983, 190)

From this perspective, it is not just the curing chants, but the whole of Kuna esoteric knowledge and practice, that should be understood as a cultural mechanism by which knowledge, and in particular knowledge of names and other detail, can be used to manage a dangerous invisible realm. If one takes this insight back to the human world, to the Kuna participation in the Swedish partnership, their contribution looks like an especially ambitious attempt to control through knowledge, to extend or transfer the core strategy of Kuna ritual to the corporeal world of politics and self-representation. The Kuna were laying claim in ethnographic form to their territory and to the place they felt they deserved in the world, insisting that they occupied their land culturally as well as physically, that they knew the names of the mountains, the names of the spirits, and the names of the great heroes.

NATIVE INTELLECTUALS

In the portrait drawn by the Swedes and their collaborators, the Kuna appear as indigenous savants and metaphysicians, Central American counterparts in the anthropological literature of the Hopi and Zuni in North America, the ancient Maya of Mesoamerica, the Dogon of West Africa, and more recently, the Yaqui of the Sonora Desert. They could have been portrayed (and have been since) in many other ways. That one representation rather than another triumphed in this case is due in part to its truth value—the Kuna have indeed elaborated a fascinating cosmology, and Nele as wise man exists in a way that Castañeda's Don Juan does not—but also to the articulation of the viewpoints, interests, and working methods that the two sides brought to their partnership. Nele and Nordenskiöld shared a devotion to learning and esoteric knowledge as the basis for prestige: they agreed on what mattered even before they met. Hayans and Pérez Kantule, moreover, by providing a ready-made wealth of texts and picture-writing, made it much easier for the Swedes to carry their research in one direction rather than others.

There is no doubt that Nordenskiöld's work is vastly more complete, reliable, and unbiased than anything on the Kuna that preceded him. If his claims are not beyond reproach, however—if the deity Tiolele is only a marginal improvement on A-oba, and if French pirates are no more plausible as culture heroes than eighteenth-century Jesuits—nonetheless Nordenskiöld and Pérez Kantule got a lot right. But Nordenskiöld was no more averse than Marsh or Gassó to ethnographic subtexts or what Clifford (1986) calls ethnographic allegory, no more able to avoid projecting himself and his own values onto his subjects or identifying with them, in what Taussig (1993) has termed the play of mimesis and alterity.

Nor could Nordenskiöld keep social class and racial antagonism out of his work. Like Richard Marsh, he differentiated between the Kuna and others in classist terms, depicting them as the remnants of a high civilization and thus as natural aristocrats. But much more than Marsh, he also insisted on vertical differentiation *within* Kuna society, on the allegedly vast gulf in knowledge and sophistication between Nele and the untaught masses of ordinary Kuna. (This even though he did not in fact know any ordinary Kuna, nor did he have the slightest idea of what they were thinking about anything.)

From my own point of view as a latter-day ethnographer who has mostly worked with ordinary Kuna, the irony is that the esoteric knowledge and ritual expertise that Nordenskiöld saw as an elite preserve have been widely shared in Kuna society. There is no doubt that some medicinalists, chanters, and chiefs are better known and more highly regarded than others, nor indeed that Nele outshone everyone else as the preeminent knower of the twentieth century. Nor is Nordenskiöld wrong to suggest that competitive knowers often deprecate others for their alleged ignorance, running down their rivals as well as the largely imaginary ignorant masses. But Nele did not constitute or embody Kuna culture all by himself, any more than Benjamin Franklin or George Washington founded the United States single-handed. My own survey of a cross-section of men in a village of middling size and prominence in the early 1970s (Howe 1974, 222–274) showed that until recently almost every adult male learned something, in effect, that just about everyone had his own niche or territory, however large or small, in the great field of knowledge. A much more recent survey by a Kuna research group in collaboration with Joel Sherzer shows that even after a long decline in recent decades, ritual knowledge is still distributed widely across the population.[36] Indeed, when leaders admonish village ritualists to forswear rivalry and invidious challenges, that is just what they emphasize, namely, that *everyone knows something*.

Equally important, while Nordenskiöld emphasized the retention or concealment of esoteric knowledge, insisting in effect on the permanence of difference between the cognoscenti and others, it is actually through sharing, either through teaching or through public performance, that knowers most fully demonstrate mastery. When traditionalists speak today of the greatness of Nele, they typically mention how many students he attracted—dozens of apprentices at one time—and how one could not walk down the streets of Ustupu in the evening without hearing chanting coming from every doorway and through the gaps in every cane wall.

When they comment on the decline of recent years, they lament their lack of students, noting that they will carry their knowledge to the grave. Rather than an imaginary Nele hoarding his symbolic riches and sneering at his lessers, it was Pérez Kantule himself, acting as teacher, sharing material with foreign interlocutors, that Nordenskiöld might have taken as his model for the flow of knowledge in Kuna society. Like Robert Redfield writing on Tepoztlán (Redfield 1930; Lewis 1963) or ethnographers disputing the nature of the Southwestern Pueblos (Bennett 1946), Nordenskiöld put the spotlight on one end of a cultural polarity or contradiction and left the other, equally real, pole in darkness.

Nordenskiöld's work was also marked by his preoccupation with antiquity and authenticity, evident not just in his regret that the Kuna wore clothes or his chagrin at finding Nele cranking a sewing machine, but in his unwavering insistence on identifying what was oldest and most traditional in indigenous lifeways. Though attuned to foreign influences (especially from the French pirates) and willing to accept and find interest in some sorts of cultural synthesis (1928b, 246–247), notably the landscape of heaven, Nordenskiöld never gave up the goal of sorting out the aboriginal from its adulterations. He was incapable of recognizing that the ancient, pure cultural core he sought was a chimera, that every aspect of Kuna society, however distinctive from its Western equivalents, had been shaped by three hundred years of struggle on an international frontier.

By no means alone among anthropologists of his generation in this search for the pristine and unacculturated, Nordenskiöld carried the tendency to an extreme. His need to return to origins and an uncorrupted past may have derived in part from the insecurities and ambiguities of his personal history, as these have been analyzed in an intellectual biography by Christer Lindberg (1996, 34–61, 460–500). It also reflected the much more general "crisis of bourgeois confidence" among European and North American elites charted by Hobsbawm (1987, 187) and Burrow (2000), in particular the antimodernist form such doubts sometimes took (Lears 1981) and the loss of confidence among sociologists and anthropologists in the nineteenth-century certainties of evolution and progress (Hobsbawm 1987, 273–275). Nordenskiöld found his touchstone, his defense against change and decay and his alternative to the stifling conformity of his own society, in unbroken ancient tradition, even if he then transmuted that tradition into the coinage of contemporary academia.[37]

Here again, the Baron and the Kuna were on converging courses. Traditionalists of Nele's generation insisted on tracing their institutions back to ancient roots, to founding culture heroes like Ibeorgun and Dad Ibe, yet as they well knew, their society had undergone radical transformation just a few years previously: Kuna men had taken over agriculture from women, who had developed a complete new costume, based entirely on foreign materials; and the move to the islands was so recent that a few laggard communities were still in transition. Chiefs like Nele sang metaphors about candlenut torches in gathering halls illuminated by kerosene.[38] Just like Nordenskiöld, the Kuna were attempting to deal with galloping change, hybridity, and social uncertainty—and indeed, with their own creative innovations—by reasserting their society's pure and ancient origins. These anxieties, shared by both parties to the collaboration, profoundly shaped the ethnography that emerged from their joint effort.

Post-Rebellion Ethnography, 1925–1950

EIGHT

During the quarter-century following the 1925 rebellion, the Kuna made their peace with Panama. In 1938, the National Assembly created a territorial reserve called the Comarca de San Blas (today the Comarca de Kuna Yala); in 1945 a constitution called the Carta Orgánica established a new system of governance uniting the whole *comarca*, with three great chiefs *(sagla dummagan)*, or caciques, and a semiannual council called the Congreso General; and in the early 1950s a law (No. 16 of 1953) officially recognized that system and established the fundamentals of Kuna autonomy in Panama. All of these reforms were promoted by a network of chiefs and scribes and hammered out in regional meetings, and all of them grew out of alliances developed with national political parties and a handful of sympathetic government officials.

Over these same years, San Blas, made notorious by the events of 1924–1925 and by Richard Marsh's widely publicized claims for the supposed "white Indians," attracted a long series of visitors—tourists, adventurers, missionaries, scholars, even a few anthropologists—some of whom felt inspired to write up their experiences and observations. The partnership that developed between the Swedes and Nele and his secretaries, as significant as it proved to be, by no means monopolized outsiders' accounts of the Kuna or their own attempts to represent themselves to the world.

Every piece of ethnographic writing from this era depended entirely on Kuna input, on their willingness to talk about themselves and display their lives, and on the mediation of native gatekeepers, who actively sought out sympathetic outsiders or else took them in hand if they showed up on their own. It is clear not only that many Kuna had come to recognize the importance of positive external relations, but that a network of mediators or brokers, including the same set of men who effected the political rapprochement with Panama, had arrived at a conscious, active policy of presenting their people and their culture to the world, either through their own autoethnographic studies or by facilitating the work of others. Indigenous agency met Western representation on the field of ethnography.

Edward Bruner has suggested that in the historical development of ethnography, each successive era has been characterized by a dominant narrative, a master account of the direction of change, with distinct "policy and political implications" (1986, 144). Such narratives, anticipating various fates for the Indians or casting members of national society as inheritors of past indigenous glories, are certainly evident in post-rebellion Kuna ethnography. In various ways, moreover, local narratives reflect the movement and evolution across the hemisphere of indigenist ideas and indigenist policies. I am struck, however, by the diversity of narratives suggested by the interests and viewpoints of different sorts of ethnographers, and by the doubts, confusion, and ambivalence shown by them all. No matter what fate each asserted or implied for the Indians, and no matter their agreement that the unstable present could not endure, few of them seemed certain where things would end up.

OLD ATTITUDES AND INCIPIENT INDIGENISM

The first publication about the Kuna to appear after the 1925 rebellion indicated just how far Panamanian attitudes had to go. *El problema indígena en Panamá* was published in 1926 by one Mateo Araúz. Araúz praised the government for restraint toward the rebels and lamented the near-total lack of knowledge about Isthmian Indians, but then went on to fill that void with four-hundred-year-old material from contact-period chroniclers, topped off with the most blatantly prejudicial stereotypes. The heart of the matter, as always, was Kuna separatism.

> The indian will never be able to submit to any sort of civilized life, since his nature, his instinct, only dictates that he live free of obligations, and all his thoughts direct him towards fulfilling his only aspiration, which is: that they leave him alone, without bothering him or imbuing him with foreign customs or ideas, within

the ancestral customs that live rooted in his being, keeping within himself all the secrets of his race, all the bad habits of the retrograde life, the same as were carried by his ancestors, transmitted from generation to generation, and practiced by those that follow, in an unchangeable manner. (1926, 1)

True, the Indian's backwards nature was not entirely his own fault:

We must accept that the unhappy denizens of the virgin American jungles would not have embraced in their miserable existence all the bad habits and defects that they now embrace, nor would they have harbored the hate towards the foreign that they profess today, were not these qualities the logical consequence of the treacherous, deceiving, and cruel conduct [of the Spanish conquistadores]. (1926, 3)

Araúz's answer was to intervene in the lives of young Indians, who were not yet sunk in their parents' bad practices and miserable existence, and to establish reserves modeled on North American Indian reservations, which he imagined to be a resounding success. After his one disquisition on the subject, he was not heard from again.

At the time Araúz wrote, signs of interest and concern about "The Indian Question" had begun to appear across Latin America, most notably in Peru, in the writing of Dora Mayer (1921), Mariátegui (1928), and others, and in the work of Manuel Gamio (1922), Moisés Sáenz (1928, 1936, 1939), and others in the so-called Mexican School of Anthropology (Marzal 1993, 377–477; Gutiérrez 1999, 90–96; De la Peña 2005, 724–727). In 1926, an International Bolivarian Congress meeting in Panama called for "the moral elevation," "intellectual and civic education," and the "definitive incorporation of the american indian to the fullness of civilization" (Quesada 1927; Puig 1948, 3)—a position that, however paternalistic and demeaning its understanding of both problem and solution, at least recognized that there was a problem.

In 1928 a geographer, Manuel María Alba, published an article entitled "Etnología y población histórica de Panamá," which consisted of a survey of names for sixteenth-century Isthmian chiefdoms, supplemented by four pages of very sketchy contemporary information. Alba reprinted the article the following year as a chapter in his book-length *Geografía descriptiva de la República de Panamá* (1929). Neutral for the most part concerning the

Indians, he did praise the coastal Kuna for their "admirable" tribal government and those of the Chucunaque—"the autochthonous type of a pure and strong race"—for their resistance to domination and intermarriage (1929, 67). Antillean Blacks, in marked contrast, were identified by Alba as a danger to Panama's "ethnic conservation, her future stability and the quality of her inhabitants" (1929, 98).

Alba displayed his pro-Indian sympathies more frankly in another article published in 1928, "Urraca, biographical sketch of a national hero," which praised a bellicose sixteenth-century chieftain of western Panama for his tenacious struggles "against the enemies of his Fatherland and his race" (1928b, 15). Urraca's emergence as a nationalist symbol had in fact begun a few years previously, when President Belisario Porras commissioned a statue of the chief from an Italian sculptor. The statue was eventually set up in the Parque Urraca, several acres set aside in the new suburb of Bella Vista, and later moved to the Normal School in the provincial town of Santiago.[1] Years later, Urraca's fierce visage found its ultimate monetary apotheosis on one side of the Panamanian centavo.

The symbolic use of Indian resistance, though a departure from recent Panamanian discourse, had a long history in Latin America, beginning with colonial-era epic poems, of which the most famous was Alonso de Ercilla's *La Araucana* (1945 [1569–1589]). A less-well-known epic, De Páramo y Cepeda's *Alteraciones del Darien* (1994 [1697]), featured the seventeenth-century Kuna.

At the beginning of the nineteenth century, independence movements and early republican governments briefly adopted the Inca, Aztec, and Araucanians as nationalist symbols. The historian Rebecca Earle, however, makes clear that this short-lived "indianesque" moment (2007, 21–67) appropriated the pre-Columbian past for creole-dominated states, most of which soon reembraced their Hispanic and colonial identities. Even in countries where ancient monuments and precolonial cultures retained some of their value, they only went to show the degraded nature of contemporary Indians and the obstacles they presented to national unity and identity. In the twentieth century, with the spread of *indianismo* and its partial revaluation of the indigenous, emphasis nonetheless fell on Indians as problem, as backwards populations to be redeemed and assimilated into national society.[2]

The disconnect between glorious past and devalued present, evident in indianesque symbolism throughout almost all eras (Earle 2007), was blatantly obvious in President Porras's actions—his memorialization of

Urraca[3] in the midst of a campaign to subdue and make over the Kuna—and even more so in the choice of another contact-period chieftain, Panquiaco, to name a gunboat purchased in 1925 to patrol the coast and overawe Kuna rebels. At the same time, the apotheosis of Urraca, along with the friendly articles by Manuel María Alba, did signal an incipient shift in national attitudes, a willingness on the part of some elites to reconsider, however tentatively, the place of the Indian in the nation, and to embrace for themselves a mixed indigenous-Hispanic identity.

Dead Indian leaders and past resistance were further eulogized in two novels from the 1930s now considered foundational to Panamanian national identity: Julio Sosa's prize-winning *La india dormida* (1936), and *Núñez de Balboa: el tesoro del Dabaibe* (1936), by the head of the recently created national university, Octavio Méndez Pereira. Of another sixteenth-century chief, Méndez Pereira wrote, "He, along with París, with Urraca, were without a doubt the predecessors of Tomás Herrera, of Morelos, of Bolívar and of San Martín" (1936, 80).

Both novels, in addition to praising Indian resistance, celebrated interethnic unions of Indian princesses, one with Balboa and the other with a lesser conquistador, both unions treated as symbols of an emergent mestizo national identity (see Earle 2007, 50–57; Szok 2001, 105–106; Sommer 1991). Of the Indian women taken as concubines by colonists, Méndez Pereira wrote: "They were the first mothers of those gallant generations that were to populate reconquered America—heroic *mestizaje*, which was later called on to effect emancipation and the new civilization of the continent" (1936, 81).

In sharp contrast with President Porras, both novelists linked indigenous past and present, explicitly identifying conquest-period peoples as Guaymí and Kuna; Méndez Pereira, in fact, went so far as to gloss *cacique* by the Kuna word *ságuila* (1936, 44–45). In equally sharp contrast, however, with the Anglophone authors discussed in Chapter 5, the armed struggle celebrated by Sosa and Méndez Pereira—an obvious metaphor for the resistance to Yanqui domination for which Panamanians yearned—was set firmly in the past. Neither author likened Urraca or París or Panquiaco to Colman or Nele, and even if enlightened officials admitted privately that in 1925 the Kuna had been driven to rebellion by unremitting abuse, no one held up the Revolución Tule as a positive nationalist model.[4]

The revalorization of indigenous culture was even more apparent—and noticeably more wholehearted—in the first published field study of the Kuna by a Panamanian, which appeared in two chapters of a folkloric survey entitled *Tradiciones y cantares de Panamá*, offered in 1930 by a prominent musician and statesman, Narciso Garay.

NARCISO GARAY'S FOLKLORIC INCLUSION

Garay, the son of Epifanio Garay, a peripatetic musician and artist, was educated first in Bogotá, Cartagena, and Panama City, later in Brussels and Paris, where he studied music with, among others, Gabriel Fauré. As a young man he performed on the violin, composed several orchestral works, and wrote journalistic criticism. With Panamanian independence from Colombia, he returned from Europe in 1904 and was appointed head the same year of a newly created national school of music, taking his place as a senior member of a cohort of foreign-educated intellectuals and activists who, as the historian Peter Szok points out (2001, 67–71, 80, 85), created many of the institutions of Panamanian national life in the first half of the century. Several years after his return, Garay began a long career in government, eventually serving as ambassador to eight different countries, Secretary or Minister of Foreign Affairs in four separate administrations from 1916 to 1940, and between times head of three other cabinet ministries. Throughout his life he combined the most wide-ranging international interests with fervent Isthmian patriotism.

Garay's book (1930), which treats the music and dance of a number of peasant and Indian groups, belongs to a well-established Latin American literary tradition called *costumbrismo*, dedicated to the discovery and preservation of rural lore as a source of national identity.[5] According to Angel Rama, this "appropriation of oral tradition" ultimately reinforced the centrality of urbanity and literacy. "Literature absorbed the multiple contributions of traditional rural culture and articulated them with other elements into a discourse on the definition, formation, and collective values of the nation" (1996, 66–67). From another perspective, however, *costumbrismo* opened up national identity to embrace previously excluded classes and ethnicities, and in Garay's case, he included the Kuna and the Guaymí of western Panama along with the campesinos of Chiriquí and the central provinces.[6]

Constructed around a chatty narrative of the author's travels and his conversations with companions and acquaintances—most of the conversations are really didactic lectures in the guise of Socratic dialogue—*Tradiciones y cantares* includes numerous musical and textual transcriptions, dozens of photographs, and four full-page color plates based on specially commissioned paintings. The tone of the book is literary, informal in a studied way, and at times a bit precious. Molas reminded Garay of gypsies and Sicilian peasants, headcloths of a painting by Jean Jacques Henner. A *nele*'s consultation with a medicinalist brought to mind a novel by Anatole France. Kuna poetry and music were compared to Pindar, Sappho, and Euripides, to *chansons de geste,* and even to symphonic tone poems. Garay quoted himself lecturing his companions on, among other topics, tone poems, alliteration, dualism, and musical intervals, all of which lends some credence to Rama's claim that in such works rural lore was being organized and disciplined by *letrado* learning and sophistication.

The two chapters dedicated to the Kuna are based on a pair of trips of a few days each that Garay made in January and February of 1929 in the company of the current intendente and other officials and friends on board the *Panquiaco*.[7] It is clear that a great deal was made of Garay, as a prominent dignitary, both on the boat and ashore. During the first visit, he transcribed panpipe and flute performances staged for him, and for the second trip he was loaned a Dictaphone machine by the national electric power company, with which he recorded and transcribed chanting, mostly associated with female puberty ceremonies.

In his investigations Garay depended on several of the usual ethnographic suspects, beginning with Charlie Nelson, Nordenskiöld's first informant from Río Azúcar two years previously, as well as the Baron's interpreters, Roberto Pérez and Samuel Morris, and a prominent young modernist, Estanislao López. Rubén Pérez Kantule, though mentioned, was either absent or uninvolved, but his father, Kantulbipi, performed for the visitors.

Garay seems to have had an excellent ear as well as a strong grounding in musicology, and he made good use of his predecessors' works, which he says he brought with him to the field. While discoursing knowledgeably about the acoustic properties of Kuna flutes and the structure of ritual poetry, he also commented on the intersections between art and politics in the post-rebellion years. After quoting at length an unnamed functionary concerning the misdeeds and provocations of Richard Marsh, Garay then disassociated himself vehemently from his own government's past repression of the Indians. Among local officials, he distinguished between hardliners and moderates, and among Nargana Kuna, between traditionalists, pro-Panamanian modernists, and pro-American adherents of the by-then banished Protestant mission. Despite urging his listeners to suspend judgment, Garay also attacked Nordenskiöld vehemently for consorting with the rebel Kuna.[8]

Toward the Indians Garay's attitudes were tinged with condescension. He mocked his informants for accepting tips and bargaining for more. He tossed off judgments about the "absolute primitiveness" of Kuna dances (Garay 1930, 58), the "puerile and primitive happiness" of carnival crowds (1930, 67), and, concerning Nordenskiöld's allies among the rebel Kuna, the "disordered and unconsidered reactions that govern the conduct of primitive man or in the state of nature" (1930, 18).

Otherwise, however, he offered support and respect. If his inclusive message was not made sufficiently obvious by the organization of the book, which afforded the Kuna and Guaymí equal billing with Latin campesinos, he announced on the opening page that his purpose on Nargana was to "get to know the indians of San Blas, Panamanians like me and my brothers by nationality" (1930, 5). A later passage in support of tradition could, except for its style, have come from James Gilbert or William Markham:

> The indians, clean and careful of their person, demanding in the cleanliness of their *bohios* [huts] and streets, as if the cult of the goddess Hygia had been reborn among them; protective of their customs and beliefs; intelligent and astute; endowed with a mythology, a science and an art of their own which provides them with the elements of a moral, intellectual, and aesthetic life indispensable to realizing their destiny on the earth . . . why should they not be good and loyal citizens of the Republic if efficacious and peaceful means of approach, education, and persuasion were used with them? (1930, 22)

Garay focused special attention, undoubtedly by design, on the two elements in native culture that the government had most sought to eradicate. Concerning women's dress, he quoted himself haranguing an unwilling audience:

> Can you imagine—I said to the Intendente—these cuna indian women, so picturesque and stimulating, attired in the fashion of New York or Paris? Isn't it a sin to Europeanize or Americanize these women, with their red headdresses, multicolored *molas*, gold noserings and vegetable or mineral necklaces, to oblige them to walk like parakeets or kangaroos with the torment of shoes on their feet and hats on their heads? Truly, our people [i.e., of the government] seem to have lost all common sense. . . . And taking the question one step further, doesn't it seem terrible to destroy

the customs and language of these aborigines, their fetishes and amulets, their superstitions and myths, in order to provide them as a substitute with what? (1930, 13)

As for puberty ceremonies, or chichas, they provided the principal research topic of Garay's second visit. Despite remarks on drunken participants and judgments on supposed ritual decadence, he devoted more than ten double-column pages to a sympathetic account (1930, 51–62), one much clearer than anything in Nordenskiöld's writing.

In Garay's narrative, puberty rituals were followed by Carnival, the two treated as exemplars of opposed tendencies. "The cult of *Ibeorgún* gave way to the cult of Momo" (1930, 66).[9] Garay and his companions participated enthusiastically in Carnival celebrations on both Nargana and its twin village of Corazón de Jesús, and he was tapped to crown one of the queens, but his strongest loyalties obviously lay with traditional culture. In another passage, he contrasted native flutes with gramophones, home-brewed chicha with rum, and puberty dancing with the fox-trot found in the dance clubs favored by modernist youth. In an obvious allegorical lesson for Panama as a whole, he urged the necessity of both tendencies, one for its dynamism, the other for defending "the knowledge acquired, the riches accumulated" (1930, 28). He described ending his first trip by calling a meeting at which he exhorted youth and age to be reconciled, and for youth to begin writing down the traditions held by age.[10] At the conclusion of the chapter about his second trip, he urged the same task on his countrymen, so that "it will then not be just the French, English, Germans and North Americans who know something of the primitive inhabitants of America," and instead "there will be a pleiad[11] of national archaeologists and ethnographers who will fulfill for the fatherland the spiritual duties that up to today have been delegated to foreigners" (1930, 80).

One discordant element in the narrative suggests that interest in the Indians was not entirely dispassionate and scientific for everyone in the party, that it might hinge on the same sort of interethnic romance attributed to Balboa. Toward the end of the first visit, one of Garay's companions confessed to an infatuation with a young woman home on vacation from schooling in Panama. "A daughter of the islands, a Cuna *india* who carries inlayed in her eyes of mystery her tribe's tragic past, looked at me several times . . . with the same sweetness and depth, I assure you, that Fulvia's first looks for Balboa must have carried." A brief exchange of words only inflamed him further. "Enchantment had done its work, friend Garay, in such a way that to resist was all in vain." When the group returned the following month, the girl told Garay's lovestruck companion that she had been waiting for him and that she would be traveling on the same boat to the city. What ultimately ensued, Garay claimed not to know (1930, 30–32, 67).

Although Garay's book undoubtedly contributed to a gradual shift in attitudes toward the country's Indian population, his exhortations to take up the work of ethnography and archaeology gained few immediate converts. Professional anthropologists did not appear until well after the Second World War, and little more was written on the Kuna by Panamanians for more than a decade. His book seems to have enjoyed less success, moreover, in defending indigenous culture than in promoting the peasant music, dance, and dress of the central provinces as the essence of national identity, a movement the Panamanian middle and upper classes found much more congenial (see Szok 2001, 106–108; Zarate 1962).

MISSIONARY ETHNOGRAPHY

The task of describing the Indians, just as Garay had feared, was left as before to foreigners, principally Swedish anthropologists, North American amateurs, and Catholic missionaries. As noted in Chapter 2, the Catholics—this time Franciscan nuns and priests from the Claretian Order—returned to Nargana and Corazón de Jesús in 1928. In addition to evangelizing the Indians and running the public school system, over the next twenty years the fathers published two grammars and a dictionary of Kuna, along with a number of histories and ethnographies.[12] The first of these works, written by José María Berengueras, was serialized during 1930 and 1931 in several issues of *El Misionero,* a Spanish journal targeting the pious laity as well as the religious. Oddly enough, Berengueras began just where Nordenskiöld did, presenting excerpts from one of the long texts later published in the Swedes' magnum opus (Nordenskiöld et al. 1938, 228–277), a history of the culture hero Ibeorgun dictated by Nele and taken down in Spanish by Pérez Kantule, which showed that even Catholic ethnography was nourished by Kuna feeding.[13]

According to Father Berengueras, Kuna myth-histories were "nothing more than a poor imitation *(remedo)* of . . . Sacred Scripture," with heroes who "are a highly distorted parody" of figures from the Bible, proving that "in the beginning there was no more than one religion and a single tradition of identical facts" (1930, no. 6, pp. 12–13). Dagargunyala, the mountain on which a handful of Kuna ancestors had escaped a universal flood, undoubtedly corresponded to Mount Ararat, and the hero Ibeorgun to Moses.

Berengueras showed the greatest interest in Ibeorgun as lawgiver, using the text as a point of departure for an ethnographic sketch that was as much moral inventory as cultural account. Kuna gender roles and marital practices he found wholly admirable, apart from the ease of divorce and a regrettable casualness in wedding ritual: rejoicing in Kuna monogamy, a relief from centuries of missionary struggle against plural marriage, Berengueras saw matrilocal residence as a laudable protection for women. "Would that these extremely wise matrimonial laws given by Ybeorgún continue in force, perfected and purified by the radiance of the Holy Gospel!" (1930, no. 80, p. 95). Favorably impressed by what he supposed was an absence of private property in land, he did not think that Kuna men worked as hard as they might.[14] In diametric opposition to all the policemen and officials who had preceded him, he much admired female costume and ornaments, which, he insisted, did no harm to women's bodies.

Less happy about the lack of streets, plazas, and other signs of municipal order, he conceded that women kept island villages superficially clean. He followed his predecessor Father Gassó in identifying *neles* and other ritualists as barriers to progress and true religion but found them less pernicious than the ethnocentric and separatist attitudes of the Kuna as a whole. Unlike Gassó, who had fulminated against the sacred gathering, Berengueras found the institution of negligible importance, probably because it had been abandoned by Nargana, where he was stationed. What most offended him was the chicha, in which "the indian is degraded to the level of brutes"[15]— which did not keep him from describing it in fascinated detail. In contrast to the indifference shown by earlier opponents of Kuna drinking to the elaborate rituals in which alcohol was embedded, Berengueras was struck by "the formality with which they accompany a thing so completely trivial and contemptible as getting drunk" (1930, no. 80, p. 96).

Father Berengueras's serialized ethnography was followed five years later by a less amiable work, a long manuscript history of secular and religious efforts to civilize the coast, struggles with the Indians, and especially the 1925 rebellion.[16] Seething with hostility against the rebel Kuna as well as missionary rivals, Berengueras mocked the Republic of Tule, condemned Coope and Purdy as co-conspirators with Marsh ("three offenders in the same crime"), and heaped praise on Gassó and Charly Robinson, while avoiding all mention of Robinson's previous collaboration with the Protestants. The bitter tone of the work was undoubtedly motivated in no small part by the Catholic mission's fierce struggles through the 1930s with an array of enemies, including Nele's coalition, a renewed native Protestant mission on Ailigandi, and a number of young scribes from Nargana.

Reflecting this decade of conflict and opposition, an official history of missionary efforts in the Darién and San Blas published in Panama in 1939 devoted twelve dense pages to an unflattering, even hostile, portrait of the Indians (Misioneros Hijos 1939, 97–110). The anonymous author or authors found the Kuna stubbornly recalcitrant and deplorably backward. Their remarks, intended to justify the slow progress of the evangelizing program, were filled with scorn and antagonism.

> Everything carries the stamp of the primitive: agriculture, commerce, education, traditions, attire, language....
>
> They blindly obey their high indigenous chiefs called Ságuilas. If one joins with these characteristics the purity of indian blood, then the enormous difficulty implicated in civilizing and missionizing them can be understood....
>
> Despite the fertility of the soil and the rich flora and fauna, agriculture, industry and commerce are ruled by rudimentary laws.... Their coin is the coconut: with it they buy merchandise, ... and with it they give themselves up to indolence....
>
> All the ... riches of the Comarca are dead, and they hardly manage to meet the most urgent necessities of life.... Outside the center of Narganá, neither education nor the average level of life reaches the most minimal level of civilization....
>
> The rest of the day [after work] they [i.e., the men] spend resting in their hammocks, spreading tobacco smoke to the four winds and caring for their own clothing. Every single day they are obliged to go to their tasks in the bush or to fish, because they consume each day everything they bring back....
>
> There are women who know nothing else of this world except their house and the river: ... they live secluded in their huts without concerning themselves with anything....
>
> The meetings tie the indian to everything old and distance them from the new....
>
> Emblematic staves and fetishistic amulets; plodding, unchanging, sad chants ...

The image-making art of our Indians is still in its infancy and has only produced grotesque *nuchus* and deformed *suar mimi* [carved wooden figures used in curing]. . . .

This profane fiesta [i.e., the chicha], which stretches over the space of several days, is completely paganized, with scandalous drinking and general drunkenness. . . . All the good qualities that the kuna indians possess [very few had so far been mentioned] are being eliminated with the frequency of these fiestas. . . .

They have an elevated concept of their race and qualities, and with it they deal with outsiders. (Misioneros Hijos 1939, 101–109, 137)

The 1939 report was followed a decade later by the first full-scale Spanish-language ethnography, *Los indios cunas de San Blas,* written by Manuel María Puig (1948). Despite carrying over verbatim a number of passages from the earlier sketch, Father Puig showed much less animus against the Indians. To be sure, he insisted on the need for civilization, as well as the Catholic religion, criticizing the indigenes harshly for resisting progress. Two long chapters devoted to the *"Acción Civilizadora"* of the Church and government (1948, 143–230) fawned on the secular powers for pouring out "their affectionate efforts onto these Benjamins of the Mother-Fatherland" (1948, 179). Ethnocentric judgments abounded, moreover: in addition to dissecting Kuna moral and linguistic defects and "idiosyncrasies" at length (1948, 29, 34–36, 41), Puig wrote that they held childish beliefs, bellowed rather than sang (1948, 91), made good servants (1948, 30), and even that they all looked alike (1948, 34). Other customs, however, he saw more sympathetically. Implicitly contradicting the 1939 report, Puig depicted Kuna men and women as working hard to produce food for guests, friends, and family (1948, 49–51). Concerning Kuna piety and morality (1948, 85, 98–101, and passim), he credited them with "norms of conduct as wholesome as can reasonably be hoped for among aborigines" (1948, 98).[17]

Puig also offered a very useful and knowledgeable account of Kuna social forms, the first to pay attention to such fundamental norms and practices as friendship, egalitarianism, gift exchange and hospitality, visiting and traveling, bathing, attitudes toward blood and the insane, and the uses of calabashes, hammocks, and domestic animals. Based on extended personal experience and thus at the opposite extreme from Nordenskiöld's short-stay, text-based research, Puig's work showed the virtues of long-term residence that Raoul Naroll (1962, 90–93; 1973, 930) finds in the best missionary ethnography.

Puig was weaker on politics and religion and on aspects of native life he had apparently not witnessed, such as agricultural labor and the inner life of households. Concerning ritual practitioners, he alternated between mostly correct accounts of their work and errors inherited from his predecessors.[18] The most dubious parts of the book consist in fact of material taken from Gassó, not always with proper attribution. Puig also had trouble shedding the ideologized preconceptions concerning progress and foresight that rationalized the civilizing project. He criticized the Kuna for not planning ahead or storing food, even quoting the same proverb as Gassó ("The way of the poor: sooner burst a gut than store"),[19] and then went on to describe Kuna storage practices (1948, 48).[20] Similarly, he saw no contradiction between claims that the Indians lacked all desire for change (1948, 9, 41, and passim) and discussion of the economic and political innovations introduced by Nele's sector (1948, 56). Overall, however, the prejudices Puig had discarded stand out as much as those he retained.

Christian ethnography has attracted surprisingly little anthropological attention, even in the best-known studies of missionization (e.g., Comaroff and Comaroff 1991).[21] Peter Pels, in a work on a late colonial Catholic mission to the Waluguru of Tanganyika, argues that the Dutch fathers wrote little cultural description and learned about the target population mostly through oral coaching and experience (1999, 282). Those few who did engage in the "hobby" of ethnography tended to blur rather than clarify ethnic and cultural boundaries, focusing attention instead on individuals and their conversion (1999, 284).

For Puig and Berengueras (and for a great many other missionaries), ethnography was much more than a hobby. In addition to the more immediate and obvious purposes of their writing—instructing successors, passing on accumulated wisdom, venting frustrations, justifying the mission's limited gains—their texts served to fix the Kuna in print and connect them inextricably to Catholic projects and purposes. Like many missionary writers, they offered a mixed report card on their charges, portraying them as a people with great potential and also great deficiencies, to be remedied only by the true faith. But even more, they sought to rationalize domination through expertise, demonstrating that only the Fathers knew the idiosyncrasies of the Kuna, their virtues and deficiencies, well enough to be entrusted with their care.[22]

Expertise also had a personal and professional dimension, concerned with self-fashioning and peer recognition in religious careers. Within the larger universe of Catholic missionary writing, found in numerous journals targeting priests, nuns, and pious lay folk, narratives of heroic struggle like Gassó's memoirs made claims to distinction, merit, and sanctity through suffering—and in earlier centuries, to saintly lives and martyrdom (Greer 2000). Ethnographic writing had a similar import, connecting author with primitive subjects through accounts of their nature and character and demonstrating praiseworthy expertise and experience. Pious ethnographers might reasonably hope to be remembered in the same way as Gassó—not as generic missionaries but as Berengueras or Puig of the Kuna mission, known not only for evangelical toil and devotion, but also for hard-won authoritative knowledge of native language and custom.

The Fathers, it should be noted, wrote for the missionized as well as the missionizers, though in quite different publications. From 1947 through 1951, Father Jesús Erice collaborated with young scribes, notably an Indian administrator named Ricardo Arango, to produce a bulletin called *Juventud Samblaseña*,[23] all part of a program to foster clubs and sodalities among Kuna converts (see Martínez Mauri 2005, 2007). Along with essays of various sorts, periodic reports from local Catholic groups, commentary on recent general congresses, and information on Catholicism and its enemies in the outside world, the bulletins featured one-page exhortations by Arango. Large blocks of text appeared in Kuna—Bible lessons, homilies, a catechism, explications of the Church calendar—all of it, however, composed by Father Erice, who also wrote much the longest piece in Spanish, a serialized history of the 1925 rebellion. Seen in retrospect, *Juventud Samblaseña* marks a waypoint in the evolution of clerical attitudes, including those of Jesús Erice himself:[24] native ethnography and religion, years later incorporated reverently into Catholic efforts (see Chapter 10), were here noticeable for their absence, and the first issue began with a tirade against attempts to revive traditional Kuna marriage. But converts were included as junior authors and workers, and the native language was conspicuously used, if only by a non-Kuna.

NATIVE AND FOREIGN AUTHORS

As a full-length Spanish-language ethnography, Father Puig's book stood alone for many years. Most serious work on the Kuna continued to be written in English and published in Sweden. As noted in previous chapters, Nordenskiöld's magnum opus, the product of his collaboration with

Rubén Pérez Kantule, was nursed to publication by Karl-Gustav Izikowitz and S. Henry Wassén, appearing in 1938, six years after the Baron's death, and remaining in print for a half-century thereafter. The work's great mass of semidigested detail and underedited texts, at the same time that it discouraged casual reading, conveyed a powerful sense of the intellectual richness of Kuna culture: what it lacked in precision and intelligibility, it more than compensated for as public relations. Published at a time when Nordenskiöld's name was still well known internationally in anthropology, the book put the Kuna on the scholarly map.

It did much the same for Nele Kantule. Nele, who had succeeded Colman in 1929 as leader of the rebel Kuna, did not need foreign help to establish him as the most prominent chief of his day or the leading teacher of several branches of ritual; nor did more than a handful of Kuna in this era have access to foreign writing about their society. But knowing that the words of Nele and his secretaries had been published abroad confirmed his preeminence and helped him to eclipse both Colman and Inabaginya as *the* great man, acknowledged both at home and abroad as the preeminent Kuna of the twentieth century.

After Nordenskiöld's death in 1932, Henry Wassén made two short research trips, in 1935 and 1947, very much in the style of his teacher but on a more modest scale, yielding two published collections of documents (Wassén 1938b, 1949). On the second trip he was accompanied by a linguist, Nils Holmer, who also spent a month on his own on Ustupu. Holmer produced an excellent dictionary of Kuna (1952a), and two very quirky grammars (1947, 1951): in the first, written before he went to the field, Holmer followed Gassó's example by filling in the lacunae in the documentation collected by Izikowitz and others with comparative material from languages as distant as Arawak, Nahuatl, and Seneca; the second grammar, though it corrected as well as supplemented the previous work, by no means shed all its idiosyncrasies.

Between 1947 and 1963, Holmer and Wassén published a series of long Kuna chant texts, which, despite a few problems in translation and sparse information on performance and social context, constitute a remarkable ethnographic contribution (Holmer 1952b; Holmer and Wassén 1947, 1953, 1958, 1963). (The most prominent of these chants, Muu igar, is discussed in Chapter 7.) Remarkable also because all of the texts were collected and translated by Guillermo Hayans, who worked with a number of knowers and sent the texts on to Sweden for publication—a long-term collaboration discussed in Chapter 10.

VISITORS AND CULTURE BROKERS

In the post-rebellion years, friendly North Americans, mostly untrained amateurs, continued to visit the Indians and write about them, gaining acceptance in the field in part on the strength of the ongoing association between the Kuna and Isthmian North Americans. This loose alliance was strengthened in the 1930s by the creation of a native Protestant church semicovertly supported from the Canal Zone, and by an agreement signed with military authorities assigning cooking and dishwashing duties on U.S. military bases to Indian workers. Tourist excursions to Indian territory continued, especially to Carti and Nargana, apparently increasing significantly during the 1940s,[25] and a handful of Zonians and North American visitors followed after William Markham on longer trips into Indian territory.[26] Five of these visitors wrote accounts of their experiences, three of which were published. (With one exception, the visitors had little if any Spanish.) Though only one contributed significantly to anthropological knowledge, the rest have much to tell about ethnographic process and Kuna agency: all five dealt with a small set of native cultural brokers, and all five reveal the articulation of outside curiosity with indigenous self-presentation.

A yachtsman named William Robinson arrived in Carti in western San Blas in August of 1928 with an introduction provided by a Kuna acquaintance in Colón (Robinson n.d., MWC). Summoned by Chief Olonibiginya, Robinson was interrogated in the Carti Suitupu gathering house. "I broke the ice by a speech upon my great and everlasting friendship for the chief's American friend M—— [undoubtedly William Markham] and my interest in the Indians and desire to give the outside world an account of their illustrious race" (Robinson n.d.).

> I . . . told him that the pen was mightier than the sword, and aroused his vanity in telling him how I would write to the American people about him and his people. . . . So finally the meeting came to a happy conclusion. . . . Thus began my friendship for the Chief, which was to prove invaluable later in giving me admission to their ceremonies and meetings, and in getting information upon their customs and beliefs. We had many a talk in the weeks that followed, and I learned much of the Indian viewpoint from Chief Olonebekinya.

As it turned out, conversations with the chief were frustrated by bad translation. Robinson's careful observations yielded much better results, especially in eleven tightly packed pages devoted to a chicha (n.d., 13–24), in part because Kuna friends kept him focused: "All the time I was there, someone always took care that if I was looking the wrong way, I would be told to 'Look see' and the event pointed out" (n.d.). Won over to admiration for the Indians (though not to optimism about their fate), Robinson later wrote up his experiences, but unhappily for Olonibiginya's hope of getting favorable notice for his people, they were never published.

Robinson was followed into Carti three years later by Matthew Stirling, head of the Bureau of American Ethnology and later known for studies of the Jivaro or Shuar. Stirling's interpreter told the chief of Carti, unnamed but undoubtedly Olonibiginya again, "how we wanted to make pictures of the village showing how the Indians lived so that the wakas [*waga*, i.e., Latins] could see that the simple life was best and as we wished to do it properly, wanted to enlist his cooperation" (Stirling n.d. [1931], NAA). After filming a house-building session, the visitors moved on to Nargana, where they repeated Garay's experiences: a pair of elderly musicians danced and played the panpipes for Stirling, while most of the rest of his party made a hit demonstrating the Charleston at a youth dance. The next day on Río Tigre, or Digir, they arranged to film chicha dancing in the streets, complete with beer and rum supplied by the visitors.

Stirling's brief involvement with the Kuna offered a snapshot of the Indians as they began, not only to perform their culture for outsiders, but also to objectify it to themselves, isolating elements and practices like chicha dancing and treating them as distinct institutions. It is surely no accident that a decade and a half later, when the Kuna created a new form of secular folkloric dancing called Noga Kope, the people of Tigre took the lead, nor that they responded in part to interest in native dances expressed in Panama and the Zone.[27]

Of the three books on the Kuna published by Zonians in this era, J. V. Tinnin's *Roughing It in the San Blas Islands* (1940) offered the least information, much of it wrong. Based on a single trip in the late 1930s made at the invitation of Nele and Alcibiades Iglesias, the latter a student of Anna Coope's who had returned from North American exile to head a native-run Protestant mission, Tinnin's account exemplifies the inspirational Protestant biography, devoted to publicizing evangelical fortitude and devotion, shown in this case by Iglesias and his North American wife Marvel. Travel narrative and a dusting of unreliable ethnography served merely to give flavor and verisimilitude to religious propaganda.[28]

Leon De Smidt, author of *Among the San Blas Indians of Panama* (1948), surpassed Tinnin by making *two* visits to the Indians in the mid-

1940s and by actually sitting down once to eat Kuna food. Also sponsored by Alcibiades Iglesias, De Smidt seems to have spent a good deal more time than Tinnin talking about Indian custom with native evangelists, and his blurry but acceptable sketch is marred only by a persistent mangling of native words.

Fred McKim, an employee of the Canal administration, began spending his vacations in San Blas in the early 1930s. During his first trip on a coconut schooner, he obtained permission to camp out on a barge used for storage anchored near an island village, very likely Nargana. On subsequent trips allowed to sleep ashore, he became close friends with Rubén Pérez Kantule, who guided and shaped his work. In 1935 McKim accompanied Henry Wassén on his trip to Nargana, and having cultivated Nele's friendship in the city, he was also able to visit several other islands.

After McKim's death in 1946, Wassén arranged for the Göteborg Museum to publish *San Blas, an Account of the Cuna Indians of Panama*, which had been carefully gone over by Pérez Kantule, along with a narrative of crossing the mountains into the Bayano with Pérez. In his writings, McKim comes across as attentive, observant, and unassuming. Despite his apparent lack of Spanish,[29] he made good use of English-speaking informants and opportunities for quiet observation. His hundred-page ethnography, though unsophisticated and sometimes oversimplified, offers a fairly reliable, well-rounded, and pleasant account of Kuna life, blemished only slightly by McKim's relentless and heavy-handed praise and defense of the Indians.[30]

In all five cases the role of Kuna middlemen or mediators in promoting research stands out. Either they invited a friendly Zonian to visit, as occurred with Tinnin and De Smidt, or else, as with McKim, Robinson, and Stirling, they readily grasped the opportunity once a visitor turned up, facilitating access, responding to questions, discoursing at length on topics of interest, and reminding their new friends to look-see when something significant was happening. Many individuals and villages may have acted out of little more than a diffuse sense that cultivating friendly outsiders couldn't hurt, but at least in the case of Nele, Olonibiginya, Alcibiades Iglesias, and Rubén Pérez, one can see a clear-cut policy and strategy to encourage positive accounts of their people that had grown out of their earlier experiences with Richard Marsh, William Markham, Minister South, and Erland Nordenskiöld.[31]

As for the amateur anthropologists, all of them were involved in the same kind of self-fashioning as Puig and Berengueras, using their connection with the Kuna to create a persona or partial identity, a major segment or element in the composite of things for which they were known to their peers.[32] In May of 1938, the *Panamá América* announced a talk at the Balboa YMCA by an employee named James Moore, a "recognized authority on the habits and customs of the San Blas Indians." Local experts like Moore and McKim may not have identified with the Indians as alter egos in the way that Marsh and Nordenskiöld did, and they may not have addressed an established professional audience, but they became known in local social circles for their special connection with an exotic group of natives. This process of individuation or self-fashioning was most apparent for McKim, whose ashes were entrusted after his death to a Kuna delegation to take back with them to the Bayano.

A FRIENDLY LATINA

It should not be thought that anyone who showed up in a Kuna village with a white face or speaking English was automatically accepted. Long-standing Kuna preferences for British and North Americans, reinforced by experiences in 1924 and 1925, did not blind them to the potential dangers posed by *any* outsider. If interested Panamanians other than Garay did not spend time with the Indians or try to learn about them firsthand in these years, it said more about *their* fears and attitudes than those of the Kuna.

That a Latin with the right attitude might be welcomed comes across clearly in a little book, *Con los indios cunas de Panamá*, written by a Guatemalan, María Albertina Gálvez (1952). Srta. Gálvez, while taking a course in library science at the University of Panama in 1950, made friends with a fellow student, Efrain Castillero, the librarian of Ustupu, and with the ubiquitous Rubén Pérez Kantule. Much taken with a public performance in the city by the newly formed folkloric dance group of Tigre, she flew out with Castillero to Ustupu (which had recently built a landing strip) for a brief but very intense introduction to Kuna culture.

Because Gálvez interlarded an hour-by-hour narrative of her stay with great masses of ethnographic information force-fed by her guides and teachers, her account conveys with special clarity the way in which the Kuna managed such visitors. After a description of two curing chanters heard from the streets on her first night, she immediately offered a chapter entitled "The chant, highest expression of Kuna sentiment" (1952, 25–29)—obviously the product of remarks dictated by her guides on their return to her lodgings.

On a subsequent evening, Gálvez was brought into the gathering house, where Nele's successor Olotebiliginya delivered a long discourse on Kuna sacred history, with Castillero struggling to keep pace in translation and Gálvez to write it all down. She repeated the lecture faithfully to her readers, with understandable small slips in the transcription of Kuna words but surprisingly few serious errors. (Like Richard Marsh before her, she misheard the Kuna pronunciation of Jehovah as a native name for God: Marsh rendered it as "A-oba," Gálvez as "Oba.")

Although the blurry illustrations show Gálvez as a middle-aged, light-skinned Latina with distinctly European features, in introducing herself to her Kuna hosts she claimed Maya ancestry, which evoked a warm response. From the remarks she attributed to Olotebiliginya, it seems that on Ustupu at least, they had fully accepted Richard Marsh's claim of a connection between their own ancestors and the ancient Maya, even the long-ago migration from the ancestral home of Tulan asserted by Marsh. With Olotebiliginya's encouragement, she followed his talk with a recitation of the major events of the *Popul Vuh* as she remembered them from published sources. Afterwards the chief took the floor again to lecture on marriage customs, chichas, and other topics, each of them given a short chapter in her book. He went on to defend Kuna patriotism, attachment to priests, nuns, and political leaders, and devotion to education, complaining "with a dolorous expression, of the bad reputation that had been given them" (1952, 92). Gálvez was also introduced to Guillermo Hayans, who was present that evening (1952, 99). All in all, she devoted more than thirty pages to what she learned in that one gathering (1952, 63–99).

On her departure from Ustupu, bearing gifts and greetings to the Indians of Guatemala, her plane touched down at Ailigandi and again at Nargana, where she visited with Rubén Pérez Kantule and fellow students from her library course in Panama. Once back in Guatemala, she sent a copy of the *Popul Vuh* to Hayans, who, she was later told, read it out in the gathering and was trying to translate it into Kuna.

Gálvez's little book was published in Guatemala in a series of popular texts. Its generosity and pro-Indian attitudes were made possible by a brief opening in that country's tortured history under the progressive president Jacobo Arbenz, soon to be ended by a CIA-promoted coup. Though Gálvez's highly feminine and Latin American writing style differed radically from that of her more restrained Anglo-Saxon counterparts, she certainly competed with Fred McKim in enthusiasm for the Kuna. (Her favorite adjectives were *maravilloso* and *encantador*.) Studiously neutral concerning indigenous religious belief and practices, she held nothing back in her praise for Kuna democracy, egalitarianism, and gender relations, and she even implied that the 1925 rebellion had been justified. The Kuna could not have asked for a more devoted friend and advocate.

RENEWED PANAMANIAN INTEREST

By the 1940s, growing international concern with the Indian Question touched Panama. The famous Peruvian politician and theorist of "Indoamérica," Haya de la Torre, passed through Panama several times during the 1930s in his restless travels,[33] and it is very likely that a few intellectuals were reading the works of José Carlos Mariátegui, José Maria Arguedas, and Mexican *indigenista* anthropologists. In April of 1940, the First Inter-American Indigenist Congress, held in Pátzcuaro, Mexico, marked the beginning of a new era in ideas on indigenous-state relations.[34] In addition to official delegates, three countries (Panama, Mexico, and the United States) sent Indian representatives: Panama dispatched Rubén Pérez Kantule, along with a government minister and Octavio Méndez Pereira, rector of the University of Panama and author of the recently published novel praising *mestizaje* and early native resistance. Méndez Pereira signed the official proceedings for his country, but it was Pérez Kantule who was elected to the conference board of directors.

The long list of resolutions taken at the Congress, though sounding in retrospect ambivalent, paternalistic, and cautiously ameliorist, especially regarding the legal rights of Indians, did call for agrarian reform, bilingual education, respect for indigenous languages and identity, cultural rather than racial conceptualizations of indigeneity, and the formation of national indigenous institutes (De la Peña 2005, 726–727; Favre 1998, 103–104). The resolutions signaled a growing international concern with the sufferings of native peoples and a partial valorization of indigenous cultures, trends reflected by increased Panamanian interest in pre-Columbian and contact-period chiefdoms and, to a lesser extent, in the Kuna and Guaymí. In the absence of professional anthropologists, the task of ethnography fell in Panama to a pair of geographers. Both dealt with Nele Kantule, and once again the efforts of Kuna brokers to facilitate sympathetic notice are immediately apparent.

In 1940, Angel Rubio, Spanish by birth but married to a Panamanian and the first professor of geography at the University of Panama, published "Indios y culturas indígenas panameñas," a review of international literature on Isthmian archaeology, ethnology, and ethnohistory, of which four pages were dedicated to the Kuna. Dry, scholarly, and neutral, the article did include long quotes from the Catholic mission report of the previous year depicting the Kuna as indolent, superstitious, and backwards. In 1944, after an interview with Nele Kantule and others on a mission to the city, Rubio spent ten days on a survey of the coast, which included a brief visit to Nele on Ustupu, as part of an official effort to determine Balboa's route to the Pacific.[35]

In 1947, Manuel María Alba, the geographer who two decades before had published the article praising Chief Urraca, brought out a new article entitled "Hombres y dioses cunas," based almost entirely on an interview with Nele and two others on a visit to the city, possibly the same encounter in which Nele had met Angel Rubio. Alba offered a few misleading remarks on the Kuna political hierarchy,[36] but his primary interest lay in native religious beliefs, which, he breathlessly told his readers, had for the very first time been entrusted to an outsider. Like Marsh and Gálvez, he misunderstood his informants' remarks on Jehovah, identifying the Kuna deity as Oba, and he inferred from their use of the Spanish word for tomb that the indigenous heaven was a place called Tummba (1947, 13).[37]

The following year Alba published *Introducción al estudio de las lenguas indígenas de Panamá*, with a forty-two-page table of basic vocabulary in eight languages and brief ethnographic sketches of the Kuna, Guaymí, and Chocó languages. Displaying considerable ambivalence, he praised the national government for its "benign policies" and its efforts to raise the Indians to "the cultural level enjoyed by other citizens of the Republic," while also regretting the "adulteration" of native custom and rejoicing that religious beliefs had survived the "tempest" of missionization (1948, 6, 9). Most of all he lavished praise on Kuna politics—"the most democratic governmental organization in any part of our continent to which a people in their cultural condition could aspire" (1948, 56)—though he still got many of the details wrong.

Not everyone shared Alba's sympathies. The following passage, directed as always against their refusal to submit or admit inferiority, comes from the first bachelor's thesis on the Kuna at the University of Panama (Páez 1941, 11).

> The years passed, and the environment and inheritance engendered in the indian a character feeble, distrustful, unsociable, resistant, cunning and apathetic.[38] He always sees in men foreign to his race a

dangerous element and from this comes the reason for his isolation and rebellion. They are crafty and fickle, a lesson taken from their persecutors, and they have repaid them with interest. Since he holds without care everything that happens in his surroundings, he only works to maintain his existence and from that comes his eternal laziness. He shows himself indolent to all movement of progress and lives only for himself and his own.

ACCULTURATION AND DECLINE

During the 1930s, probably the most widely read works on the Kuna were an absorbing but anthropologically naïve summary of secondary sources, "Cuna Folk of Darien," offered as an appendix to the pirate Wafer's narrative (in Joyce 1934), the other an unreliable and in places mendacious narrative of his adventures by Richard Marsh (1934), which portrayed the Kuna much as he had in his 1925 Declaration of Independence. The first doctoral dissertation devoted to the Kuna, also the first work based on an extended field trip and the first informed by anthropological theory, David Stout's *San Blas Cuna Acculturation: An Introduction,* did not appear until 1947.

Stout had in fact carried out his research several years earlier while a doctoral student at Columbia University, first during a visit to Göteborg in 1939–1940, and then in three or four months of fieldwork in Carti, Tigre, and Nargana, with Rubén Pérez, Alcibiades Iglesias, and Fred McKim as three of his key informants. After military service during World War II, Stout published his monograph with the Viking Fund in 1947, and the following year Columbia accepted it unchanged as his dissertation.

Stout's slim volume, a study of social change under the acculturation rubric then dominant in North American anthropology, began with a succinct, dispassionate ethnographic survey, one much clearer than Nordenskiöld's great volume. Soon consulted widely as the most approachable English-language summary of Kuna culture, its one notable defect was the lack of distinction between Stout's own field results and information from his predecessors. The historical analysis that followed, the first serious attempt to analyze the principal changes in Kuna society since the sixteenth century, displayed both the strengths and the limitations of the acculturation model.

Acculturation, meaning the processes by which members of one society took on cultural traits from another, was the concept adopted in the

1930s and 1940s, first to recast the old notion of diffusion as a dynamic and historically documented process, and second to come to terms with cultural change, especially among native North Americans (Herskovits 1937, 1938). Although a formative "Memorandum for the Study of Acculturation" (Redfield, Linton, and Herskovits 1936) pointed to mutual influence between groups in contact, most studies in fact described a unidirectional process by which small indigenous societies or peasant and immigrant communities accepted elements from the West or from national society (Beals 1953, 628–629). Although acculturation studies often noted the agency shown by recipient peoples as they adapted, synthesized, or outright rejected traits from a dominant culture, change was largely understood in terms of modifications to the cultural repertoires of subordinate groups or sectors, with an assumed endpoint of assimilation or at best marginalization in a cultural enclave. Lacking clear explanatory principles or a dynamic model of change, students of acculturation, to the extent that they went beyond historical particularism, often fell back on individualist psychology.[39] Though distinctively North American as an academic focus, the acculturation concept strongly influenced Mexican scholarship and indigenist policies through anthropologists like Manuel Gamio, Moisés Sáenz, Aguirre Beltrán, and others who trained in the United States (De la Peña 2005).

Very much in this mold, Stout's analysis of Kuna acculturation struggled to fit a complex regional history into an accountant's column of cultural addition and subtraction, balancing elements lost over time against borrowings from dominant outsiders, especially English and North Americans. He assumed a continuum of acculturation among contemporary Kuna communities much like the one posited by Robert Redfield (1934, 1941) for the Yucatán, treating Nargana as the endpoint toward which other villages were tending (Stout 1947, 7). Like his teacher, Ralph Linton (1936, 343), Stout accounted for borrowings in terms of the relative prestige of donor groups (Stout 1947, 72, 109) and, in particular, an urge on the part of the Kuna, "largely unconscious, to identify themselves through imitation and emulation with English-speaking whites" (1947, 108).

Why the warm and open Kuna affection for North Americans had to be excavated from their collective unconsciousness was never made clear. While Stout gave due attention to Kuna relations with the government, newspapers, and political parties, he made so much of their North American leanings and connections as to obscure determined Kuna efforts to make a place for themselves in Panamanian national society. In a modified, attenuated, scholarly form, Stout was still following Nordenskiöld and the amateurs from the Zone in defining the Kuna in terms of their separatism, characterizing them as essentially *not-Panamanian*.

Like many acculturation theorists, Stout expressed little confidence in the survival of indigenous lifeways, and he claimed that among the Kuna "the general trend has been one of deculturation" (1947, 107), a conclusion endorsed in the *Handbook of South American Indians* (Steward 1948; 1949, 765) and again a few years later in a textbook published by Julian Steward and Louis Faron (1959, 224–230), both of which depicted the Kuna as the culturally impoverished remnants of what Steward termed "Circum-Caribbean chiefdoms." Part of a salutary recognition that many surviving native polities were much smaller and simpler than their pre-Columbian predecessors, this model nonetheless misrepresented the trajectory of change among the Kuna: after the initial sixteenth-century holocaust and the colonial wars, their society had if anything grown in size, complexity, and vigor.[40] While avoiding explicit predictions, Stout's gloomy account pointed toward continued loss and assimilation, a conclusion in which his theoretical presuppositions were undoubtedly validated by experience in the field: during his months in San Blas, which were mostly divided between Nargana and Carti, the changes Stout observed in Nargana would have been condemned repeatedly by his informants in Carti as they voiced the pessimism about change and cultural decay (and the antipathy to Nargana) typical of Kuna traditionalists.

Stout's one-sided account underlines native vulnerability in the ethnographic process: the Kuna could influence the field situation, feeding a visitor interpretation as well as fact, making friends and enlisting sympathy, but once the visitor returned home, they had no control over what ended up in print. Had they known of their portrayal as the washed-out remnants of past greatness, they might not have been pleased, but there was absolutely nothing they could do about it.

At mid-century, the constellation of Panamanian researchers called for by Narciso Garay had yet to appear; the corpus of ethnographic writing on the Kuna was still modest; and with the exception of Stout, the Swedes, and Garay himself, amateurs still predominated. Within a few years, all this would change. Amateurs and foreigners, far from disappearing, would increase exponentially. But a professionalized national anthropology would also gain hold, in public discourse and government policy as well as the Panamanian university system. Indigenous cultures would play a much larger role in the national consciousness than ever before. And thousands of pages would be written about the Kuna, by Latin Panamanians, by Europeans and North Americans, and by the Kuna themselves.

The Ethnographic Boom, 1950–

NINE

From mid-century on, the ethnographic picture grew immensely more complicated, as improved access, amateur interest in native cultures, and the growth of anthropology as a discipline brought dozens of anthropologists and hundreds of aficionados of exotica into San Blas, turning Kunaology into a cottage industry. A growing fascination with mola blouses refocused attention on the work of indigenous women, in the process regendering ethnographic representations and moving the Kuna and their art to the center of Panamanian national iconography. An influx, first of Peace Corps volunteers and then of foreign anthropologists, added new strands to external alliances and dialogues, while the professionalization and politicization of the human sciences thrust anthropologists into the world of policy and activism. Given the complexity of these developments and the proliferation of ethnographers and ethnography in this era, I have had to pick and choose ruthlessly in this chapter, excluding or slighting works of great value, some by close colleagues and friends, in favor of research and texts that in my judgment best illustrate the evolution of the field.

JOSÉ REVERTE, THE AMATEUR PROFESSIONAL

Interest in and concern for indigenous cultures grew in postwar Panama, but only slowly. A wide-ranging volume of essays commemorating the Republic's fiftieth anniversary in 1953 included but a single entry on anything indigenous, a brief glimpse of pre-Columbian art (A. Méndez 1953).

A key essay by Hernán Porras (1953) on ethnic, regional, and class-based groups ignored other Indians altogether, while alluding to the Kuna only as a people who, except in 1925, had stood apart from national life.

In 1956, Panama held its first and only Indigenist Congress (Comisión Permanente 1959). In addition to prominent politicians and scholars with Indian connections or interests such as ex-intendente and friend of the Kuna Félix Oller and the geographer Angel Rubio, delegates included twenty-one Guaymí, three Chocó, and forty-six Kuna, among them most leading Kuna intellectuals other than Guillermo Hayans. After tense discussion of the nature of the congress (would it be *indígena* or *indigenista?*) and the proper ethnic makeup of its governing body, Alcibiades Iglesias was chosen to preside over the sessions, but the *mesa directiva,* except for Rubén Pérez Kantule, was constituted entirely of Latin Panamanians. Resolutions and addresses, showing the same mix of concern, respect, and condescension evident in previous international congresses, condemned the Spanish conquest, defended recent Catholic missions, and questioned treatment of indigenous plantation workers and Kuna children boarding in the city. It was agreed that Nele Kantule, Urraca, and Benito Juárez should be declared *"genios tutelares"* of the Congress, that the eloquence of Kuna speakers demonstrated their great potential, and that university programs in anthropology and more *indigenista* congresses were badly needed.

Although the Congress was in fact never repeated, within a few years the University of Panama and the Catholic University of Santa María la Antigua had indeed established positions in anthropology, providing bases for the country's first professionals, Reina Torres de Araúz and José Manuel Reverte Coma. Reverte, a Spanish medical doctor and self-trained anthropologist, lived in Panama from 1950 to 1968, during which time he participated in exploration and fieldwork both in San Blas and elsewhere while also working in medicine, public health, and radio. Endowed with immense energy, curiosity, and self-confidence, Reverte felt entitled to write on almost any subject. Publications on the Kuna included a long chapter in *Río Bayano* ("región de mañana")(1961a, 71–130) and a number of articles and pamphlets on marriage, curing, navigation, and "sexual life."[1]

After returning to Spain, Reverte carried on at the same pace, based since 1994 at a Madrid museum named for himself, the Museo de Antropología Médica-Forense Paleopatología y Criminalistica Profesor Reverte Coma.[2] In addition to publishing works on Voodoo, the "Curse of the Pharaohs," and many other topics, Reverte continued writing on Panama. A return to the Isthmus in 1974 to film a television series led to the semi-autobiographical *Operación Panamá*, with several chapters devoted to experiences with the Kuna (1977, 89–177). Much more recently, Reverte has published an annotated gazetteer of Kuna place names (2001) and a study of the Emberá called *Tormenta en el Darién* (2002).

Scattered hints and anecdotes in Reverte's Kuna writing suggest he went often to the field for busy visits lasting days or weeks. Apart from the anecdotal *Operación Panamá*, his ethnographic descriptions were mostly straightforward and—except for the article on marriage, which cited antiquated sources like Lubbock and Frazer—largely devoid of theory. The exception was his longest and most ambitious work, *Literatura oral de los indios cunas* (1968), in which native texts and ethnography were swamped by European rhetoric, folklore theory, a priori assumptions, guesswork, and displays of erudition.

Reverte, it should be acknowledged, was the first after Narciso Garay to argue that Kuna oral poetry merited stylistic analysis or to recognize its extensive use of parallelism. In his tireless way he elicited useful summaries of a great many chants. But his understanding of roles, genres, and performance was confused, and he doubly distorted Father's Way, first by insisting that all Kuna texts are fixed, anonymous, and performed from memorization (cf. Chapin 1983; Sherzer 1983, 1990), and second by recording historical episodes as if they were discrete chants. Compounding the recurrent confusion caused by Kuna pronunciation of Jehovah, Reverte asserted that Eoba (Gálvez's and Alba's Oba, Marsh's A-oba) was the god of corn *(oba)* (1968, 51, 141–145).

Reverte's strikingly ambivalent account mixed high praise for Kuna verbal art and frequent allusions to his friends among the Indian elite with the most antiquated and derogatory evolutionism, in which archaism was offered as the key to almost every aspect of their oral poetry.[3] The nadir in this respect was reached in the chapter entitled "Primitive Mentality" (1968, 37–45), in which Reverte invoked Lucien Lévy-Bruhl and a work called *Pioneering on the Congo* (Bentley 1900) as contemporary sources proving the mental deficiencies of natives—"the difficulty they have in understanding abstractions . . . and the fatigue that the act of thinking produces" (1968, 39).[4]

Concerning his own intellectual accomplishments, Reverte wrote that the Kuna tongue was: "sonorous and easy, . . . simple for a Spanish-speaking man" (1968, 108), and he claimed to have delivered several speeches in the language (1977, 168). His written use of Kuna is actually quite variable, correct in many places if oversimplified, wildly wrong in others.[5] *Sulup mas kunne,* "eat eagle," a metaphor for marrying, for instance, is mistranslated as "eat lobster" *(dulup),* as if newlyweds were sitting down to a shellfish dinner (1977, 115).[6] Most of all, in the volume on oral literature Reverte blindly followed his informants and translators, reproducing text excerpts written down for him that he did not himself understand more than partially.[7]

Johannes Fabian's claim (1983) that anthropology places peoples like the Kuna "out of time," whether valid for the field as a whole, applies perfectly to Reverte, who quoted with approval the German theorist Erich Kahler characterizing primitives as "blind alleys broken off from human evolution" (Reverte 1968, 40). For Reverte, the Kuna were survivals from a past age whose greatest utility was to serve as living laboratories for investigators like himself. Although, like Nordenskiöld, Reverte did allow for outstanding individuals among Kuna savants, he was sure that their simplemindedness, failure to assimilate, and general backwardness were racially determined and thus unchangeable, as was demonstrated by the failures of literate Indians, who should otherwise show the improving effects of education:

> There is something within them that makes them feel a strong tug towards their own . . . the same as the little tiger raised since a cub . . . feels the call of the jungle and flees or takes a swipe at someone . . . it is common in Panama and there are even proverbs that recognize it, considering the Indian as ungrateful. (1968, 41)

With this astounding invocation of a racist proverb to prove Indian atavism and inferiority,[8] Reverte slandered not just the Kuna as a whole, but in particular the very assistants and translators who, to an extent he never acknowledged, made his own studies possible.

REINA TORRES AND THE INSTITUTIONALIZATION OF PANAMANIAN ANTHROPOLOGY

For all his energy and his many connections with Panamanian elites, José Reverte never achieved the influence of his female rival, Reina Torres de Araúz. Having taken her training in history and anthropology at the University of Buenos Aires in a program staffed by European refugees (A. Araúz 1982, 7), Torres de Araúz received her bachelor's degree in 1955 and her doctorate in 1963. She began teaching in the Instituto Nacional after her return home in the mid-1950s, but soon moved to the University of Panama, where she presided over the field of anthropology for a quarter-century.

Torres de Araúz published assiduously on a wide variety of anthropological, archaeological, and ethnohistoric topics, and her ethnographic research paid most attention to the Emberá and Wounán Chocó. Her culminating work, *Panamá indígena,* published in 1980 two years before her early death at age 49, encompassed all of the country's native peoples. The Kuna case, however, drew her back repeatedly and seems to have deeply marked her intellectual evolution and indigenist policies.[9]

Torres de Araúz's first monograph, *La mujer cuna* (1957), was solicited by the Instituto Indigenista Interamericano as part of a projected comparative study of Indian women in Peru, Mexico, and Panama (see Pereira de Padilla and Segura 1983, 84). For this brief work, she depended on previous publications as much as her own fieldwork, during which she apparently kept mostly to the relative security of Nargana and Ustupu. She criticized some conditions in the lives of Kuna women (too much hot pepper in the diet), but overall she called them a cultural aristocracy. "The indigenous Cuna woman is, thus, the queen of her household and the outstanding *(señera)* figure in her culture" (1957, 4). Torres de Araúz's exaggeration of female prominence and her blindness to the moderate but quite obvious male domination of Kuna public life suggests that *La mujer cuna* must be seen, among other things, as a veiled ethnographic allegory (Clifford 1986), a metaphorical depiction of the author's own goals as an emerging female leader in Panamanian national society.

Thereafter Torres de Araúz worked most frequently in the Bayano and Darién, often in the company of her husband Amado, an engineer and explorer. In 1959, Amado led a four-month motorized expedition across the then-roadless Darién and on to Bogotá, during which Reina gathered information for her doctoral dissertation on the Chocó.[10] Later she took student groups for work-visits to Indian villages in the Bayano (Anonymous 1964, 144) while continuing to visit the region with her husband, sometimes by helicopter.

Perhaps her greatest opportunity arose when the United States entertained the bizarre and dangerous idea of building a sea-level canal using nuclear explosives. The Battelle Institute contracted with Torres de Araúz to carry out environmental impact investigations (1966–1968) for what was called Route 17, to run from Mulatupu-Sasardi in eastern San Blas across the low mountains and the Chucunaque basin to the Pacific (Torres de Araúz 1967, 1968). Her report, *Human Ecology of Route 17* (1970), based on demographic and subsistence surveys with Kuna, Chocó, and nonindigenous groups on both sides of the cordillera, provided information still useful today.

Torres de Araúz's Germanic professors, in addition to a willingness to work in all branches of anthropology, seem to have imbued her with a devotion to facts scrubbed clean of theory or interpretation. Apart from *La mujer cuna*, in which she insistently pushed her feminist theme, Reina's cultural descriptions were bland and impersonal. The Route 17 report, translated and edited by the Battelle Institute, took impersonality to an extreme, which in the context of deciding whether to explode nuclear bombs in Indian territory, is distinctly unsettling. Her other work reads in much the same way, however, as a kind of scientific inventory or survey. Even in *El Darién, etnoecología de una región histórica* (1975), she seldom treated one cultural or natural fact as causally or analytically prior to another.

But Torres de Araúz emphatically saw anthropology as a policy discipline, inspiring her to speak out concerning archaeological and historic preservation, integration of indigenous peoples, and, more cautiously, the environmental impact of development. After the idea of an atomic canal was abandoned, she touted her study as the kind of safeguard needed to screen out harmful projects.[11] In the Route 17 report itself, however, all but six pages of it devoted to a studiously neutral research summary, she avoided firm conclusions on "a Possible Population Transfer" (1970, 167), and concerning the Kuna in particular, she suggested that their rebellious history might have created "a sort of collective psychosis" (1970, 168). Despite her environmental concerns, moreover, she supported dam and highway projects and mass relocations. Like the first generations of British anthropologists in Africa, Torres de Araúz evidently saw her function as guiding and informing, not challenging, government programs.

In her classes, writings, and public statements, the great policy question for Torres de Araúz was always the nation, its integration, and its component peoples.[12] According to her husband Amado, "she did not participate greatly in indigenist politics. Perhaps the sociological orientations and the administrative problems of this movement did not attract her for being so time-consuming and frequently under the control of demagogues" (1982, 15). In her writings, living peoples sometimes seemed most valuable as components, along with archaeological remains and historic documents, of a shared national patrimony. She did, nonetheless, speak out on behalf of ethnic minorities. Exercising considerable influence in the Torrijos government, with the General himself as well as with ex-students and other elites,[13] she helped shape the Indianist policies central to the regime's populist program (Martínez Mauri 2007, 113). She played a leading role as delegate and vice president of a commission that produced a revised national constitution adopted in 1972, which called for protection of Indian lands and set aside seats for them on a new representative council, an innovation she felt would strongly encourage political integration.[14]

An immensely energetic empire-builder, Torres de Araúz successively headed the old Museo Nacional (1969–1970) and the Patrimonio Histórico (1970–1980), the latter a key agency in the Ministry of Culture. Frustrated in early attempts to promote a national indigenous institute (González 1986, 110), she founded a Centro de Investigaciones Antropológicas (with the unfortunate acronym CIA); two journals, *Hombre y Cultura* and *Patrimonio Histórico;* and a new national center, the Museo del Hombre Panameño (later renamed in her honor after her death), as well as several specialized museums (González 1986, 114). Through the 1970s she sponsored a series of large-scale scholarly conferences, and at least at the undergraduate level, she actively encouraged research and thesis-writing (McKay 1964; Pereira de Padilla and Segura 1983, 235–296). In an era in which North American anthropologists found their work thwarted or even excluded in much of Latin America, Reina was invariably welcoming, helpful, and gracious to foreign scholars.

She did less well, however, at mentoring the next generation of Panamanian anthropologists. Keeping tight control of teaching and administration, she blocked and sidetracked potential rivals and successors. She did not, moreover, inculcate the ideals of long-term fieldwork or learning native languages, nor did she always encourage other Panamanians to carry out serious research where she had worked before herself, which excluded much of the country. With one or two notable exceptions, the most productive ethnographers of the next generation were largely trained abroad, studied nonindigenous groups, and found employment in agencies outside Reina's control. In 1971, a majority of junior anthropologists in the country created an alternative group called the Asociación Panameña de Antropología, with its own short-lived journal, in an unsuccessful attempt to break her hold on the field (see F. Herrera 1989, 104–105).

In her publications Torres de Araúz treated the Kuna sympathetically on the whole: though she depicted the "Revolución Tule" as unfortunate and Richard Marsh as a self-deluded fool (Torres de Araúz 1973), she also blamed the 1925 rebellion on misguided and coercive culture change (in

Pereira de Padilla and Segura 1983, 333-334). It could be argued, however, that she did the Kuna the most good not when she singled them out for special attention, but rather when she included them in a larger national mosaic, as she did in the Museo del Hombre Panameño, which included exhibits on twentieth-century urban immigrants as well as ancient and contemporary native cultures. Reina's final book, *Panamá indígena*, offered a strikingly pluralist vision:

> In our judgment, an indigenist policy should not tend towards ethnic elimination—in its most complete sense, cultural and racial—as a means of complete and final integration to the "national culture", but rather towards the conservation of the essentials of those cultures ... within the political context of a pluricultural nation. In that way, they persist as a substratum of the "national culture" and exhibit their own individuality in the economic, social and political game of the nation to which they belong. (1980, 337)

As Francisco Herrera has pointed out (n.d. [2004]), Torres de Araúz's publications never moved beyond description and social classification to an historical analysis of ethnic groups in Panama's political evolution, nor did she offer a clear plan for reconciling ethnic and national identity. Nonetheless, she did more than anyone else to justify the persistence of indigenous territories and lifeways and to confirm Panama as a multiethnic and multicultural nation.

If Torres de Araúz was coming to grips with thinking about the Kuna and their place in the national mosaic, neither she nor any other national anthropologists were spending much time with them in the field. With some notable exceptions—a handful of articles and BA theses, a dissertation on the Bayano Kuna by a Mexican-born anthropologist (Brizuela 1973), and much more recently, fine studies of hunting, migrants, and urban Kuna discourse by Jorge Ventocilla (1992), Raúl Leis (1992), and Marta de Gerdes (1998), as well as distinguished but mostly archival ethnohistorical works by Francisco Herrera (1984, 1987, 1989) and Alfredo Castillero Calvo (1995)—few non-Indian Panamanians have devoted themselves to Kuna ethnography. This absence can be explained in various ways: by a perennial lack of funding, discouragement from Torres de Araúz in her day, the predominance of jobs in applied anthropology (F. Herrera n.d. [2004]), and the intensely urban orientation of the national middle class.[15] But it is hard to avoid the conclusion that many Latin Panamanians still found daunting the prospect of learning an indigenous language or living with Indians as assertive and unyielding as the Kuna.[16]

AMATEUR ENTHUSIASM

During the period in which Reina Torres and Reverte began working with the Kuna, foreign anthropologists were notable for their absence. The Kuna had emerged in postwar North American anthropology as a well-known ethnographic case, a staple in the samples of numerous comparative studies, based primarily on the work of Stout and Nordenskiöld and two secondary accounts by Elliot Joyce and Donald Marshall.[17] Allotted one of the earliest and largest entries in the new cross-cultural database, the Human Relations Area Files, the Kuna also appeared prominently in the *Handbook of South American Indians*, a massive ethnological survey brought out between 1946 and 1950 under the direction of Julian Steward (1948). However, the deculturation model adopted by Stout, combined with his often quite dispiriting depiction of recent social change, left the impression that little of interest remained to be studied, and with one or two marginal exceptions,[18] North American and European professionals mostly left the Kuna alone for two decades.[19]

They abandoned the field to amateur enthusiasts, first among them a geneticist from Georgia named Clyde Keeler (known to the Kuna as Kilobipi, or "Little Uncle"). Drawn to San Blas for biological investigation of Kuna albinos, Keeler soon began branching out into imaginative ethnography. Like many enthusiastic autodidacts, Keeler personally embodied Tyler's doctrine of survivals, faithfully preserving theory from a previous anthropological age. His first and most modest book, *Land of the Moon-Children* (1956), usefully reported results of Keeler's privileged access to the Kuna under the informal sponsorship of Alcibiades Iglesias and the Baptist mission. Subsequent works like *Secrets of the Cuna Earthmother* (1960) and *Apples of Immortality from the Cuna Tree of Life* (1961; see also 1969, 1987) cast aside all restraint in favor of a mélange of nineteenth-century evolutionism and radical diffusionism, portraying the Kuna as a matriarchal society with an ancient Middle Eastern religion—notions that had a powerful impact on subsequent amateur work and at least one professional study (Holloman 1969).

Keeler was accompanied on later trips by Robert VandeCastle, a parapsychologist from the University of Virginia interested in testing the paranormal abilities of Kuna seers (VandeCastle 1975); VandeCastle subsequently returned several times on his own, sometimes assisted by a psychic and a woman diagnosed with multiple personalities, whom he later married.

Keeler and VandeCastle were followed by a horde of adventure tourists and aficionados of native artisanry and exotica, drawn to a culture simultaneously exotic and accessible. Regional tourism had picked up since the late 1940s, with construction of a modest inn on El Porvenir and visits to Carti and Mandinga by cruise ships; several Kuna villages built airfields for light planes, opening the region to flights from Panama City. Through the 1950s and 1960s, the number of air strips, cruise ship visits, and tourists all increased greatly, and an international market opened for the mola blouses worn by Kuna women and the front and back panels cut loose from blouses or sewn specially for the tourist trade. By 1970 two Americans had opened small resorts, a third was guiding day-trippers on boat tours, two Kuna entrepreneurs had built simple *posadas* near El Porvenir, and numerous yachtsmen began cruising the archipelago.[20]

Dozens of popular articles also appeared, most written for the travel sections of Sunday newspapers, based on brief visits and a few conversations with the same crew of English-speaking guides, resort proprietors, and other local experts, each article offering variations on a small set of persistent themes—San Blas as a mysterious outpost of the Vikings or Mesopotamia, or more often as a matriarchal paradise comprising exactly 365 coconut-covered islands slumbering in the past until shortly before the author arrived. Some articles carried on the theme of Kuna independence, but in this less outspoken era, the matter of native racial consciousness was typically euphemized or omitted.[21]

The more adventurous travelers struck out on their own, staying in rented rooms or arranging to live for a few weeks with a Kuna family. Others made contact through the Baptist Church in the Canal Zone, through the mission hospital founded in 1966 on Ailigandi, or else, like William Markham and others before them, through friendships with Kuna men working on U.S. installations. Mola buyers began touring the region, some snapping up hundreds of panels per trip, and a handful of Zonians and others carried out informal fieldwork, returning to stay each time with the same Indian families.[22]

A number of travel books and ethnographic sketches in the tradition of Tinnin and De Smidt followed, such as Joanne Kelly's *Cuna* (1966) and Hanns Ebensten's *Volleyball with the Cuna Indians and Other Gay Travel Adventures* (1987)—and even more, a slew of publications on mola

FIGURE 9.1 Panamanian stamp

blousework: books and articles on mola art, mola motifs, molas for children, mola patterns to sew oneself, even two mola coloring books.[23] While no single moment can account for this fascination with Kuna needlework, much followed from two exhibits in New York City in 1968–1969 and a review by the *New York Times* critic John Canaday (12/29/68, p. D25), in which he called molas "brilliant artifacts at the very least" and "very often works of fine art." Also influential was an engaging coffee-table book produced by two devoted folklorists, Ann Parker and Avon Neal (1977), whose striking illustrations displayed the range and creativity of mola designs. Molas also began attracting serious study by anthropologists, eventually including Mari Lyn Salvador, Lawrence Hirschfeld, Joel and Dina Sherzer, Herta Puls, Gunther and Ursula Hartmann, Mary Helms, Karin Tice, Renée Sweig, Michel Perrin, Louise Agnew, and Paolo Fortis.[24]

The mola craze, a prominent part of the developing global market in non-Western art and handicrafts, contributed to a thorough regendering of Kuna anthropology, which had been anticipated by Reina Torres's study of Kuna women (1957). Before World War II, students of Kuna culture, all but two of them men, had worked almost exclusively with male informants on male-dominated institutions.[25] Now, however, mola-consciousness began to give Kuna women and female creativity their due, and indeed, in popular writing, to obscure that of Kuna men, a trend reinforced by attention to Kuna matrilocal residence, which was easily misinterpreted as matrilineality or even (in the case of amateurs like Keeler) as matriarchy. Unlike Panamanian nationals—who were regularly exposed to Kuna men working in restaurants, banana plantations, and the Canal Zone, as well as to frequent newspaper reports on general congresses and other male-dominated events—foreign tourists, mola-buyers, and amateur anthropologists largely dealt with Kuna women, often with those women at their most outspoken and demanding as they sold their handiwork, leaving a strong imprint on the new version of gender. Rather than a male leader or ritualist, the prototypical imagined Kuna was now an assertive and highly creative matriarch.[26]

The new generation of popular works about the Kuna, as they recycled the same ideas and "facts," seldom added to understanding as amateurs like McKim had, except on the technical details of mola-sewing. Moreover, although the old Kuna-Zone alliance was carried on by the Southern Baptists and the U.S. military, amateur anthropologists no longer acted as advocates or intermediaries in the way that Markham and McKim had once done. The growing interest in molas and mola-makers, nonetheless, did contribute significantly to making a place for the Kuna in Panama, reversing the value of indigenous women, their bodies, and their dress from tokens of a stigmatized barbaric identity to positive national symbols. Latin Panamanians were much slower than Zonians to buy molas or to cultivate an interest in contemporary indigenous cultures, but as the international market in native artisanry and the number of cruise ships visiting Carti and Mandinga grew through the 1970s, mola designs and the faces of Kuna women began turning up in Panama City on place mats, postage stamps, gas station walls, and even on plastic sheeting, offered as emblems of Isthmian local color and, over time, of Panama itself. During the 1980s and early 1990s, while the turmoil of the Noriega era and the aftermath of the U.S. invasion kept tourists away from the rest of Panama, cruise ships continued to transit the canal and call in Kuna Yala (as San Blas is now called), reinforcing international interest in Kuna art and in the process consolidating its place in the national iconography.[27]

A PLETHORA OF *MERGIS*

Amateur dominance of foreign ethnography could not last. With the great expansion of graduate programs in the United States and Europe, it was inevitable that a people as accessible, colorful, and well known as the Kuna would again begin attracting academic attention. First to come was Regina Holloman, a doctoral student at Northwestern University, who carried out seven months of fieldwork in 1966 and 1967. Holloman's dissertation, "Developmental Change in San Blas" (1969), a study of social networks and adaptive transformation in the framework of modernization theory, covered a tremendous range of previously unexamined topics—from demography and ecology through household organization, economic cooperatives, local and regional politics, to relations with the Peace Corps and the U.S. military—as if Holloman felt impelled to make up for all the social and economic omissions of past ethnographers. Although she wrote only a handful of articles on her research (1971, 1975, 1976) and never published her thesis, Holloman nonetheless reshaped the field by offering the first serious, multistranded analysis of Kuna external relations and the first representation of Kuna culture as a continuously changing adaptive mechanism.

Holloman was followed in the 1970s by a large cohort of young fieldworkers, beginning with two couples from the University of Pennsylvania, Joel and Dina Sherzer and James and June Howe, who were directed toward San Blas by Olga Linares, a Harvard-educated Panamanian anthropologist then at Penn.[28] During 1970 and 1971, the Howes studied kinship and political organization on Niatupu, the Sherzers the ethnography of speaking on Mulatupu, while Richard Costello from the University of California investigated political economy and change on Río Azúcar. These were the first ethnographers (other than Catholic missionaries and the Kuna themselves) to stay in the field for a year or more, and in the case of the Howes and Sherzers, the first to work in the native language. In publications since then, Joel Sherzer and James Howe, together with Mac Chapin, have in different ways pushed Kuna studies away from Nordenskiöld's concern with private knowledge toward the public sphere and an emphasis on events, discourse, practice, and performance, all concerns of contemporary anthropology.

Other dissertations and theses, several of strikingly high quality, appeared through the 1970s and early 1980s.[29] Notable contributions were made by Frances Stier, who wrote a pioneering quantitative dissertation on agriculture and household form (1979); Alexander Moore,[30] the first to treat Nargana as a significant subject in its own right; and Mac Chapin, whose comprehensive and widely consulted dissertation on cosmology and curing (1983) cleared up the confusions in Nordenskiöld's work. The generation of the 1970s was followed by others, notably Alaka Wali and Karin Tice.[31] Although some have moved on to other regions and topics or fallen victim to the dearth of jobs in anthropology, a half dozen continue to write on Panama and the Kuna.

European anthropology also rediscovered the Kuna in these years, and on much the same scale. France has been represented by the well-known novelist J. M. LeClezio; by Carlo Severi (Italian by birth but based in Paris), who has published a series of elegant structural analyses of ritual texts and pictography;[32] and more recently, by studies of albinism by Pascale Jeambrun and molas by Michel Perrin (Jeambrun and Sergent 1991; Perrin 1999). Several German anthropologists have published widely on the Kuna,[33] and Massimo Squillacciotti from the University of Siena has led a sizeable and productive group of Italian researchers.[34] A large number of Colombians have published studies, mostly on the small Colombian Kuna populations off the Isthmus around the Gulf of Urabá.[35] Several more ethnographers and linguists from France, Italy, Spain, Colombia, New Zealand, and the United States are currently at work.

One of the most important studies produced by foreign anthropologists in recent decades, representative of both the changes and continuities in Kuna ethnography, is Joel Sherzer's *Kuna Ways of Speaking* (1983). Like many late-twentieth-century ethnographies, Sherzer's study zeroed in on just one aspect of culture, and like many others, it addressed a body of theory, in this case "the ethnography of speaking," a movement promoted by Sherzer and others in anthropological linguistics. Focusing on different domains and varieties of Kuna speech, particularly those characteristic of the gathering, curing, and puberty ceremonies, Sherzer paradoxically conveyed a vivid and comprehensive sense of Kuna society as a whole.

Ways of Speaking is filled with texts (Sherzer's later work even more so), but the textual tradition derives, not from Nordenskiöld, but from North Americanist anthropology and Sherzer's teacher, Dell Hymes. Sherzer's texts, moreover, are based on natural speech recorded in mostly unstaged live performance rather than on dictation or native writing, an approach impossible until the development of lightweight field recorders. Sherzer most resembled Nordenskiöld in giving fulsome credit to native performers and teachers, beginning his book with a photo gallery of Kuna knowers identified by name. And like many of his predecessors and contemporaries, he offered an admiring and affectionate cultural portrait representing the Kuna in the most positive possible terms.

Among North Americans who have written on the Kuna since the 1970s, several had previously worked in San Blas for the Peace Corps. One of them, Mac Chapin, began his ethnographic studies while still a volunteer, bringing out a booklet (Chapin 1970) and a phonograph record (Méndez 1970) that, by simultaneously addressing native and non-native audiences, opened a new ethnographic era. The disk, "Tad Ibe gi namaket" ("A chant about the Sun"), captured a chiefly performance by Horacio Méndez, a leading teacher of tradition. One hundred fifty copies, underwritten by a Panamanian development agency,[36] were given away to interested Kuna in 1970, and for months afterward the recording, played on battery-powered record players, could be heard all over the region. Encouraging Kuna ethnic pride, the recording also did for Horacio Méndez what the Swedes had done for Nele Kantule, confirming him as the preeminent traditionalist of his generation.

Chapin's other contribution, *Pab igala* ("Father's Way") (1970), was a substantial collection of narratives encompassing most of the episodes in the cycle of mythology or sacred history, the whole cleaning up the gaps and confusions in Nordenskiöld's 1938 volume and providing the first clear picture of Father's Way. Underwritten by the U.S. Information Service and sponsored by Reina Torres's Centro de Investigaciones Antropológicas, 150 copies were mimeographed for distribution in San Blas and sale at the national museum in the form of a large stapled booklet of seventy single-spaced legal pages. Reprinted two decades later in book form by an Ecuadorian press (1989), *Pab igala* has been extensively mined by other researchers[37] and widely read by the Kuna themselves, many of whom have learned their own traditions from the volume. While quite conservative in one respect, in that it continued the tradition of locating Kuna culture in the learning of outstanding men, Chapin's volume broadened and transformed the ethnographic dialogue by addressing the Kuna themselves, and for better or worse it furthered the process of moving tradition from the spoken word to the printed page.

By the end of the 1970s foreign anthropologists had become a fact of Kuna life. European and North American ethnographers occupied a niche—that of resident *mergi*—opened for them by their anthropological predecessors, and even more by the Peace Corps volunteers who had blanketed the region in the 1960s. Resident *mergis* stood out from other outsiders in their intention to stay for months or years, their attempts to speak *dulegaya*, and their willingness to go barefoot, eat *dulemasi*, and live in Kuna homes. A number of villages took on ethnographers as mascots, in some cases for years or decades, while a few communities, such as Tigre, Tupile, and Suitupu, received a succession of long- and short-term researchers. Many Kuna took it for granted that the traditions and lifeways of the Golden People (Olotule) should be recorded, and as traditional knowledge and practices faded, they often looked to resident *mergis* to preserve their heritage for posterity. If few communities or individuals were as self-conscious or relentless as Nele, Alcibiades, and Rubén had been in promoting favorable notice abroad, the interest in external validation and the assumption that ethnographic study would help Kuna public relations informed relationships with the hairy inquisitive foreigners.

The fieldwork of this era depended as well on long-term individual relationships like those of Nordenskiöld, Wassén, and Holmer with Nele, Pérez Kantule, and Hayans, relationships that were patterned in part on traditional apprenticeship in ritual and Father's Way. Indeed, as fewer and fewer young men took on traditional learning and aging masters lamented their lack of Kuna students, foreign anthropologists were recruited in part to fill the apprentice gap, while those like Sherzer who actively used tape recorders in their work also found themselves fulfilling a function going back to Nordenskiöld by providing an audience and permanent record for chiefs and ritualists who wished to perform for posterity as well as their fellows. Teachers applied the same rigor with foreign anthropologists that they did in drilling their Kuna students: through the summer of 1975, my own mentor listened critically each night as I read him a Spanish paraphrase of my dissertation, while Mari Lyn Salvador remembers watching nervously as members of the mola co-op pored over her field notes.[38]

Which is not to say that relations were always perfect. As early as the 1930s, Wassén (1938b, 7) noted objections to Rubén Pérez's insistent questioning. Some conservative villages, especially in eastern San Blas, remained closed to anthropologists through the early 1970s. More than one ethnographer was rejected by a prospective field site or even ejected after initially being accepted (see Howe 1986, 201). And as in other countries, questions of profit, credit, and First World domination sometimes provoked discord and suspicion (see Martínez Mauri 2007, 6).[39]

Tensions concerning the commodification of tradition were probably inevitable, given that Kuna apprentices already compensated their teachers and that some foreigners were all too ready to offer dollars for arcane wisdom.[40] The monetary value of culture was confirmed by an influx of mola-buyers, journalists, and filmmakers, most of all in the case of the French cinematographer Pierre Gassieu, who in the mid-1970s paid the town of Ustupu large amounts to stage a chicha and a mass exorcism, leaving turmoil, resentment, and raised expectations in his wake.[41] And as university students learned about academic careers, but not about the paltry returns typical for scholarly publication, some concluded that foreigners were growing rich on the native patrimony.

Apart even from financial considerations, some educated Kuna argued that outsiders were taking credit for indigenous accomplishments, a conclusion that the numerous Swedish publications of Kuna texts could be interpreted as confirming. In a lengthy diatribe against anthropologists delivered at a general congress in 1985, a young intellectual (who was standing next to me, sometimes, I imagined, gesturing in my direction) offered an extended analysis of the problematics of the word author, one that would have done Foucault proud. And as Kuna began to publish regularly, Mac Chapin's *Pab igala,* in particular, as the only foreign work available to many Kuna readers, attracted criticism from indigenous rivals, some of whom argued that the study of Kuna sacred tradition should be reserved for the Kuna.[42]

One source of tension was the persistent conflation of fieldwork with traditional apprenticeship. No matter how widely a researcher might recruit consultants and assistants, no matter how much a project might depend on observation or survey questionnaires, the fallback assumption was that he or she was acquiring esoteric knowledge, part of the native intellectual patrimony, from Kuna "knowers of things." As ordinary Kuna increasingly abandoned ritual apprenticeship to foreigners and to self-conscious literate Indian intellectuals, and as indigenous researchers began publishing (see Chapter 10), the divisions that had held in Nordenskiöld's time between native subject and outside investigator, always blurry in the Kuna case, began to dissolve, leaving foreign and native ethnographers as colleagues and potential competitors.

In an era of tension and conflict between Panama and the United States, relations were also colored by anti-Americanism.[43] Many older Kuna retained their fondness for North Americans, sometimes referred to as *iamar*, "older brothers." Kuna men continued working on U.S. bases until the end of the century, and in 1977, during a plebiscite on the canal treaty, Ailigandi caused an uproar by briefly flying both the American flag and the banner of the 1925 revolution, while a majority of Kuna voted No on the treaty. But high school and university students embraced the politics of the Left, and the longest-running indigenous organization, the Movimiento de la Juventud Kuna, was for years closely linked with the Panamanian communist party, the Partido del Pueblo (see Martínez Mauri 2007, 346–355). Even Kuna with less radical leanings were eager to rebut the long-standing allegation that they were dupes of the gringos. Anthropologists were sometimes accused of working for *La CIA*, and in the 1980s, during the period of greatest international tension before the U.S. invasion, it became difficult or impossible to do research on the largest islands with major student populations like Ailigandi and Ustupu.[44]

But relations never deteriorated as far as they did in some parts of Latin America. So long as foreign anthropologists exercised reasonable tact, and so long as they agreed to cooperate with Kuna researchers and authorities, most continued to gain permission to work.[45] Perhaps even more surprising, though Kuna have occasionally taken issue with outsiders' ethnographies, major public controversies between Indians and anthropologists like those that have surfaced repeatedly in North America (e.g., concerning Gutiérrez 1991; see also Landsman and Ciborski 1992) have been notable for their absence. The fierce social critic and indigenous activist Arysteides Turpana, not shy about correcting anthropological studies (1996), has also rejoiced at the work of foreign ethnographers: "In the great, sophisticated, and civilized . . . cities of the world, the dule culture is . . . admired and applauded thanks to the work of propaganda done by Nordenskiöld [and others]" (1982, 55). Recently, in an impassioned response to the assassination of three Kuna men by Colombian paramilitaries in January of 2003, Turpana contrasted these outrages with the honor shown Kuna culture in European centers of learning, and he evoked his pleasure at conversing in his own language on a visit to MIT and at finding his poems being read by a colleague in Brazil.[46]

ADVOCACY AND ACTIVISM

If Reina Torres had reservations about pro-indigenous agitation, others did not. In the late 1970s a collective of liberationist priests brought out seven tracts—long pamphlets or short books—whose radical critique of the status quo was clearly signaled by titles such as *Indígena y proletario; Tierra para el guaymí;* and *El indio y las clases sociales.*[47] Fourth and fifth in the series were two works by Father Ricardo Falla on the Kuna: *El tesoro de San Blas* (1979b), on a recent political crisis over tourism, and *Historia kuna, historia rebelde* (n.d.), a study of the 1925 rebellion and its antecedents, which was critical of all parties concerned—Catholic, Protestant, Panamanian, and North American—everyone except perhaps the Kuna rebels themselves.[48]

On the whole, however, the late-twentieth-century Kuna—relatively well fed, well educated, and well represented, at least by the standards of indigenous groups in the Americas—inspired less concern among anthropologists and activists than other, more desperate rural populations in Panama, especially the campesinos of the central provinces and the Guaymí, or Ngöbe-Buglé, to the west. In addition to authoring distinguished works on the marginalization and impoverishment of *interiorano* peasant communities, such as those by Steven Gudeman (1978), Stanley Heckadon Moreno (1983), and Gloria Rudolf (1999), anthropologists have critiqued the forces impinging on indigenous and nonindigenous groups in studies of a massive copper mine (Gjording 1991), a hydroelectric project (Wali 1984, 1989, 1995), and ethnicized labor on banana plantations (Bourgois 1988, 1989). During the 1980s, the political journal *Diálogo Social* hammered away at the oppression of the Guaymí (as did several monographs and edited volumes),[49] but had much less to say about the Kuna or Emberá-Wounán.

Academic studies of the Kuna, less outspoken on the whole and less immediately crisis-oriented than those on other Panamanian groups, have nonetheless consistently taken their side in analyzing relations with the state and the world economy, in one recent case (Howe 1998, 2004b) even overtly justifying the 1925 rebellion. The advocate's stance, however, has shown itself most clearly, just as it did with Nordenskiöld, McKim, and Gálvez, in the very positive, sometimes adulatory tone in which everything Kuna—from verbal and visual art to the indigenous sense of humor—has been depicted in works with titles such as *Yer Dailege!* ["Beautiful!"] (Salvador 1978), *The Art of Being Kuna* (Salvador 1997), and *Magnificent Molas* (Perrin 1999). As difficult as it may be to assess in detail the impact of such intensely positive representations, they have undoubtedly strengthened the hand of the Kuna. No single work has transformed perceptions in the way that Nordenskiöld and Pérez's magnum opus did, but taken together with tourism and popular writing, academic ethnography has done just what Nele and Rubén and Alcibiades hoped for, helping to consolidate the position of the Kuna at home and abroad.

Since the early 1990s, moreover, commentary and analysis have grown more pointed and direct. The most substantial ethnographic portrayal of the Kuna from this era, nominally a work of fiction in a genre called socioliterature, was published by a prominent sociologist, Raúl Leis. Heavily didactic, with few stylistic pretensions, *Machi: un kuna en la ciudad* (1992) takes its title from the native word for boy, a term often used for Kuna urban laborers.[50] It identifies the prototypical Kuna not as a native intellectual or poet but as a struggling urban migrant, a survivor rather than an object lesson. The Kuna, as Leis depicts them, enjoy cultural resources unavailable to most migrants, but otherwise they are just like other rural Panamanians struggling to get along in an unjust urban world.

Francisco Herrera (n.d. [2004]) has rightly lamented what he sees as the marginalization of anthropology in Panama: certainly, no individual exercises anything like the influence once held by Reina Torres, and a brief opening in the aftermath of the American invasion, in which several well-qualified anthropologists headed environmental and indigenist agencies, soon closed again. But Latin, Kuna, European, and North American colleagues now communicate and cooperate in a way unknown years ago; critical and activist works (Instituto and Diócesis 1991; Rudolf n.d. [2001]; Leis 2004) outnumber purely academic monographs; and outspoken anthropologists and sociologists make their opinions heard.

LITERARY ETHNOGRAPHY

In addition to appearing in popular and academic writing, the Kuna have been portrayed a number of times in novels, poetry, and film. Each literary and cinematic representation takes a stance on the nature of the Kuna and their place in the world, offering an ethnographic model or theory of Indian essence and Indian realities.

Alfredo Cantón (1910–1967), a novelist and educator with a PhD from Washington University, had at some point been a teacher in San Blas, and like Father Puig before him, he put his extended residence to good use. In his ethnographic novel, *Nalu-Nega* (1962), a sympathetic but critical reading of their situation, Cantón attempted to resolve the contradictions he perceived between tradition and progress in Kuna life. His story begins with a highly implausible love story—one of Doris Sommer's (1991) interethnic romances—in which a lovestruck Latin from Chiriquí Province wins the right to marry and settle down with a young Kuna girl. Although the Chiricano and his bride soon die mysteriously, their daughter, Nalu Nega,[51] grows into the most beautiful, accomplished, and self-confident of women, ending up despite her mixed ancestry as a nativist patriot and hero of her people.

The chronicle of Nalu Nega's early years provided Cantón with the vehicle for a cultural diagnosis. Misleading on some points, especially concerning curing and cosmology, and heavy-handed in his clumsy and often incorrect use of Kuna phrases to establish verisimilitude, Cantón otherwise gave a lively and reliable sense of the events and rhythms of village life, one fuller and more revealing than most conventional ethnographies, especially concerning the gathering, or *congreso*.[52] Through the interventions of his heroine, who convinces reluctant elders to establish the village's first school and name her as teacher (at fifteen!), Cantón sorted out the good and not so good in Kuna culture. Negative votes went to native curing, the chicha (depicted as much drunkenness and little ritual), parental control of marriage, gerontocracy in general, and the dead hand of tradition, while native "legends," mourning, ethnic pride, and especially village democracy were praised unreservedly.

The story is permeated with questions of desire and romantic connection, beginning with the love match between Chiricano and *india* that marks their child as a cultural mediator. Much of the story is played out in the context of the gender politics and intergenerational tensions of Kuna marriage, as well as the historic legacy, well known to Cantón, of Latin sexual predation in the years before 1925. Nalu Nega, courted and desired by almost every non-Indian she meets, also spends much of the narrative worrying either that her chosen career as teacher will be cut short by an arranged marriage or that she will be unable to marry at all because a selfish uncle refuses to finance her puberty ceremony—an issue she resolves by publicly cutting her own hair.

In striking contrast to most Panamanian authors, Cantón showed great sympathy for Kuna rebelliousness. Toward the end of the book, Nalu Nega's grandmother justifies the suspicions of change and outsiders shown by Kuna elders by telling her of the abuses that led to the 1925 rebellion,[53] a story Nalu Nega vows to incorporate into her school teaching. The precocious heroine also observes electoral fraud by Panamanian officials, scathingly described by Cantón, and she persuades her village to trade with Colombian *contrabandistas*, a controversial stance in the 1950s and 1960s.

As the narrative reaches its conclusion, Nalu Nega opens her school, and the massed men and women of the island drive off a government patrol boat intent on capturing a Colombian vessel.[54] While a delegation including the chief goes off to Panama to resolve the contraband issue with the government (just as a Kuna village would in fact have done), Nalu Nega and progressive youths hatch plans to build a village airstrip. On the chief's return, he arranges to have Nalu Nega married to her sweetheart, and in the inaugural flight from the new airfield, the young pair flies off to a summer course for beginning teachers. Love, school, and the gathering conquer all.

Unlike Cantón, the next littérateur to contemplate the Kuna saw only good. In 1963 or 1964, Ernesto Cardenal, Nicaraguan poet and Christian Marxist, met with Chief Yabiliginya, successor to Inabaginya, at a Catholic boarding school for Indian children in Medellín (Cardenal 1992, 48–49). Yabiliginya was in Colombia to complain about the terms of the coconut trade, Cardenal to study for the priesthood. Soon thereafter, he published an article, "Los indios cunas, 'una nación soberana,'" in the Panamanian journal *Lotería,* with numerous borrowed quotes and text excerpts marked by what Cardenal called "the naiveté and enchanting erroneousness with which [the Indians] translate into Spanish" (1964, 89). Quoting Nele:

> Now you see . . . God left his best words among us. Therefore Panama can't make a stupid people out of us. . . . The Panamanians boast and they are teaching us that we don't know anything. . . . Now you see that we know everything in this land that God left for us. . . . We don't know how to read and write. We keep everything in our head and thus we never forget about what our ancestors left us on this earth.

Cardenal found these "wise words" a "reproach for all of us . . . because all of us, the 'civilized,' have sinned from lack of understanding" (1964, 94).

Famous in later years as Sandinista minister of culture, Cardenal had been pursuing a religious vocation since 1957, first in Kentucky with the prominent mystic Thomas Merton, and then in Mexico and Colombia. Following a suggestion by Merton (Cardenal 2003, 37), "who revealed the wisdom, the spirituality, and the mysticism of the indians to me," Cardenal began spending vacations from the Colombian seminary immersing himself in indigenous subjects at the Ethnographic Museum in Bogotá, thus initiating a theme that has since run through his poetry for more than three decades in works such as *El estrecho dudoso* (1966), *Mayapán* (1968), *Homenaje a los indios americanos* (1969), *Quetzalcoatl* (1985), and *Los Ovnis de oro: Poemas indios* (1988, 1992). *Homage to the American*

Indians opens with a hagiographic tribute to Nele, while the much longer *Ovnis de oro* ("Golden UFOs"), which takes its name from the disks on which Kuna culture heroes descended to earth, includes four poems on the Kuna.[55] Since the rest of Cardenal's indigenist oeuvre derives almost entirely from his wide-ranging readings (except for visits to San Blas, he seems to have spent little time with living Indians), the Kuna poems anchor the whole and strengthen the thematic connection between past and present central to the work.

Cardenal's poetry takes a proselike form, much influenced by Ezra Pound, that he calls *exteriorismo*, "subjective poetry, narrative and anecdotal, made with the elements of real life and with concrete things" (in Salmon 1992, xiii). In a long poem about a visit to Mulatupu, observations from Cardenal's experiences alternate with snippets taken from his readings, both framed by the poet's sweeping conclusions (1992, 4–28):[56]

> The men on rough benches in the dark
> Behind, the women sewing with oil lamps while
>   they listened,
> sewing *molas*,
> refulgent the gold on their faces (noserings and
>   earrings)
> in the lamplight
> *Molas:* the blouses of the women:
> orange and red and pink and black and green and
>   yellow.
> They read the list of those who would go to work
>   next day
> on the communal lands.
> They chose new policemen.
>   No money circulates . . . (1992, 4–5)

> They have been socialists for 2000 years.
> Together they all construct houses for all.
>   The land, for all the tribe.
> The deer, the great fish, divided among everyone.
>   Perfect interisland harmony . . . (1992, 12–13)

> They talk in secret of the tree of life.
>   the tree Palu-wala (the mother who gave birth to
>   us all) (1992, 28–29)[57]

Like more prosaic visitors, Cardenal depended on Kuna readiness to explain themselves. In the words he quoted from Binigdi, one of the Mulatupu chiefs:

And that which I said was for it to be recorded on that magnetic tape; it was so that the voice of San Blas goes to other nations, and so they know that we have faith in God that God created us. (1992, 8)

Cardenal's portrait of the Kuna as mystics and communitarian socialists depended in fact on a kind of implicit conspiracy with his interlocutors, in which their most idealized and unrealistic claims (no theft, no conflict, perfect sharing and equality), assertions of a sort the Kuna sometimes air for short-term visitors, confirmed the poet's fondest wishes and preconceptions. Not that he needed much encouragement. The subjects of his other Indian poems are, like the Kuna, treated as alternatives to corrupt, brutal capitalism (the Inca Empire as socialist welfare state; the Iroquois and Classic Maya as pacifists), or else as analogues for opposed modern tendencies. Every people, every civilization is turned into an object lesson, a reproach to a modern world dominated by money and violence. Though the sweep and power of Cardenal's vision can carry away even skeptical readers, ultimately the poet shows greater devotion to his own idée fixe of socialist mystics than he does to anyone as adept at using money and as imperfectly harmonious as flesh-and-blood Kuna.

If Cardenal stands more or less alone in terms of the poetic form of his work, in other respects he joins a large standing ethnographic corps devoted to scrutinizing the Kuna. Even as some members of this class of permanent observers and interlocutors die, retire, or move on, others take their place, and online accounts of encounters with the Kuna tribal world, in particular, seem to increase each month. For better and for worse, the Kuna will never lack for bloggers, filmmakers, tour guides, and social scientists to tell the world who they are. As this chapter suggests, however, Kuna authorities and scribes increasingly control access to the field, at least by serious social scientists, and they influence (though by no means control) what is said about their people. As Chapter 10 shows, moreover, with the development of a more complete and self-conscious intercultural dialogue, native intellectuals play an increasingly active and assertive role, not just as facilitators, assistants, consultants, subjects, and junior colleagues, but as ethnographers in their own right.

Native Ethnography

TEN

This chapter takes up once again the story of indigenous self-representation—ethnography by as well as about the Kuna—in the years since Rubén Pérez Kantule's trip to Sweden. I begin with a cohort of "birds," or scribes, who mixed politics and salaried employment with uncredentialed but devoted efforts at recording and preserving their people's culture and history, first among those scribes Rubén's colleague, the long-term collaborator with Swedish anthropologists, Guillermo Hayans. The chapter then traces the growth of indigenous ethnographic agency, with the late-twentieth-century appearance of university-trained native anthropologists and historians and the evolution of their roles in research and publication from subordination to partnership and autonomous initiative. I conclude by considering the shape and content of Kuna auto-ethnography, with special attention to the vexed question of so-called indigenous essentialism.

NEW DEFENSIVE ETHNOGRAPHY

After Pérez Kantule's return from Sweden, he wrote several articles for a bilingual newspaper sympathetic to the Indian cause, the *Panamá América*.[1] In one long piece entitled "Estudios sobre la vida de los indios de San Blas" (6/18/33), Rubén lauded his people and defended them from almost every accusation ever leveled against them. Not only were San Blas men hardworking agriculturalists, they were so honest that anything mislaid by a visitor would be returned. Monogamous, respectful to their elders, kind to women, incapable of lying, and friendly to well-intentioned outsiders, the Indians "abominate perversions of all sorts," and they were also "entirely free from certain secret diseases." Their religious beliefs, which "do not depart from those of civilized people," centered on a supreme power encompassing "the universal concept of God." (No mention of Great Mother.)

Rubén took on several contentious issues directly. Insisting that a majority of Kuna wore Western dress, he pointed out that women wore molas and long skirts because they considered them healthy, beautiful, moral, and a contribution to their physical development. He apologetically described belief in evil spirits as typical of the "restive spirit of investigation found even in the highest civilizations."[2] As for chichas, "it is true that [participants] do become inebriated," but only on special ceremonial occasions, and their remarkably benign behavior while drinking is joyful rather than "nasty or quarrelsome."

A good deal of ambivalence between tradition and modernity surfaces intermittently in the article. In a section entitled "How the Indians should be governed," Pérez condemned police violence and forced culture change, which had produced a rebellion in 1925 characterized as lamentable but inevitable, and he called for a separate legal and cultural regime for the region. But he also praised the education that had produced men like himself, and which in time could instill "the precepts and obligations of life prevalent in urban communities." The Indians, he said, aspired to be like other Panamanian citizens, and with the new growth of schools, "I believe that our people will become artistic, cultivated, noble, and civilized."

These newspaper pieces seem to have sated Pérez Kantule's thirst for publication, apart from an article on molas in the Mexican journal *América Indígena* (1942), which was probably solicited during the international conference in Pátzcuaro (see Chapter 8). Continuing for many years to mentor foreign anthropologists and cultivate other international connections, Rubén seems to have largely given up on publication in favor of other pursuits—regional politics, an extended and frustrating campaign to become chief of Nargana, a village library, and his own private archive. Although his first effort at archive-building was thwarted when Nele and Ustupu insisted on keeping all the books and papers Pérez brought back from Sweden, on his return to Nargana he soon began anew, continuing on for the rest of his life.

ARCHIVISTS AND CHRONICLERS

As archivist, Rubén was not alone. At least two others, Guillermo Hayans and Estanislao López, accumulated materials over thirty, forty, or more years, collecting thousands of pages each.[3] All three saved personal and political correspondence, contracts, clippings, and *actas*, or minutes, from general congresses and other meetings. The *actas* in particular fill major gaps in the historical record, since the Intendencia, at least in the early years, does not seem to have consistently filed or collected minutes, and until recently the General Congress itself lacked systematic procedures for long-term document retention.[4] López's archive has the largest number of newspaper clippings, many concerned with the later stages of his long career; Rubén Pérez's seems to have the most systematic and complete holdings in *actas* and other official documents; while particularly in the Hayans and López archives, many of the documents were produced by the archivists themselves.

To varying extents, all three men generated as well as collected documents. Estanislao López—before 1925 a modernist radical, later an ally of Nele and other leaders, and finally chief of all the Kuna—kept a personal diary for decades, which has not been seen outside his family.[5] López also wrote a considerable number of village histories and biographies of leaders like Nele, Charly Robinson, Colman, and Inabaginya, based apparently on conversations and interviews during his travels. He also typed out a number of chronicles of events and personalities in twentieth-century Kuna history, based on his own experience, as well as the experience of others, with titles like "Nombres de los personajes olvidados . . ." and "Algunos relatos reseñas historicos de los congreso generales. . . ." One long typescript, "Apuntes historicos de los sucesesos sangientas de la Comarca de San Blas de años de 1908–1917–1921 . . . 1977 . . . ," includes extended remarks on his own participation in the events of February 1925 and their aftermath. The manuscripts, messy, misspelled, and sometimes a bit confused, were obviously produced by laborious hunt-and-peck typing and never edited or corrected, which has not negated their value for latter-day researchers.

In all of his work, López showed the same concern with preserving names apparent in Colman's 1913 letter and in the great Swedish compendium, names that in this case included the men who brought back the Panamanian flag in 1904, the first boys sent off to school in 1906, eighty men who stood with Charly Robinson in 1910, the youths led by Claudio

Iglesias in 1918, the leadership hierarchy of one or another village in a particular year, Nargana people living in Panama in the 1980s, the first graduates of urban schools, the first Kuna BAs, the first MD, and so forth.

Without falling into the grip of "archive fever" (Derrida 1995) or getting lost in the voluminous literature on the colonial archive (see Stoler 2002b), which cannot be fully engaged in this chapter, one can readily see that the Kuna archives are more than random collections of documents. Like Kuna censuses, legislation, and yes, ethnography, they represent an attempt to think like a state, to appropriate and use the forms of national power in self-defense. For their creators—López, Pérez Kantule, and Hayans—they also functioned as assertions of personal mastery, written substitutes or replacements for the oral knowledge held in memory by unlettered Kuna knowers. Just as traditional knowers typically mastered several different branches of ritual and esoteric knowledge, so the archives range across several kinds of documents. For the Kuna as a whole, the archives assert collective mastery and legitimacy, suggesting by their very existence the reality and the worthiness of all the events, practices, and ideas their documents record.

GUILLERMO HAYANS, THE COMPLETE NATIVE ETHNOGRAPHER

As researchers, even López and Pérez Kantule were surpassed by Guillermo Hayans, who continued recording Kuna culture and history for most of his adult life. The many hundreds of pages Hayans generated followed models already apparent in his early work with Nele and Rubén. They included short village profiles like those he sent to Sweden in 1931, longer local histories, and biographies of Kuna leaders. He wrote narratives and chronological lists of events from the nineteenth and twentieth centuries, based on both oral and written sources, such as "Historia de los Antíguas Ságuilas el tiempo cuando reinaban el Colombia." He also collected mytho-historical narratives and cosmology, such as "Las guerras de Ibelele contras los pony e reyes en este mundo"[6] and "Los monumentos históricos del Río Tuile."[7] And he continued recording chants used in curing and other ritual—more than his Swedish correspondents could possibly publish. For the Swedish publications, Hayans provided Spanish translations and sometimes picture-writing, but the never-published texts often consist only of the Kuna original taken down in a Spanish-derived orthography.[8] The transcriptions are orthographically unsystematic and inconsistent, but perfectly readable by anyone who knows the Kuna language. Hayans also copied laws, made excerpts from books and other texts, and archived letters and lists that came into his possession, such as "Lista de los viajeros para el Partido Liberal Renovador [in 1932]."[9]

As for his ongoing relationship with the Scandinavian anthropologists, Hayans found the association deeply meaningful but also lonely and frustrating. María Albertina Gálvez, the Guatemalan who visited Ustupu in 1950 (see Chapter 8), met Hayans during a long evening in the gathering house: Chief Olotebiliginya called him a *"gran historiador,"* but she found him "sad and embittered" (1952, 134).

> "They do not know of me in Panama," he told me with deep sadness in a tone of humility, which changed to a look of pride when he told of his constant relations with distinguished personalities of the scientific world in Sweden. He spoke to me with great praise of Baron Nordenskiol, of Denmark [sic]. "The Baron put me in contact with other learned men of Europe who still write me; he also sent me his writings; in them are our customs and our traditions. I would like to show you these books, the very same that I have tried to compile, since I have no one here to show it, and it is sad to write for oneself." (1952, 134)

She later visited Hayans at home:

> With great pride which radiated from his countenance, he began to show me his most beautiful jewels: the books from his friends in Sweden, increased in value by polite words of dedication, which for him represent his greatest treasure; afterwards in a humble manner he showed me his notebooks of jottings written in Spanish.

Finally, after a long conversation:

> He would not bid us farewell without showing us some notes on their traditions and chants, written by him in the ideographic form of the indians of San Blas . . . which according to the words of the writer "represent a distinct advance over the writings of many primitive peoples." (1952, 136)

Hayans's sadness may have been caused in part by his obscurity relative to Rubén Pérez, especially in Panama: no matter how many texts Hayans sent off for publication, Rubén was the one who had traveled to Sweden, the one whose picture and story appeared in the great compendium and who was named to international conferences and scholarly academies. Hayans may also have come to regret his inability to publish on his own and the relatively humble position to which he was assigned in the ongoing collaboration. Holmer and Wassén never failed to credit each text to both Hayans and the knower from whom he had collected it, but they reserved the title of author for themselves, and they never explicitly acknowledged (as Nordenskiöld for his part had done) that Hayans was the ethnographer and they merely his editors and publishers.[10] In some instances they offered fulsome credit; in others, when they criticized Hayans's translations or reserved the title page entirely for themselves,[11] they seemed to be treating questions of credit as a competition or zero-sum game. Regardless of how they apportioned tribute for each work, moreover, almost every subsequent bibliography, database, or card catalogue credits Rubén Pérez Kantule with just one publication, the article on molas he wrote for *América Indígena* (1942),[12] and none of them mentions Guillermo Hayans at all.

A NEW GENERATION

Hayans and a few others continued working through the 1950s and 1960s. A scattering of schoolteachers and students published articles, pamphlets, and library theses on Kuna biography and history, and in 1972, with Reina Torres's backing, a man named Lino Smith began teaching the Kuna language at the University of Panama (L. Smith 1975). These few exceptions aside, a new generation of native ethnography and native historians and ethnographers did not emerge until later in the 1970s and into the 1980s, with the growth of anthropology as a discipline, the appearance of opportunities to study abroad, and a nativist revival among the Kuna.

At the beginning of the 1970s, many schoolteachers and other educated Kuna, reflecting the attitudes absorbed in their own schooling, spoke of indigenous *tradición* with impatience or condescension, treating it as an obstacle to *desarrollo* and *progreso*. By mid-decade, however, as the indigenous rights movement gained momentum across the Americas, many had changed their minds, embracing *cultura*—at least in the abstract—as a token of ethnic identity and source of pride.[13] By 1980 San Blas had been renamed Kuna Yala,[14] and over the following years, several islands followed suit by re-indigenizing Hispanic names: San Ignacio de Tupile became Danakwe Dupir, Corazón de Jesús, Akkwanusatupu.

Another place name gained much wider circulation: Abya Yala, which originally referred either to a specific location prominent in Kuna sacred history[15] or to Kuna territory as a whole, was taken up by the international indigenous movement to replace the Eurocentric name America. Since then, Abya Yala has been adopted as the name of a publishing house in Ecuador, a theater group in Costa Rica, the stage name of a Basque musician, a fund for indigenous development, at least two activist information sites, several international conferences, a support network for Latin American art in the New York metropolitan area, and a short-lived Kuna journal.[16]

Indigenous activists also began returning to Kuna names for themselves and their children. By this time, only a few older individuals were still known in daily life by traditional long names, which begin with one of four prefixes (*Olo*—"gold," *Mani*—"silver," *Ina*—"medicine," or *Igwa* [a tree]) followed by a series of nonmeaningful syllables: for example, Manidiwinappi or Olowisobdili.[17] Hispanic and Anglophone names predominated so thoroughly that many men and women could not remember their Kuna names or lacked them altogether. In the new wave of ethnic renaming, prominent senior men rediscovered or reinvented traditional names, while young activists departed sharply from past practice by choosing strongly emotive names with links to characters and events in sacred history.

In the new generation of native anthropologists, the initial cohort of four was divided evenly both between priests and laymen and between highly educated amateurs and credentialed professionals. Arnulfo Prestán, trained in Mexico, published a pioneering ethnographic monograph, entitled *El uso de la chicha y la sociedad kuna* (1975). Divided into two distinct halves, one devoted to puberty ceremonies, the other to a comprehensive account of Kuna society, Prestán's study displays nothing noticeably indigenous in its orientation or interpretations. But the advantages of native ethnographers—linguistic mastery, rapport with informants, childhood socialization—combined in this case with Prestán's dogged persistence and attention to detail, yielded a wealth of new ethnographic information.

The first Kuna to be ordained a priest, Padre Juan José Davies, who styles himself Ibelele (after the great culture hero also called Dad Ibe), has worked mostly in linguistics, and after retiring from the priesthood, Davies for several years headed a one-man Academia de la Lengua Kuna (Davies n.d. [c. 1978]). The littérateur Arysteides Turpana, educated in Costa Rica, Panama, France, and Brazil, author of volumes of poetry (1968, 1979, 1983), a book of traditional narratives (1987), and several short historical and ethnographic studies (1987, 1996), has arguably made his greatest contribution in impassioned social commentary and defense of indigenous rights (e.g., 1982, 1983, 1985, 1991, 1995).

Padre Victoriano Smith, now better known as Aiban Wagwa, obtained a doctorate in anthropology from the Salesian University in Rome with a dissertation on native and modern education (Smith 1981, 1982). Since then he has published several volumes of poems and collections of Kuna narratives—including a comprehensive volume of Father's Way[18]—as well as an oral history of the 1925 rebellion (Inakeliginia 1997). By studying with prominent teachers such as Carlos López and Horacio Méndez, Aiban, more than anyone else, has blended the roles of modern investigator and traditional knower of things.

Other native anthropologists soon followed. Since the 1960s and especially since the 1970s, several hundred Kuna men and woman, encouraged by the ferment and populist policies of the Torrijos years, have gained bachelor's degrees from the University of Panama, some in anthropology or sociology, while a smaller number won scholarships for advanced study in Europe, the United States, Latin America, and the Soviet Union. In the mid-1970s Kuna students and professionals founded a new organization, the Centro de Investigaciones Kunas (CIK), which encouraged indigenous research and published a few issues of a journal, *Abya Yala*, while exercising a modicum of supervision over foreign investigators in the name of the General Congress. In the roughly ten years of its existence, CIK never achieved organizational stability, but it did provide a base for promising young social scientists, notably Jesús Alemancia, Cebaldo de León, and Eligio Alvarado, and in the process it galvanized interest in autoethnography and cultural defense.

In the same years, another nucleus of urban Kuna, led by Guillermo Archibold—alarmed at incursions by mestizo peasants, part of a wave of colonization encouraged by eastward extension of the Panamerican Highway—established a station at a spot called Udirbi where a dirt feeder road crossed the cordillera into the Kuna reserve. In the late 1970s Archibold and company organized a much more ambitious project with international funding called PEMASKY (Proyecto de Estudio para el Manejo de Areas Silvestres de Kuna Yala).[19] With a thoroughly mixed record—strong on border demarcation and consciousness-raising, much weaker on self-organization—by the early 1980s PEMASKY, pressed to develop too fast, too far, had more or less collapsed. Even in ruins, however, the project yielded positive results, establishing the Kuna with foreign foundations

FIGURE 10.1 Kuna anthropologist Cebaldo Iwinapi de León speaking at the International Congress of Americanists, Seville, July 2006

as worthy recipients of financial support. Equally important, in the early 1990s the project's example helped inspire new indigenous NGOs, including Napguana and the Fundación Dobbo Yala (Wickstrom 2001, 194; Martínez Mauri n.d. [2003], 2005, 2007), both of which have in turn published on Kuna society. By 1995, seventeen more Kuna NGOs had charter applications pending (Ventocilla, Núñez, F. Herrera, H. Herrera, and Chapin 1995, 113), and since the turn of the century still more have appeared (Martínez Mauri 2007).

A third ethnographic line grew from indigenous religious origins. In the 1960s, the Kuna began formalizing traditional interisland singing gatherings into regularly scheduled *congresos tradicionales* (see Howe 1986, 72–78; B. Castillo 1995, 2005). Out of this system grew a Congreso General de la Cultura Kuna, or Onmaked Dummad Namakaled, "Great Singing Gathering," with its own set of three ranked great chiefs, or caciques, taking responsibility for religion and culture in general as well as singing congresses in particular. Despite a fuzzy division of labor with the administrative General Congress and *its* three great chiefs, the Cultural Congress persisted and in 1992 created its own research institute called Koskun Kalu, which also oversaw work by non-Kuna. Koskun, which has very recently been merged with IDIKY, the technical and managerial agency of the secular General Congress, has published books, magazines, and newsletters; sponsored workshops and conferences; and collaborated with foreign investigators.

A fourth line had its origins in the doctrine advanced in recent decades by left-leaning Catholic missionaries called *inculturation,* which channels their work through the cultures and languages of evangelized peoples and attempts to reconcile the Gospel with preexisting beliefs (Shorter 1988; Schineller 1990). From the late 1970s through the early 1990s, several Catholic priests and social activists, indigenous and nonindigenous, held a series of semiannual *Encuentros de comunidades de base de Kuna Yala,* dedicated to documenting, preserving, and analyzing Kuna sacred history (A. Martínez 1998, 2–3; Olonagdiginia 2000). Workshop sessions featured narratives from Father's Way spoken rather than sung by prominent chiefs and *argars,* mixed with commentary and consciousness-raising on the situation of the Kuna and Panama; paraphrased in Spanish by Aiban Wagwa, they were distributed in a series of photocopied bulletins called *Kuna Yargi.*[20] The meetings and bulletins led eventually to a long honors thesis by Atilio Martínez (1998) and publications on Father's Way by Aiban Wagwa (1994, 1995, 2000). The same model, combining myth with commentary and conscientization, was later employed in a series of national meetings of clergy and laity, *Encuentros nacionales de pastoral indígena,* sponsored by the Catholic organization CONAPI[21] (González, Quiróz, Endara, and Quintero 2003).

All of this work by university-educated elites, much of it under the sponsorship of official organizations, has coexisted with a humbler but vigorous strain of independent research and writing carried on by grassroots intellectuals using school notebooks, ballpoint pens, portable typewriters, and the truly revolutionary technology of cheap cassette recorders. One of my early research consultants, Camilo Layan, has for three decades extracted an annual donation from me of one hardbound "Record" notebook, in which he has been recording the complete cycle of puberty chants. An ex-assistant, Faustino Rodriguez, for many years kept up a chronicle of village events, while Laurentino Salcedo, the son of my principal teacher and consultant, has taken up the task of tape-recording his father Gonzalo's chants and narratives. Elsewhere, a retired teacher named Juan Colman collects information on his ancestor Cimral Colman, while a schoolteacher, Simón Herrera, has written a long biography of Chief Inabaginya (n.d. [2003]). Young secretaries take down village histories, and actors in annual commemorations of 1925 interview their elders in search of dramatic authenticity. So pervasive has the idea of research become that orators who wish to suggest that their facts and opinions are in order sometimes declare that they have been carrying out an *estudio* on the topic in question.[22]

Of all these homegrown investigators, by far the most important was Carlos López, or Inakeliginia (1913–2000), *argar,* or chief's spokesman, in the village of Tupile, or Dannakwe Dupir, consultant to a number of anthropologists, and in his later years a great chief of Kuna Yala.[23] López systematically interviewed participants and eyewitnesses to the 1925 rebellion and the years leading up to it, holding their accounts in his head and narrating them at regional meetings. Although he could read and write, and though his chronicle was eventually taped at least twice and published in Spanish by Aiban Wagwa (Inakeliginia 1997), López's own method remained uncompromisingly oral.

FROM COLLABORATION TO AUTHORSHIP

As individuals and organizations, Kuna intellectuals gained experience, training, and funds through collaborative ventures, in which, over time, their own influence and agency moved toward rough parity with their foreign partners. Some external connections have persisted for decades, in particular the long-running alliances between the women's Cooperativa de Molas and North American friends such as Mari Lyn Salvador and Karin Tice, and between Mac Chapin, godfather of PEMASKY, and a whole generation of Kuna *técnicos*. Collaborative projects range from the language course developed by Aiban Wagwa with his Italian colleague, Massimo Squillacciotti (1984), to annual festivals of children's art run by Smithsonian staffer Jorge Ventocilla with the artist Ologuagdi. Alexander Moore and the photographer Levon Mardikyan combined with Eligio Alvarado to videotape the chicha of Alvarado's daughter, while James Howe, egged on by Alvarado and backed by the Cultural Congress, worked with Rodolfo Herrera to microfilm Kuna archives. A number of agencies and individuals, including the museologist Mari Lyn Salvador, have assisted in the development of community-based museums, while Joel Sherzer, who has run annual linguistic seminars with Kuna colleagues, sponsored an ambitious project with Koskun Kalu to inventory and record all surviving chants and chanters (see Price 2005, 48–49). The artist Ologuagdi, a one-man interethnic bridge, has illustrated numerous works by Kuna, Latin Panamanians, and foreigners (see Ventocilla 1997). One of the most involved collaborations, for a traveling exhibit and companion volume curated by Mari Lyn Salvador entitled *The Art of Being Kuna* (1997), involved indigenous consultation and input over more than a decade.

In 1995, an ethnically mixed team produced a landmark publication addressed to both indigenous and nonindigenous audiences, *Plantas y animales en la vida del pueblo kuna*, which has since gone through three editions in Spanish and English (Ventocilla, Herrera, and Núñez 1995, 1997, 1999). In 125 pages and twelve brief chapters, the work paints a fascinating but unromantic portrait of a people struggling to reconcile the declining health of the forest and ocean with their own destructive practices and involvement in the world economy. Another ambitious interethnic project, financed by UNESCO and the Spanish government, entitled *Pueblos indígenas de Panamá: Hacedores de cultura y de historia* (Picón, Alemancia, and Gólcher 1998), situates indigenous peoples in the mainstream, rhetorically uniting native cultures and Panamanian scholars and activists—but conspicuously *not* foreigners—in an emergent national project.

The gap between foreign-language publications and indigenous subjects has also narrowed. Koskun Kalu systematically collects foreign writings on Kuna culture, and at least three studies—Severi's *La memoria ritual*

(1993b, 1996), Sherzer's *Kuna Ways of Speaking* (1983, 1992), and Howe's *A People Who Would Not Kneel* (1998, 2004)—have been translated into Spanish. Copies of Howe's book, for which the Cultural Congress is principal sales agent, have been distributed to every village in Kuna Yala.

Today at the beginning of the twenty-first century, in addition to a good many university theses, a number of Kuna-authored publications have appeared, bankrolled by international NGOs and European governments. One set, authored by Kuna *técnicos*, addresses practical and political questions, typically following external models from natural and social science disciplines. Representative examples include a volume of indigenous law, *Anmar igar: normas kunas* (Congreso General Kuna 2001), an opinion poll concerning threats to Kuna Yala's western border (IDICA/GRET n.d.), and Eligio Alvarado's comprehensive survey, *El perfil de los pueblos indígenas de Panamá* (2001). Another set of more overtly culturalist publications, of primary concern here, is dedicated to preserving and defending indigenous identity.[24]

THE SHAPE OF INDIGENOUS ETHNOGRAPHY

Almost any aspect of traditional culture, from taboos (A. Hernández 1996b) to basket-making (Morris 1995) to jokes and play (Brown and Martínez 2006), can be taken into the culturalist embrace. In practice, however, some elements and domains have been embraced fervently, while others have been ignored or neglected. In making sense of this patchy ethnographic mosaic and of the cultural identity it promotes, I have found it useful to examine Kuna writings not just in the light of my own understanding of their society but also in contrast with the best-known and most thoroughly analyzed case of American nativist intellectual activism, the thought and practice of pan-Mayanists in Guatemala, as analyzed by Edward Fischer (1999, 2001) and others (Fischer and Brown 1996; Warren 1998; Nelson 1999; Hale 2002; Montejo 2005).

Unmentionables

In native ethnography, omissions are as revealing as inclusions. In Guatemala and Chiapas, traditional women's dress, or *traje*, is a salient as well as fundamental symbol of indigeneity, now being reworked and reconfigured to signal pan-Maya as well as local and regional identity (Hendrickson 1995, 1996; Fischer 2001, 117–119; Greenfield 2004). One might have expected the same of molas, and indeed of the whole colorful ensemble of Kuna women's dress, especially since outsiders have so insistently taken noserings and molas as *the* signs of Kuna identity. In native ethnography, on the other hand, molas are seldom mentioned and (as far as I know) never studied.[25]

The answer is probably simple: molas are female, and Kuna public intellectuals and students of culture are almost all male (see Price 2005, 26–28). Native ethnographers, like other Kuna, take great pride in molas, but needlework lies outside their domain, and studying or writing about molas would provoke discomfort.[26] As far as I know, members of the women's mola cooperative and other mola-sewers do not write much about their craft either, probably because they are focused on production and sale rather than interpretation. Thus what is celebrated, discussed, and endlessly analyzed by outsiders remains stubbornly visual, implicit, and unspoken among both mola makers and wearers and their male kin. Jackson and Warren's observation (2005, 559–560) that indigenous women are often taken as prototypical representatives of their people applies with full force to popular *external* images of the Kuna, but for nativist ethnographers, the heart of their culture so far seems to be mostly male.

Other things notable for their scarcity in native ethnography include traditional kinship and marriage, and agriculture, from all of which the Kuna intelligentsia has struggled to break free. A few village-based intellectuals still work part-time in the forest, but men with secondary and university education have mostly forsaken agricultural labor for salaried employment, and so far only one article-length study, by an author firmly in the *técnico* camp, has appeared on traditional agricultural production (G. Castillo Díaz 1985). In affairs of the heart, young urban intellectuals, like all Kuna today, choose their own lovers and spouses, who often come from different home-islands, and many couples reside neolocally: thus the traditional marriage and household system based on village endogamy, parental choice of spouses, marriage by capture, matrilocal residence, and labor service to fathers-in-law would offer an uncomfortable ethnographic topic (see Howe 1985, 2004a).[27]

Molas and male agricultural labor are also historically problematic, given their nineteenth-century origin and, in the case of molas, their complete dependence on foreign-made tools and materials. In 1970, my oldest female informant, born at the end of the previous century, discussed molas frankly in much the same terms as do outsiders' accounts, as an art form that in her youth was still new and evolving. This uncomfortably brief history, though undoubtedly well known to some senior men and women today, has never been acknowledged publicly in any Kuna accounts that I have heard or read: instead, native historians hark back to the pre-Columbian use of barkcloth and the role of female culture heroes in bringing traditional designs; one published narrative unabashedly moves mola origins back a millennium and attributes them entirely to Iboergun and his sister Kikadiryai (C. López, in Salvador 1997, xxv). The change to male agriculture, though perhaps less disconcerting, is also passed over, as an obvious example of recent and fundamental social change (see below), though the nineteenth-century move to the islands and the riverine origins of the Kuna (obvious throughout the narratives of Father's Way) are frankly acknowledged.

Language Politics

In strong contrast with these ethnographic and historical unmentionables, the mother tongue, *dule*, or *dulegaya*, is insistently foregrounded, just as it is in what McKenna Brown (1996) calls the "language loyalty movement" and Fischer (2001) the "political linguistics" of pan-Mayanists in Guatemala—and for that matter, in nativist and nationalist writing worldwide.[28] Like other indigenous peoples, Kuna activists and literati react against the imposition of a national language and to the stigmatization of their own tongue, identified, like many other indigenous Latin American languages, as a mere *dialecto*.

The Kuna case differs from the Maya in many ways: in the absence of colonial-era texts and pre-Columbian writing and the presence of only a single language divided by minor dialectical differences. The challenges in Guatemala—of uniting multiple contemporary and archaic languages and their dialects, reconciling hotly contested orthographic systems, and bringing pre-Columbian hieroglyphics under linguistic and ideological control—are greater than those in Panama, as is the anti-Indian opposition (Fischer 2001, 120–127, 201–205). Nora England (1996, 189) suggests, moreover, that Guatemalan Indian languages carry an extra ideological burden as "almost the only attribute of contemporary Maya culture that can be claimed to be unequivocally *Maya* in genesis and development." On the national stage, the goal of gaining official status for native languages is simultaneously more plausible and more politically threatening in Guatemala, where indigenous peoples represent a much larger portion of the national population than they do in Panama.

The Kuna case also differs in the lighter impact of professional linguistics. Several native Protestants of earlier generations received training from the Summer Institute of Linguistics. More recently, Aiban Wagwa and Abadio Green have published systematic text analysis and language instruction (Méndez, Santacruz, Peláez García, and Green 1996; Aiban Wagwa and Squillacciotti 1984). Joel Sherzer has run informal linguistics seminars, and his student, Kayla Price (2005, 2006), has sat in on sessions of a Kuna task force struggling toward a standard orthography. But very few contemporary Kuna have received professional linguistic training. The vacuum has been filled in part by practices typical of academic scholasticism, including traditional school grammars, linguistic purification and hypercorrection, etymologizing, and folk-Whorfianism. Generic Whorfian analysis, found all around the world, treats key words as expressions of *cosmovisión* and core cultural values: for Kuna intellectuals, this interpretive strategy undoubtedly has multiple origins, including *argars'* spoken recapitulations of chiefly chanting, mission sermons, outsiders' ethnographies, and school and university studies in humanistic disciplines. Etymology, most prominent in the oft-repeated claim that the name Panamá derives from *banaba*, "far off," is used to explain away apparent linguistic borrowing and to uncover deep meanings of words (e.g., Turpana 1987, 36–38; 1996; Davies n.d. [c. 1978], 45). The procedure, characteristic of many ethno-nationalist movements, probably owes a great deal to Western scholasticism and folk linguistics. It does, however, reflect a distinctively Kuna concern with *origins,* one obvious as well in Father's Way, traditional curing chants, and today in orthographic standardization.

Efforts to establish standardized spelling, though by no means as conflict-ridden as in Guatemala and elsewhere, have met obstacles and delays. An early attempt in the 1970s by a Soviet-trained Latin Panamanian linguist to impose a complex orthography only produced confusion (see Chapin 1991). The system produced much more recently in 2004 and 2005 by a special task force of Kuna intellectuals (Price 2005, 2006) is notable for its simplicity, for the marked but mostly unacknowledged influence of Spanish orthography, and for an insistence on showing origins and derivations rather than pronunciation.[29]

Kuna ethnographic writings are peppered with native words and phrases, but sentences and paragraphs, not to mention entire works written in Kuna, are seldom seen. Aiban Wagwa, Abadio Green, and several indigenous colleagues have published a volume of texts and translations in Colombia (Méndez, Santacruz, Peláez García, and Green 1996). Reuter

Orán has prepared several bilingual primers (Orán 1992), and Aiban, Turpana, and one or two others write poetry in Kuna as well as Spanish. Very recently, a Kuna journalist and artist have produced a charming trilingual children's book, *Niiskuamar Ebised Dule (The Star Counter)* (Kubiler and Cole-igar 2007). But historical and ethnographic works and nativist essays almost always appear in Spanish. Only one indigenous intellectual, Iguaniginappi Kungiler, makes a practice of publishing in Kuna, and so far almost no one else has heeded his exhortations to do likewise.

This absence can be attributed to the long delays in establishing an official orthography and conventions for written Kuna discourse (see Price 2005, 100–101). More positively, ethnographers probably publish in Spanish to reach non-native audiences and monolingual urban Kuna. The strongest impediment, however, is the long-standing identification of writing with Spanish. Legislation promoting bilingual education passed in 1953 and the 1970s has until recently received little serious attention from the education ministry, and it is only now, several years into the twenty-first century, that the Kuna themselves have mounted a major campaign, heavily financed by foreign donors, to establish a standard bilingual curriculum (Aiban Wagwa 2005). Although the effort includes remedial classes to teach scribes to write in their own language, the outcome remains in doubt. The *técnicos* and culturalists of today, like their predecessors of the 1920s, still speak two languages but write only one.

Etymology and Numerology

Kuna native linguistics has given special prominence to the indigenous counting system, which lost ground in the twentieth century to its Spanish equivalent, partly through the influence of schools, partly through the greater simplicity and ease of use of Spanish numbers. Kuna numerals join together long strings of syllables, and as in quite a few indigenous American counting systems, each number requires a numeral classifier. (To take one example, thirty-nine smallish fish would be *ua uka-durgwengakambegakabakebak*.)[30] Although some native speakers still know and use parts of the traditional system, Spanish numerals increasingly predominate, despite recent efforts at revival. The third week of August of 2004 was proclaimed "Semana de Numeración Kuna" (*Kika* 11/10/2003), with what effect is unclear.

As the element of everyday speech that has most obviously lost ground to Spanish, the indigenous counting system presents an obvious target for revindication and revitalization. Efforts to restore, describe, and analyze Kuna numerals also follow in part from their relative accessibility and manageable size as a research topic, and very likely from the influence both of foreign scholars, who have published studies of the Kuna number system (Montalván 1976; Severi 1987; Squillacciotti 1987; 1998, 149–168; Burgoa 1993), and of pan-Mayanists and *their* fascination with numbers (see Fischer 2001, 203–204). Going one step further, several Kuna nativists—foremost among them Abadio Green, well known as an indigenous activist and leader in Colombia—treat indigenous counting as a prime field for the discovery of deep structure and meaning through etymology and numerology.[31]

> This system helps us to deepen knowledge of the culture since the ancestors; therefore the study of words becomes an act of commitment to history, because to this extent we are coming closer to the true history that is deposited in the ancestral speech that is languages of the indigenous cultures of . . . Apya Yala (América). (Green 2004, 331)

In this form of analysis, each number is understood in terms of the presumed meanings of its component syllables and its connection to other words and concepts. Thus both Green (2004, 334–335) and Paredes de León (n.d. [2004]) derive *nerkua (nergwa),* "six," from *nele,* "wise man/ wisdom," and *kua (gwa),* "heart." *Kukle,* or *gugle,* "seven," similarly, supposedly comes from *kuli (gulli),* a bamboo flute, and *nele,* "wise man/ wisdom." This procedure leads to frequent analytical contortion: since the *kuli* flute has six holes, not seven, the number must be derived from the melody it produces along with the flute itself (thus one plus six). Nor do theorists agree on every number: Green glosses "nine" *(pakkepak)* as "*abstenerse-abstenerse-abstenerse,*" Paredes de León as "*hacerse padres +padres,*" an allusion to the nine months of pregnancy. The latter breaks down *kuensak,* "one," into *único* and *saka,* "father-in-law," while Green, who ties the number to the authority of the chief *(sakla)* rather than of fathers-in-law, glosses it as "the wisdom of the mother to make order in the community" (2004, 332), which requires an analytical leap from syllables supposedly meaning disorder to their implied opposite.

Even if many of these word derivations often seem forced or implausible (cf. Price 2005, 110), and even if the program as a whole lacks traditional roots, this attempt to etymologize indigenous numbers, really a new form of symbolic classification, reinterprets and resacralizes Kuna language and culture, drawing on elements from domestic and community life. It shows the same creativity apparent in Nele's narrative about French pirates, in the new uses for picture-writing found by Rubén and Guillermo Hayans, and for that matter, in the work of the handful of nineteenth-century chiefs who systematized the corpus of narratives in Father's Way and taught them to the next generation.

Rebellious History

For the Kuna, history and culture are inextricably intertwined. The major institutions and practices—from house-building to kin terms, sanitation, and puberty ceremonies—have their historical thesis, their origin, in celestial immigrants like Ibeorgun, who came to earth to teach the ancestors and predecessors of the Kuna. They have their antithesis in the government's ethnocidal program of the early 1920s, and their reaffirmation in the 1925 rebellion, understood as a defense of traditional ways, as well as of land and autonomy. Not surprisingly, Kuna nativist writings freely mix culture and history, embedding one within the other, and not surprisingly, they return insistently to the story of 1925, the very model of their own activism and cultural assertion.

The Kuna rebellion is portrayed in poetry, oral history (esp. Inakeliginia 1997), short written narratives, and particularly in annual commemorative dramas in which young men recreate in bloody detail their people's suffering and struggle. The recreations I know best, from the village of Niatupu/Tigantiki, consist of a series of vignettes, each one showing a Kuna practice such as puberty ceremonies or medicinal curing, followed by its suppression at the hands of loudly bigoted police agents. The drama thus explicitly and self-consciously frames elements of traditional culture as distinct institutions emblematic of the boundary between Kuna and national society.

The greatest interpretative challenge concerning 1925 is the role of the explorer Richard Marsh and the U.S. Legation, especially in light of Panamanian insistence on Marsh's malign role in events,[32] and more broadly, the long-standing Kuna connection with North Americans and other English-speakers. Indigenist writings and dramas, in addition to rehearsing in detail the abuses that justified rebellion in 1925, emphasize Kuna agency and autonomy, minimizing, ignoring, or contextualizing the U.S. role in events.[33] Concerning the longer run of Kuna history since the conquest, native accounts have until very recently had little to say about the

FIGURE 10.2 Mural celebrating Kuna leaders and the rebellion of 1925, Ustupu, 1981

colonial era or about relations with either English- or Spanish-speaking outsiders.

The other great interpretive challenge, noted above, is change: how to reconcile claims to millenarian roots and ancient tradition with the recent origin of village dance groups, general congresses, and island villages, as well as molas and male agriculture. In broad terms, the dominant response has been to insist on the ancient origin of cultural fundamentals and to ignore or explain away innovation, but the basis for more complex interpretations is also at hand, a topic discussed further below.

Native Environmentalists

Like other indigenous peoples throughout the hemisphere, the Kuna claim a special connection with the earth and the forest, evident in self-portrayals of all sorts (H. Herrera 1995). In the Kuna case, this assertion combines and synthesizes several strands, including European and North American stereotypes of Indians as at one with nature, which grew and flourished under New Age and environmentalist influence; recent pan-Indian ideology, which eagerly embraces those stereotypes; the specifics

FIGURE 10.3 Poster of Great Mother as the Earth, PEMASKY Project, 1980s

of the PEMASKY project, for which environmentalism was fundamental; and even firmly established Kuna values and beliefs. Chiefs traditionally sing to their followers that "we have come here to care for the world" *(yal akwega an nonimala),* and in Nan Dummad, the Kuna really do have a beloved mother earth. In the short life of the PEMASKY project, its staffers went from village to village with a cleverly designed audiovisual presentation that raised environmental consciousness by presenting new ideas like watersheds and the circulation of water through the atmosphere by dressing them in traditional cosmology. Destructive practices, like commercial overfishing of lobsters, while impossible to deny, have been understood as recent departures from traditional balance and respect for nature.

The problematics of identification as natural environmentalists, regardless of its partial validity in the Kuna case, are now widely recognized. On the positive side, it offers native activists a powerful role as mediators between the developed world and tropical nature, as is insightfully explored in a thesis on Kuna intellectuals by Mònica Martínez Mauri (2007). As Brysk (1994) and Assies (2000) point out, however, such identifications can subordinate politics and struggle to an essentializing and even infantilizing natural identity. Support for indigenous groups and alliances with NGOs based on unrealistic expectations of environmentalist purity have led to controversy and disappointment (Conklin and Graham 1995; Dove 2006; Hames 2007), and recently to a sweeping wholesale rejection of such partnerships by some of the largest environmental organizations (Chapin 2004).

Even in its internal effects, moreover, it might be argued that the stereotype of oneness with the earth, reinforced by its twin, the spirituality of indigenous being, has shaped Kuna self-representation in unfortunate ways. Unlike recent ideology, the village gathering has always combined the celestial with the mundane and material, anchoring people to the forest and sea in practice as well as imagination: when chiefs invoke Kuna responsibility for the land, they mean agriculture as well as forestry, and in the dry season, village leaders harangue men to feed their families by producing more. Kuna men are farmers even more than ritualists and politicians, and generations of villagers have found environmental stewardship compatible with private property and production for external markets. In politically correct native ethnography, however, only usufruct and subsistence agriculture should be mentioned, cutting or burning the forest must be euphemized, and the relationship with the land is epitomized by herbal medicine. The result is to reinforce implicit divisions among urban intellectuals between culturalists and more pragmatic *técnicos* and to encourage further alienation from agriculture and village economies, thus denying moral support to the men and women still in Kuna Yala struggling to maintain their families by their own labor. Here again, however, complications and countercurrents require further discussion below.

The Centrality of Father's Way

In the light of earlier chapters, it should come as no surprise that Kuna indigenous ethnography gives most attention to ritual and esoteric knowledge—the basis of prestige ranking in Kuna society, the element highlighted in external self-presentation as early as Colman's 1913 letter, and the core subject of the Swedish collaboration, as well as the closest equivalent to Western academic learning. The long, more or less fixed texts, or *igar*, that I have referred to by the shorthand designation of "curing chants" (which include several texts devoted to mourning, hunting, and other nonmedical ends) are often mentioned with pride but seldom studied in depth (see S. Brown 1995, 1996). In the 1980s it seemed as if every young educated Kuna claimed, with the aid of a notebook and tape recorder, to be learning one chant or another, but almost none of them persevered.[34] More recently, the research arm of the Cultural Congress, Koskun Kalu, under the sponsorship of Joel Sherzer, has carried out an exhaustive inventory of surviving chants and chanters (see Hernández n.d. [2004]; Price 2005, 48–49), along with a program of scholarships for traditional apprenticeships. As one result, Koskun Kalu has recently published one of the lesser curing chants, *Sia igar kialed* ("Way of cacao, short-form") (Hernández 2005), with the text given in colloquial Kuna rather than the language of the spirits. It may be that more texts will follow, but overall, the great effort required to learn the chants—and perhaps also, increased concern about their divulgation and publication—have pushed research in other directions.[35]

The female puberty ceremonies known as *inna* in Kuna and chicha in Spanish have over the years received a great deal of attention in constructions and interpretations of Kuna culture, both positive and negative. In the early 1920s, chichas were, along with women's dress, a primary target of the government ethnocide (though it was drinking and not ritual that worried officials). After 1925, the chicha, as an accessible and colorful element in indigenous practice, seems to have been regularly offered up as an exhibit to visitors like Narciso Garay and Matthew Stirling. Today, village dance groups import elements of chicha dancing into their folkloric routines, and urban Kuna return to the islands to participate in chichas and even to sponsor them for their own daughters. In the field of indigenous ethnography, however, almost nothing has been written on puberty ceremonies since Arnulfo Prestán's *El uso de la chicha* (1975), now more than thirty years old. Although lingering sensitivities concerning drinking may persist, once again it is probably the scale and complexity of the subject matter—the four days of rituals, profusion of symbolism, and immensely long chants—that have for so long discouraged would-be researchers. Very recently, in June 2005, Koskun Kalu held a workshop supported by UNESCO (as yet unpublished) to initiate a systematic study of this field of ritual.

Center stage in native ethnography is occupied by Father's Way (Bab igar), the set of mytho-historical narratives, cosmology, metaphor, and conventional wisdom carried on by chiefs and their interpreter-spokesmen called *argars*. Publicly performed in a linguistic variety much closer to everyday speech than the spirit language of the curing chants, amplified and explicated in *argars*' spoken sermons, Father's Way is also much more accessible to students and apprentices than are curing chants.[36] Just as a chief or *argar* can in a night or two learn one history or set of metaphors from a teacher or senior colleague, so a young nativist researcher can tape chants and spoken narratives during a short field trip or regional meeting.

Father's Way also unites city with country and youth with age in a way that curing chants cannot. Urban intellectuals return regularly to Kuna Yala for workshops and singing meetings, while the Cultural Congress, by preserving the old partnership between chiefs and scribes, sublimates generational tensions that have in the past sometimes led to conflict (Howe 1998; also Chapter 2). Authority in the Congress hierarchy is apportioned between traditional chiefs and educated secretaries and staff, and in the organization's periodic meetings and published works, young literate men can acknowledge and even pay homage to elders' wisdom, treating it as the very essence of Kuna identity, while at the same time avoiding the more direct and onerous generational subordination they would experience at home in their natal villages.

Father's Way, moreover, has great ideological appeal. To progressive Catholic missionaries embracing the doctrine of inculturation, it represents the religious Other they now wish to engage rather than replace. In historiographic terms, given the absence of monuments, calendrics, written records, or ancient artifacts, the continuity and time depth of Kuna culture can best be demonstrated by the long sequence of episodes, eras, and culture heroes in Father's Way. As a genre explicated as well as performed in the gathering house, the narratives have their own exegetical tradition. Most important of all, Kuna ethnic identity, claims to territory, and resistance to domination have always been expressed and rationalized through Father's Way: contemporary speakers and writers invoking the example of militant figures like Twiren or Dad Ibe, who fought evil spirits or taught the ancestors to resist predatory neighbors, also call to mind more recent forebears like Nele or Colman, who in their time sang about those same heroes.[37]

Like the Christian Bible, Father's Way has undergone a process of editing and standardization, with the excision of noncanonical narratives. Through the early 1970s, the eastern sector once led by Inabaginya carried on an alternative syncretic narrative tradition, which inspired opposition and embarrassment on the part of other Kuna. Rather than Iberogun or Dad Ibe, chiefs in this eastern group sang about Jesus Christ, Simón Bolívar, culture heroes who lived in Bogotá or the Cauca Valley, and a canoe-load of Kuna who paddled to Rome (Howe 1986, 48–49, 76–77).[38] In recent years the minority tradition has disappeared from sight: although men from the eastern sector have served as great chiefs of both Kuna congresses, the alternate narratives have to my knowledge never been published or even acknowledged in print.[39]

In written interpretations of Father's Way, an insistence on literal truth coexists, somewhat uneasily, with didactic interpretation emphasizing ethnic solidarity, cultural retention, and connections with nature, evident in such evocative titles as *Spirit of the Earth, Our Spirit* (Kungiler 1997), *History of My Fathers, My Beloved History* (Aiban Wagwa 1995), and *In Defense of Life and Its Harmony* (Aiban Wagwa 2000). A few authors have taken interpretation further, schematizing Father's Way and adapting it to Western academic writing, notably Juan Pérez Archibold in an article entitled "Historic Memory, Social Structure, and Theology of the Kuna Nation." An honors thesis by Atilio Martínez (1998) treats the eight Ibelergan ("Great Shamans/Seers") who came to earth after Ibeorgun as knowledge-bringers and "prophets" like their counterparts in the Old Testament.

The Old Testament analogy underlines a crucial point, the largely text-based representation of Kuna religion. Attention is all but monopolized by aspects of belief readily codified in writing, whether by foreigners or native activists, elements thought to deserve the world's respect in no small part because of their equivalence to the Bible and Christian theology.[40] Other aspects of Kuna religion less readily textualized—moralism, apocalyptic fears, recurrent crises with the invisible world, homely teachings, and control of women—receive short shrift. Most neglected is the central rite itself, the singing gathering, and its role in countering threats, restoring balance, communicating with the deities, and constituting villages as congregations. Overall, textual representation of Kuna religion, despite its intellectual sophistication and its fidelity to the mytho-historical narratives, is nearly as flat or one-dimensional sociologically as was Nordenskiöld's work in its day.

INDIGENOUS IDENTITY AND THE NATION

In all of the areas discussed above, Kuna nativist intellectuals have faced a much less daunting national environment than their compatriots in Guatemala or Colombia have until very recently. Among educated Latin Panamanians, some (though by no means all) are now willing to hear indigenous cultural claims, and newspapers and official sources regularly acknowledge the General Congress and Kuna participation in national affairs. Panama, though it has seen invasion and turmoil, has not experienced anything like the extremes of violence that have wracked Guatemala and Colombia. In late February each year, when the Kuna celebrate their rebellion, newspaper columnists sometimes lament Indian disloyalty and the glorification of policemen's murders, but the events of 1925 lie much further in the past than the brutal civil wars of the other two countries, one of them still ongoing. Whether Kuna claims are accepted or not, native intellectuals can voice them loudly without fear of reprisal.

Panama, moreover, has become a more thoroughly multiracial and multicultural country than it was a few decades ago. As the role of tourism in the national economy grows exponentially, that multiplicity is also crucial to the image constructed for foreign visitors (Guerrón-Montero 2006). The government has a major stake in preserving rather than suppressing the exoticism of the Kuna, who rank just below the canal itself as a tourist attraction, especially for cruise ships. As the Kuna put their lives on display for tourists, moreover, they have so far not had to change their clothes or take them off or otherwise depart far from their daily routines. More fundamentally, their prominence gives them influence that other groups—indigenous, campesino, or Afro-Panamanian—can only attempt to emulate.

But multiculturalism, as Charles Hale (2002, 2006) has argued for Guatemala, has its own limits. According to Hale's diagnosis, widely accepted multiculturalist discourses constrain at the same time that they empower, "separating acceptable demands for cultural rights from inappropriate ones, recognizing the former and foreclosing the latter" (2002, 507). In Panama, where Indians do not constitute a large enough proportion of the national population to inspire deep fear or to seriously threaten the political dominance of white and mestizo elites, questions of identity are not so much self-limiting as irrelevant: in the final analysis, indigenous culture and history simply do not matter as much as material claims. What many Latin Panamanians resent, apart from Kuna assertiveness, is Indian control of lands that they feel should belong to the country as a whole—and to private developers. In Kuna Yala, outside interests have repeatedly attempted to take control and to breach the territorial integrity of the reserve (Falla n.d. [c. 1975]; Howe 1982, 2002; Pereiro Pérez and De León Smith 2007). In the Bayano and the Darién, adamant defense of indigenous *comarcas* by the Emberá, Wounán, and interior Kuna has led to resentment and even counterorganizing on the part of campesino colonists and timber and ranching interests. Except for the mola trade, indigenous culture matters much less to national elites than do land, trees, and beaches.

INDIGENOUS ESSENTIALISM?

In anthropological works concerned with self-representation by native intellectuals, one of the most vexed questions is that of so-called indigenous essentialism: "discourses of enduring commonalities—common ethnic roots and historical pasts, cultural essences, and experiences that are seen as naturally binding people together."[41] Whereas indigenous spokesmen assert primordial identities and cultures, in some cases using concepts taken from anthropology, many social scientists have come to see such essences as constructed, fractured, partial, and contingent on present needs and conflicts—a difference of viewpoint fundamental enough to provoke uneasiness and even conflict. Non-Indian anthropologists struggle not only to find models for making analytical sense of such constructions but also to balance analysis with support, especially in places where anti-Indian critics have seized on imputations of inauthenticity to attack indigenous activism. In Jean Jackson's now-classic phrasing, "Is there a way to talk about making culture without making enemies?" (1989; see also Herzfeld 2001, 34).

Discomfort and the potential for conflict have been exacerbated by two foundational concepts in recent social science: Benedict Anderson's "imagined communities" (1983) and invented culture or tradition (or as it is often popularly construed, anti-authenticity), which originated in an influential volume edited by Hobsbawm and Ranger (1983). Although both works focus primarily on nationalism and nationalist ideologies, as does Handler's (1988) widely read deconstruction of Quebecois culturalism, their relevance to indigenous versions of history and culture is obvious, as a number of heated controversies have shown.[42]

In the literature on this topic, "essentialism" sometimes seems to function as a cover term for several discomfiting aspects of indigenous ideology, which include a literalist or fundamentalist stance toward tradition, obvious with the Kuna insistence on the exact historical truth of Father's Way, and a seemingly passive acceptance of received ideas from pan-Indian ideology, summed up by such catchphrases as spirituality, oneness with the earth, primordial "millenarian" origins, enduring tradition, elders' wisdom, egalitarianism, heroic resistance, and culture itself. This collection of images, stereotypes, and simplifications—a synthesis of nineteenth-century nationalist ideology, enduring visions of the noble savage, antimodernism, outdated anthropology, and environmentalist rhetoric—often seems imposed on, rather than emergent from, local realities, with a potential for "replacing the distinctive timbre of each . . . society with a pan-Indian monotone" (Brown 1993, 319).

Some scholars have doubted the legitimacy of questioning or scrutinizing indigenous essentialism, on the grounds that such critiques depend on intellectual resources and perspectives privileging the metropole, and that whatever may be intended, they end up undercutting the "discursive authority" of subaltern intellectuals (Briggs 1996, 462; Rappaport 2005b, 36). To extend a free pass, however, to anyone claiming indigenous identity (itself a problematic category), or more truthfully, to extend it to anyone indigenous of whom the writer approves, only trivializes and patronizes those it purports to defend. Does one respect Kuna or Aymara or Lakota intellectuals by denying their claims the same kind of serious consideration and critique extended to Quebecois, Greeks, Serbs, bio-prospectors, or colleagues at home? Given that indigenous intellectuals form part of a much wider conversation, and given that some of today's essentialisms derive from last week's academic theories, sympathetic nonindigenous scholars should be joining that conversation, albeit from a position of equality rather than authority, even if it means risking occasional discomfort or angry rejection (see Linnekin 1991, 448).

As for indigenous essentialism itself, several things should be noted. First, one should not be too hasty in imputing construction, imaginaries, and inventions: some things, even some cultural things, have existence and persistence outside anyone's self-conscious recognition of them. As Edward Fischer argues persuasively for pan-Mayanists, "cultural actors' self-interests and the ways they see fit to pursue them are . . . conceived in relation to perceived cultural forms and normative patterns" (Fischer 2001, 16; see also 1999): what at first glance may seem contingent, ad hoc, or borrowed may be shaped and guided in less obvious ways by enduring cultural logics and structures of feeling (see also Friedman 1992). By the same token, the superficial rhetoric of terms like spirituality and mother earth may gloss long-standing and deeply felt values and attachments. The closer one gets to local actors and cultural specifics, the more likely this is to be so.

Second, one may sometimes need to separate, however provisionally, culture and its secondary representations in ethnography and ideology. Jean Jackson, in an article on the rhetoric of indigeneity in the Colombian Vaupés (1989), discusses Tukanoan activists' claims concerning territory, land tenure, and communal labor, which, she suggests, misrepresent local practices. As she points out in a later article, however, those practices (however much they, too, may have changed) presumably continue to have their own existence, and "the creation of a highly self-conscious ideology about practice has a different ontological status than the part of culture that informs the practice" (1995, 19). Both village life and indigenist rhetoric form part of larger and increasingly diverse cultural wholes, but one is a depiction of and claim about the other. For the Kuna, Father's Way may at some point in the future survive only on the printed page, but so long as villages assemble to hear chiefs chant, it has a reality subsumed only partially by its portrayal in writing.

Finally, as a number of authors have noted, essentialism and fundamentalism are by no means the whole story. Essentialisms are often invoked strategically by indigenous actors as needed, and claims made at one moment or in one context may be complicated or contradicted at another (Warren and Jackson 2002; Jackson and Warren 2005). Concerning their relations with the forest and the sea as discussed above, for instance, there can be no doubt that the Kuna have often put on the mantle of indigenous environmentalism. But ideology did not blind them for long to their own participation in environmental degradation. In addition to undertaking empirical studies of hunting practices (López Vivar 2002) and the commercialization of scarce resources (H. Herrera 1995; A. Castillo n.d. [2000]), indigenous biologists and their allies have offered a judicious assessment of the situation in a comprehensive review article, "Los indígenas kunas y la conservación ambiental" (Ventocilla, Núñez, F. Herrera, H. Herrera, and Chapin 1995), as well as in *Plants and Animals in the Life of the Kuna* (Ventocilla, Herrera, and Núñez 1995, 1997). A published interview with one Kuna *técnico*, Nicanor González (1992), appeared under the telling title "We Are Not Conservationists."

The same cross-currents are apparent in historical consciousness. The polarization between oral and written sources (and for that matter, between native and non-native authors) that often characterizes indigenous historiography is much less evident with the Kuna. Although oral tradition has special value for the Kuna as an embodiment of generational continuity and repository of *anmar danikid* ("our coming/our history"), the written record, preserved by local archivists and avidly mined by both urban and village-based researchers, is also given weight. Past leaders, though idealized as exemplars of Kuna greatness, have had their actions and motives scrutinized using models of indigenous agency more complex than elders' wisdom and heroic resistance. A recent synthesis of Kuna history published by Koskun Kalu, "Origen del pueblo kuna desde la memoria

FIGURE 10.4 Poster of Kuna History, PEMASKY Project, 1980s

histórica" (Brown 2005), devotes fourteen dense pages to a summary of events between 1571 and 1888, most taken from written sources.

Even more fundamentally, recent studies, whether by urban intellectuals, local chroniclers, or actors in village commemorative dramas, rest on the assumption that historical understanding is open-ended, that more remains to be discovered about the past. The events of the early twentieth century, moreover, far from slipping into a vague, amorphous dimness as their protagonists pass from the scene, are being fixed permanently in oral and written memory, and the temporal range of that record is being extended back into the nineteenth century, notably concerning the treaty of 1870 with Colombia mentioned in the preface to this book: this accord, first discussed by Arysteides Turpana (1985), now informs Kuna understanding of their territorial rights—on the grounds that their reserve antedates Panamanian independence—and it has recently been investigated more fully in the Colombian archives by Bernal Castillo.

Models of change and development display the same complexity. In the sequence of narratives making up Father's Way, institutions and knowledge, rather than appearing full-blown in a single moment, were introduced by one or another culture hero and then in many cases rejected or forgotten by recalcitrant proto-Kuna, only to be later reintroduced or rediscovered; the sum total of knowledge and practice evolved over time, with successive teaching by figures like Dad Ibe, Ibeorgun, and the eight great shamans. The same evolutionary teleology is evident in understandings of how Kuna political institutions matured over the course of the twentieth century, with the successive creation of a legal reserve in 1938, the constitution of 1945 and its institutionalization of the high chiefs and General Congress, the fundamental law of 1953, and further additions and developments of recent years (Castillo 2000, 2005). As a model of change and innovation, this scheme of gradual perfection even offers hope for reconceptualizing molas and other innovations, a way of seeing them as distinctively Kuna even if they do not come from the beginnings of time.

Whatever its structure or content, it should not be assumed that ideology always determines action. Just as affirmation of their millenarian origins has not kept the Kuna from innovating and changing, so an insistence on cultural and historical autonomy and the obfuscation of their centuries of ties with outsiders do not prevent them from establishing new ties as needed with NGOs and government agencies. It is hard to see how indigenous intellectuals could assert an identity for their people—in the case under consideration here, how they could characterize themselves in their auto-ethnographic writing—without essentialisms of one sort or another. For some individuals and some movements, such claims may act as blinders, limiting their vision or even trapping them in ideological dead ends. But it need not always be so.

Since its beginnings with Nele, Rubén Pérez, and Guillermo Hayans, Kuna auto-ethnography has addressed both internal and external audiences, attempting to preserve and codify indigenous culture, as well as to defend and represent it to the outside world. In the new century, external audiences have by no means been written off: Kuna intellectuals still demand the respect of the nation and the world. Today, however, culturalist writing primarily targets fellow-Kuna, reminding them of past glories and helping them reconnect in a more self-conscious way with their heritage. With half the population now in the city, and with traditional practices fading even in Kuna Yala, the task of preservation and self-understanding becomes ever more pressing and ever more difficult.

Chapin's Lament

ELEVEN

Edward Bruner argues cogently that "ethnographies are guided by an implicit narrative structure" (1986, 139), and in particular that each ethnography presupposes an outcome, a fate anticipated for its subjects, whether assimilation and cultural loss or resistance and resurgence. In Chapter 8 I took issue with Bruner, at least concerning Kuna ethnographies written between 1925 and 1950, which, it seems to me, reveal a variety of interpretive viewpoints and frameworks, and indeed, basic disagreement and uncertainty concerning the character and fate of the Indians. But Bruner has a point. Ethnographic consensus, however partial, can emerge at various moments and eras, and lines of interpretation do thread their way from one work to another. I would depart from Bruner only in suggesting that narrative schemes coexist and intermingle with essentialist readings of character, efforts to sum up the nature of a people as well as their fate.

In postwar Kuna ethnography, the old story of stubborn isolation and endogamy characteristic of early-twentieth-century popular Anglophone writing has resurfaced in new form as an exceptionalist narrative of success, a celebration of resistance, adaptive change, and even florescence in the face of threats that have pushed other indigenous groups to the wall. The Kuna have become in effect the happy exception that proves the dismal rule. This story of atypical success has been told by the Kuna themselves, in auto-ethnographic writing and searches for outside funding, and by a great many sympathetic outsiders. The story, moreover, has a large element of truth, even if success consists of holding-on and digging-in, of small victories in the face of relentless threats, rather than ultimate triumphs. When the Spanish government created the Premio Bartolomé de Las Casas, it seemed inevitable as well as appropriate that one of the first recipients (in 1998) was the Kuna General Congress.

Triumphalist narratives (however muted and qualified in this case) often mask their opposites: worries about disrespect, inadequacy, defeat, decay, loss, and extinction. Kuna scribes, a century after their first appearance, still seem caught in the contradiction between the written and spoken word. Thoroughly literate themselves and connected only tangentially with the oral practices and traditions they wish to defend as the essence of their patrimony, they tack back and forth, sponsoring oral but largely nontraditional events such as workshops and seminars whose ultimate product is a printed text. Abadio Green (2004) tries to resolve this contradiction through denial, by asserting that "the writing of indigenous peoples is life itself," that is, that oral and written are one and the same.

> It has been said in various academic circles that indigenous languages are purely oral *(ágrafas)*, that is, that they have no writing, because they are not within the system of alphabetic writing. . . .
>
> In this context we can affirm in the light of different scientific disciplines that indigenous languages have their own system of writing, which they have constructed over the course of their existence. . . .
>
> The body of a person, his way of walking, jumping, running and swimming are writings that only his pueblo can read. . . . Writing is a sign not only of speech, but rather it is the art of painting, weaving, seeing, feeling, hearing, dressing oneself. (Green 2004, 324–328)

As James Clifford points out, this contradiction and its attendant anxieties encompass all the parties to ethnographic conversations.

> Since Socrates' refusal to write, itself powerfully written by Plato, a profound ambivalence towards the passage from oral to literate has characterized Western thinking. And much of the power and pathos of ethnography derives from the fact that it has situated its practice within this crucial transition. (Clifford 1986, 116)

Almost every kind of ethnographic study (with the partial exception of filmmaking and photography) effects a transformation into writing, which occurs regardless of the ethnographer's position in or outside the group in question, regardless even of whether members of the group are literate or illiterate. "Whatever else an ethnography does, it translates experience into text" (Clifford 1986, 115). Much of the anxiety and doubt about textuality that pervades contemporary anthropology is concerned with the legitimacy, validity, authorship, and faithfulness to the original of such translations, questions that apply with equal force to ethnography by insiders and outsiders. Like all contradictions, this one can never be mediated more than partially, and it is not likely to go away anytime soon.

Kuna anxieties, as I have argued throughout this book, focus heavily on their reputation in Panama and the world. Despite the undeniable success of their efforts and those of foreign allies, their long-term propaganda campaign and the negative attitudes it seeks to counter show no signs of letting up. When tensions erupt, as happened recently when one village punished an errant Latina teacher with stinging nettles, or when indigenous interests clash with those of miners, dam-builders, or peasant colonists, then anti-Indian sentiment and stereotypes—and often resentment directed specifically at the Kuna—break through the thin crust of tolerance and acceptance in Panamanian public discourse.

For better or worse, public images and attitudes in Panama, both positive and negative, often single out the Kuna. The Emberá may be colorful, but they have no molas. The Wounán may have shamans and mythology, but biographies of Wounán ritualists and leaders do not appear in the national media. The Ngöbe may fight tenaciously against intrusion and exploitation, but it is Kuna assertiveness and Kuna violence that outsiders resent and fear. The national integration of all indigenous groups may be called into doubt, but it is Kuna independence and Kuna alliances with imperialist foreigners that people remember. Each *etnia* now has its own *comarca*, caciques, and *carta orgánica*, but everyone knows who demanded and got them first.

Being singled out has its costs, as was evident in the 1920s when the government unleashed its ethnocidal campaign against the Kuna but ignored other Indians. The Kuna sense of their own uniqueness, moreover, has undoubtedly impeded pan-Indian solidarity and organizing, as Philippe Bourgois (1989, 160–178), for one, has lamented. If the Kuna did reach out to their kin more consistently and wholeheartedly, and if an effective national-level organization were to emerge, it might respond more effectively to the current orgy of neoliberal exploitation of tourism and natural resources, and to the threats it presents to almost every indigenous and campesino group. The Kuna would be wise, nonetheless, not to submerge their identity too far into a pan-Indian soup, not to dilute or neglect their Kunaité or the culturalist work that feeds it. Every success they have enjoyed—and even more, every episode of internal crisis and division successfully resolved—has depended on the understanding that, yes, they are Indians and loyal Panamanians, but first and last, they are Kuna. More than that, the alternatives being offered will not inevitably strengthen their cause. A wide variety of concerned publications, which (quite rightly) focus on the malnutrition, disease, child labor, and other social ills afflicting all of Panama's poor, typically portray Indians as objects of concern, or worse, as *victims* in need of rescue.[1] Victimhood, whether true to the facts in many cases, and whether it effectively promotes outside intervention, is a poor substitute for a sense of one's own agency and identity, especially for those who struggle to oppose threats as collectivities as well as individuals.

Kuna anxieties focus on internal change and cultural loss as well as external challenges. Loss of territory and autonomy or lack of respect can be blamed on someone else, but the waning and disappearance of old ways—however much one points the finger at schooling and urbanization—are ultimately recognized as *natukin*, one's own doing. Everyone is aware of cultural loss and of his or her own role in the process, even if it is euphemized in print: homemakers lament the decline in free exchange of food as they send children out to buy fish or coffee; nativist publications analyze a system of numerals few people use; young men support themselves through wage labor or lobster-diving rather than agriculture; scribes write on computers in praise of oral specialties practiced by a handful of knowers; old men lament their lack of apprentices; and few people dare to describe themselves or their friends as "true Kuna" *(Tule sunnat)*, except in nervous jest.

Among foreign anthropologists, few since Stout have written about cultural loss as frankly as Mac Chapin, who has worked with the Kuna over four decades. In an article entitled "Losing the Way of Great Father" (1991), Chapin noted with dismay the waning of interest in traditional pursuits and traditional learning on the part of young Kuna, the ever-increasing dominance of Western education, and most of all what he saw as the failure to connect young activists with older traditionalists in the PEMASKY project, an alliance he had himself helped to foster. One can argue with the details and even some of the fundamentals of Chapin's analysis—in a society that has never stopped evolving, institutions have been added as well as deleted, and the late 1960s and early 1970s, the implicit baseline for his comparisons, were a moment not of stasis but of headlong change. But Chapin is right about the increasing pace of change, which has accelerated still more since he wrote, and he is right that much has already gone.

The sentiments voiced by Chapin, the lament for things lost, could hardly be more academically incorrect. One of the most cruelly dismissive things one can say about a field study—or about a whole era in anthropological work—is that it is mere "salvage ethnography," a foolish and self-contradictory attempt to reconstruct a vanished and largely imaginary past. Such laments are seen, moreover, as the imposition of a standard schema or interpretive framework rather than a response to the world. James Clifford identifies "the theme of the vanishing primitive, of the end of traditional society," as a "structure of feeling" and of "narrative."

> Ethnography's disappearing object is, then, in significant degree, a rhetorical construct legitimating a representational practice: "salvage" ethnography in its widest sense. The other is lost, in disintegrating time and space, but saved in the text. . . . I . . . question the assumption that with rapid change something essential ("culture") . . . vanishes. And I question, too, the mode of scientific and moral authority associated with salvage, or redemptive, ethnography. (Clifford 1986, 112–113)

Worse accusations than academic self-justification or interpretive dogmatism have been aimed at those who lament the past. In the nineteenth century, it is often pointed out, "expressions of melancholic grief for the 'vanishing Indian'" (Sayre 2005, 4) rationalized dispossession or attempts to symbolically appropriate the indigenous connection with the American land. As Gordon Sayre notes, even that great foe of the Indians, Andrew Jackson, could offer "melancholy reflections" on their disappearance while simultaneously arguing for its inevitability (Sayre 2005, 4).

The argument is taken one step further by Renato Rosaldo, who, in a widely influential essay, asserts that ethnographic tristesse is merely a variant on what he calls imperialist nostalgia: "one kills somebody, and then mourns the victim," or "in attenuated form," one deliberately alters something and then laments the change, thus concealing a "complicity with often brutal domination" (1989, 69–70). Nostalgia, whatever its object, is according to Rosaldo a suspect sentiment, one peculiar to the West (he cannot have been reading much Chinese poetry) and "even in its origins . . . associated with processes of domination" (1989, 71). Anthropologists who mourn the passing of traditional society or even fondly remember how things were during their first field trip "attempt to use the mask of innocence to cover their involvement with processes of domination" (1989, 86).

Arguments in this form, one kind of antiessentialist essentialism, condemn sentiments, ideas, practices, institutions, and even whole disciplines for the uses to which they have sometimes been put. If ideologies posit spurious differences, then all recognition of difference is suspect. If early ethnographies denigrated or condescended, then all ethnography denigrates. If nineteenth-century anthropology was racist, then racism is anthropology's eternal nature. If regret for change and loss was appropriated by imperialism or manifest destiny, then all nostalgia or regret is tainted. Following the same logic, one would have to reject all law, all government, and every known political position, left, right, and center, because at one time or another every one has been turned to oppression. One would also have to blind oneself to the plasticity and mutability of nostalgia, which can focus on pasts as various as the joys of Franco's Spain or time on the barricades in 1848, 1871, or 1968.

It is very often pointed out that doomsayers, whether salvage anthropologists or proponents of manifest destiny, were wrong, that people and cultures failed to disappear as predicted. For that, one can only cheer. But some were indeed erased, through genocide or ethnocide. (Even Clifford [1986, 112] concedes that "ways of life can, in a meaningful sense, 'die'; populations are . . . sometimes exterminated.") Others have rebounded, demographically and culturally, but only after the most severe losses. And almost all have undergone wholesale change, sometimes past all recognition. One may acknowledge that change is inevitable and ceaseless, even that supposedly timeless traditional cultures represent just a moment abstracted from the flow of change, shaped in many cases by the colonial encounter. One may understand that cultures are not organisms or even clearly bounded entities. One may respect today's inheritors of proud cultural traditions. But Kuna who live in the city and learn both Father's Way and the latest news from Venezuela through the printed word, or Lakota who drive pickups, live in trailers, and work for wages, live lives radically different from their ancestors', and one does them no disrespect to say so.

More than just studying the present—which is, after all, what ethnographers have mostly done in all eras—Clifford urges them to conceptualize it not as "present-becoming-past" but as "the cultural future of the planet" (1986, 115). This projection into the future—really a form of prediction—is not something anthropologists have ever been good at, and the next best thing, the insistence on the radical newness of the present globalized world and the irrelevance of any past other than colonial oppression, has limited and controlled interpretation every bit as much as salvage-consciousness. Clifford argues further that ethnographies treating the present as "a passing reality" constitute a "withdrawal from any full response to an existing society" (1986, 114). Why this should be so, why awareness of change, change not always for the better, is incompatible with engaging the present, never becomes clear. Nor is it clear how one is to escape such consciousness, any more than a photographer taking a family snapshot, who knows that by tomorrow the event recorded today will be in the past.

I am not arguing that Kuna studies (with the marginal exception of Chapin's lament) have embraced the narrative of salvage ethnography. Quite the contrary. I am suggesting that concerns about loss and change, like concerns about others' respect or disrespect, or about how the Kuna can belong to the nation but still remain themselves, run through the whole literature, sometimes as text, more often as subtext, pervasive even when denied, obfuscated, or left unmentioned. I also see these preoccupations crossing the ethnographic divide, bringing together collaborators like Markham and Olonibiginya, Nele, Rubén, and Nordenskiöld, even contemporary culturalists and their foreign interlocutors, uniting them in complex and ambivalent articulations of partly shared viewpoints. And if writing culture can never hold off loss and change in any but the most partial and contradictory ways, it is still worth doing.

NOTES

CHAPTER 1

1. See Blommaert 2005; Kroskrity 2000; Irvine and Gal 2000, and references in those works.

2. Brown 1993; Jackson 1989, 1991, 1995; Conklin and Graham 1995; Conklin 1997; Graham 2002; Warren and Jackson 2002; Langer and Muñoz 2003; Jackson and Warren 2005. The list could be *much* longer.

3. See Boyer and Lomnitz (2005) and the works they cite.

4. See Kupperman (2000, 11) and Liebersohn (1998, 23) concerning heterogeneous colonial writing on native North America; Sayre (2005) on genre differences in nineteenth-century fiction about Indians; and Doris Sommer's critique (1991, 30–41) of Foucault's neglect of the bourgeois novel (Foucault 1980). For a blatant example of such selectivity, see Rapport and Overing (2000, 13): after introducing the famous Sepúlveda–Las Casas debate, they treat Sepúlveda's anti-Indian stance as entirely representative of European attitudes.

5. In using the term hegemony, authors often demonstrate only its weak senses (domination in general, predominant but disputed discourses) but assume or imply the strongest.

6. That Spivak's essay has, through its several incarnations, inspired discrepant interpretations is due in part to its density and tortuous argumentation. Taking it only to represent a certain position, I disregard its complexities and place in the development of Spivak's later thought.

7. I omit, for the sake of brevity, discussion of the claim that subaltern groups cannot resist on their own terms, or worse, that a particularly insidious form of hegemonic control renders them able to resist but only in ways that ultimately reinstate the dominant ideology and their own subordination (see Keesing 1992, 225–238; Thomas 1994, 55–58, 210). I do believe that groups like the Kuna may

be caught by the discourses against which they struggle, but not that such traps are necessarily unavoidable.

8. Cohn 1987; Anderson 1983; Scott 1998; Thomas 1994, 37–39; Metcalf 1995, 113–159; Kertzer and Arel 2002.

9. Casagrande 1960; Liberty 1978; Sanjek 1993; Szasz 1994.

10. See below, however, on Southwestern ethnography.

11. My interest was first inspired by hearing of a course taught by Thomas Beidelman devoting a whole semester to reading Nuer ethnography.

CHAPTER 2

1. Cullen 1853, 71.

2. Regina Holloman (1969, 169–170) first noted the importance of boarding with Panamanian families. Marta de Gerdes (1995, 114–120) has corrected Holloman's misunderstanding of the Spanish term *acudiente*. Neither takes note of the term *criado* or the wide distribution of the practice in Latin America.

3. According to an oral history by Ricardo Thompson (OH 4/14/85), his father, Pilip Thompson, said that two literate men preceded Charly Robinson in San Blas at the turn of the century: Jim Barkley and Manuel Jesús Soo. The latter was said to have studied in Colombia.

4. In a previous work, I concluded from the ambiguous sources that Abisua was high chief of the coast until about 1900 (Howe 1998, 25–26), a question I now see as ambiguous and unresolved.

5. Gassó 1911–1914, XII, 275; VI, 85; XV, 64.

6. Sisnett 1956, 151, 252, 257; Céspedes 1985, 46–80, 207–313; Szok 2001, 67–71; 2004, 60–61; Bernal 2004; Howe 1998, 97–98, 181–182.

7. Intendente Humberto Vaglio, 6/30/21, "Informe semestral" (ANP), courtesy of Francisco Herrera.

8. Gassó's published diary indicates that this idiom was already current in 1907, though he incorrectly interpreted *karta* [his spelling] to refer to a messenger rather than the message (1911–1914, X, 207). Elsewhere he more correctly connected the word with messages and writing (VI, 86).

9. "Knower of things" *(immar wisid)* is the generic term for ritualist that I most often heard in my work. Today many young Kuna intellectuals use the term *gana* and even *abisua*, both of which were previously confined largely to ritual speech. By "knower" or "knower of things" I mean just what they mean by *gana*.

10. Intendente Humberto Vaglio opined that Chiefs Colman and Olonibiginya resisted schools because they would end "their ridiculous traditions" and ultimately their own positions of power ("Informe semestral . . ." MGJ 1920, p. 240).

11. Manuel Hernandez for Colman to Belisario Porras n.d., ANP, courtesy of Francisco Herrera.

12. OH Samuel Morris of Nargana, 1/28/89.

13. The most important source on Kuna scribes and their role as mediators is the thesis of Mònica Martínez Mauri (2007).

14. Citations in this book of letters and newspaper articles take the form month/day/year. Years in the twentieth century have two digits, those in the twenty-first century, four. Thus, "2/26/25" and "3/06/2004."

15. "Philippe Thompson (Felipe Thomson) 1895–1961, Bilip Tansin," privately printed pamphlet, courtesy of Bernal Castillo.

16. The reports of the Claretian missionaries make clear that the Catholic Church took the initiative in applying for control of schools in San Blas, and that they were surprised when "by an inexplicable miracle" the application was approved (Misioneros Claretianos, "Historia de la misión," Introducción, 1928).

17. Misioneros Claretianos, "Historia de la misión," passim.

18. Misioneros Hijos 1939, 120–122; Puig 1948, 182–187; V. Smith 1982, 294–303; Misioneros Claretianos, "Historia de la misión"; Calvo Población 2000, 303–349, 474–478.

19. J. J. Enderton to Nele 6/23/31, 7/20/31; Nele and Samuel Morris to Enderton 7/10/31, ARPK.

20. Peña 1959, 70–73.

21. The 1970 figures derive from an unpublished data sheet, which I was allowed to copy in the offices of Reina Torres de Araúz's research team for her studies of proposed Canal Route 17 (see Chapter 8). The 1960 figures, copied at the same time, probably derive from a published census volume, but they might come from unpublished data sheets. Thirty-seven years later, I cannot remember. The much higher literacy figures given by Holloman (1969, 89) are in error.

Literacy varied widely in 1970. On Mirya Ubigandup, of 343 individuals ten and older, only 13 could read and write, and only 4 out of 99 children were enrolled in school. On Nargana, out of 647 individuals ten and older (not counting urban migrants), only 100 were illiterate, and all but 8 out of 224 children were in school. On Carti Suitupu, 63 percent of the over-ten population was illiterate, and 55 percent of school-age children were enrolled.

22. República de Panamá, Dirección de Estadística y Censo 2001, vol. 2, *Población*, cuadro 8. I report the national rather than the regional figures for the Kuna in 2000 because so many of them, especially those most dedicated to education, were by then living in the city. See also República de Panamá, Dirección de Estadística y Censo 1998, which indicates that in Kuna Yala in 1990, the proportion of illiterates aged ten and up was still 40 percent, compared to 10.7 percent for the Republic as a whole.

CHAPTER 3

1. In my experience, Kuna leaders usually insist on speaking through interpreters even when they are fluent in Spanish, especially in formal meetings or interviews.

2. Sancurman, i.e., Sam Colman. Colman, who most often used the name Cimral, sometimes used Sam or his Kuna name, Inagindibipilele.

3. Kwepti, Gwebdi, or Río Azúcar, today called Wargandi.

4. Tigandiki, also known as Niatupu.

5. Concerning the three leaders mentioned for Playón Chico, or Ukkup Senni, see Howe 1998, 146–149, and Chapter 2.

6. I.e., passes provided by the government for free travel on the Panama Railroad from Colón to Panama City.

7. Charles Lewis was or had recently been the first chief of Nusatupu, or Cora-

zón de Jesús. It was very unlikely that Garrido would make Lewis head of the two islands, first because he would not have brooked any interference in local affairs, and second because Lewis had already run afoul of the police.

8. I.e., Colman's secretary used the adjective *policial* instead of the noun *policía*.

9. Gassó (1911–1914) noted that the Panamanian government received a collective letter against him, and it is likely that nineteenth-century Kuna leaders occasionally communicated on paper with the Colombian government. Such letters were of necessity dictated to non-Indians.

10. Informe Semestral del 10 de julio al 31 de diciembre de 1920, que el Intendente de la Circunscripción de San Blas presenta al Señor Secretario de Gobierno y Justicia, ANP, courtesy of Francisco Herrera.

11. The sample of available letters is skewed, since numerous letters from Inabaginya to intendentes occur in files in El Porvenir, but the originals of Colman's complaints to higher functionaries remained in government files in Panama. Colman's political use of letters and interviews nonetheless emerges clearly from the documentary record.

12. This is not to say that the relative importance of various class markers may not vary significantly between cultures, as Michèle Lamont (1992) has persuasively argued: "My data suggest that Bourdieu greatly underestimates the importance of moral boundaries while he exaggerates the importance of cultural and socioeconomic boundaries" (1992, 5), and indeed that much of what Bourdieu's admirers have taken as universal aspects of boundary-marking are distinctively French. On the importance of schools to bourgeois society in setting social boundaries and allowing social mobility, see Hobsbawm (1987, 174–179).

13. References to the extensive sociolinguistic literature on these topics can be found in Blommaert's incisive discussion (2005). It is striking that the cases Blommaert examines of "texts that do not travel well," which involve Africans struggling to master the forms of European personal and bureaucratic discourse (2005, 58–60, 78–83), are remarkably similar to the trials of Kuna scribes.

14. See Locke's famous dicta on gentlemen and letters (Locke 2000 [1693], section 189).

15. Different orthographies of Kuna represent these stops either as K/G, P/B, and T/D or KK/K, PP/P, and TT/T. These stops are variably voiced and unvoiced in ways different and more complex than for their Spanish equivalents, they vary more by word position, and one set (K, T, P) functions as doubles of the other (GG, DD, BB). Thus interference with the closest consonants in Spanish is all but guaranteed (see Price 2005, 2006).

16. Although, in Goffman's terms (1959), chiefs and secretaries constituted a team, their interests were not identical: the latter may have concealed the limits of their knowledge of Spanish and English from the former.

17. It is also instructive that when intendentes endorsed Kuna letters or introduced them as evidence in reports or case files, they revised them heavily, cleaning up their stylistic and grammatical errors and inconsistencies.

18. Informe semestral que presenta el Jefe de la Circunscripción de San Blas al Señor Secretario de Gobierno y Justicia 7/19, ABP; also MGJ 1920; Howe 1998, 134.

19. Here I am influenced by sad experience with academic infighting: sophisticated professors put themselves and their profession in a bad light through the intemperance of their attacks on opponents.

20. I consulted Porras's letters in the Archivo Belisario Porras at the University of Panama.

21. R. J. Alfaro to H. Alfaro 3/13/25, ARJA.

22. "Indios" in the newspaper *Crítica Libre*, 10/13/03. Anelio Merry, Aiban Wagwa, in *Crítica Libre*, 10/28/03.

CHAPTER 4

1. Properly *gandule* or *kantule*.

2. Wafer 1934 [1699]; Balburger n.d. [1748]; Ariza 1971 [1774]. In my opinion, which some colleagues may find overcritical, most of these sources offer fragmentary, unreliable information, whose interpretation depends heavily on extrapolation from recent ethnography. Useful bits and pieces turn up in other pirate memoirs (Dampier 1927; Esquemeling 1924; Ringrose in Esquemeling [1924, 299–331]) and missionary reports (Requejo Salcedo 1908 [1640]; Severino de Santa Teresa 1956, 27–72, 81–101, 174–195, 260). An epic poem, *Alteraciones del Darien* (De Páramo y Cepeda 1994 [1697]), has yet to be systematically analyzed.

3. Ernesto Restrepo Tirado demonstrated Reclus's plagiarism almost immediately (1971 [1887], 81–84; also in V. Restrepo 1888, 113–115). Restrepo Tirado's own observations (1971, 84–95; also in V. Restrepo 1888, 113–129), though more original, full, and reliable, were hampered by a short stay, reticent informants, and his own prejudices. See also Pinart (1887, 1890).

4. Early-twentieth-century knowledge of the Kuna was summed up in a school text, *Geografía de Panamá*, by Ramón Valdés (1905, 41–44); a brief Smithsonian monograph (Bell 1910, 625–632); and a *National Geographic* article (Pittier 1912, 643–657)—all notable for fragmentary information, received notions (some going back to Ariza), and egregious errors.

5. Informe del Sr. Agustín Vélez de J., Inspector del Puerto, Jefe del Resguardo Nacional de Colón, a su Señoría el Ministro de Hacienda de la República de Colombia, año de 1891, Gaceta de Panamá, Año IV, Número 561, Panama, 30 de Abril de 1892, página 2464. Courtesy of Bernal Castillo.

6. For references on Gassó's long series of published letters, see Howe 1998 or Howe 2004b.

7. Gassó 1911–1914, IV, 56; XIV, 18, 43; XXI, 39, 66; Howe 1998, 49, 309.

8. Nordenskiöld et al. 1938, 5–6; Joyce 1934, 178–184.

9. Sources included a report by Gassó, briefs and memoranda from interested parties, a 1913 fact-finding mission, and Kuna letters and delegations (see Howe 1998, 61, 95–107).

10. *Diario de Panamá* 8/12, 8/17, 8/18, 8/19/10; *Panama Journal* 8/12, 8/17, 8/18, 8/19, 8/20/10; Anonymous 1916; Howe 1998, 61–62, 101–107.

11. Said 1978; Stoler and Cooper 1997; Comaroff and Comaroff 1991; Thomas 1994.

12. The coherence in the government's civilizing program for which I have ar-

gued (Howe 1991a; 1998, 177–187), though real, did not constitute a systematic discourse or body of knowledge about the Indians.

13. In one report, Vaglio did offer six unfavorable paragraphs on other aspects of Indian life ("Informe semestral . . ." MGJ 1920, pp. 241–242).

14. On colonial ideologies of lack, see Thomas 1994, 54.

15. Informe del Intendente Jefe de la Circunscripción de San Blas, MGJ 1916, pp. 461–462. My translation. Most excerpts from Spanish-language texts in this chapter were translated by Ana Ríos Guardia; I have made numerous small editorial changes and take responsibility for the translations' accuracy.

16. Throughout his memoirs (1911–1914), Leonardo Gassó railed at third parties—West Indian sailors, Protestants, North Americans, Masons, Liberals, fickle governments, Kuna from the Bayano.

17. See Porras's subsequent letter against the merchants (Porras to Secretary 12/28/19, in Calvo Población 2000, 553, no. 86, document pages, p. 132).

18. How far officials would go to fault Coope is evident in strained efforts to blame her for Claudio Iglesias's death (Mojica, "Informe . . ." for July 1921–July 1922, ABP) and, later, even for the 1925 rebellion.

19. Bourne 1990; Pulsipher 2005; White 1991, 223–268; Wallace 1993, 37–38; Merrell 1999; Weber 2005. On Indian-White relations and antagonisms among colonists, see especially Peter Silver's persuasive analysis (2008).

20. Today the spelling *sahila* is more common. Variant spellings are encouraged by complications in Kuna phonology. The stop represented by G or K is transformed to the vowel I or Y when followed by a consonant. Thus *saka-mala,* "parents-in-law," is shortened to *saimar.* However, when the G or K is followed by an L, the transformation is only partial, and to capture the raspy semivowel, the word for chief has variously been written *ságuila* or *sahila* or *sagla,* as well as *saila.*

21. On exploiting *sailas* for indirect rule, see Intendente Vaglio, "Informe semestral . . ." MGJ 1920, p. 238.

22. E.g., Intendente Vaglio to Porras 6/29/19, ABP; Santiago Castillo, Head 2d Police Detachment, to Intendente Mojica 5/26/21, AI; Police agent Guillermo Denis to Intendente Mojica 9/27/23, AI.

23. See also Informe semestral, Intendente [Vaglio] to Secretary 1/30–6/30/19, ABP.

24. See also Informe del Intendente [Hurtado], MGJ 1916, p. 464; Intendente Vaglio to President Porras 11/26/19, 1/20/20, ABP; Informe semestral, Intendente to Secretary 1/30–6/30/19, ABP.

25. In the blurry microfilm of the letter, this word appears to be "impludible": whether a misspelling, an improvised neologism, or a misreading, it can fairly confidently be taken to mean undeniable, unassailable.

26. See also Lt. Linares to Secretary 12/30/20, AI; Howe 1998, 130–149, 167–176.

27. Informe semestral, Intendente [Mojica] to Secretary 1/01–6/30/19 [6/30/19], AI.

28. Informe semestral, Intendente [Mojica] to Secretary 1/01–6/30/21.

29. Untitled report for two periods, July–December 1921 and January–July of 1922, ABP.

30. See also Intendente Vaglio to Secretary 12/01/19, ABP; Informe semestral, Intendente Mojica to Secretary 7/01/20–12/31/20, AI; Intendente Mojica to Jefe 2d Destacamento 5/31/21, AI; S. Castillo, Jefe 2d destacamento to Intendente 6/6/21, AI.

31. República de Panamá, Dirección General del Censo 1922. San Blas was included in the volume for the Province of Colón.

32. The five sites were the border village Puerto Obaldía, three branches of the Mandinga banana plantations, and the administrative headquarters at El Porvenir.

33. Eight individuals were counted in what appear to be work camps.

34. It is easy to imagine possible screw-ups and fudging as immediate causes of the truncated census reporting.

35. Kertzer and Arel 2002, 23–25; Goldscheider 2002; Blum 2002; Uvin 2002.

36. Intendente Mojica to Secretary 6/30/22 [untitled report for two periods, July–December 1921 and January–July of 1922], ABP.

37. Secretary to Intendente 2/04/21, AI.

38. On the intervention by Latin goldworkers, see Howe 1998, 125, 320n. 25. On use of analogy as cultural defense, see Howe 1998, 49–50, 309nn. 34–36; Gassó 1911–1914, I, 203; VI, 86; XX, 280; XXI, 66–67. Gassó's Indian opponents and Colman used analogy in different ways, one arguing for separate dispensations, the other that Kuna customs were worthy counterparts of national institutions or harmless variants on fundamental types.

39. Colman to Porras 1/31/13, ANP, courtesy of Francisco Herrera. See also the letter excerpted in Chapter 2: Manuel Hernandez for Colman to Belisario Porras n.d., ANP, courtesy of Francisco Herrera.

40. Unlike the sample letters given in Chapter 3, in this letter the line breaks have not been retained.

41. The active principle in each carving derives, not from its outward form, but from the virtues of the wood from which it is fashioned.

42. Colman's secretary also added to the confusion by putting "alone" in the singular *(solo)*.

43. As previously noted, the preposition *a* and the verb form *ha* were often confused by Kuna scribes.

44. *Gandule niga bipi,* literally "flute-man young nephew/young man"—possibly the everyday name of a man of the village.

45. Colman probably recognized Latin American use of *Doctor* as a generalized honorific but failed to see that its use for Indian ritualists would be unacceptable. More recently, the Kuna have reserved *Doctor* exclusively for *neles,* or seers, the most prestigious of all specialists.

46. On which, see Chapter 2; also Howe 1998, 153–166.

47. Estrella 9/30/21, courtesy of Francisco Herrera. The passages quoted were preceded and followed by several paragraphs devoted to violence and the recent court case. The names given at the bottom of the document were of Colman and five other chiefs.

48. Guha 1983, 225–238; Keesing 1992, 225–238; Thomas 1994, 55–58, 210.

Keesing's 1992 discussion is more open and flexible on the point than his previous talks.

49. It may be that the statement fit Colman's private sentiments to the extent that he saw some changes, such as schools, as inevitable in the long run.

50. Not that the issue would be solved anytime soon, given the enduring tension in both discourse and state policies between universal, mostly individual human rights and special collective rights for indigenous peoples, or indeed, for any category or sector within national populations (Assies 2000, 14, 18; Stavenhagen 1994, 2002; Sieder 2002; Jackson and Warren 2005, 560; Jackson 2007). In early-twentieth-century Panama the notion of special rights or ancestral claims was largely absent.

51. E. T. Lefevre to Sec. R. J. Alfaro, in Sec. to Intendente 7/06/20, AI; Howe 1998, 146.

52. "The Indians of San Blas, in their mayority [*sic*], are [con]sidered yet as savages and semi-savages, and therefore are [governed] by a certain system of special laws,—very different to the [oth]er laws in force in the other parts of the republic of Panamá" (Intendente Vaglio to Anna Coope 6/10/20 [in English], AI; see also Intendente Mojica, "Informe . . ." June 1922, p. 10, ABP). In 1923 the Secretary of Government and Justice rejected Mojica's demand to suspend laws in San Blas, because the measure was not needed to control the *"barbaros"* (Secretary to Intendente 6/30/23, AI). Even concerning land rights, though special claims were occasionally acknowledged, priority and duration of tenure and a universal moral right to adequate subsistence mattered, not special indigenous connection with the land. Officials objected vociferously when the Kuna asserted a right to exclude outsiders or control access to the forest (Howe 1995, 1998).

CHAPTER 5

1. Verrill 1921, 204–205; ms. "The San Blas Region and Its Customs," 80-A-15. Flyers for a tourist excursion date from a few months after the 1925 rebellion (6/30, 7/29/25); see also a clipping (Star & Herald 6/28/25) and another flyer the following year (5/11/26) (80-A-15, USNA).

2. See the photograph of one branch of the IORM, the Cholo Tribe No. 5 (http://www.czimages.com/CZMemories/Photos/photoof123.htm). The *Canal Zone Pilot* of 1908 (Anonymous 1908, 463–464) listed seven "tribes" across the Zone. See also Lemke 1964, 674; *Panama Canal Review* (11/06/53, in http://www.czbrats.com/Towns/gatun.htm). On the IORM in general, see also http://www.abaris.net/freemasonry/marin_red_men.htm; P. Deloria 1998.

3. Verner (1920, 23) wrote of the Kuna that "every visitor to the Canal Zone hears of their peculiarities."

4. Information on Gilbert comes from Grigore (1987), from short pieces appended to the reprint edition (Grigore 1987), and from a Web site (http://www.angelfire.com/tx/CZAngelsSpace/JSGilbert.html).

5. "Arzoguete" and "tulete" should properly be *absogedi* (an exorcist-chanter) and *inaduledi* (medicine-man).

6. *Ome,* "woman, wife," *bunagwa,* "girl, sister [man speaking]."

7. A distortion of *machigwa*, "boy."

8. Iterations of this theme are ubiquitous: Nicholas 1903, 232; Pearson 1904, 210; Forbes-Lindsay 1906, 94; Anonymous 1908, 429; Bell 1910, 629–630; Anderson 1911, 321; Collins 1912, 138; Gause and Carr 1912, 228, 239–240; Allen 1913, 346; Browne 1913, 81; Avery 1915, 299; Verner 1920, 24, 27; Lutz 1924, 19; Joyce 1934, 166, 170; Core 1941, 175; Feeney 1941, 193–195; Minter 1948, 30–32. Writers with friendly experience of the Indians, in Colón or San Blas, offered variants, either contrasting their fearsome reputation with their real inoffensive amiability, or else portraying exclusionism as a reasoned policy, or locating the true holdouts among the Chucunaque River Kuna (Weir 1909, 46–47; Pittier 1912, 648–649; Abbott 1913, 311–312; Beach 1917, 1940; Verrill 1921, 183, 185–186; 1922, 32–38; 1924, 54, 58; Feeney 1941).

9. Bell 1910, 629; Anderson 1911, 321; Pittier 1912, 649; Avery 1915, 301; Verner 1920, 26; McCullough 1977, 594. Although I identify the themes of self-immolation and refusal to sell sand with North Americans, it should be noted that the port captain (see Chapter 4) and Leonardo Gassó both mentioned the threat to kill women and children (1911–1914, II, 205); Otto Lutz, a European-born scholar teaching at the Instituto Nacional, recounted the sand incident (1924, 20); and Father José Berengueras (1930–1931) mentioned both. Ideas about racial purity reemerge in Carles's pamphlet (1965) from the 1960s.

10. For other statements on Kuna racial purity, see Gause and Carr 1912, 239–240; Browne 1913; Avery 1915, 299; Verner 1920, 24; Verrill 1921, 185–186; Robinson n.d., 1; Nordenskiöld 1928b, 232–234; Joyce 1934, 166, 170; McKim 1947b, 18, 110; Beach 1940, 138; Core 1941, 175; Feeney 1941, 197; Minter 1948, 30.

11. Figueroa Navarro 1978, 1987.

12. On tourism, see note 1.

13. The document appears in two versions: "The San Blas Region," in RG84, and "The San Blas Region and Its Customs," 80-A-15. Both versions excerpt a *Star and Herald* article from June 1919 concerning conflict over noserings; they note that Coope's mission, which began in 1913, had been in place seven years. The accession date for the version in Canal Authority files is November 25, 1929. Although the author refers to himself several times, his name only appears, ambiguously, at the foot of the last page.

14. "Native" typically referred to non-Indian locals.

15. Markham to Porras 2/01/24, with Markham n.d. 1. Markham to Porras 2/08/24, Enclosure 4, Dispatch 659, 3/13/25, 819.00/1180, USNA.

16. Porras to Markham 3/10/24, with Markham n.d. 1. Porras to Secretary 3/22, 4/26/24; Secretary to Porras 3/24/24, ABP (courtesy of Francisco Herrera).

17. Intendente to Head 1st Police Detachment 9/19/24; Intendente to Head Second Detachment 9/17/24, AI. I have not seen the petition itself.

18. For fuller accounts see Howe 1998; Marsh 1934; Taussig 1993.

19. Copies of the Declaration are in NAA; State Department Records (Enclosure 4, Dispatch 651, 2/28/25, 819.00/1176); Star & Herald 2/27/25; and Puig 1948, 205–223.

20. Concerning possible eugenicist influence, see communications from Davenport (in 819.00/1162, 1166). Marsh had previously tried out some elements of his portrayal in a manuscript promoting the 1924 expedition, a magazine article, and various statements and press releases (see Howe 1998). The Declaration does not mention Viking explorers, a theme to which Marsh later returned.

21. Marsh himself had previously called limb binding "barbaric" (see Howe 1998).

22. See South to State 3/13/25, 819.00/1180.

23. Panamanian newspapers had mocked Marsh mercilessly in 1924 for elaborate theories about Kuna racial origins and the white Indians (Howe 1998, 240–242).

24. Resolución 38 de 1925, República de Panamá, in Records of Legation, R800, RG84, USNA; Governor Panama Canal to Secretary of War 3/04/25, 80-A-15; *New York Times*, editorial "The Republic of Tala [sic]," 3/01/25; Garay 1930, 10; Nordenskiöld et al. 1938, 418–419; Castillero Reyes 1946.

25. Markham n.d. 2. The content of Kuna complaints in this meeting were also discussed by Marsh (ROM diaries 1925, second part, pp. 7–9, NAA); by Minister South (South to State 3/13/25, 819.00/1180); and in notes apparently taken down by another U.S. official (Records of Legation, RG84, USNA).

26. South to State 3/02/25, 819.00/1164.

27. Variability in North American attitudes became evident when South went on leave in late 1925: the chargé d'affaires received renewed Indian appeals but pressed them to submit to Panamanian authority and even colluded with a secret agent of the government (Howe 1998, 293).

28. Major 1993, 151–153; Pizzurno Gelós and Araúz 1996, 153–158.

29. De la Ossa's report of March 9 is in Diario (3/12/25) and in translation in 80-A-15.

30. H. Alfaro to R. J. Alfaro 3/24/25, ARJA.

31. *Sia bibi*, literally "little niece," an everyday name for a Kuna woman.

32. Markham n.d. 2.

33. South did praise the English of the interpreter on Suitupu (South to State 3/13/25, 819.00/1180).

34. Rebels did write several letters to authorities (see Howe 1998, 223), two of which moved South. He might have been less affected if not already persuaded by Kuna oratory.

35. H. Alfaro to R. J. Alfaro 3/24/25, ARJA. Navas's flawed critique of a Catholic grammar (1935) suggests that his mastery of Kuna was imperfect.

36. Markham n.d. 2.

37. E.g., Dilworth 1996, 189.

38. *El Tiempo* 3/13/25, in 80-A-15. The claim was implausible because the government had already welcomed foreign-owned banana plantations without the necessity of plotting or uprisings, and because the company in Mandinga lent a vessel to help suppress the rebels. Though Marsh himself had tried in 1923 to secure a huge concession in the Darién, his 1925 intervention came at the cost of renouncing any such schemes.

39. See Howe 1998, 279–291, 351nn. 50, 51.

40. Star & Herald 2/27/25. The lines are from Thomas Babington Macaulay's "Horatius," stanza xxvi.

41. Estrella 8/21/25.

CHAPTER 6

1. Nordenskiöld 1928b, 226. A handwritten copy of a newspaper article on the expedition stamped with Rubén Pérez's seal (ARPK) seems to date from the end of the trip.

2. For Nordenskiöld's biography, I rely principally on Lindberg's study (1996), which was paraphrased and translated for me by Tor Schoenmeyr and Karin Antoni, and on the essays in the volume published by Alvarsson and Agüero (1997), especially those by Alvarsson, Wassén, Hellbom, Isacsson, and Lindberg, also on Wassén 1987–1988 and personal communications from Bo Ernstson.

3. Nordenskiöld himself carried out archaeological investigations, but his sort of distributional analyses of technology only made sense until archaeology matured and supplanted them.

4. *Indianlif i El Chaco* (1910), *Indianer och Hvitai nordöstra Bolivia* (1911), *Forskningar och äventyr I Sydamerika 1913–14* (1915).

5. *Svenska Dagblat* 7/07/32, in Lindberg 1996, 529.

6. See Lindberg 1996, 34–61, 460–500. Alvarsson (1997) notes Nordenskiöld's positive attitude toward Indians. His antipathy to Blacks (see Lindberg 1996, 460–500) is apparent throughout his narrative of the 1927 expedition (Nordenskiöld 1928b).

7. Bo Ernstson, personal communication.

8. All information on the Berkeley stay from Lindberg 1996, 374–378.

9. Information on the voyage and fieldwork comes from the trip narrative (1928b) and Lindberg's biography (1996), both published in Swedish. Also Linné's unpublished logbook and brutally frank field diary (MWC). Nordenskiöld's field notes and many of his other papers were not available, apparently scattered among family members and some sold or lost (Bo Ernstson, personal communication).

10. Lindberg 1996, 380–383; Linné diary, MWC.

11. Nordenskiöld 1928b, 120–191. See especially the anti-Black diatribe on p. 191.

12. Kainora, predecessor village of present-day Achutupu.

13. That Nele's acceptance and encouragement of the project was a matter of policy is suggested by the suspicion and even hostility encountered in other Kuna villages (1928b, 215–218).

14. In this era, he spelled his name Haya and only later changed it to Hayans, the form used throughout here.

15. Concerning the life of Pérez Kantule, I have relied on taped interviews of descendants by Bernal Castillo, also on B. Castillo 2000, 148–157; Martínez Mauri n.d. [10/29/2003]; 2007, 315–332; Velarde 1996. Martínez Mauri's detailed biography analyzes in depth numerous aspects of Pérez Kantule's life not covered here. Sources for Guillermo Hayans include a brief autobiography by Hayans

(ms. 9/15/52, MWC); a biography copied and signed by Hayans's son-in-law, Chany Edman (AGH); and various manuscript fragments (AGH).

16. Pérez Kantule n.d., trip diary (see note 28).

17. 1928b, 228–229; statement by Nordenskiöld, Estrella 8/07/27.

18. 1927; 1928b, 230, 276–282; Nele and Pérez Kantule 1928, 13; Nordenskiöld et al. 1938, xii; Lindberg 1996, 512–514.

19. According to Lindberg (1996, 514–515), Nordenskiöld was unable to study the documents in the depth he would have liked, in part because of the time devoted to collecting artifacts.

20. "[Kuna culture is] *los restos de una gran cultura semejante a la de los mayas u otra de las encontradas en Centro America*" (Estrella 8/07/27).

21. Nordenskiöld later saw the light: his posthumous magnum opus (Nordenskiöld et al. 1938, 320) notes that "unfaithfulness within marriage is not unusual." Amusingly, Guillermo Hayans wrote Rubén during his stay in Sweden to pass on news of a scandal on Ustupu involving another secretary (Haya to Pérez Kantule 6/30/31, AGH).

22. I have not been able to determine the exact number of days spent at Ustupu, perhaps as few as two or three. Nordenskiöld's account (1928b) is vague; his notes are unavailable; and Linné's logbook lacks crucial dates.

23. Nordenskiöld (1928b, 221) correctly interpreted a lone Panamanian flag on Ustupu as a sign of political division, but failed to recognize the existence of a second community on the island affiliated with Inabaginya, and thus the presence close at hand of unfriendly observers.

24. Emphasis in original. Nordenskiöld to RPK 1/12/31, MWC.

25. Pérez Kantule n.d., trip diary (see note 28). I have not found the original of his criticisms.

26. Pérez Kantule to Nordenskiöld 2/09/31, MWC.

27. Nordenskiöld to Pérez 4/02/31, MWC.

28. In the 1960s, Pérez Kantule produced a typewritten copy of the diary, illustrated with his own photographs, Swedish postcards, and illustrations taken from Nordenskiöld's publications. The manuscript, entrusted to the former intendente, Napoleón Salazar, was turned over to Rubén's descendants in about 2000; they made copies available to Koskun Kalu, research arm of the Congreso General de la Cultura Kuna. With the family's permission, Koskun Kalu provided me with a photocopy in 2001 (Pérez Kantule n.d.). For the Swedish sojourn, I also depend on Lindberg (1996), articles by Wassén (see bibliography), and several Swedish newspaper articles. Plans are underway to publish the diary.

29. Wassén, article in *La Prensa* [Argentina] 10/06/32 (MWC).

30. Newspaper articles (all at MWC) include *Ny Tid* 6/27/31; *Svenska Dagbladet* 8/03/31; *Minareten* n.d.; *Julskeppet* [Christmas annual] 12/n.d./31 (this last by Wassén). Newspaper articles by Nordenskiöld himself include *Svenska Dagbladet* 8/06/31, 3/13/32; *Sandels Tidningen* 1/30/32.

31. Bo Ernstson, personal communication. Museum files contain a manuscript of Valery's remarks (MWC). Lindberg (1996, 522–524) has a full account of the tour, which also included lectures on non-Kuna topics.

32. Pérez Kantule n.d.

33. Estrella 7/21/33; *Panamá América* 11/10/33, n.d./33 (in the MWC), 6/30/34, 7/01/34, 1/20/39; Star & Herald 12/24/33, 5/24/34, 9/24/34—all in MWC.

CHAPTER 7

1. Although Wassén took public credit, Izikowitz made it known privately that he had played a major role in pulling the volume together (Bo Ernstson, personal communication).
2. Nordenskiöld et al. 1938, 1-7, 28-58, 79-89, 334-388, 393-398, 414-455, 479-481, 485-493, 506-509.
3. Other miscellaneous items include a law text and political letters (pp. 104-121); extracts from a health survey (pp. 481-485); catalogue descriptions for artifacts associated with puberty ceremonies (pp. 69-78); diagrams of puberty ceremonies (pp. 65-69); a glossary of Kuna words (pp. 657-679); and a table of characters in Kuna sacred history (pp. 323-332).
4. Nordenskiöld et al. 1938, 399-414, 455-478, 555-611, 614-619, 623-642, 644-656. Medicine admonishments are short chanted texts that instruct and animate the spirits in medicines.
5. Although Pérez did a conscientious job on the interlinear glosses, they cannot convey even the most superficial meaning of the chanted lines, let alone the import and symbolism of the chant as a whole. The only texts in Kuna with paraphrases—but not true translations—are found on pp. 446-478, 650-656.
6. Nordenskiöld et al. 1938, 8-28, 58-65, 89-91, 125-322, 494-506.
7. I could not find the twenty-one-page manuscript at the MWC. In the volume, several shorter texts on Ibeorgun are also included as addenda to the third long text (1938, 263-277).
8. As an added source of confusion, the kin terms mix archaisms with current usage.
9. One reason why the overall progression of Kuna mythic history was never clarified—and why Dad Ibe and other culture heroes received short shrift—was that Nele, Pérez, and Nordenskiöld all concentrated on the hero Ibeorgun.
10. My translation.
11. It is interesting, however, that Nordenskiöld insisted that Nele doubted many aspects of Kuna cosmology and history (see below, this chapter) and that he offered a kind of apology for ideas accepted by Nele that Nordenskiöld considered mystical or credulous (1932b, 468-469; Nordenskiöld et al. 1938, xviii-xx, 88).
12. 1928b, 194-195, 247, 258; Nele et al. 1930, 6-7; Nordenskiöld et al. 1938, 3, 438-439; Nordenskiöld to Reginald Harris n.d., MWC.
13. Nordenskiöld identified light-skinned nonalbino Kuna (almost certainly heterozygotes for albinism) as French descendants. In a press statement (Estrella 8/07/27), Nordenskiöld discussed the French at length, claiming that Olga had identified a Kainora Indian as French-looking. Nordenskiöld's predecessor, Father Gassó, gave credit for every Kuna virtue to the eighteenth-century Jesuit, Father Walburger, or Balburger, though in fact Balburger's charges, after rejecting his teaching, mostly died in an epidemic (Balburger n.d. [1748]; Castillero Calvo 1995,

215–224; Severino de Santa Teresa 1956, 279–286; Gallup-Díaz 2004). Scholars favoring the Scots' influence ignore the brevity and superficiality of Scots colony relations with the Kuna. Christian influences on Kuna religion, if any, probably derive in fact from *Dominican* missionaries (see Castillero Calvo 1995).

14. As noted in Chapter 10, young Kuna historians have recently begun paying close attention to colonial history and written sources, but this material has not formed any part of the histories in Father's Way.

15. The expedition went ashore very briefly at four other communities, with satisfactory results only on Isla Pino.

16. Nordenskiöld mentions Gassó (Nordenskiöld et al. 1938, 5–6). On the gathering house as "the house of errors," see Howe 1998, 51, 309n. 46; Gassó 1911–1914, XXII, 134–135, also passim.

17. During my own brief research in Sweden, I went over the manuscript essay on individuals with Bo Ernstson, who provided a running précis and commentary.

18. Nordenskiöld said Nele doubted elaborations of Kuna cosmology and culture heroes preceding Ibeorgun (Nordenskiöld et al. 1938, xviii). These doubts, possibly true, do not belie Nordenskiöld's need to distinguish Nele from the masses.

19. As an added complication, Nordenskiöld discusses the name Diolele (Nordenskiöld et al. 1938, 434), but Wassén (1989/90, 20) says Nordenskiöld used another name, Tiosaila, though in the same paragraph he also mentions Tiolele. Another esoteric name for God is Olokuppilele.

20. As Chapin notes (1983, 181), many of the names in the chants are strictly speaking not substitutions for everyday names, but the names of their spiritual counterparts.

21. On Kuna belief in Father's intervention in life, see Howe 1986, 51–78; 1998, 47; Gassó 1911–1914, I, 57; IX, 162; XX, 16; XXI, 39, 136–137.

22. Here again, Nordenskiöld's reliance on the curing chants misled him. In the chants' inner secrets, the deities create objects or beings sexually, evidence he thought for the priority of creation and for morality as a late foreign overlay (Nordenskiöld et al. 1938, 432–444), but in fact a function of religious division of labor: morality belongs, not to curing chants, but to the gathering, home of Father and Mother together.

23. Also Nordenskiöld to Pérez 1/09/31 (MWC).

24. The chant's unintelligibility was mentioned in the 1953 publication but not the earlier 1947 version, which is what Lévi-Strauss drew on. Questions of intelligibility, it should be noted, must be treated with care. It is often asserted that *argars* translate into ordinary language chiefly chants that nonchiefs cannot understand. In fact, the most common items of chiefly vocabulary are widely known, and most verses are immediately understandable, even by me. Similarly, knowledgeable Kuna, including some women, can follow many of the most obvious verses in curing chants. Nonetheless, it is highly unlikely that the women for whom Muu igar is performed are following along as it is chanted.

25. Nordenskiöld noted that Charlie Nelson had no pictography at hand but made some for him (1928b, 208–209). The admonishment for stones called *akkwalele* (Nele and Pérez Kantule 1928, 53–75, plates 3–5; Nordenskiöld et al.

1938, 557–575, plates VII–VIII), with picture-writing specially drawn by Pérez Kantule (Nele and Pérez Kantule 1928, 3; Nordenskiöld et al. 1938, 557), served as one of Nordenskiöld's prime examples (see figure 7.1). He noted (1938, xiv) that "only in exceptional cases has Pérez actually copied the picture-writing" made by others. Concerning the documents in Spanish and English produced by the Kuna, Nordenskiöld pointedly noted that almost all of them "have not been written at my request but were already present in the tribe before my arrival" (1928b, 148), but it did not seem to worry him that the same could not be said of the picture-writing.

26. Nele and Pérez Kantule 1928; Nele et al. 1930; Nordenskiöld et al. 1938.

27. Nele and Pérez Kantule 1928, 25–48, plates 1, 2; 53–75, plates 3–5; Nordenskiöld et al. 1938, plates II–IX, XI, XIII, XV, following p. 686. Among these drawings by Nelson and Pérez Kantule, at least two, depicting characters and entities from Kuna sacred history, are obviously nontraditional (1938, plate I).

28. A knower and friend named José Solis allowed me to copy his graphic pictures of the spiritual birth of scissors in the *purba* to Tisla igar (see also Holmer and Wassén 1963, 82–85).

29. As for the painted boards displayed during puberty ceremonies, it would require thousands of boards to represent the verses of the puberty chant cycle. Nordenskiöld's claims (Nele et al. 1930, 14) that death chanters carry with them a picture script, and that they continue chanting on the trip to the graveyard, do not match my experience.

30. Though Nordenskiöld touted Pérez's claims for picture-writing calendars, relief-carved wooden tablets, and pictography resembling Aztec hieroglyphics, neither he nor any later ethnographer ever saw such things (1932a, 7; Nordenskiöld et al. 1938, xxv, 421–423).

31. 1938, 12–14. The census figures have caused problems. Totals given in the six community profiles contradict Pérez Kantule's census, likely distorted to favor Nele and Colman's alliance. Wassén missed this discrepancy but noticed that Pérez Kantule's figures disagreed with Hayans's count for Ustupu (Wassén 1938b, 17). Unfortunately, he cast doubt on Hayans rather than Pérez (see Hirschfeld, Howe, and Levin 1978; Stout 1947, 59).

32. Many of the category headings used by Hayans (*Situación, Límites, Costas*, etc.) also appear in the Valdés text. Geographic volumes by Manuel María Alba (1929) (see Chapter 8) and José Crespo (1928), with very different formats, are not likely models.

33. Cohn 1987; Scott 1998; Anderson 1983; Kertzer and Arel 2002.

34. On Colman's cooperation with the census: Jefe del segundo destacamento to Teniente encargado en Porvenir 5/08/20, AI. For other sources on the 1920 census, see Howe 1998, 321n. 5. The Kuna were probably complacent about census-takers in 1920 because, as they were nontaxpayers, the information did not threaten their interests.

35. See Sherzer's alternate analysis (1990, 249), which supplements rather than contradicts Chapin's explanation.

36. Artinelio Hernández n.d. [May 2004].

37. Lindberg's extended discussion of Nordenskiöld's social philosophy and his attitudes toward primitivism (1996, 34–61, 460–500) shows that he was able

to combine down-to-earth views of the unpleasant realities of Indian life in the Chaco with idealization of traditional ways and a call for their return to Swedish society.

38. Even the supposedly eternal traditions of Father's Way may have been reworked and rearranged into a new mytho-historical synthesis by the handful of nineteenth-century Kuna teachers in Colombia and the Tuira Valley from whom they derive. On variant traditions and editing in the later twentieth century, see Chapter 10.

CHAPTER 8

1. De Tapia 1971, 55. Ernesto Castillero Reyes (1970, 70) notes that Urraca's statue was moved but not the dates for its placement or displacement. The space, rededicated to Ricardo Miró, is still known as the Parque Urraca.

2. See also de la Peña 2005, 724; Weber 2005, 261–263; Sayre 2005, 17–19.

3. On Urraca, see also De Tapia 1971; Russo Berguido 1973; Alemancia 1998.

4. A great deal more remains to be written about *mestizaje* in Panama than can be encompassed here. Although questions of intermarriage and race-crossing were foregrounded in the local struggles between police and Kuna villagers between 1919 and 1925, and apparently in the Indian policies of the Porras government (Howe 1998, 186–187), they do not appear to have been nearly so salient after 1925. Questions of past colonial *mestizaje* as an aspect of modern national identity had little direct bearing on current relations with Indian populations. Contemporary race relations, either as practice or as national ideology or problem, were concerned more with Afro-Panamanian populations, especially of Antillean origin, than with the Kuna or other Indians.

5. Pupo-Walker 1996, 490–503; Swanson 2004, 13–14.

6. Garay's researches were solicited by the government (Gasteazoro 1979, 17; Garay to Nordenskiöld 7/23/29, MWC), but publication of the expensive volume in Brussels was likely at the author's expense and initiative.

7. Garay, artfully vague about dates, first arrived on January 3, 1929, and returned a month later (Gasteazoro 1979, 36; Misioneros Claretianos 1928–1945).

8. Garay 1930, 9–11, 22, 28, 14–19. Despite his attack on Nordenskiöld, Garay wrote to ask to present his results in Sweden (Garay to Nordenskiöld 7/23/29, MWC). Garay also harshly criticized Frances Densmore's monograph (1926) on Kuna music.

9. As noted elsewhere, Ibeorgun is one of the greatest of Kuna culture heroes, founder of (among many other things) puberty ceremonies; Momo is the titular deity of Carnival.

10. The effects of Garay's exhortations are unknown. By this time, of course, Nele, Pérez Kantule, and Hayans were all hard at work on Ustupu.

11. *Una pléyade*, i.e., a distinguished cohort of researchers.

12. For reasons of space, I do not discuss grammars and dictionaries of Kuna in this work.

13. Even more puzzling, Berengueras said he had obtained the text not from

Pérez or Hayans, but the secretary of Nele's rival Inabaginya. Among signs of the common origin of the two texts, both begin identically: *"Hace muchos años hubo un gran diluvio en este país"* (Nordenskiöld et al. 1938, 228; Berengueras 1930, no. 76, p. 12).

14. Kuna agriculturalists had in fact been alienating land permanently for years.

15. Berengueras 1930, no. 80, p. 96. Both Garay (1930, 66) and the Claretians (Misioneros Claretianos 1928–1945) noted missionary opposition to chichas and Carnival.

16. J. M. Berengueras n.d.

17. Like Gassó, Puig (1948, 98) credited Kuna virtues to an eighteenth-century missionary, Jacobo Balburger, though less insistently than Gassó.

18. Puig, following Gassó, sometimes assigns correct functions to the roles of *absogedi* (mass exorcist) and *gandule (kantule)* (puberty chanter) and sometimes uses the words (incorrectly) as cover terms for singers and ritualists in general. He also attributes to *neles* and *absogedis* functions in village governance they do not in fact hold.

19. "Lo del pobre: antes reventar que sobre" (Puig 1948, 13, 41). The English version is from an unpublished translation by Ned Brierley.

20. It never occurred to Puig that the primary staple, bananas, cannot be stored for more than a few days, or that agriculturalists, in the functional equivalent of storage, anticipated needs by managing multiple fields and staggering plantings.

21. Published missionary writings from *past* centuries, especially the famous *Jesuit Relations* (Kenton 1954), on the other hand, have attracted great attention.

22. For similar claims to authority through ethnography and competitiveness with secular ethnographers by Capuchins in the Orinoco delta, see Briggs (1996, 453).

23. Thanks to the very amiable Claretian fathers who allowed me to study the publication in their Panama City library.

24. Erice, known affectionately in later years as *Nono arrat,* "Green/blue head" (see Chapin 1992; Howe 1998, 298), republished his history (1975), as well as a grammar and a dictionary (1980, 1985), but apparently no ethnography.

25. Star & Herald 8/27/25, in 80-A-15; *Panamá América* (11/11/38); Feeney 1941; Puig 1948, 11, 26, 51–52, 58, 65, 83–84, 91; Martínez Mauri 2007, 86; Pereiro Pérez and De León Smith 2007.

26. I neglect some relevant but peripheral writings, including La Varre's (1940) whacky account and Theodore Humphries's blatantly racist survey (1944)—the latter having little to say on the Kuna, none of it based on field experience.

27. Holloman 1969, 479–480n. 20; Howe 1974, 346–347; Smith 1984, 191–194, 245–264; 1997.

28. Tinnin included a chapter on Kuna marriage closely based on an interview with Rubén Pérez.

29. In a rare linguistic error, McKim mentioned a canoe called a *chinga*. The vessel he had in mind, called *panga* in Panamanian Spanish, is not used by the Kuna.

30. In an appreciation of McKim's contribution, Reina Torres noted that it was

"saturated with the immense admiration that this man felt for the Cuna culture and its human exponents" (1962a, 24). For examples, see McKim (1947b, 24, 43, 44, 72, 103).

31. It is striking how often culture brokers displayed puberty ceremonies, despite the stigma under which chichas had previously suffered. The Kuna missionary Alcibiades Iglesias probably kept puberty ceremonies off the program for De Smidt and Tinnin—the latter wrote that "the chee-chee [sic] is San Blas' one social vice" (1940, 105)—but Robinson, McKim, Garay, and Stirling were all invited to observe. If some sensitivities remained, chichas, which already involved intracultural performances of all sorts, were pivotal events in Kuna culture.

32. Stirling was of course a professional, but his manuscript was sketchy and superficial.

33. Francisco Herrera, personal communication.

34. United States Office of Indian Affairs 1941.

35. Rubio sent a questionnaire concerning Balboa's route (Rubio to Haya 8/01/44, AGH). The Claretians recorded his party's arrival in Nargana March 21, 1944 ("Historia de la misión," ms.). Miró (1975) notes that little resulted except a newspaper article giving Nele's views on Balboa's route.

36. The Kuna, Alba wrote, were governed by a coterie of chiefs headed by a *nele*—unaware that a seer was paramount only by chance, that Nele Kantule had actually never been paramount, or apparently even that Nele had died three years previously.

37. In Alba's confused sketch of Father's Way, the great hero Dad Ibe, or Tat Ipe, is nowhere mentioned, and his long name, Olowaibipilele, is mistakenly applied to the Kuna deity.

38. "*Un carácter endeble, desconfiado, huraño, refractario, astuto e indiferente*" (Páez 1941, 11). Such sentiments were slow to disappear: the authors of another bachelor's thesis on the Kuna rebellion written twenty years later noted that "The indians lived a miserable life submerged in their own ignorance" (Castillo and Méndez 1962, 10).

39. Gillin 1942; Hallowell 1945; Beals 1953, 634–636.

40. I neglect the issue of whether the Kuna really descend from contact-period Darién societies (see Howe 1977)—Stout (1947, 1948), Joyce (1934), Sauer (1966), and others concluded, with qualifications, that they did; many recent authors believe the Kuna migrated onto the Isthmus *after* the sixteenth-century holocaust (Torres de Araúz 1974; Romoli 1953, 1987; Stier 1979, 54, 110–115; Castillero Calvo 1995, 37–40, 74, 77; Martínez Mauri 2007, 28–30).

CHAPTER 9

1. Reverte 1961a, 1961b, 1962a, 1962b, 1963, 1966.

2. Concerning Reverte's highly controversial role in the investigation of the murder in Guatemala of Bishop Juan Gerardi, see Goldman 2007.

3. "If the Cuna people still lives with a neolithic technology, their literature must go equally, and it must also be neolithic, rudimentary" (1968, 24, 34). "One of the most striking characteristics of Cuna poetry is *repetition* and *reit-*

eration . . . a primitive rhythm . . . consubstantial with man, innate, precultural" (1968, 85).

4. "When the indian is forced to try to reflect, right away he gets a headache" (1968, 43).

5. Numerous remarks (e.g., 1968, 65, 97–98) show that Reverte did not understand Kuna phonology or long and short word forms. The recent volume on place names (2001)—edited by Rubén Pérez, Jesús Erice, and others—is better.

6. *Warkaed,* or "tobacco-holder," a role in puberty ceremonies, is rendered as *markaed,* literally "lightning-grabber" (1977, 126). The warning shouted in the singing gathering—*Kabitamalarye! Nwebalitomarye!* "Don't sleep! Listen well!"—is rendered as *Ká bila marga . . . No bali tumalarga* (1977, 168), i.e., Reverte missed the basic verbs for sleep and listen. Wassén wrote a scathing review of Reverte (1963b). In one place, Reverte (1968, 66) mentions the Tonga Islanders of the Pacific but cites Junod's study (1927) of the South African Thonga [*sic*].

7. To illustrate a point on poetic style, Reverte introduced a chant fragment (1968, 90–91) recycled from a previous work (1961b, 117–123). His translator, Manuel Hernandez, struggling with multiline verses, improvised glosses for several fillers, of which Reverte was blithely unaware. *Ibidi kuyé* ("Things are [that way]") was rendered as "*está predicando en el cielo,*" while *Taile sunyé obargué* (roughly, "Is truly seen I say") was given as "*Es cierto que nos ha dejado aquí en la tierra.*"

8. "There are three ungrateful animals: the cat, the dove, and the Indian."

9. Francisco Herrera (personal communication) agrees concerning the importance of the Kuna to Torres's work. For her accession to the Panamanian academy of history she published a brief Kuna ethnohistory (1974).

10. A. Araúz 1982; Torres de Araúz 1966, 1967–1968; González 1986, 109.

11. In Pereira de Padilla and Segura 1983, 332–333; also González 1986, 113.

12. Francisco Herrera n.d. [2004]; also personal communications.

13. Torres de Araúz 1980; F. Herrera 1989, 103; n.d. [2004].

14. Torres de Araúz 1980; Pereira de Padilla and Segura 1983, 317–377; F. Herrera 1989, 103–104.

15. On Panamanian urbanism, see Velásquez Runk 2005, 400–477. Today, nonindigenous Panamanians may feel pressure to leave Kuna studies to the Kuna, though young Latin researchers, teachers, and health and development personnel now work in Kuna Yala.

16. Torres de Araúz and Reverte, like Garay, apparently spent only brief periods in the field and invoked their privileged positions in dealing with the Kuna. The great exception is Francisco Herrera, who has worked with every group in every remote corner of the country.

17. Marshall 1950 was a Harvard undergraduate thesis based on secondary sources by an ex-serviceman who had been stationed in San Blas during World War II.

18. Exceptions include Shatto 1972; Agnew 1956.

19. When my advisor at Penn, Olga Linares, suggested that I consider fieldwork among the Kuna, she urged me to disregard the impression left by Stout that nothing worthwhile remained to be studied.

20. On Kuna tourism, see Martínez Mauri 2007, 86; Pereiro Pérez and De León 2007; Chapin 1990; Doggett 1999; Falla 1979b; Howe 1982, 2002; Snow and Wheeler 2000; Swain 1977, 1989; Tice 1995; Zydler and Zydler 1996.

21. E.g., D. Davis, "Getting to Know the Cuna Indians," *New York Times* 11/09/75; E. Todras-Whitehill, "San Blas Islands, Panama: A Haven for Ancient Ways," *International Herald Tribune* 1/10/2008.

22. The Canal Zone anthropological society was a center of amateur anthropology and apparently of pot-hunting.

23. Isthmian Anthropological Society 1969; Corin n.d. [c. 1970]; Kapp 1972; Mueller 1973; Auld 1977; Shaffer 1982; Patera 1984, 1995; Caraway 1981, 1982; Calkins-Bascom n.d. [c. 1991]; Presilla 1996; Mathews 1998.

24. See Salvador (1976, 1978, 1997); Dina and Joel Sherzer (1976); Hirschfeld (1976, 1977a, 1977b); Puls (1978, 1988); Gunther Hartmann (1980a, 1980b); Ursula Hartmann (1985, 1986, 1988); Helms (1981); Tice (1989, 1995); Sweig (1987); Perrin (1999); and Fortis (2002). Two decades earlier, Louise Agnew wrote a recently rediscovered dissertation on molas (1956).

25. Lady Richmond Brown's mendacious account (1925) is discussed in Howe 1998, 191–193. Frances Densmore (1926) studied music in Washington in 1924, though only with male informants. The only non-androcentric male writer, William Markham, was obsessed with women's dress. His manuscript (Markham n.d. 1) was never published.

26. Serious studies of gender *were* produced, notably by Mari Lyn Salvador (1976, 1978), Margaret Swain (1977, 1978), Karin Tice (1995), and James Howe (2004a).

27. The bar at the Holiday Inn in Panama City is called the Inna Nega (chicha house); a health food restaurant is Café Nabguana, after a Kuna name for the earth.

28. Joel Sherzer had in 1970 recently taken a position at the University of Texas; James Howe was carrying out his doctoral fieldwork. I write of myself in the third person for simplicity of exposition.

29. Robert Alvarez wrote on an economic co-op (1972); Sandra Smith McCosker on music and dance (McCosker 1974, 1976; S. Smith 1984); Nancy Brennan Hatley on enculturation (1973, 1976); Margaret Swain (1977, 1978) on gender; Mari Lyn Salvador on mola aesthetics (1976, 1978); Trude Lawrence Lowenbach (1977) on deviance; and Gloria Garvin (1983) on psychotherapeutics.

30. Moore 1978, 1980, 1981, 1983, 1984. Moore was already a veteran fieldworker.

31. Gary Hasbrouk studied fishing (1985); Alaka Wali included the Bayano Kuna in a multiethnic study of a hydroelectric project's impact (Wali 1984, 1989, 1995); Karin Tice's analysis (1989, 1995) of handicraft production and marketing illuminated gender and political economy; Eric Moeller (1997) wrote on millenarianism among the Bayano Kuna. While most learned at least a little Kuna, to my knowledge, until recently only Sherzer, Howe, Chapin, Stier, Wali, and possibly Moeller carried out much or all of their work in the language.

32. Severi 1981, 1982a, 1982b, 1985, 1987, 1988, 1993a, 1993c, 1996, 1997.

33. Brokhaus 1974; G. Hartmann 1980a, 1980b, 1985, 1988; U. Hartmann

1985, 1986, 1988; Helbig 1983, 1985; Herrmann 1964, 1969, 1975, 1977, 1980a, 1980b; Maurer and Huber 1977; Werner 1984.

34. Almagioni 1992; Berti 1985; Di Giovanni 1992; Fiore 1985; Fortis 2002; Franciosi 1985; Hohenegger 1985; Ongaro 1992; Squillacciotti 1983, 1984, 1988, 1992, 1998; Stefanoni 1984, 1987, 1988. Spain and Britain have been more lightly represented—Calvo Buezas 1990; Gómez Parra and Martínez 1992; Pando Villaroya 1987; Puls 1978, 1988.

35. Carmona Maya 1989; Díaz Granados, Herrera, and Cardale de Schrimpff 1974; Díaz Vélez 1988; Gómez 1969a, 1969b; Leonor Herrera 1969; Jaramillo 1986; Llerena Villalobos 1987; Morales Gómez 1969, 1972, 1975, 1992; Peñaherrera de Costales and Costales 1968; Perefán Simmonds 1995; Severino de Santa Teresa 1959; Vargas 1993. In recent years, an Italian group has sponsored a Web site on Kuna research (http://lettere.media.unisi.it/kuna/biblio.php).

36. The Panamanian anthropologist Francisco Herrera organized funding and participated in work on the record project (personal communication).

37. Helms 1979; Vargas 1993; Taussig 1993; Gallup-Díaz 2004.

38. Mari Lyn Salvador, personal communication.

39. Kuna artifacts in foreign museums, lacking grave goods, skeletal material, sacred objects, or items of great individual value, have provoked little contention (though see Howe 1986, 54). Kuna recognize that had this material remained in the tropics, it would have disintegrated or been discarded.

40. Kuna knowers now levy hefty fees on both native and foreign students, even for Father's Way.

41. Gassieu's film, promoted by Margaret Mead and shown a few times, apparently never entered commercial distribution (Lawrence Hirschfeld, personal communications).

42. Many younger Kuna seem unaware that Chapin's *Pab igala,* reprinted in 1989, first appeared in 1970.

43. I emphasize factors internal to Panama. Francisco Herrera (personal communication) points out that Kuna intellectuals were also responding to critiques of North American anthropology by activists in Mexico and elsewhere. Much remains to be written, hopefully by Herrera, on Panamanian anthropology.

44. In 1985, while I was interviewing an ancient veteran of the Kuna revolution on Achutupu, a group of young Ailigandi men began shouting from the street, urging him not to cooperate or else to charge me high prices.

45. At the same 1985 General Congress at which the young man lambasted anthropologists, I later presented research plans for myself and a colleague, which were received with friendly enthusiasm. Significantly, our projects, already approved by the Centro de Investigaciones Kunas, involved Kuna collaboration.

46. Arysteides Turpana Iguaigliginya, "Los martires de la frontera" (http://dulenega.nativeweb.org/martires.html). See also Kungiler's appreciation, "Howe and la memoria colectiva de 'Un pueblo que no se arrodillaba'" (n.d., at that time on the Web); also *Mundo Kuna* March 2008 (http://www.mundokuna.ya.st/).

47. Cabarrús 1979; Sarsanedas 1978; Falla 1979a. Also Bilbao et al. 1978, 1979.

48. The rebellion study, also written in 1975, lacks a publication date.

49. Sarsanedas 1978; Comité Patrocinador 1982; Guionneau-Sinclair 1987, 1988.

50. *Machi* carefully acknowledges its sources (Kuna leaders' speeches, recent short studies, Catholic workshops, advice from indigenous colleagues) (1992) and makes telling and error-free use of Father's Way.

51. Nalu Nega is the name of an island, given to the heroine because her father drowned nearby.

52. Cantón, concerned with talking gatherings and democratic decision-making, must not have observed sacred gatherings or household life: see his errors concerning meals (1962, 37–39). His clumsy use of Kuna phrases is often incorrect.

53. Cantón's account of the causes of the 1925 rebellion, though compressed, oversimplified, and sometimes confused, is generally sound.

54. Most of the regional coconut output was sold to Colombian vessels, at various times opposed or tacitly accepted by the government. In 1962 a shootout occurred at Tigre (Digir) when a patrol boat apprehended a Colombian vessel. The less violent fictional incident narrated by Cantón was likely added to the story between winning the national literary prize for 1960–1961 and the book's final publication.

55. The second edition of *Ovnis* (1992) combined the poems from the first edition with those previously published in *Homenaje* (1969).

56. I have retranslated the poem from Spanish to English to correct what seem to me errors and weaknesses in the translation by the editors, Carlos and Monique Altschul (Cardenal 1992).

57. *Paluwala*, literally, "salt-tree."

CHAPTER 10

1. I work from both English- and Spanish-language versions of this article, using a photocopy, MWC. I have not yet found Pérez's other articles in the *Panamá América*.

2. The apology for spirit beliefs and the defense of molas seem to echo Marsh's declaration of independence (see Chapter 5), from which either Pérez or the newspaper editors may have borrowed. Just as with Colman's 1921 statement to the press (see Chapter 4), it is difficult to disentangle various parties' contributions to this document.

3. Other archives, including the papers of Alcibiades Iglesias, have not been surveyed or catalogued. Unfortunately, some private archives, especially those stored in closed boxes, may not survive the humid climate.

4. For both the General Congress and village gatherings, documents have typically been taken home by one or another secretary, and their survival depends on the secretary's judgment or whim. Unfortunately, all three private archives discussed here have been dispersed among family members. All three have been studied by historical researchers and repeatedly photocopied, microfilmed, and scanned, though probably not in their entirety.

5. In the mid-1980s, López's daughter, Hildaura López de Iglesias, told me that the diary would have to be kept private until all the women mentioned in it had died.

6. Ibelele, also known as Dad Ibe and Machi Olowaibipilele, fought against the evil spirits called *boni* and their kings *(errey)* (see Chapin 1983; Aiban Wagwa 2000).

7. This is a list of spirit strongholds, called *galu (kalu)*, from the Tuira River watershed, with brief descriptions of their inhabitants and other characteristics.

8. *Wiboet Ikala* (The Way of Sobering-up), for instance, includes 174 numbered but untranslated lines.

9. The manuscripts mentioned here are from AGH (courtesy of Chany Edman and Bernal Castillo) or the MWC.

10. One publication, "New Kuna Myths, According to Guillermo Hayans" (Wassén 1952), gives the native collector credit in its title.

11. *The Complete Mu-Igala* (1953) is shown as "*by* Nils Holmer and Henry Wassén" [emphasis added].

12. Even for the 1938 magnum opus, whose title page acknowledges that it was published in collaboration with Pérez, in later references Nordenskiöld is almost invariably credited as sole author.

13. Mac Chapin, Joel Sherzer, and I (personal communications) all noted the change in attitudes toward tradition that occurred in the mid-1970s. See also B. Castillo 2000, 113.

14. As previously noted, I use the name San Blas for the years before 1980 because the neologism Kuna Yala would be anachronistic. The name Kuna Yala was not accepted officially by the government until 1998.

15. Abyayala was the area on and around Dagargunyala, the mountain on which proto-Kuna ancestors end up after the world flood that forms one episode in Father's Way.

16. Different Web sites give different translations for Abya Yala (all of them wrong), such as "land in its full maturity" or "continent of life." Some identify the term as Aymara or Quechua. Rather than list the dozens of sites that use the name Abya Yala, I recommend that the reader carry out a Web search.

17. That is, some syllables are gender-specific, and some could be glossed for meaning, but the names as a whole do not form meaningful phrases or titles in the way popularly associated with Native North American names. Hundreds of beings in the invisible world and characters in Kuna sacred history have names formed on the same pattern, but I never noted a case in which a human—other than a foreign anthropologist—was given the name of a spirit or mythical personage (see Howe and Sherzer 1986). Quite a few Kuna have also had more informal indigenous names based on everyday titles and kin terms, such as *Machi,* "Boy," or *Gandur,* "puberty chanter."

18. Aiban Wagwa 1976, 1994, 1995, 2000, 2002; Méndez, Santacruz, Peláez García, and Green 1996.

19. Chapin and Herrera 1998; Chapin n.d.; Castillo 1987.

20. *Kuna Yargi* 22 (on Ibeorgun, Ustupu, April 1989), 23 (on Twiren, Kuebdi, November 1989), 24 (on Piler and Pursob, Akuanusadup, March 1990), all courtesy of Mònica Martínez Mauri.

21. Coordinación Nacional de Pastoral Indígena.

22. A very few homegrown investigators have found wider audiences, notably Tomás Herrera, a university-educated Kuna who collaborated with a North Amer-

ican amateur, Anita McAndrews, on a volume of Kuna "legends" (Herrera and McAndrews 1978). McAndrews translated Herrera's spoken Spanish into emotive English, with interpolated dialogue. Herrera's interpretations attempt to reconcile tradition and literate modernity, while McAndrews's confused afterword (1978, 83–102) obsesses about Kuna sexual and racial separatism. To her credit, McAndrews gave Herrera top billing on the title page.

23. See the obituary of Carlos López in *La Prensa* 8/09/2000.

24. Although here I mostly stick to works in print, the Kuna also represent and disseminate their culture and history in dances, street theater, workshops, radio broadcasts, even a multiethnic musical ensemble, El Proyecto Banaba.

25. The Cultural Congress newsletter *Onmaked* for February 1995 shows a "Mujer Kuna cosiendo mola," but all the articles concern male-dominated institutions.

26. The discomfort might be especially acute because the few men who do sew molas are mostly homosexuals, some of them quite flamboyant in their dress and behavior.

27. Unlike discussions of kinship practice, fond remembrances of beloved parents and other senior kin, with implicit invocation of their authority and wisdom, are commonplace.

28. R. M. Brown 1996; Fischer 2001, 96–98, 120–127, 201–205; England 1996; Maxwell 1996; Richards and Richards 1996.

29. "Don't know," for instance, is written *wissuli* rather than *wichuli*, indicating its derivation from *wisi-suli* rather than its pronunciation.

30. Counting money in Kuna is, in particular, complicated and confusing. A base unit of the monetary system was *ton-*, equivalent to a Colombian peso. In adapting to the decimal system of Panama, fifty cents was designated as *suiton-*, or "long *ton*," and higher amounts are counted in that unit, abbreviated to *suit-*. Thus amounts as counted in Kuna are always twice their value in balboas or dollars: five balboas is *suitambe*, "ten-*suit*." Multiples of ten balboas are counted in *tula-* or *tur-*, "twenty," and multiples of fifty balboas are counted as *tulatar*, "five-twenties," with a multiplier, *ila-*. Thus one hundred balboas or dollars is *tulatar-irbogwa*, "five twenties, two times."

31. Ochoa and Peláez 1995, 59–63; Paredes de León 2001, n.d. [2004]; Green 2004; see also Price 2005, 108–110.

32. E. Castillero Reyes 1946; E. Castillero Reyes and Arce 1948, 205; A. Castillo and Méndez 1962; Carles 1965, 32–36.

33. Kungiler 1994; A. Martínez 1996; Smith Kantule 1996; Aiban Wagwa 1997b; S. Herrera n.d. [2003], 68–79; Smith Kantule and Iglesias 2001.

34. The film *Spirit of Kuna Yala* shows a PEMASKY staffer practicing in the forest.

35. This delicacy about publishing the "sacred" words of the chant itself, very different from the stance taken by Hayans and other collaborators with the Swedes, may reflect ideas acquired from other indigenous groups with whom Kuna activists are in contact, but it may also reflect long-standing attitudes that Hayans ignored.

36. However, many teachers of Father's Way are now charging money, even

to fellow-Kuna, which did not happen in the past. Many younger chiefs are now reportedly using writing and tape-recording to learn histories.

37. Aiban Wagwa 1994; Howe 1991b; 1998, 173–176; Howe, Alemancia, de León, López, Solís, and Morris 1994.

38. In the late 1960s, Kuna espousing the dominant tradition worried that the great chief, Igwa-Yabiliginya, from the eastern sector might misrepresent Kuna religion to outsiders; the issue influenced the choice of his successor in 1971 (Howe 1986, 76–77).

39. The narratives were thoroughly Kuna-ized: Jesus travels after death through the Kuna underworld; the intrepid voyagers are greeted in Rome by a host of knowers descending from heaven on a golden staircase.

40. As Mac Chapin points out (personal communication), Kuna interest in parallels between Father's Way and the Bible long antedates recent native ethnography.

41. Warren and Jackson 2002, 8; Warren 1998, 19, 77–79, 145–147; Fischer 2001, 9–11, 83–84; Rappaport 2005b, 36–40; Herzfeld 2001, 32–34.

42. See Handler and Linnekin 1984; Hanson 1989; Thomas 1997; Keesing 1992; Linnekin 1983, 1991.

CHAPTER 11

1. Leis 1992, 2004; Rudolf n.d. [2001]; Instituto & Diócesis 1991; L. Herrera 1994; Olguín Martínez 2006.

ABBREVIATIONS

80-A-15	File Numbers of Records of the Panama Canal Executive Office, General Records 1914–1934, Record Group 185, U.S. National Archives, Washington, D.C.
819	File numbers for Records of the Department of State Relating to the Internal Affairs of Panama, Record Group 59, U.S. National Archives, Washington, D.C.
ABP	Archivos Belisario Porras, Universidad de Panamá
AEL	Archivos de Estanislao López, Nargana (Kuna Yala) and Panamá
AGH	Archivos de Guillermo Hayans, Ustupu (Kuna Yala) and Panamá
AI	Archivos de la Intendencia, El Porvenir, Kuna Yala
ANP	Archivos Nacionales de Panamá
ARJA	Archivos de Ricardo J. Alfaro, Panamá
ARPK	Archivos de Rubén Pérez Kantule, Nargana (Kuna Yala) and Panamá
Diario	*El Diario de Panamá*
Estrella	*La Estrella de Panamá / Panama Star and Herald*
MGJ	Memorias de Gobierno y Justicia, Gobierno de Panamá
MWC	Museum of World Culture (Världskulturmuseet), Göteborg, Sweden (formerly Göteborg Ethnographic Museum)
NAA	National Anthropology Archives, Smithsonian Institution, Washington, D.C.

OH	Oral History (recorded but unpublished)
RG84	Records of the U.S. Legation in Panama, Record Group 84, U.S. National Archives, Washington, D.C.
Secretary	Secretario de Gobierno y Justicia, Gobierno de Panamá (unless other government secretary indicated)
Star & Herald	*Panama Star and Herald*
USNA	United States National Archives and Record Service, Washington, D.C.

BIBLIOGRAPHY

Abbot, Willis. 1913. *Panama and the Canal in Picture and Prose*. London: Syndicate Publishing.

Abu-Lughod, Lila. 1991. "Writing against Culture." In *Recapturing Anthropology: Working in the Present*, ed. Richard Fox, pp. 137–162. Santa Fe: School of American Research.

Agnew, Louise. 1956. "Symbolic Communication and Decoration of the San Blas Cuna." Ph.D. diss., Illinois Institute of Technology.

Aiban Wagwa (see also Victoriano Smith). n.d. *Desde el silencio indio*. Panamá: Fe y alegría.

———. 1976. *A la manera kuna (poemas)*. Panamá: n.p.

———. 1994. *¡Noticias de sangre de nuestro pueblo! Nuestros padres nos lo relatan así*. Kuna Yala, Panamá: Congreso General de la Cultura Kuna.

———. 1995. *La historia de mis padres, mi querida historia*. Panamá: Publicaciones EMISKY.

———. 1997a. *Kaaubi: selección de algunos poemas, 1972–1992*. Kuna Yala, Panamá: n.p.

———. 1997b. Preface. In *Así lo vi y así me lo contaron*, Inakeliginia (Carlos López), ed. Aiban Wagwa, pp. 15–17. Kuna Yala, Panamá: Congreso General de la Cultura Kuna.

———. 2000. *En defensa de la vida y su armonía*. Kuna Yala, Panamá: Congreso General de la Cultura Kuna.

———. 2002. *Mor ginnid*. Guatemala: Editorial Nojib"sa.

———. 2005. *Los kuna entre dos sistemas educativas: propuesta educativa de los congresos generales kunas y rasgos de la Educación Bilingue Intercultural*. Panamá: Congresos Generales Kunas.

Aiban Wagwa and Massimo Squillacciotti. 1984. *Corso Elementare di Lingua Cuna in Cassette, con l'Ausilio del Testo Scritto*. Siena, Italy: Dipartimento di Filosofia e Scienze Sociali, Università degli studi di Siena.

Alba, Manuel María. 1928a. "Etnología y población histórica de Panamá." Panamá: Imprenta Nacional.
———. 1928b. "Urraca: semblanza de este héroe nacional." Panamá: Imprenta Nacional.
———. 1929. *Geografía descriptiva de la República de Panamá.* Panamá: Bendetti Hermanos.
———. 1947. "Hombres y dioses cunas: la creación del mundo cuna." Panamá: Imprenta Nacional. Reprinted 1965, in *Revista Lotería* 11 (22): 72–81.
———. 1948. *Introducción al estudio de las lenguas indígenas de Panamá.* Panamá: Imprenta Nacional.
Alemancia, Jesús. 1998. "'Urracá': señor del viento, la lluvia y el trueno." In *Pueblos indígenas de Panamá: Hacedores de cultura y de historia,* ed. César Picón, Jesús Alemancia, and Ileana Gólcher, pp. 44–45. Panamá: UNESCO.
Allen, Emory Adams. 1913. *Our Canal in Panama.* Cincinnati: United States Publishing.
Almagioni, G. 1992. "Immagine Ed Identità Dei Cuna." In *America: Cinque Secoli Dalla Conquista,* ed. Massimo Squillacciotti, pp. 33–48. Siena, Italy: Saggi dal seminario Interdisciplinare della Facoltà di Lettere e Filosofia, Università di Siena.
Alvarado, Eligio. 2001. *El perfil de los pueblos indígenas de Panamá.* Panamá: Fundacíon Dobbo Yala.
Alvarez, Robert. 1972. "A Cuna Indian Cooperative: A Voluntary Association as a Vehicle for Change." Master's thesis, San Diego State University.
Alvarsson, Jan-Åke. 1997. "El humanitarismo de Nordenskiöld." In *Erland Nordenskiöld, investigador y amigo del indígena,* ed. Jan-Åke Alvarsson and Oscar Agüero, pp. 81–108. Quito: Ediciones Abya-Yala.
Alvarsson, Jan-Åke, and Oscar Agüero, eds. 1997. *Erland Nordenskiöld, investigador y amigo del indígena.* Quito: Ediciones Abya-Yala.
Anderson, Benedict. 1983. *Imagined Communities: Reflections on the Origin and Spread of Nationalism.* London: Verso.
Anderson, Charles. 1911. *Old Panama and Castilla del Oro.* Boston: Page Co.
Andreve, Guillermo. 1926. *Directorio general de la Ciudad de Panamá.* 2nd ed. Panamá: Andreve y Compañia.
Anonymous. 1908. *Canal Zone Pilot: Guide to the Republic of Panama and Classified Business Directory.* Panamá: A. Bienkowski.
Anonymous. 1916. *Excursión á la costa de San Blas en Panamá.* Madrid: Publicaciones del Boletín de la Real Sociedad Geográfica.
Anonymous. 1927. "Panama Chief Writes History." *Palacio* 23:617–618.
Anonymous. 1962. "Una visita á la región del Río Bayano." *Lotería* 7:107.
Anonymous. 1964. "Una excursión al Río Bayano." *Hombre y Cultura* 1 (3): 144–145.
Apter, Andrew. 1999. "Africa, Empire, and Anthropology: A Philological Exploration of Anthropology's Heart of Darkness." *Annual Review of Anthropology* 28:577–598.
Araúz, Amado. 1982. ". . . Fue reina en el sentido real o imaginable." *Revista Lotería* 314–318:5–17.

Araúz, Mateo. 1926. *El problema indígena en Panamá*. Panamá: Imprenta Nacional.

Archibold, Juan Pérez. 2004. "Memoria histórica, estructura social y teología de la nación kuna." *Abisua v. 5*, in http://www.geocities.com/TheTropics/Shores/4852/teolo.html.

Ariza, Andrés de. 1971. "Comentos de la rica y fertílisma provincia del Darién año de 1774." *Hombre y Cultura* 2:107–115.

Assies, Willem. 2000. "Indigenous Peoples and Reform of the State in Latin America." In *The Challenge of Diversity: Indigenous Peoples and Reform of the State in Latin America*, ed. Willem Assies, Gemma van der Haar, and André Hoekema, pp. 3–22. Amsterdam: Thela Thesis.

Atkinson, Paul, Amanda Coffey, Sara Delamont, John Lofland, and Lyn Lofland, eds. 2001. *Handbook of Ethnography*. London: Sage Publications.

Auld, Rhoda. 1977. *Molas: What They Are, How to Make Them, Ideas They Suggest for Creative Appliqué*. New York: Van Nostrand Reinhold.

Avery, Ralph Emmett. 1913. *America's Triumph in Panama: Panorama and Story of the Construction and Operation of the World's Giant Waterway from Ocean to Ocean*. Chicago: L. W. Walter.

———. 1915. *The Panama Canal and Golden Gate Exposition*. n.p.: n.p.

Axtell, James. 1985. *The Invasion Within: The Contest of Cultures in Colonial North America*. New York: Oxford University Press.

Bailey, F. G. 1969. *Stratagems and Spoils: A Social Anthropology of Politics*. New York: Schocken.

Balburger [or Walburger], Jacobo. n.d. [1748]. "Breve noticia de la Provincia del Darién, de la ley y costumbres de los indios, de la poca esperanza de plantar nuestra fe y del número de sus naturales." Copies found in various archives; see Castillero Calvo 1995, Capítulo 9. My copy courtesy of Carl Langebaeck.

Barton, David, and Nigel Hall, eds. 1999. *Letter Writing as a Social Practice*. Amsterdam: John Benjamins.

Bazerman, Charles. 1999. "Letters and the Social Grounding of Differentiated Genres." In *Letter Writing as a Social Practice*, ed. David Barton and Nigel Hall, pp. 15–33. Amsterdam: John Benjamins.

Beach, Rex. 1917. "The San Blas People." *Cosmopolitan*, January, pp. 143–145.

———. 1940. *Personal Exposures*. New York: Harper & Brothers.

Beals, Ralph. 1953. "Acculturation." In *Anthropology Today: An Encyclopedic Inventory*, ed. Alfred Kroeber, pp. 621–641. Chicago: University of Chicago Press.

Bell, Eleanor Yorke. 1910. "The Republic of Panama and Its People, with Special Reference to the Indians." In *Annual Report for 1909*, pp. 607–637. Washington, D.C.: Smithsonian Institution.

Bennett, John. 1946. "The Interpretation of Pueblo Culture: A Question of Values." *Southwestern Journal of Anthropology* 2 (4): 361–373.

Bentley, W. Holman. 1900. *Pioneering on the Congo*. New York: F. H. Revell.

Ben-Yehuda, Nachman. 1995. *The Masada Myth: Collective Memory and Mythmaking in Israel*. Madison: University of Wisconsin Press.

Berengueras, José María. 1930–1931. "Misión católica de San José de Narganá." *El Misionero*, nos. 76, 78–80, 82, 85, 87–89, 91, 93–99.

———. n.d. [1930s]. "Kuna Yala: Historia contemporánea" [not original title]. Archives of the Claretian Order, Vic, Spain; courtesy of Mònica Martínez Mauri.

———. 1934. *Rudimentos de gramática caribe-kuna*. Panamá: n.p.

Bernal, Juan Bosco. 2004. "La educación en Panamá: antecedentes, tendencias y perspectivas." In *Panamá: cien años de República*, pp. 47–76. Comisión Universitaria del Centenario de la República. Panamá: Manfer.

Berti, P. 1985. "I Cayuco Degli Indios Cuna di San Blas." *Modellistica* 6:591–594.

Beverley, John. 1999. *Subalternity and Representation: Arguments in Cultural Theory*. Durham, N.C.: Duke University Press.

Bhabha, Homi. 1985. "Signs Taken for Wonders: Questions of Ambivalence and Authority under a Tree Outside Delhi, May 1817." In *"Race," Writing, and Difference*, ed. Henry Louis Gates, pp. 163–184. Chicago: University of Chicago Press.

Biesanz, John, and Mavis Biesanz. 1955. *The People of Panama*. New York: Columbia University Press.

Bilbao, Ion, Ricardo Falla, Jorge Sarsanedas, Stefan Turcios, and Eduardo Valdés. 1978. *La patria del indio: Panorámica comparativa de las areas indígenas*. Serie El Indio Panameño. Panamá: Centro de Capacitación Social.

Bilbao, Ion, Ricardo Falla, and Eduardo Valdés. 1979. *Darién: indios, negros y latinos: El Valle del Río Sambú/conflicto interétnico en el Darién*. Serie El Indio Panameño. Panamá: Centro de Capacitación Social.

Bishop, Farnham. 1920. *Panama Past and Present*. New York: Century Co.

Blommaert, Jan. 2005. *Discourse: A Critical Introduction*. Cambridge: Cambridge University Press.

Blum, Alain. 2002. "Resistance to Identity Categorization in France." In *Census and Identity: The Politics of Race, Ethnicity, and Language in National Censuses*, ed. David Kertzer and Dominique Arel, pp. 121–147. Cambridge: Cambridge University Press.

Boon, James. 1977. *The Anthropological Romance of Bali, 1597–1972: Dynamic Perspectives in Marriage and Caste, Politics and Religion*. Cambridge: Cambridge University Press.

Bourdieu, Pierre. 1984. *Distinction: A Social Critique of the Judgement of Taste*. Cambridge, Mass.: Harvard University Press.

Bourgois, Philippe. 1988. "Conjugated Oppression: Class and Ethnicity among Guaymí and Kuna Banana Workers." *American Ethnologist* 15:328–348.

———. 1989. *Ethnicity at Work*. Baltimore: Johns Hopkins University Press.

Bourne, Russell. 1990. *The Red King's Rebellion: Racial Politics in New England, 1675–1678*. Oxford: Oxford University Press.

Boyer, Dominic, and Claudio Lomnitz. 2005. "Intellectuals and Nationalism: Anthropological Engagements." *Annual Review of Anthropology* 34:105–120.

Brennan Hatley, Nancy. 1973. "Cooperativism and Socialization among the Cuna Indians of San Blas." Master's thesis, University of California, Los Angeles.

———. 1976. "Cooperativism and Enculturation among the Cuna Indians of San Blas." In *Enculturation in Latin America,* ed. Johannes Wilbert, pp. 67–94. Los Angeles: UCLA Latin American Series 37.

Breslin, Patrick, and Mac Chapin. 1984. "Ecología estilo kuna." *Desarrollo de Base* 8:26–35.

Briggs, Charles. 1996. "The Politics of Discursive Authority in Research on 'The Invention of Tradition.'" *Cultural Anthropology* 11 (4): 435–469.

Brizuela Absalon, Alvaro. 1973. "Bayana dule gan—los kunas del Bayano (el mito como modelo de vida)." Master's thesis, Universidad Autónoma Nacional de México.

Brokhaus, P. 1974. *Bild der volker: die Cuna.* Wiesbaden: Brokhaus Völkerkunde.

Brown, Judith K. 1970. "Sex Division of Labor among the San Blas Cuna." *Anthropological Quarterly* 43:57–63.

Brown, Michael F. 1993. "Facing the State, Facing the World: Amazonia's Native Leaders and the New Politics of Identity." *L'Homme* 33 (2–4): 307–326.

Brown, R. McKenna. 1996. "The Mayan Language Loyalty Movement in Guatemala." In *Maya Cultural Activism in Guatemala,* ed. Edward Fischer and R. McKenna Brown, pp. 165–177. Austin: University of Texas Press.

Brown, Simión. 1995. "Igargan: cantos curativos kunas." *Onmaked* 1:57–58.

———. 1996. "Masar igar: canto-guia á la morada de Paba." *Onmaked* 2:7–8.

———. 2005. "Orígen del pueblo kuna desde la memoria histórica." Panamá: Congreso General de la Cultura Kuna.

Brown, Simión, and Atilio Martínez. 2006. "Dodomalad igala: Dodoged igar y la memoria colectiva de mis abuelos y abuelas." Kuna Yala, Panamá: Congreso General de la Cultura Kuna.

Browne, Edith. 1913. *Peeps at Many Lands: Panama.* London: Adam and Charles Black.

Bruner, Edward. 1986. "Ethnography as Narrative." In *The Anthropology of Experience,* ed. Victor Turner and Edward Bruner, pp. 139–155. Urbana: University of Illinois Press.

Brysk, Alison. 1994. "Acting Globally: Indian Rights and International Politics in Latin America." In *Indigenous Peoples and Democracy in Latin America,* ed. Donna Lee Van Cott, pp. 29–51. New York: St. Martin's.

Bullard, Arthur. 1918. *Panama: The Canal, the Country and the People.* New York: MacMillan.

Burgoa, Lydia. 1993. "Estudio comparativo del sistema de numeración kuna." *Scientia* 8:97–129.

Burrow, J. W. 2000. *The Crisis of Reason: European Thought, 1848–1914.* New Haven, Conn.: Yale University Press.

Buzard, James. 1993. *The Beaten Track: European Tourism, Literature, and the Ways to Culture, 1800–1918.* New York: Oxford University Press.

Cabarrús, Carlos Rafael. 1979. *Indígena y proletario: proletarización y lucha política del indígena bocatoreño.* Serie El Indio Panameño. Panamá: Centro de Capacitación.

Calkins-Bascom, Willow. n.d. [c. 1991]. *Islands and Rainforests: Living in the Tropics with the Kuna Indians.* Athens, Ga.: Willowworks.

Calvo Buezas, Tomas. 1990. *Indios cunas: la lucha por la tierra y la identidad.* Madrid: Libertarias.

Calvo Población, Gaspar Félix. 2000. "La educación kuna: introducción del sistema educativo occidental en la cultura kuna de Panamá. Ph.D. diss., Universidad de Salamanca.

Cantón, Alfredo. 1962. *Nalu-Nega.* Madrid: Susaeta. Reprinted Panamá: Editorial de la Nación, 1971.

Caraway, Caren. 1981. *Mola Design Book.* Owings Mills, Md.: Stemmer House.

———. 1982. *The Mola Design Coloring Book.* Owings Mills, Md.: Stemmer House.

Cardenal, Ernesto. 1964. "Los indios cunas, una 'nación soberana.'" *Revista Lotería* 104:79–97.

———. 1966. *El estrecho dudoso.* Madrid: Ediciones Cultura Hispánica.

———. 1968. *Mayapán.* Managua: Editorial Alemana.

———. 1969. *Homenaje a los indios americanos.* Managua: Editorial Universitaria, Universidad Nacional Autónoma de Nicaragua.

———. 1973. *Homage to the American Indians.* Baltimore: Johns Hopkins University Press.

———. 1979. *Antología de poesia primitiva.* Madrid: Alianza Editorial.

———. 1985. *Quetzalcoatl.* Managua: Editorial Nueva Nicaragua.

———. 1988. *Los ovnis de oro.* México: Siglo XXI Editores.

———. 1992. *Los ovnis de oro/Golden UFOs: Poemas indios/The Indian Poems.* Translated and edited by Carlos Altschul and Monique Altschul. Bloomington: Indiana University Press.

———. 2003. *Las ínsulas extrañas memorias II.* México: Fondo de Cultura Económica.

Cardenal, Ernesto, and Jorge Montoya Toro. 1964. *Literatura indígena americana; antología.* Medellín: Editorial de la Universidad de Antioquia.

Carles, Rubén Dario. 1965. *San Blas, tierra de los cunas.* Panamá: Editora Humanidad.

Carmack, Robert, Janine Gasco, and Gary Gossen. 1996. *The Legacy of Mesoamerica: History and Culture of a Native American Civilization.* Upper Saddle River, N.J.: Prentice Hall.

Carmona Maya, Sergio. 1989. *La música, un fenómeno cosmogónico en la cultura kuna.* Medellín: Editorial de la Universidad de Antioquia.

Casagrande, Joseph. 1960. *In the Company of Man; Twenty Portraits by Anthropologists.* New York: Harper.

Castillero Calvo, Alfredo. 1995. *Conquista, evangelización, y resistencia: ¿Triunfo o fracaso de la política indigenista?* Panamá: INAC.

Castillero Reyes, Ernesto. 1946. "Historia de la extraña República de Tule." *Biblioteca Selecta* 1 (10): 17–36.

———. 1970. "La ciudad de estatuas peregrinas." *Revista Lotería* 16:67–70.

Castillero Reyes, Ernesto, and Enrique Arce. 1948. *Historia de Panamá.* Buenos Aires: n.p.

Castillo, Angélica, and Micaela Méndez. 1962. "La Revolución de Tule, 1925." B.A. thesis, Universidad de Panamá.

Castillo, Arcadio. n.d. [2000]. *Analisis de la pesca actual de la langosta espinosa.* Panamá: Smithsonian Tropical Research Institute.

Castillo, Bernal. 1995. "Una visión histórica de los kunas en el periodo colonial de los siglos XVI–XVII." *Onmaked* 1:5–6.

———. 1996. "Intendencia: su orígen." *Onmaked* 2:4–5.

———. 2000. "Transformaciones socioculturales de la Comarca de Kuna Yala: caso de la comunidad de Yandup (1907–1945)." Honors thesis, Universidad de Panamá.

———. 2005. "La autonomía indígena en Kuna Yala frente al impacto de la globalización: Un análisis de los retos del autogobierno indígena." Master's thesis, Universidad de Costa Rica.

Castillo, Bernal, and Iguayoikiler Ferrer. 2004. *Abisua, Inakailibaler: el gran guía espiritual y organizador de los Congreso Generales Kunas.* Panamá: Instituto de Investigaciones Koskun Kalu.

Castillo, Gubiler (Geodisio). 1985. "El sistema de 'nainu' en Kuna Yala: perspectivas para el desarrollo." *Abya Yala* 1 (1): 2–12.

———. 1987. "Proyecto de ecodesarrollo en Kuna Yala: alternativa válida para promover el desarrollo económico y social." *Revista Lotería* 368:55–75.

Céspedes, Francisco. 1985. *La educación en Panamá: panorama histórico y antología.* Biblioteca de la Cultura Panameña. Panamá: Universidad de Panamá.

Chapin, Mac. 1970. *Pab igala: historias de la tradición kuna.* Panamá: Centro de Investigaciones Antropológicas.

———. 1976. "Muu Ikala: Cuna Birth Ceremony." In *Ritual and Symbol in Native Central America,* ed. Philip Young and James Howe, pp. 57–65. Eugene: University of Oregon Anthropological Papers No. 9.

———. 1983. "Curing among the San Blas Kuna of Panama." Ph.D. diss., University of Arizona.

———. 1985. "UDIRBI: An Indigenous Project in Environmental Conservation." In *Native Peoples and Development: Six Case Studies from Latin America,* ed. Theodore McDonald, pp. 39–53. Cambridge, Mass.: Cultural Survival.

———. 1989. *Pab igala: historias de la tradición kuna* [reprint of Chapin 1970]. Quito: Abya Yala.

———. 1990. "The Silent Jungle: Ecotourism among the Kuna Indians of Panama." *Cultural Survival Quarterly* 14 (1): 42–45.

———. 1991. "Losing the Way of Great Father." *New Scientist* 10:40–44.

———. 1992. "The Final Journey of Padre Jesús: A Narrative for the Quincentenary." *Encounters* 10:31, 37, 48.

———. n.d. [1998]. "Defending Kuna Yala: The Study Project for the Management of Wildland Areas of Kuna Yala (PEMASKY)." Report.

———. 2004. "A Challenge to Conservationists." *World Watch* 17 (6): 17–31.

Chapin, Mac, and Heraclio Herrera. 1998. "Defending Kuna Yala: The Study Project for the Management of Wildland Areas of Kuna Yala (PEMASKY)." In *Bridging Traditional Ecological Knowledge and Ecosystem Science,* ed. Ronald Trosper, pp. 81–96. Flagstaff: Northern Arizona School of Forestry.

Clifford, James. 1986. "On Ethnographic Allegory." In *Writing Culture: The*

Poetics and Politics of Ethnography, ed. James Clifford and George Marcus, pp. 96–121. Berkeley: University of California Press.

Cohn, Bernard. 1987. "The Census, Social Structure and Objectification in South Asia." In *An Anthropologist among the Historians and Other Essays,* pp. 224–254. Delhi: Oxford University Press.

Colley, Linda. 2002. *Captives.* New York: Pantheon Books.

Collins, James. 1995. "Literacy and Literacies." *Annual Review of Anthropology* 24:75–93.

Collins, James, and Richard Blot. 2003. *Literacy and Literacies: Texts, Power, and Identity.* Cambridge: Cambridge University Press.

Collins, John. 1912. *The Panama Guide.* Panamá: J. L. Maduro, Jr.

Comaroff, Jean, and John Comaroff. 1991. *Of Revelation and Revolution: Christianity, Colonialism, and Consciousness in South Africa, Vol. 1.* Chicago: University of Chicago Press.

Comisión Permanente del Primer Congreso Indigenista Panameño. 1959. *Memoria del Primer Congreso Indigenista Panameño, 18 a 22 de abril de 1956.* Panamá: Ministerio de Educación.

Comité Patrocinador del "Foro sobre el pueblo Guaymí y su futuro," eds. 1982. *El pueblo guaymí y su futuro.* Panamá: CEASPA.

Congreso General de la Cultura Kuna. 1994. "¡Noticias de sangre de nuestro pueblo!: Nuestros padres nos lo relatan así." Translated by Aiban Wagwa. San José, Costa Rica: Ediciones COOPA.

Congreso General Kuna. 2001. *Anmar igar: normas kunas.* Kuna Yala Panamá: Congreso General Kuna.

Conklin, Beth. 1997. "Body Paint, Feathers, and VCRs: Aesthetics and Authenticity in Amazonian Activism." *American Ethnologist* 24:711–728.

Conklin, Beth, and Laura Graham. 1995. "The Shifting Middle Ground: Amazonian Indians and Eco-Politics." *American Anthropologist* 97:695–710.

Conniff, Michael. 1985. *Black Labor on a White Canal, 1904–1981.* Pittsburgh: University of Pittsburgh Press.

Coope, Anna. 1917. *Anna Coope: Sky Pilot of the San Blas Indians.* New York: American Tract Society.

Cooper, Frederick, and Ann Laura Stoler. 1997. "Between Metropole and Colony: Rethinking a Research Agenda." In *Tensions of Empire: Colonial Cultures in a Bourgeois World,* ed. Frederick Cooper and Ann Laura Stoler, pp. 1–56. Berkeley: University of California Press.

Core, Sue. 1941. *Panama's Trails of Progress: The Story of Panama and Its Canal.* New York: North River Press.

Corin, Georgia. n.d. [c. 1970]. *All about the Mola.* Panamá: n.p.

Costello, Richard. 1975. "Political Economy and Private Interests in Río Azúcar: An Analysis of Economic Change in a San Blas Community." Ph.D. diss., University of California, Davis.

Crehan, Kate. 2002. *Gramsci, Culture, and Anthropology.* Berkeley: University of California Press.

Crespo, José. 1928. *Geografía de Panamá.* Boston: Heath.

Cronon, William. 1983. *Changes in the Land: Indians, Colonists, and the Ecology of New England.* New York: Farrar, Strauss.

Cullen, Edward. 1853. *Isthmus of Darien Ship Canal*. London: Effingham Wilson.
Curtin, Philip D. 2000. *The World and the West*. New York: Cambridge University Press.
Dampier, William. 1927. *A New Voyage Round the World*. London: Argonaut Press [original 1697].
Darnell, Regna. 2001. *Invisible Genealogies: A History of Americanist Anthropology*. Lincoln: University of Nebraska Press.
Davies, Ibelele Nikktiginya (Juan José). n.d [c. 1978]. *Gramática kuna, conforme a los planes del Congreso General Kuna*. Panamá: Academia de la Lengua Kuna.
De Gerdes, Marta. 1995. "Constructing Kuna Identity through Verbal Art in the Urban Context." Ph.D. diss., University of Texas, Austin.
De la Peña, Guillermo. 2005. "Social and Cultural Policies towards Indigenous Peoples: Perspectives from Latin America." *Annual Review of Anthropology* 34:717–739.
Deloria, Philip. 1998. *Playing Indian*. New Haven, Conn.: Yale University Press.
Densmore, Frances. 1926. "Music of the Tule Indians of Panama." In *Smithsonian Institution, Miscellaneous Collections* 77. Washington, D.C.
De Páramo y Cepeda, Juan Francisco. 1994. *Alteraciones del Dariel: Poema Épico*. Edited by Héctor Orjuela. Bogotá: Editorial Kelly.
Derrida, Jacques. 1995. *Archive Fever: A Freudian Impression*. Chicago: University of Chicago Press.
De Smidt, Leon. 1948. *Among the San Blas Indians of Panama*. Troy, N.Y.: n.p.
De Tapia, Lola. 1971. "El indio Urraca, defensor de una raza." *Revista Lotería* 187:55–57.
Díaz Granados, Alfonso, Leonor Herrera, and Marianne Cardale de Schrimpff. 1974. "Mitología cuna: los kalu." *Revista Colombiana de Antropología* 17:203–247.
Díaz Vélez, Margarita. 1988. "Estructura política actual de las comunidades cuna, habitantes de la Isla Sasardi Mula tupo." Thesis, Universidad de Antioquia, Medellín.
Dicks, Bela. 2003. *Culture on Display: The Production of Contemporary Visibility*. Maidenhead, UK: Open University Press.
Dierks, Konstantin. 1999. "The Familiar Letter and Social Refinement in America, 1750–1800." In *Letter Writing as a Social Practice*, ed. David Barton and Nigel Hall, pp. 31–41. Amsterdam: John Benjamins.
Diez de la Cortina, R. 1915. *Modelos para cartas en Español y en Inglés*. New York: R. D. Cortina.
Di Giovanni, M. 1992. "I Cuna Nei Resoconti Dei Primi Viaggiatori." In *America: Cinque Secoli Dalla Conquista*, ed. Massimo Squillacciotti, pp. 21–29. Siena, Italy: Saggi dal seminario Interdisciplinare della Facoltà di Lettere e Filosofia, Università di Siena.
Dilworth, Leah. 1996. *Imagining Indians in the Southwest: Persistent Visions of a Primitive Past*. Washington, D.C.: Smithsonian Institution Press.
Dirks, Nicolas. 2001. *Castes of Mind: Colonialism and the Making of Modern India*. Princeton, N.J.: Princeton University Press.

Doggett, Scott. 1999. *Panama*. Hawthorn, Australia: Lonely Planet.
Dove, Michael. 2006. "Indigenous People and Environmental Politics." *Annual Review of Anthropology* 35:191–208.
Dunham, Jacob. 1850. *Journal of Voyages*. New York: Hucstis and Cozans.
Earle, Rebecca. 2007. *The Return of the Native: Indians and Myth-Making in Spanish America, 1810–1930*. Durham, N.C.: Duke University Press.
Ebensten, Hanns. 1987. *Volleyball with the Cuna Indians and Other Gay Travel Adventures*. New York: Penguin Books.
Elliott, J. H. 1970. *The Old World and the New, 1492–1650*. Cambridge: Cambridge University Press.
———. 1995. "Final Reflections: The Old World and the New Revisited." In *America in European Consciousness, 1493–1750*, ed. Karen Kupperman, pp. 391–402. Chapel Hill: University of North Carolina Press.
England, Nora. 1996. "The Role of Language Standardization in Revitalization." In *Maya Cultural Activism in Guatemala*, ed. Edward Fischer and R. McKenna Brown, pp. 178–194. Austin: University of Texas Press.
Ercilla y Zúñiga, Alonso de. 1945. *The Araucaniad: A Version in English Poetry of Alonso de Ercilla y Zúñiga's La Araucana*. Translated and edited by Charles Lancaster and Paul Manchester. Nashville: Vanderbilt University Press.
Erice, Jesús. 1950. "A la memoria de Nele." *Juventud Sanblaseña* 3:90–99.
———. 1951. "El trágico episodio de Río Azúcar." *Juventud Sanblaseña* 3.
———. 1961. "Primer etapa de la civilización de San Blas." *Lotería* 65:66–68.
———. 1975. "Historia de la revolución de los indios kunas de San Blas." *Estudios Centroamericanos* 319–320:283–304; 321:362–388 [reprinted in *Hombre y Cultura* 3:135–167].
———. 1980. *Gramática de la lengua kuna*. Panamá: Impresora de la Nación.
———. 1985. *Diccionario de la lengua kuna*. Panamá: Impresora de la Nación.
Esquemeling, John [or Alexandre]. 1924. *The Buccaneers of America*. New York: E. P. Dutton.
Estados Unidos de Colombia. 1871. *Civilización de los indios Tules*. Bogotá: Imprenta de Medardo Rívas.
Fabian, Johannes. 1983. *Time and the Other: How Anthropology Makes Its Object*. New York: Columbia University Press.
Falla, Ricardo. n.d. [c. 1975]. *Historia kuna, historia rebelde: la articulación del archipielago kuna a la nación panameña*. Serie El Indio Panameño. Panamá: Centro de Capacitación Social.
———. 1979a. *El indio y las clases sociales: El indígena panameño y la lucha de clases/pista para la intelección de los grupos étnicos*. Serie El Indio Panameño. Panamá: Centro de Capacitación Social.
———. 1979b. *El tesoro de San Blas: turismo en San Blas*. Serie El Indio Panameño. Panamá: Centro de Capacitación Social.
Favre, Henri. 1998. *El indigenismo*. Translated by Glenn Amado Jordán. México: Fondo de Cultura Económica.
Feeney, Corinne. 1941. "Arch-Isolationists, The San Blas Indians." *National Geographic* 79:193–220.

Feierman, Steven. 1990. *Peasant Intellectuals.* Madison: University of Wisconsin Press.

Field, Les. 1994. "Who Are the Indians? Reconceptualizing Indigenous Identity, Resistance, and the Role of Social Science in Latin America." *Latin American Research Review* 29 (3): 237–248.

Figueroa Navarro, Alfredo. 1978. *Dominio y sociedad en el Panamá colombiano (1821–1903).* Panamá: Impresora Panamá.

———. 1987. *Los grupos populares de la ciudad de Panamá a fines del siglo diecinueve.* Panamá: Impretex.

Fiore, Barbara. 1985. "La Percezione Della Forma Tra i Cestai Cuna." *La Ricerca Folklorica* 12:103–111.

Fischer, Edward. 1999. "Cultural Logic and Maya Identity: Rethinking Constructivism and Essentialism." *Current Anthropology* 43:473–499.

———. 2001. *Cultural Logics and Global Economies: Maya Identity in Thought and Practice.* Austin: University of Texas Press.

Fischer, Edward, and R. McKenna Brown, eds. 1996. *Maya Cultural Activism in Guatemala.* Austin: University of Texas Press.

Forbes-Lindsay, C. H. 1906. *Panama: The Isthmus and the Canal.* Philadelphia: John C. Winston.

Fortis, Paolo. 2002. "La 'Mola' Dei Cuna di Panamá Come Linguaggio Figurativo." Thesis, Università degli Studi di Siena.

Foucault, Michel. 1980. *The History of Sexuality.* New York: Vintage Books.

Franciosi, Paola. 1985. "Cuna: Identita Culturale e Partecipazione Politica." *LatinoAmerica* 20:62–68.

Freeman, Joanne. 2002. *Affairs of Honor.* New Haven, Conn.: Yale University Press.

Friedman, Jonathan. 1992. "The Past in the Future: History and the Politics of Identity." *American Anthropologist* 94 (4): 837–859.

Fuentes, Ventura, and Alfredo Elías. 1918. *Manual de correspondencia.* New York: MacMillan.

Galbraith, Douglas. 2001. *The Rising Sun.* New York: Atlantic Monthly Press.

Gallup-Díaz, Ignacio. 2004. *The Door of the Seas and Key to the Universe.* New York: Columbia University Press.

Gálvez, María Albertina. 1952. *Con los indios cunas de Panamá.* Biblioteca de Cultura Popular. Guatemala: Ministerio de Educación Pública.

Gamio, Manuel. 1922. *La población del Valle de Teotihuacan.* México: Talleres Gráficos de la Nación.

Garay, Narciso. 1930. *Tradiciones y cantares de Panamá: ensayo folklórico.* Panamá: n.p. Reprinted 1982.

Garvin, Gloria. 1983. "Cuna Psychotherapeutics: A Psychological, Social, and Theoretical Analysis (San Blas Islands, Panama)." Ph.D. diss., University of California, Los Angeles.

Gaspar, P. C. 1938. "Les Indiens de San Blas." *Bulletin de la Societé Des Américanistes de Belgique* 26:75–85.

Gassó, Leonardo. 1908a. *Doctrina y catecismo popular en castellano y karibekuna.* Barcelona: Tipografía Católica.

———. 1908b. *Gramática karibe-kuna.* Barcelona: Tipografía Católica.

———. 1910. "Informe sobre la catequización de los indios karibes de la Costa de San Blas y del Río Bayano, en la República de Panamá." *Las Misiones Católicas* 18:152–153, 163–165.

———. 1911–1914. "La Misión de San José de Nargana entre los karibes (República de Panamá)." *Las Misiones Católicas* 19–22. Barcelona (intermittent serial publication).

Gasteazoro, Carlos Manuel. 1979. "Presentación de Narciso Garay." *Revista Lotería* 281:1–45.

Gause, Frank, and Charles Carr. 1912. *The Story of Panama.* Boston: Silver, Burdett.

Gilbert, James Stanley. 1891. *Gilbertianae: Isthmian Rhymes.* Great Barrington, Mass.: Douglas Brothers.

———. 1894. *The Fall of Panamá, and Other Isthmian Rhymes and Sketches.* New York: n.p.

———. 1905. *Panama Patchwork.* Panamá: Star and Herald.

Gillin, John. 1942. "Acquired Drives in Culture Contact." *American Anthropologist* 44:545–554.

Gjording, Chris. 1991. *Conditions Not of Their Choosing: The Guaymí Indians and Mining Multinationals in Panama.* Washington, D.C.: Smithsonian Institution Press.

Goffman, Erving. 1959. *The Presentation of Self in Everyday Life.* Garden City, N.Y.: Doubleday.

———. 1963. *Stigma.* Englewood Cliffs, N.J.: Prentice-Hall.

Goldberg, David. 1997. *Racial Subjects: Writing on Race in America.* New York: Routledge.

Goldman, Francisco. 2007. *The Art of Political Murder: Who Killed the Archbishop?* New York: Grove Press.

Goldscheider, Calvin. 2002. "Ethnic Categorizations in Censuses: Comparative Observations from Israel, Canada, and the United States." In *Census and Identity: The Politics of Race, Ethnicity, and Language in National Censuses,* ed. David Kertzer and Dominique Arel, pp. 71–91. Cambridge: Cambridge University Press.

Gómez, Antonio. 1969a. "El cosmos, la religión, y creencias de los indios cuna." *Boletín, Universidad de Antioquia* 3:55–98.

———. 1969b. "Los cuna: Aspectos culturales de su adaptación al medio ambiente." Ph.D. diss., Universidad de los Andes, Bogotá.

Gómez Parra, R., and A. Martínez. 1992. "El nuevo nombre de América está escrito en kuna, Abya Yala." In *Los indios a la reconquista de América,* ed. Angeles Martínez Miguélez, pp. 191–203. Madrid: Editorial Fundamentos.

González, José Tomas, Marinelda Quiróz, Héctor Endara, and Blas Quintero. 2003. *VII Encuentro Nacional de Pastoral Indígena: misión y misioneros siglo XXI: diálogo pastoral y diálogo entre culturas.* Panamá: CONAPI.

González, Nicanor. 1992. "'We Are Not Conservationists': Interview with Nicanor González." *Cultural Survival Quarterly,* Fall, pp. 43–45.

González, Raúl. 1986. "Semblanza de Reina Torres de Araúz (una evocación en el aniversario de su muerte)." *Revista Lotería* 361:107–117.

Goody, Jack. 1986. *The Logic of Writing and the Organization of Society.* Cambridge: Cambridge University Press.

———. 1987. *The Interface between the Written and the Oral.* Cambridge: Cambridge University Press.

———. 2000. *The Power of the Written Tradition.* Washington, D.C.: Smithsonian Institution Press.

Goody, Jack, ed. 1968. *Literacy in Traditional Societies.* Cambridge: Cambridge University Press.

Goody, Jack, and Ian Watt. 1963. "The Consequences of Literacy." *Comparative Studies in Society and History* 5:304–345.

Gordon, Robert. 1992. *The Bushman Myth: The Making of a Namibian Underclass.* Boulder, Colo.: Westview.

Grafton, Anthony. 1992. *New Worlds, Ancient Texts: The Power of Tradition and the Shock of Discovery.* Cambridge, Mass.: Harvard University Press.

Graham, Laura. 2002. "How Should an Indian Speak? Amazonian Indians and the Symbolic Politics of Language in the Global Public Sphere." In *Indigenous Movements, Self-Representation, and the State in Latin America,* ed. Kay Warren and Jean Jackson, pp. 181–288. Austin: University of Texas Press.

Gramsci, Antonio. 1971. *Selections from the Prison Notebooks.* Translated and edited by Q. Hoare and G. N. Smith. London: Lawrence and Wishart.

Grant, Madison. 1916. *The Passing of the Great Race, or the Racial Basis of European History.* New York: Scribner's.

Green, Abadio. 2004. "La lengua como legado de los dioses." In *Voces Indigenas Universitarias,* ed. Zayda Sierra, pp. 323–340. Medellín: Universidad de Antioquia.

Greene, Eleanore. 1940. *Panama Sketches.* Boston: Bruce Humphries.

Greenfield, Patricia. 2004. *Weaving Generations Together: Evolving Creativity in the Maya of Chiapas.* Santa Fe: School of American Research.

Greer, Allan. 2000. "Colonial Saints: Gender, Race, and Hagiography in New France." *William and Mary Quarterly,* 3d ser., 57 (2): 323–348.

Grigore, Julius. 1987. Introduction. In *Panama Patchwork,* James Stanley Gilbert, pp. i–v. Venice, Fla.: Canal Zone Images.

Gudeman, Stephen. 1978. *The Demise of a Rural Economy.* London: Routledge.

Guerrón-Montero, Carla. 2006. "Tourism and Afro-Antillean Identity in Panama." *Journal of Tourism and Cultural Change* 4:65–84.

Guha, Ranajit. 1983. *Elementary Aspects of Peasant Insurgency in Colonial India.* Delhi: Oxford University Press.

Guionneau-Sinclair, Françoise. 1987. *Movimiento profético e innovación política entre los ngobe (guaymí) de Panamá, 1962–1984.* Panamá: Universidad de Panamá.

———. 1988. *Proceso de cambio en la sociedad ngobe (guaymí) de Panamá.* Panamá: Universidad de Panamá.

———. 1991. *Legislacion ameríndia de Panamá.* Panamá: Imprenta Universitaria.

Gutiérrez, Natividad. 1999. *Nationalist Myths and Ethnic Identities: Indigenous Intellectuals and the Mexican State.* Lincoln: University of Nebraska Press.

Gutiérrez, Ramón. 1991. *When Jesus Came, the Corn Mothers Went Away: Mar-*

riage, *Sexuality, and Power in New Mexico, 1500–1846.* Stanford, Calif.: Stanford University Press.
Hale, Charles. 2002. "Does Multiculturalism Menace?: Governance, Cultural Rights and the Politics of Identity in Guatemala." *Journal of Latin American Studies* 34:485–524.
———. 2006. *Más Que un Indio: Racial Ambivalence and Neoliberal Multiculturalism in Guatemala.* Santa Fe: School of American Research.
Hallowell, A. Irving. 1945. "Sociopsychological Aspects of Acculturation." In *The Science of Man in the World Crisis,* ed. Ralph Linton, pp. 171–200. New York: Columbia University Press.
Halverson, John. 1991. "Olson on Literacy." *Language in Society* 20:619–640.
———. 1992. "Goody and the Implosion of the Literacy Thesis." *Man* 27:301–317.
Hames, Raymond. 2007. "The Ecologically Noble Savage Debate." *Annual Review of Anthropology* 36:177–190.
Handler, Richard. 1988. *Nationalism and the Politics of Culture in Quebec.* Madison: University of Wisconsin Press.
Handler, Richard, and Jocelyn Linnekin. 1984. "Tradition, Genuine or Spurious." *Journal of American Folklore* 97:273–290.
Hanson, Alan. 1989. "The Making of the Maori: Cultural Invention and Its Logic." *American Anthropologist* 91:890–902.
Harris, Reginald. 1922. "Eugenics in South America." *Eugenical News* 7:17–42.
Hartmann, Gunther. 1980a. *Molakana: Volkskunst der Cuna, Panama.* Berlin: Museum für Völkerkunde.
———. 1980b. *Textilkunst der Cuna-Indios Im Grenzgebiet von Kolumbien un Panama* [Ausstellungskatalog]. Koblenz: Museum für Völkerkunde.
———. 1985. "Bei Den San Blas Cuna in Panama." *Mitteilungen der Berliner Gesellschaft für Anthropologie, Ethnologie, und Urgeschichte* 6:39–41.
———. 1988. *Gold und Silber: Gold von der Kuna, Panama, Silberschmuck von der Mapuche, Chile.* Berlin: D. Raimer.
Hartmann, Ursula. 1985. "Klassiche Molakana Im Durchbrochenen Silhouettenstil bei Den Kuna, Panama." *Zeitschrift für Ethnologie* 110:99–111.
———. 1986. "Stilrichtungen bei Den Molakana der Kuna-Indianerinnen Panamas Am Beispiel der Schildkrötendarstellung." *Zeitschrift für Ethnologie* 111:259–270.
———. 1988. "Das Ake-Motiv in Den Molakana der Kuna-Indianerinnen Panamas." *Zeitschrift für Ethnologie* 113:265–281.
Hasbrouck, Gary. 1985. "Subsistence Fishing among the San Blas Kunas, Panama." Master's thesis, University of California, Berkeley.
Healy, David. 1988. *Drive to Hegemony: The United States in the Caribbean, 1898–1917.* Madison: University of Wisconsin Press.
Heckadon Moreno, Stanley. 1983. *Cuando se acaban los montes.* Panamá: Smithsonian Tropical Research Institute.
Helbig, Jörg Wolfgang. 1983. *Religion und Medizinmannwesen bei Den Cuna.* Hohenschäftlarn: K. Renner.

———. 1985. "Einige Bemerkungen Zum 'Muu Ikala,' einem Medizingesang der Cuna Panamas." *Indiana* 10:323–339.

Hellbom, Anna-Britta. 1997. "Las personas en la investigación de Nordenskiöld." In *Erland Nordenskiöld, investigador y amigo del indígena,* ed. Jan-Åke Alvarsson and Oscar Agüero, pp. 109–126. Quito: Ediciones Abya-Yala.

Helms, Mary. 1979. *Ancient Panama: Chiefs in Search of Power.* Austin: University of Texas Press.

———. 1981. "Cuna Molas and Coclé Art Forms: Reflections on Panamanian Design Styles and Symbols." *Working Papers in Traditional Arts* No. 7. Philadelphia: Institute for the Study of Human Issues.

———. 1988. *Ulysses' Sail: An Ethnographic Odyssey of Power, Knowledge, and Geographical Distance.* Princeton, N.J.: Princeton University Press.

Hendrickson, Carol. 1995. *Weaving Identities: Construction of Dress and Self in a Highland Guatemalan Town.* Austin: University of Texas Press.

———. 1996. "Women, Weaving, and Education in Maya Revitalization." In *Maya Cultural Activism in Guatemala,* ed. Edward Fischer and R. McKenna Brown, pp. 156–164. Austin: University of Texas Press.

Hernández, Artinelio. 1996a. "Acta de la revolución kuna de 1925." *Onmaked* 2:6–9.

———. 1996b. "Tabu como metodo de enseñanza." *Onmaked* 2 (6): 5–6.

———. n.d. [May 2004]. "Informe del mes de mayo, Proyecto Igargan." Report. Instituto de Investigaciones Koskun Kalu.

———. 2005. *Sia igar kialed: versión en lenguaje común.* Panamá: Instituto de Investigaciones Koskun Kalu.

Herrera, Francisco. 1984. "La Revolución de Tule: antecedentes y nuevos aportes." Honors thesis, Universidad de Panamá.

———. 1987. "La Rebelión de Tule y el papel de la Legación Norteamericana." *Revista Panameña de Antropología* 3:40–56.

———. 1989. "Indian-State Relations in Panama, 1903–1983." Master's thesis, University of Florida, Gainesville.

———. n.d. [2004]. "La antropología y el desarrollo de la nacionalidad." Manuscript.

Herrera, Heraclio. 1995. "The Ueruk Palm." In *Plants and Animals in the Life of the Kuna,* ed. Jorge Ventocilla, Heraclio Herrera, and Valerio Núñez, pp. 98–109. Austin: University of Texas Press.

Herrera, Leonor. 1969. "Arquía: la organización social de una comunidad indígena cuna." Ph.D. diss., Universidad de los Andes, Bogotá.

Herrera, Ligia. 1994. *Regiones de desarrollo socioeconomico de Panamá, 1980–1990.* Panamá: Centro de Estudios Latinamericanos "Justo Arosemena."

Herrera, Simón. n.d. [2003]. "La verdad oculta del General Inapakiña." Manuscript.

Herrera, Tomás, and Anita McAndrews. 1978. *Cuna Cosmology: Legends from Panama.* Washington, D.C.: Three Continents Press.

Herrmann, Adolf. 1964. "Der Irresein-Komplex bei Den Insel-Kuna: Studienreise San Blas Panama 1963." *Zeitschrift für Ethnologie* 89:277–281.

———. 1969. "Kuna-Indianer und Ihr Kulturerbe Im Sog der Gegenwart." *Zeitschrift für Ethnologie* 94:131–135.

———. 1975. "Das Onmaket Nega, die Zentrale Institution der Kuna-Kultur in der Comarca de San Blas." *Zeitschrift für Ethnologie* 100:264–271.

———. 1977. "Die Kuna-Proklamation 1925 in der Comarca de San Blas–Panama." *Zeitschrift für Ethnologie* 102:297–307.

———. 1980a. "Kleine Grammatik Des Karibe-Kuna." *Zeitschrift für Ethnologie* 105:157–182.

———. 1980b. "Wörterliste Deutsch-Kuna." *Zeitschrift für Ethnologie* 105:183–255.

Herskovits, Melville. 1937. "The Significance of the Study of Acculturation for Anthropology." *American Anthropologist* 39:259–264.

———. 1938. *Acculturation: The Study of Culture Contact*. New York: J. J. Augustin.

Herzfeld, Michael. 2001. *Anthropology: Theoretical Practice in Culture and Society*. Oxford: Blackwell.

Higham, John. 1966. *Strangers in the Land: Patterns of American Nativism, 1860–1925*. New York: Atheneum.

Hinsley, Curtis. 1989. "Zunis and Brahmins: Cultural Ambivalence in the Gilded Age." In *Romantic Motives: Essays on Anthropological Sensibility*, ed. George Stocking, pp. 169–207. Madison: University of Wisconsin Press.

Hirschfeld, Lawrence. 1976. "A Structural Analysis of the Cuna Arts." In *Ritual and Symbol in Native Central America*, ed. Philip Young and James Howe, pp. 43–56. Eugene: University of Oregon Anthropological Papers No. 9.

———. 1977a. "Art in Cunaland: Ideology and Cultural Adaptation." *Man*, n.s., 12:104–123.

———. 1977b. "Cuna Aesthetics: A Quantitative Analysis." *Ethnology* 16:147–166.

Hirschfeld, Lawrence, James Howe, and Bruce Levin. 1978. "Warfare, Infanticide, and Statistical Inference: A Comment on Divale and Harris." *American Anthropologist* 80 (1): 111–115.

Hobsbawm, Eric. 1987. *The Age of Empire, 1875–1914*. New York: Pantheon.

Hobsbawm, Eric, and Terence Ranger, eds. 1983. *The Invention of Tradition*. Cambridge: Cambridge University Press.

Hochschild, Adam. 1999. *King Leopold's Ghost: A Story of Greed, Terror, and Heroism in Colonial Africa*. Boston: Houghton Mifflin.

———. 2005. *Bury the Chains: The British Struggle to Abolish Slavery*. London: Macmillan.

Hohenegger, Mergherita. 1985. "Analisi di un Universo Semiotico: Le Mola Dei Cuna di San Blas." Honors thesis, Universita di Roma "La Sapienza."

Holloman, Regina. 1969. "Developmental Change in San Blas." Ph.D. diss., Northwestern University.

———. 1971. "Ritos de pubertad masculina, matrimonio, pre-pubertad, y couvade entre los cunas de Panamá: algunas notas etnohistóricas." *Hombre y Cultura* 2:41–49.

———. 1975. "Ethnic Boundary Maintenance, Readaption, and Societal Evolution in the San Blas Islands of Panama." In *Ethnicity and Resource Competition in Plural Societies*, ed. Leo Despres, pp. 27–40. Paris: Mouton.

———. 1976. "Cuna Household Types and the Domestic Cycle." In *Frontier Adaptations in Lower Central America*, ed. Mary Helms and Franklin Loveland, pp. 133–149. Philadelphia: Institute for the Study of Human Issues.

Holmer, Nils. 1947. *Critical and Comparative Grammar of the Cuna Language*. Etnologiska Studier 14. Göteborg: Etnografiska Museum.

———. 1951. *Cuna Chrestomathy*. Etnologiska Studier 18. Göteborg: Etnografiska Museum.

———. 1952a. *Ethno-Linguistic Cuna Dictionary*. Etnologiska Studier 19. Göteborg: Etnografiska Museum.

———. 1952b. *Inatoipippiler, or the Adventures of Three Cuna Boys, According to Maninibigdinapi (Belisario Guerrero)*. Etnologiska Studier 20. Göteborg: Etnografiska Museum.

———. 1953. "Some Semantic Problems in Cuna and Kaggaba." *International Anthropological and Linguistic Review* 1:195–200.

Holmer, Nils, and S. Henry Wassén. 1947. *Mu-Igala or The Way of Muu. A Medicine Song from the Cuna Indians of Panama*. Göteborg: Elanders Boktryckeri Aktiebolag.

———. 1953. *The Complete Mu-Igala in Picture Writing. A Native Record of a Cuna Indian Medicine Song*. Etnologiska Studier 21. Göteborg: Etnografiska Museum.

———. 1958. *Nia-Ikala, canto mágico para curar la locura*. Etnologiska Studier 23. Göteborg: Etnografiska Museum.

———. 1963. *Dos cantos shamanísticos de los indios cunas*. Etnologiska Studier 27. Göteborg: Etnografiska Museum.

Howe, James. 1974. "Village Political Organization among the San Blas Cuna." Ph.D. diss., University of Pennsylvania.

———. 1977. "Algunos problemas no resueltos de la etnohistoria del este de Panamá." *Revista Panameña de Antropología* 2:30–47.

———. 1979. "The Effects of Writing on the Cuna Political System." *Ethnology* 18:1–16.

———. 1980. "Introducción: guia a la literatura del congreso kuna." In *Cantos y oraciones del congreso cuna*, Horacio Méndez, Gonzalo Salcedo, Olowitinappi, and Mastayans; ed. James Howe, Joel Sherzer, and Mac Chapin, pp. 6–30. Panamá: Editorial Universitaria.

———. 1982. "Kindling Self-Determination among the Kuna." *Cultural Survival Quarterly* 6:15–17.

———. 1985. "Marriage and Domestic Organization among the San Blas Kuna." In *The Botany and Natural History of Panama*, ed. William Darcy and Mireya Correa, pp. 317–331. St. Louis: Missouri Botanical Garden.

———. 1986. *The Kuna Gathering: Contemporary Village Politics in Panama*. Austin: University of Texas Press.

———. 1990. "Mission Rivalry and Conflict in San Blas, Panama." In *Class, Politics, and Popular Religion in Mexico and Central America*, ed. Lynn Stephen and James Dow, pp. 143–166. Society for Latin American Anthropology Publication Series 10. Washington, D.C.: American Anthropological Association.

———. 1991a. "An Ideological Triangle: The Struggle over San Blas Kuna Culture, 1915–1925." In *Nation-States and Indians in Latin America*, ed. Greg Urban and Joel Sherzer, pp. 19–52. Austin: University of Texas Press.

———. 1991b. "Star Girls and Star Man: A Comparative Analysis of Paired Kuna Myths." *Journal of Latin American Lore* 17:225–266.

———. 1992. "Protestants, Catholics, and 'Gentiles': The Articulation of Missionary and Indigenous Culture on the San Blas Coast of Panama." *Journal of the Anthropological Society of Oxford* 23:139–155.

———. 1995. "La lucha por la tierra en la Costa de San Blas (Panamá), 1900–1930." *Mesoamérica* 29:57–76.

———. 1998. *A People Who Would Not Kneel: Panama, the United States and the San Blas Kuna*. Washington, D.C.: Smithsonian Institution Press.

———. 2002. "The Kuna of Panama: Continuing Threats to Land and Autonomy." In *The Politics of Ethnicity: Indigenous Peoples in Latin American States*, ed. David Maybury-Lewis, pp. 81–106. Cambridge, Mass.: David Rockefeller Center for Latin American Studies.

———. 2004a. "Kuna." In *Encyclopedia of Sex and Gender*, ed. Carol Ember and Melvin Ember, pp. 581–591. New York: Kluwer Academic/Plenum.

———. 2004b. *Un pueblo que no se arrodillaba: Panamá, los Estados Unidos, y los kunas de San Blas*. Guatemala: CIRMA/Plumsock Mesoamerican Studies.

Howe, James, with Jesús Alemancia, Cebaldo de León, Carlos López, Jimmy Solís, and Samuel Morris. 1994. "Sounds Heard in the Distance: Poetry and Metaphor in the Kuna Struggle for Autonomy." *Latin American Indian Literatures Journal* 10:1–21.

Howe, James, and Lawrence Hirschfeld. 1981. "The Star Girls' Descent: A Myth about Men, Women, Matrilocality, and Singing." *Journal of American Folklore* 4:292–322.

Howe, James, and Joel Sherzer. 1986. "Friend Hairyfish and Friend Rattlesnake, or Dealing with Anthropologists through Humor." *Man* 21:680–696.

Hrdlička, Aleš. 1926. "The Indians of Panama and Their Physical Relation to the Mayas." *American Journal of Physical Anthropology* 9:1–15.

Humphries, Theodore. 1944. *The Indians of Panama: Their History and Culture*. Panamá: Pan American Publishing.

IDICA/GRET (Instituto para el Desarrollo Integral de la Comarca de Kuna Yala/Group de Recherché et d'Echanges Technologiques). n.d. [August 1995]. "Invasión de terrenos comarcales: la percepción de las comunidades kunas del sector Cartí (Kuna Yala, Panamá)." Report.

Iglesias, Marvel. 1958. *I Married a San Blas Indian: The Story of Marvel Elya Iglesias*. New York: Vantage Press.

Inakeliginia [Carlos López]. 1997. *Así lo vi y así me lo contaron*. Translated and edited by Aiban Wagwa. Kuna Yala, Panamá: Congreso General de la Cultura Kuna.

Inden, Ronald B. 1990. *Imagining India*. Bloomington: Indiana University Press.

Instituto de Estudios Nacionales (Universidad de Panamá) and Diócesis Misionera de Colón. 1991. *Colón y Kuna Yala: desafío para la Iglesia y el gobierno*. Panamá: Diócesis Misionera de Colón, Talleres de Materiales de Evangelización.

Irvine, Judith, and Susan Gal. 2000. "Language Ideology and Linguistic Differentiation." In *Regimes of Language: Ideologies, Polities, and Identities*, ed. Paul Kroskrity, pp. 35–80. Santa Fe: School of American Research.

Isacsson, Sven-Erik. 1997. "Nils Erland Herbert Nordenskiöld." In *Erland Nordenskiöld, investigador y amigo del indígena*, ed. Jan-Åke Alvarsson and Oscar Agüero, pp. 29–58. Quito: Ediciones Abya-Yala.

Isthmian Anthropology Society. 1969. *About Molas/Hablando de molas*. Panamá: Panama Canal Press.

Jackson, Jean. 1989. "Is There a Way to Talk about Making Culture without Making Enemies?" *Dialectical Anthropology* 14 (2): 127–144.

———. 1991. "Being and Becoming an Indian in the Vaupés." In *Nation-States and Indians in Latin America*, ed. Greg Urban and Joel Sherzer, pp. 131–155. Austin: University of Texas Press.

———. 1995. "Culture, Genuine and Spurious: The Politics of Indianness in the Vaupés, Colombia." *American Ethnologist* 22 (1): 3–27.

———. 2007. "Rights to Indigenous Culture in Colombia." In *The Practice of Human Rights: Tracking Law between the Global and the Local*, ed. Mark Goodale and Sally Engle Merry, pp. 204–241. Cambridge: Cambridge University Press.

Jackson, Jean, and Kay Warren. 2005. "Indigenous Movements in Latin America, 1992–2004: Controversies, Ironies, New Directions." *Annual Review of Anthropology* 34:549–573.

Jacobs, Margaret. 1999. *Engendered Encounters: Feminism and Pueblo Cultures, 1879–1934*. Lincoln: University of Nebraska Press.

Jaramillo, José Antonio. 1986. "El legado de ibeorgum: La música como factor de supervivencia cultural en la comunidad cuna de Caimán Nuevo." Thesis, Universidad Nacional de Colombia, Bogotá.

Jeambrun, Pascale, and Bernard Sergent. 1991. *Les Enfants de la Lune: L'Albinisme Chez les Amérindiens*. Paris: Éditions INSERM.

Joyce, L. E. Elliott, ed. 1934. "Introduction, Appendices, and Notes." In *A New Voyage and Description of the Isthmus of America*, Lionel Wafer, Series 2, Vol. 73, pp. xi–lxxi, 166–201. Oxford: Hakluyt Society.

Junod, Henri. 1927. *The Life of a South African Tribe*. London: MacMillan.

Junta Nacional del Cincuentenario. 1953. *Panamá, 50 años de República*. Panamá: n.p.

Kalman, Judy. 1996. "Joint Composition: The Collaborative Letter Writing of a Scribe and His Client in Mexico." *Written Communication* 13 (2): 190–220.

———. 1999. *Writing on the Plaza*. Cresskill, N.J.: Hampton Press, Inc.

Kapp, Kit S. 1972. *Mola: Art from the San Blas Islands*. North Bend, Ohio: K. S. Kapp Publications.

Karttunen, Frances. 1994. *Between Worlds: Interpreters, Guides, and Survivors*. New Brunswick, N.J.: Rutgers University Press.

Keeler, Clyde. 1956. *Land of the Moon-Children*. Athens: University of Georgia Press.

———. 1960. *Secrets of the Cuna Earthmother*. New York: Exposition Press.
———. 1961. *Apples of Immortality from the Cuna Tree of Life*. New York: Exposition Press.
———. 1969. *Cuna Indian Art*. New York: Exposition Press.
———. 1987. *Timeless Threads in the Fabric of Cuna Indian Culture*. Milledgeville, Ga.: n.p.
Keesing, Roger. 1992. *Custom and Confrontation: The Kwaio Struggle for Cultural Autonomy*. Chicago: University of Chicago Press.
Kelly, Joanne. 1966. *Cuna*. South Brunswick, N.J.: A. S. Barnes.
Kenton, Edna, ed. 1954. *The Jesuit Relations and Allied Documents*. New York: Vanguard Press.
Kertzer, David, and Dominique Arel. 2002. "Censuses, Identity Formation, and the Struggle for Political Power." In *Census and Identity: The Politics of Race, Ethnicity, and Language in National Censuses*, ed. David Kertzer and Dominique Arel, pp. 1–42. Cambridge: Cambridge University Press.
———, eds. 2002. *Census and Identity: The Politics of Race, Ethnicity, and Language in National Censuses*. Cambridge: Cambridge University Press.
Kingsley, Charles. 1866. *Hereward, the Last of the English*. Boston: Ticknor and Fields.
Krieger, Herbert. 1926. *Material Culture of the People of Southeastern Panama, Based on Specimens in the United States National Museum*. U.S. National Museum Bulletin 134. Washington, D.C.: Smithsonian Institution.
Kroskrity, Paul, ed. 2000. *Regimes of Language: Ideologies, Polities, and Identities*. Santa Fe: School of American Research Press.
Kubiler [Leadimiro González] and Cole-igar. 2007. *Niiskuamar Ebised Dule / El contador de estrellas / The Star Counter*. Miami/Panamá: Piggy Press.
Kungiler, Iguaniginape. 1994. *Ologindibipilele: caminante y guerrero de 1925 (biografía de Simral Colman)*. Colectivo de Editores Kunas. Panamá: Instituto Cooperativo Interamericano.
———. 1997. *Yar burba, anmar burba: espíritu de tierra, nuestro espíritu*. Panamá: Congreso General de la Cultura Kuna.
Kupperman, Karen Ordahl. 1995. "Introduction: The Changing Definition of America." In *America in European Consciousness, 1493–1750*, ed. Karen Ordahl Kupperman, pp. 1–32. Chapel Hill: University of North Carolina Press.
———. 1997. "Presentment of Civility: English Reading of American Self-Presentation in the Early Years of Colonization." *William and Mary Quarterly* 54:193–228.
———. 2000. *Indians and English*. Ithaca, N.Y.: Cornell University Press.
Lamont, Michèle. 1992. *Money, Morals, and Manners*. Chicago: University of Chicago Press.
Landsman, Gail, and Sara Ciborski. 1992. "Representation and Politics: Contesting Histories of the Iroquois." *Cultural Anthropology* 7:425–447.
Langer, Erick, and Elena Muñoz. 2003. *Contemporary Indigenous Movements in Latin America*. Wilmington, Del.: SR Books.
La Varre, William. 1940. *Southward Ho! A Treasure Hunter in South America*. New York: Doubleday, Doran.

Lavender, Catherine Jane. 2006. *Scientists and Storytellers: Feminist Anthropologists and the Construction of the American Southwest*. Albuquerque: University of New Mexico Press.
Lawrence Lowenbach, Trude. 1977. "Physical and Social Deviance: A Study of Health-Related Attitudes, Perceptions and Practices within a San Blas Cuna Village, Panama." Ph.D. diss., University of North Carolina, Chapel Hill.
Lears, T. Jackson. 1981. *No Place of Grace: Antimodernism and the Transformation of American Culture*. Chicago: University of Chicago Press.
Leis, Raúl. 1992. *Machi: un kuna en la ciudad*. Panamá: CEASPA.
———. 2004. "La casa es de forma de totuma y el infierno está de fuera de la casa: los pueblos indígenas de Panamá, carencias y potencialidades." In Proceedings (on CD) of the 25th Congress of the Latin American Studies Association, Las Vegas, Nevada, April 2004.
Lemke, Carl, ed. 1964. *Official History of the Improved Order of Red Men*. Waco, Tex.: Davis Brothers.
Lepore, Jill. 1998. *The Name of War*. New York: Alfred A. Knopf.
Lévi-Strauss, Claude. 1963. "The Effectiveness of Symbols." In *Structural Anthropology*, pp. 186–205. New York: Basic Books.
Lewis, Oscar. 1963. *Life in a Mexican Village: Tepoztlán Re-Studied*. Urbana: University of Illinois Press.
Liberty, Margot. 1978. *American Indian Intellectuals*. St. Paul: West Publishing.
Liebersohn, Harry. 1998. *Aristocratic Encounters: European Travellers and North American Indians*. Cambridge: Cambridge University Press.
Lindberg, Christer. 1996. *Erland Nordenskiöld Ett Indianlif*. Stockholm: Natur och Kultur.
———. 1997. "El museo—como libro y situación de campo: el visionero Erland Nordenskiöld." In *Erland Nordenskiöld, investigador y amigo del indígena*, ed. Jan-Åke Alvarsson and Oscar Agüero, pp. 59–79. Quito: Ediciones Abya-Yala.
Linnekin, Jocelyn. 1983. "Defining Tradition: Variations on the Hawaiian Identity." *American Ethnologist* 10:241–252.
———. 1991. "Cultural Invention and the Dilemma of Authenticity." *American Anthropologist* 93:446–448.
Linton, Ralph. 1936. *The Study of Man: An Introduction*. New York: Appleton-Century.
———, ed. 1940. *Acculturation in Seven North American Indian Tribes*. New York: Appleton-Century.
Llerena Villalobos, Rito. 1987. *Relación y determinación en el predicado de la lengua kuna*. Bogotá: Colciencias.
Locke, John. 2000. *Some Thoughts Concerning Education / by John Locke*, ed. John Yolton and Jean Yolton. Oxford: Clarendon Press.
Lomnitz, Claudio. 2001. *Deep Mexico, Silent Mexico: An Anthropology of Nationalism*. Minneapolis: University of Minnesota Press.
López, Carlos. See Inakeliginia.
López, Delio, Julio Pérez, and Archivaldo López. 2007. *Igargan/cantos/songs: La cosmovisión kuna y la biodiversidad marina*. Panamá: CODESTA.

López Hernandez, Heraclio. 1995. "Madre tierra: un modo de vida." *América Indígena* 15:113–117.
López Paniagua, Rafael. 1943. *El libro del corresponsal.* Guatemala: Tipografía Nacional.
López Vivar, Yadibaler. 2002. "Estudio de la cacería de fauna silvestre en dos comunidades kunas del Caribe panameño." Honors thesis, Universidad de Panamá.
Lutz, Otto. 1924. "Los habitantes primitivos de la República de Panamá." Leipzig: n.p.
McCosker, Sandra [see also Sandra Smith]. 1974. *The Lullabies of the San Blas Cuna Indians of Panama.* Etnologiska Studier 33. Göteborg: Etnografiska Museum.
———. 1976. "San Blas Cuna Indian Lullabies: A Means of Informal Learning." In *Enculturation in Latin America,* ed. Johannes Wilbert, pp. 29–66. Los Angeles: UCLA Latin American Series 37.
McCullough, David. 1977. *The Path between the Seas: The Creation of the Panama Canal, 1870–1914.* New York: Simon and Schuster.
McFeely, Eliza. 2001. *Zuni and the American Imagination.* New York: Farrar, Strauss and Giroux.
McKay, Alberto. 1964. "Los Trabajos de graduación sobre antropología presentados en la Universidad de Panamá." *Hombre y Cultura* 1 (3): 99–101.
McKim, Fred. 1947a. *The Forbidden Land. Reconnaissance of Upper Bayano River, R.P. in 1936.* Etnologiska Studier 15:115–186. Göteborg: Etnografiska Museum.
———. 1947b. *San Blas, an Account of the Cuna Indians of Panama.* Etnologiska Studier 15:3–113. Göteborg: Etnografiska Museum.
McLoughlin, William. 1986. *Cherokee Renascence in the New Republic.* Princeton, N.J.: Princeton University Press.
Major, John. 1993. *Prize Possession: The United States and the Panama Canal, 1903–1979.* Cambridge: Cambridge University Press.
Malinowski, Bronislaw. 1929. *The Sexual Life of Savages.* New York: Harcourt Brace.
Mariátegui, José Carlos. 1928. *7 ensayos de interpretación de la realidad peruana.* Lima: Biblioteca Amauta.
Markham, William. n.d. 1. "Markham Narrative." IF 2905, Tioga Point Museum, Athens, Pennsylvania.
———. n.d. 2. "Markham's Account of Uprising." IF 2907, Tioga Point Museum, Athens, Pennsylvania.
Marsh, Richard. 1925. "Blond Indians of the Darien Jungle." *World's Work,* March, pp. 483–497.
———. n.d. [1925]. "Declaration of Independence and Human Rights of the Tule People of San Blas and the Darien." NAA.
———. 1934. *White Indians of Darien.* New York: Putnam.
Marshall, Donald. 1950. "Cuna Folk: A Conceptual Scheme Involving the Dynamic Factors of Culture, as Applied to the Cuna Indians of Darien." Honors thesis, Harvard College.

Martínez, Atilio. 1996. "Acta de la Revolución Kuna de 1925." *Onmaked* 2:6–9.
———. 1998. "Historia de los profetas kunas ('nelegana')." Honors thesis, Universidad de Panamá.
———. 1999. *La educación en el pueblo kuna / Education among the Kuna Peoples*. Panamá: Congreso General de la Cultura Kuna.
Martínez Mauri, Mònica. n.d. [October 29, 2003]. "Rubén Pérez Kantule: la diplomatie autochtone avant les ONGS." Manuscript.
———. 2005. *Indigenous NGO and Cultural Mediators: Kuna Yala (Panama) 1925–2004*. World Public Forum "Dialogue of Civilizations" Bulletin 2. Moscow.
———. 2007. *De Tule Nega a Kuna Yala: mediación, territorio, y ecología en Panamá, 1903–2004*. Barcelona/Paris: Universidad Autónoma de Barcelona / École des Hautes Études en Sciences Sociales.
Marzal, Manuel. 1993. *Historia de la antropología indigenista: México y Perú*. Barcelona: Anthropos Editorial del Hombre.
Mathews, Kate. 1998. *Molas! Patterns, Techniques, and Projects for Colorful Appliqué*. Asheville, N.C.: Lark Books.
Maurer, Ingeborg, and M. Huber. 1977. *Die San Blas Cuna: Ein Indianerstamm in Panama*. Cologne: Museen de Stadt.
Maxwell, Judith. 1996. "Prescriptive Grammar and Kaqchikel Revitalization." In *Maya Cultural Activism in Guatemala*, ed. Edward Fischer and R. McKenna Brown, pp. 195–207. Austin: University of Texas Press.
Mayer, Dora. 1921. *El indígena peruano a los cien años de república libre e independiente*. Lima: Imprenta Peruana de E. Z. Casanova.
Méndez, Alejandro. 1953. "El arte de nuestros antepasados indígenas." In *Panamá, 50 años de República*, ed. Junta Nacional del Cincuentenario, pp. 311–318. Panamá: n.p.
Méndez, Horacio. 1970. "Tad Ibe gi namaket." Long-playing record. Panamá.
Méndez, Horacio, Gonzalo Salcedo, Olowitinappi, and Mastayans. 1980. *Cantos y oraciones del congreso cuna*. Edited by James Howe, Joel Sherzer, and Mac Chapin. Panamá: Editorial Universitaria.
Méndez, Horacio, Manuel Santacruz, Victor Peláez García, and Fred Green. 1996. *La historia de mis abuelos*. Transcribed and translated by Aipan Wakua [Aiban Wagwa], Abadio Green Stocel, and Jorge Peláez. Colombia: Asociación de Cabildos Indígenas de Antioquia.
Méndez Pereira, Octavio. 1936. *Núñez de Balboa: el tesoro del Dabaibe*. Madrid: Ediciones Nuestra Raza.
Merrell, James. 1999. *Into the American Woods*. New York: W. W. Norton & Company.
Metcalf, Thomas R. 1995. *Ideologies of the Raj*. Cambridge: Cambridge University Press.
Miller, George. 1919. *Prowling about Panama*. New York: Abingdon Press.
Minter, John. 1948. *The Chagres: River of Westward Passage*. New York: Rinehart.
Miró, Rodrigo. 1975. "Angel Rubio, explorador de nuestra realidad física e histórica." *Revista Lotería* 228:38–43.

Misioneros Claretianos [numerous authors]. 1928–1945. "Historia de la misión de San Blas (Segunda época)." Courtesy of Mònica Martínez Mauri.

Misioneros Hijos del Corazón de Maria. 1939. *Memoria del Vicariato Apostólico del Darién, Panamá*. Panamá: Imprenta Acción Católica.

Mitchell, Timothy. 1988. *Colonizing Egypt*. Cambridge: Cambridge University Press.

Moeller, Eric J. 1997. "Identity and Millenarian Discourse: Kuna Indian Villagers in an Ethnic Borderland." Ph.D. diss., University of Chicago.

Montalván, Ana. 1976. "Formación de los numerales kunas." *Revista Nacional de Cultura* 2:45–50.

Montejo, Víctor. 2005. *Maya Intellectual Renaissance: Identity, Representation, and Leadership*. Austin: University of Texas Press.

Moore, Alexander. 1978. "Mayas y Cunas: ensayo comparativo." *Patrimonio Histórico* 2:73–114.

———. 1980. "Planners, Tourists, and Indians: National Planning, Regional Development Projects, and the San Blas Cuna." *Practicing Anthropology* 2:5–6, 19–20.

———. 1981. "Basilicas and Kingposts: A Proxemic and Symbolic Event Analysis of Competing Public Architecture among the San Blas Cuna." *American Ethnologist* 8:259–277.

———. 1983. "Lore and Life: Cuna Indian Pageants, Exorcism, and Diplomacy in the Twentieth Century." *Ethnohistory* 30:93–106.

———. 1984. "From Council to Legislature: Democracy, Parliamentarianism, and the San Blas Cuna." *American Anthropologist* 86:28–42.

Morales Gómez, Jorge. 1969. "Los indios cuna del Golfo de Urabá y sus contactos culturales." Ph.D. diss., Universidad de los Andes, Bogotá.

———. 1972. "Contactos culturales en el Golfo de Urabá: La evangelización de los cunas." *América Indígena* 32:1197–1210.

———. 1975. "Notas etnográficas sobre la tecnología de los indios cuna." *Revista Colombiana de Antropología* 19:79–102.

———. 1992. "Tres episodios en la historia de los indios cuna." *Boletín de Historia y Antiquedades* 79:393–408.

———. 1995. "El convenio de 1870 entre los cunas y el estado colombiano: Sentido de una acción de resistencia." *Revista Colombiana de Antropología* 32:187–196.

Morgan, Christine. 1958. *I Married a San Blas Indian: The Story of Marvel Elya Iglesias*. New York: Vantage Press.

Morris, Anacleto. 1995. *Karba dardaled: aprenda ud. sin maestro*. Panamá: Congreso General de la Cultura Kuna.

Mueller, Jeannette. 1973. *Molas: Art of the Cuna Indians*. Washington, D.C.: International Exhibitions Foundation.

Murphy, Elizabeth, and Robert Dingwall. 2001. "The Ethics of Ethnography." In *Handbook of Ethnography*, ed. Paul Atkinson, Amanda Coffey, Sara Delamont, John Lofland, and Lyn Lofland, pp. 339–351. London: Sage Publications.

Nagel, Joane. 2003. *Race, Ethnicity, and Sexuality*. New York: Oxford University Press.

Naroll, Raoul. 1962. *Data Quality Control.* New York: Free Press.

———. 1973. "Data Quality Control in Cross-Cultural Surveys." In *A Handbook of Method in Cultural Anthropology,* ed. Raoul Naroll and Ronald Cohen, pp. 927–945. New York: Columbia University Press.

Navas, Narciso. 1935. "Un esfuerzo: a propósito de 'Rudimentos de gramática karibe-kuna,' del Reverendo Padre José Berengueras." *Boletín de la Academia Panameña de la Historia* 2 (7): 107–115.

Nele Kantule and Rubén Pérez Kantule. 1928. *Picture-Writings and Other Documents by Néle, Paramount Chief of the Cuna Indians, and Rubén Pérez Kantule, His Secretary.* Comparative Ethnographical Studies, ed. Erland Nordenskiöld. Göteborg: Elanders Boktryckeri Aktiebolag.

Nele Kantule, Charles Slater, Charlie Nelson, et al. 1930. *Picture-Writings and Other Documents by Néle, Charles Slater, Charlie Nelson and Other Cuna Indians.* Comparative Ethnographical Studies, ed. Erland Nordenskiöld. Göteborg: Elanders Boktryckeri Aktiebolag.

Nelson, Diane. 1999. *A Finger in the Wound: Body Politics in Quincentennial Guatemala.* Berkeley: University of California Press.

Nicholas, Francis. 1903. *Around the Caribbean and across Panama.* Boston: H. M. Caldwell.

Nordenskiöld, Erland. 1910. *Indianlif i El Gran Chaco Sydamerika.* Stockholm: Albert Bonniers Förlag.

———. 1911. *Indianer Och Hvita i Nordöstra Bolivia.* Stockholm: Albert Bonniers Förlag.

———. 1915. *Forskningar Och Äventyr i Sydamerika 1913–1914.* Stockholm: Albert Bonniers.

———. 1927. "Cunaindianernas Bildskrift." *Göteborgs Handels-Och Sjöfartstidning,* November 26.

———. 1928a. "Cuna Indian Conceptions of Illness." In *Festschrift. Publication d'Hommage offerte au P. W. Schmidt,* ed. W. Koppers, pp. 527–529. Wien: n.p.

———. 1928b. *Indianerna På Panamanäset.* Stockholm: Åhlén & Åkerlunds Förlag.

———. 1929. "Les Rapports Entre l'Art, la Religion et la Magie Chez les Indiens Cuna et Chocó." *Journal de la Societé Des Américanistes de Paris,* n.s., 21:141–158.

———. 1932a. "La Conception de l'Âme Chez les Indiens Cuna de l'Isthme de Panamá (la Signification de Trois Mots Cuna, Purba, Niga Et Kurgin)." *Journal de la Societé Des Américanistes de Paris,* n.s., 24:5–30.

———. 1932b. "Faiseurs de Miracles et Voyants Chez Les Indiens Cuna." *Revista del Instituto de Etnología, Tucumán* 2:459–469.

———. 1999. *The Cultural History of the South American Indians.* New York: AMS Press.

Nordenskiöld, Erland, with Rubén Pérez Kantule. 1938. *An Historical and Ethnological Survey of the Cuna Indians,* ed. S. Henry Wassén. Göteborg: Etnografiska Museum.

Ochoa, Reinaldo, and Jorge Peláez. 1995. *An Mal Epistele Nekka Kuepur Purpa*

Seyelkin Pinsaelkkepe. Colombia: Asociación de Cabildos Indígenas de Antioquia.

Olguín Martínez, Gabriela. 2006. *Trabajo infantil y pueblos indígenas: el caso de Panamá.* San José, Costa Rica: Oficina Internacional de Trabajo.

Olien, Michael. 1988. "After the Indian Slave Trade: Cross-Cultural Trade in the Western Caribbean Rimland, 1816–1820." *Journal of Anthropological Research* 44:41–66.

Oliver, Frederick. n.d. [1916]. "The San Blas Indians of Darien." NAA.

Olson, David. 1994. *The World on Paper.* Cambridge: Cambridge University Press.

Ong, Walter. 1982. *Orality and Literacy: The Technologization of the Word.* London: Methuen.

Ongaro, S. 1992. "L'Immagine Dei Cuna Nei Massmedia." In *America: Cinque Secoli Dalla Conquista,* ed. Massimo Squillacciotti, pp. 29–33. Siena, Italy: Saggi dal seminario Interdisciplinare della Facoltà di Lettere e Filosofia, Università di Siena.

Orán, Reuter. 1992. *Ue an ai (Este es mi amigo): Libro de lectura para niños kunas, primer grado.* Panamá: Ministerio de Educación.

Páez, Gumersinda. 1941. "Los indios de San Blas y la rebelión indígena del año 1925." Honors thesis, Universidad de Panamá.

Pagden, Anthony. 1993. *European Encounters with the New World: From Renaissance to Romanticism.* New Haven, Conn.: Yale University Press.

Pando Villaroya, José Luis de. 1987. *Diccionario de la lengua cuna.* Madrid: Pando ediciones.

Paredes de León, Hernán. 2001. *La enseñanza de la numeración kuna en primero y segundo grado de la escuela primaria en las poblaciones kuna.* Panamá: Universidad de Panamá.

———. n.d. [2004]. *Tulakuen, tule cuenta: numeración en lengua kuna.* Paredes de León 2001, edited and revised for primary school teaching by Eyra Harbar and Alibel Pizarro. Panamá.

Parker, Ann, and Avon Neal. 1977. *Molas: Folk Art of the Kuna Indians.* Barre, Mass.: Barre Publishing.

Patera, Charlotte. 1984. *Mola Making.* Piscataway, N.J.: New Century.

———. 1995. *Mola Techniques for Today's Quilters.* Paducah, Ky.: Collector Books.

Pearson, Henry. 1904. *What I Saw in the Tropics.* New York: India Rubber Publishing.

Pels, Peter. 1999. *A Politics of Presence: Contacts between Missionaries and Waluguru in Late Colonial Tanganyika.* Amsterdam: Harwood.

Peña, Concha. 1959. "El problema de los menores indigenas." In *Memoria del Primer Congreso Indigenista Panameño, 18 a 22 de abril de 1956,* pp. 70–76. Panamá: Ministerio de Educación.

Peñaherrera de Costales, Piedad, and Alfredo Costales. 1968. *Cunas y chocós: proyecto de ecología humana (Ruta 25, Colombia).* Quito: Instituto Ecuatoriano de Antropología.

Perefán Simmonds, Carlos César. 1995. *Sistemas jurídicos paez, kogi, wayuu y tule*. Bogotá: Instituto Colombiano de Cultura, Instituto Colombiano de Antropología.

Pereira de Padilla, Joaquina, and Ricardo Segura, eds. 1983. *Aproximación a la obra de Reina Torres de Araúz*. Panamá: INAC.

Pereiro Pérez, Xerardo, and Cebaldo De León Smith. 2007. *Los impactos del turismo en Kuna Yala (Panamá): Turismo y cultura entre los kuna de Panamá*. Madrid: Editorial Universitaria Ramón Areces.

Pérez Kantule, Rubén. n.d. "Libro Diario de Mi Viaje a Suecia, 2 de Mayo a 15 de Diciembre, 1931." Archives of Koskun Kalu, Congreso General de la Cultura Kuna, Panamá.

———. 1942. "Las molas de los indios cunas." *América Indígena* 2:84–85.

Perrin, Michel. 1999. *Magnificent Molas: The Art of Kuna Indians*. Paris: Flammarion.

Picón, César, Jesús Alemancia, and Ileana Gólcher, eds. 1998. *Pueblos indígenas de Panamá: Hacedores de cultura y de historia*. Panamá: UNESCO.

Pike, Frederick. 1992. *The United States and Latin America: Myths and Stereotypes of Civilization and Nature*. Austin: University of Texas Press.

Pinart, Alphonse. 1887. "Les Indiens de l'Etat de Panamá." *Revue d'Ethnographie* 6:1–24, 117–132.

———. 1890. *Vocabulario castellano-cuna, Panamá, 1882–1884*. Paris: E. Leroux.

Pitcock, Ronald. 2000. "'Let the Youths Beware!': The Sponsorship of Early 19th-Century Native American Literacy." *Written Communication* 17 (3): 390–426.

Pitkin, Hanna. 1972. *Wittgenstein and Justice: On the Significance of Ludwig Wittgenstein for Social and Political Thought*. Berkeley: University of California Press.

Pittier, Henry. 1912. "Little-Known Parts of Panama." *National Geographic Magazine* 23 (7): 627–662.

Pizzurno Gelós, Patricia, and Celestino Araúz. 1996. *Estudios sobre el Panamá republicano*. Panamá: Manfer.

Porras, Hernán. 1953. "Papel histórico de los grupos humanos en Panamá." In *Panamá, 50 años de República,* ed. Junta Nacional del Cincuentenario, pp. 63–109. Panamá: n.p.

Pratt, Mary Louise. 1992. *Imperial Eyes: Travel Writing and Transculturation*. London: Routledge.

Prebble, John. 1968. *The Darien Disaster*. London: Secker and Warburg.

Presilla, Maricel. 1996. *Mola: Cuna Life Stories and Art*. New York: Henry Holt.

Prestán, Arnulfo. 1975. *El uso de la chicha y la sociedad kuna*. Ediciones Especiales 72. México: Instituto Indigenista Interamericano.

Price, Kayla. 2005. "Kuna or Guna? The Linguistic, Social, and Political Implications of Developing a Standard Orthography." Master's thesis, University of Texas, Austin.

———. 2006. "Kuna or Guna?: The Linguistic, Social, and Political Process of Developing a Standard Orthography." *Texas Linguistic Forum* 49:170–180.

Puig, Manuel María. 1948. *Los indios cunas de San Blas: su origen, tradición, costumbres, organización social, cultura, y religión*. Panamá: n.p.

Puls, Herta. 1978. *The Art of Cutwork and Appliqué, Historic, Modern, and Kuna Indian*. Newton, Mass.: Charles T. Branford Co.

———. 1988. *Textiles of the Kuna Indians of Panama*. Aylesbury, UK: Shire.

Pulsipher, Jenny Hale. 2005. *Subjects unto the Same King: Indians, English, and the Contest for Authority in Colonial New England*. Philadelphia: University of Pennsylvania Press.

Pupo-Walker, Enrique. 1996. "The Brief Narrative in Spanish America: 1835–1915." In *The Cambridge History of Latin American Literature*, Vol. 1, *Discovery to Modernism*, ed. Roberto González Echevarría and Enrique Pupo-Walker, pp. 490–535. Cambridge: Cambridge University Press.

Quesada, Ernesto. 1927. *El panamericanismo bolivariano*. Buenos Aires: Imprenta Mercatali. Offprint from *Nosotros* (Argentina) 20, no. 211 (1926).

Rama, Angel. 1996. *The Lettered City*. Translated and edited by John Charles Chasteen. Durham, N.C.: Duke University Press.

Ramos, Alcida. 1998. *Indigenism: Ethnic Politics in Brazil*. Madison: University of Wisconsin Press.

Rappaport, Joanne. 1990. *The Politics of Memory: Native Historical Interpretation in the Colombian Andes*. Cambridge: Cambridge University Press.

———. 1994. *Cumbe Reborn: An Andean Ethnography of History*. Chicago: University of Chicago Press.

———. 2005a. "Alternative Knowledge Producers in Indigenous Latin America." *LASA Forum* 36 (1): 11–13.

———. 2005b. *Intercultural Utopias: Public Intellectuals, Cultural Experimentation, and Ethnic Pluralism in Colombia*. Durham, N.C.: Duke University Press.

Rapport, Nigel, and Joanna Overing. 2000. *Social and Cultural Anthropology: The Key Concepts*. London: Routledge.

Reclus, Armand. 1881. *Panama et Darien: Voyages d'Exploration*. Paris: Librarie Hachette.

———. 1972. *Exploraciones a los Istmos de Panamá y Darién en 1876, 1877, y 1878*. San José, Costa Rica: Editorial Universitaria Centroamericana.

Redfield, Robert. 1930. *Tepoztlán: A Mexican Village*. Chicago: University of Chicago Press.

———. 1934. "Culture Change in Yucatan." *American Anthropologist* 36:57–69.

———. 1941. *The Folk Cultures of Yucatan*. Chicago: University of Chicago Press.

Redfield, Robert, Ralph Linton, and Melville Herskovits. 1936. "Memorandum for the Study of Acculturation." *American Anthropologist* 38:149–152.

República de Panamá, Dirección de Estadística y Censo. 1998. *Compendio estadístico, Comarca de San Blas (Kuna Yala), años 1992–1996*.

———. 2001. *Censos nacionales de población y vivienda, 14 de mayo de 2000*. Vol. 2, *Población*.

República de Panamá, Dirección General del Censo. 1922. *Boletín No. 2. Censo demográfico de la Provincia de Colón 1920*. Panamá: Imprenta Nacional.

Requejo Salcedo, Juan. 1908. "Relación histórica y geográfica de la Provincia de Panamá." *Colección de Libros y Documentos Referentes a la Historia de América* 8:85–136. Madrid.

Restall, Matthew. 1997. *The Maya World*. Stanford, Calif.: Stanford University Press.

Restall, Matthew, Lisa Sousa, and Kevin Terraciano, eds. 2005. *Mesoamerican Voices: Native Language Writings from Colonial Mexico, Yucatan, and Guatemala*. Cambridge: Cambridge University Press.

Restrepo, Vicente. 1888. Prologue, Introduction, Notes, and Appendices. In *Viajes de Lionel Wafer al Istmo del Darién (Cuatro meses entre los indios)*, trans. and ed. Vicente Restrepo, pp. v–xi, 55–129. Bogotá: Silvestre y Compañia.

Restrepo Tirado, Ernesto. 1971. "Un viaje al Darién." *Revista Lotería* 68:57–95.

Reverte, José Manuel. 1961a. *Río Bayano: un ensayo geográfico e histórico sobre la región de mañana*. Panamá: Ministerio de Educación.

———. 1961b. "Vida sexual de los indios cunas de Panamá." *Revista Lotería* 67:36–42.

———. 1962a. "La medicina entre los indios cuna de Panamá." *Anales de Arqueología y Etnología* 17/18:137–150.

———. 1962b. "Vida sexual y creencias religiosas entre los indios cuna de Panamá." *Boletín, Universidad de Antioquia* 2:57–103.

———. 1963. "Curación y magia entre los indios cunas de Panamá." *Cuadernos Hispanoamericanos* 167:276–294.

———. 1966. *El pacto médico-hechicero*. Panamá: Imprenta Nacional.

———. 1967. "El matrimonio entre los indios cuna de Panamá." Panamá: n.p.

———. 1968. *Literatura oral de los indios cunas*. Panamá: Ministro de Educación.

———. 1977. *Operación Panamá: por la ruta de las descubridores*. Madrid: EDAF.

———. 2001. *Bioetnogeografía de los indios cuna (toponimia cuna)*. Madrid: Museo "Profesor Reverte Coma" de Antropología Médica-Forense, Paleopatología y Criminalística.

———. 2002. *Tormenta en el darién: vida de los indios chocoes en Panamá*. Madrid: Museo "Profesor Reverte Coma" de Antropología Médica-Forense, Paleopatología y Criminalística.

Richards, Julia, and Michael Richards. 1996. "Maya Education: A Historical and Contemporary Analysis of Mayan Language Education Policy." In *Maya Cultural Activism in Guatemala*, ed. Edward Fischer and R. McKenna Brown, pp. 208–221. Austin: University of Texas Press.

Richmond Brown, Lady Lilian Mabel. 1925. *Unknown Tribes, Uncharted Seas*. New York: Appleton.

Robinson, William. n.d. [1930s?]. "Along the Mulatas Archipelago. A True Account of the Present Day Life of the Little Known San Blas Indians." Manuscript, MWC.

Romoli, Kathleen. 1953. *Balboa of Darién*. Garden City, N.Y.: Doubleday.

———. 1987. *Los de la lengua Cueva: las tribus del istmo oriental al tiempo de la conquista española*. Bogotá: ICAN.

Rosaldo, Renato. 1989. *Culture and Truth: The Remaking of Social Analysis*. Boston: Beacon Press.
Rubio, Angel. 1940. "Indios y culturas indigenas panameñas." Panamá: Imprenta Panamá America.
Rudolf, Gloria. 1999. *Panama's Poor: Victims, Agents, and Historymakers*. Gainesville: University Press of Florida.
———. n.d. [2001]. "Vidas indígenas y desarrollo humano: una mirada desde las comarcas y la ciudad." Report to INDH. Panamá, December 2001.
Rus, Jan. 2004. "Rereading Tzotzil Ethnography: Recent Scholarship from Chiapas, Mexico." In *Pluralizing Ethnography: Comparison and Representation in Maya Cultures, Histories, and Identities*, ed. John Wantanabe and Edward Fischer. Santa Fe: School of American Research.
Russo Berguido, Alejandro. 1973. "Ubarragá Maniá Tigrí (Urracá)." *Revista Lotería* 19.
Sáenz, Moisés. 1928. *Reseña de la educación pública en México en 1927*. México, D.F.: Talleres graficos de la nacion.
———. 1936. *Carapan: bosquejo de una experiencia*. Lima: Libreria Imprenta Gil.
———. 1939. *México integro*. Lima: Imprenta Torres Aguirre.
Sahlins, Marshall. 2002. *Waiting for Foucault, Still*. Chicago: Prickly Paradigm Press.
Said, Edward. 1978. *Orientalism*. London: Routledge.
Salemink, Oscar. 2003. *The Ethnography of Vietnam's Central Highlanders: A Historical Contextualization, 1850–1990*. London: Routledge.
Salmon, Russell. 1992. Introduction. In *Los ovnis de oro/Golden UFOs: Poemas indios/The Indian Poems*, Ernesto Cardenal, pp. ix–xxxv. Bloomington: Indiana University Press.
Salvador, Mari Lyn. 1976. "Molas of the Cuna Indians: A Case Study of Artistic Criticism and Ethno-Aesthetics." Ph.D. diss., University of California, Berkeley.
———. 1978. *Yer Dailege! Kuna Woman's Art*. Albuquerque: Maxwell Museum of Anthropology.
———, ed. 1997. *The Art of Being Kuna: Layers of Meaning among the Kuna of Panama*. Los Angeles: UCLA Fowler Museum of Cultural History.
Sanjek, Roger. 1993. "Anthropology's Hidden Colonialism: Assistants and Their Ethnographers." *Anthropology Today* 9 (2): 13–17.
Sarsanedas, Jorge. 1978. *Tierra para el guaymí: La expoliación de las tierras guaymies en Chiriquí*. Serie El Indio Panameño. Panamá: Centro de Capacitación Social.
Sauer, Carl O. 1966. *The Early Spanish Main*. Berkeley: University of California Press.
Sax, William. 1998. "The Hall of Mirrors: Orientalism, Anthropology, and the Other." *American Anthropologist* 100 (2): 292–301.
Sayre, Gordon. 2005. *The Indian Chief as Tragic Hero: Native Resistance and the Literatures of America, from Moctezuma to Tecumseh*. Chapel Hill: University of North Carolina Press.

Schineller, Peter. 1990. *A Handbook on Inculturation*. New York: Paulist Press.
Schultz, Lucille. 1999. "Letter-Writing Instruction in 19th Century Schools in the United States." In *Letter Writing as a Social Practice*, ed. David Barton and Nigel Hall, pp. 109–130. Amsterdam: John Benjamins.
Scott, James. 1985. *Weapons of the Weak: Everyday Forms of Peasant Resistance*. New Haven, Conn.: Yale University Press.
———. 1990. *Domination and the Arts of Resistance: Hidden Transcripts*. New Haven, Conn.: Yale University Press.
———. 1998. *Seeing Like a State*. New Haven, Conn.: Yale University Press.
Selfridge, Oliver. 1874. *Reports of Explorations and Surveys to Ascertain the Practicability of a Ship Canal between the Atlantic and Pacific Oceans*. Washington, D.C.: U.S. Government Printing Office.
Severi, Carlo. 1981. "Image d'Étranger." *Res* 1:88–94.
———. 1982a. "Le Chemin Des Métamorphoses: Un Modèle de Connaissance de la Folie dans un Chant Chamanique Cuna." *Res* 3:33–67.
———. 1982b. *Nia-Igar-Kalu (Le Voyage de Nele Ukkurwar Aux Villages de la Folie): Le Traitement de la Folie Chez les Indiens Cuna de San Blas (Panama)*. Paris: L'École des Hautes Études en Sciences Sociales.
———. 1985. "Penser par Séquences, Penser par Territoires: Cosmologie et Art de la Memoire dans la Pictographie Des Indiens Cuna." *Communications* 41:169–190.
———. 1987. "Il Numero Negli Studi Etnoantropologici. Per una Ricerca Sul Sistema di Numerazione Presso i Cuna di Panama." In *Numerare, Contare, Calcolare: Per un Approccio Interdisciplinare Allo Studio Della Quantificazione*, ed. Claudio Pizzi, Serena Veggetti, Massimo Squillacciotti, and Aiban Wagwa, pp. 35–93. Roma: Cadmo Editore.
———. 1988. "L'Étranger, l'Envers de Soi et l'Echec Du Symbolisme: Deux Représentations Du Blanc dans la Tradition Chamanique Cuna." *L'Homme* 28 (2–3): 174–183.
———. 1993a. "La Mémoire Rituelle. Expérience, Tradition, Historicité." In *Mémoire de la Tradition*, ed. A. Monod and A. Molinié, pp. 327–364. Paris: Societé d'Ethnologie.
———. 1993b. *La memoria rituale: Follia e immagine del Bianco in una tradizione sciamanica amerindiani*. Florence, Italy: La Nuova Italia Editrice.
———. 1993c. "Talking about Souls: On the Pragmatic Construction of Meaning in Cuna Chants." In *Cognitive Aspects of Religious Symbolism*, ed. Pascal Boyer, pp. 165–181. Cambridge: Cambridge University Press.
———. 1996. *La memoria ritual: Locura e imagen del blanco en una tradición chamánica amerindia*. Quito: Ediciones Abya-Yala.
———. 1997. "Kuna Picture Writing: A Study in Iconography and Memory." In *The Art of Being Kuna: Layers of Meaning among the Kuna of Panama*, ed. Mari Lyn Salvador, pp. 245–270. Los Angeles: UCLA Fowler Museum of Cultural History.
Severi, Carlo, and Enrique Gómez. 1983. "Los pueblos del camino de la locura: canto chamanístico de la tradición cuna." *Amerindia* 8:129–179.
Severino de Santa Teresa, Padre. 1956. *Historia documentada de la Iglesia en*

Urabá y el Darién, IV, Segunda Parte, América española, 1550–1810. Bogotá: Editorial Kelly.

———. 1959. *Los indios catios—los indios cuna.* Medellín: Imprenta Departamental de Antioquía.

Shaffer, Frederick. 1982. *Mola Design Coloring Book: 45 Authentic Designs from Panama.* New York: Dover.

Shatto, Gloria. 1972. "The San Blas Cuna Indian Sociedad as a Vehicle of Economic Development." *Journal of Developing Areas* 6 (3): 383–398.

Sherzer, Dina, and Joel Sherzer. 1976. "Mormaknamaloe: The Cuna Mola." In *Ritual and Symbol in Native Central America,* ed. Philip Young and James Howe, pp. 21–42. Eugene: University of Oregon Anthropological Papers 9.

Sherzer, Joel. 1983. *Kuna Ways of Speaking.* Austin: University of Texas Press.

———. 1990. *Verbal Arts in San Blas: Kuna Culture through Its Discourse.* Cambridge: Cambridge University Press.

———. 1992. *Formas del habla kuna: una perspectiva etnográfica.* Quito: Abya Yala.

———. 1994. "The Kuna and Columbus: Encounters and Confrontations of Discourse." *American Anthropologist* 96 (4): 902–924.

———. 2003. *Stories, Myths, Chants, and Songs of the Kuna Indians.* Austin: University of Texas Press.

Shorter, Aylward. 1988. *Toward a Theory of Inculturation.* Maryknoll, N.Y.: Orbis Books.

Sieder, Rachel. 2002. Introduction. In *Multiculturalism in Latin America: Indigenous Rights, Diversity, and Democracy,* ed. Rachel Sieder, pp. 1–23. New York: Palgrave MacMillan.

Silver, Peter. 2008. *Our Savage Neighbors: How Indian War Transformed Early America.* New York: W. W. Norton.

Sisnett, Manuel Octavio. 1956. *Belisario Porras, o la vocación de la nacionalidad.* Panamá: Imprenta Universitária.

Smith, Lino. 1975. "La enseñanza de la lengua cuna en la universidad." *Hombre y Cultura* 3:179–181.

Smith, Sandra [see also Sandra McCosker]. 1984. "Panpipes for Power, Panpipes for Play: The Social Management of Cultural Expression in Kuna Society." Ph.D. diss., University of California, Berkeley.

———. 1997. "The Musical Arts of the Kuna." In *The Art of Being Kuna: Layers of Meaning among the Kuna of Panama,* ed. Mari Lyn Salvador, pp. 293–310. Los Angeles: UCLA Fowler Museum of Cultural History.

Smith, Sherry L. 2000. *Reimagining Indians.* Oxford: Oxford University Press.

Smith, Victoriano [aka Aiban Wagwa]. 1981. "Los kuna entre dos sistemas educativas." Ph.D. diss., Universidad Pontificia Salesiana, Rome.

———. 1982. "Principios de la teofanía kuna." Extract from Ph.D. diss., Universidad Pontificia Salesiana, Rome.

Smith Kantule, Jesús. 1996. "Na uisgumala: conozcamos lo nuestro." *Onmaked* 2:10–11.

Smith Kantule, Jesús, and Flaviano Iglesias. 2001. *La Revolución Kuna de 1925.* Colección Pequeño Formato. Panamá: Editorial Portobelo.

Snow, Steven, and Cheryl Wheeler. 2000. "Pathways to the Periphery: Tourism to Indigenous Communities in Panama." *Social Science Quarterly* 81 (3): 732–749.

Sommer, Doris. 1991. *Foundational Fictions: The National Romances of Latin America*. Berkeley: University of California Press.

Sosa, Julio. 1936. *La india dormida*. Panamá: Manfer.

Spencer, Jonathan. 2001. "Ethnography after Post-Modernism." In *Handbook of Ethnography*, ed. Paul Atkinson, Amanda Coffey, Sara Delamont, John Lofland, and Lyn Lofland, pp. 443–452. London: Sage Publications.

Spivak, Gayatri Chakravorty. 1988. "Can the Subaltern Speak?" In *Marxism and the Interpretation of Culture*, ed. Cary Nelson and Lawrence Grossberg, pp. 271–313. London: Macmillan.

Spurr, David. 1993. *The Rhetoric of Empire: Colonial Discourse in Journalism, Travel Writing, and Imperial Administration*. Durham, N.C.: Duke University Press.

Squillacciotti, Massimo. 1983. "Note Etnografiche Sui Cuna." *Etnologia Antropologia Culturale* 11:11–20.

———. 1984. "I Cuna: Immagini di una Ricerca." *La Ricerca Folklorica* 10:121–129.

———. 1987. "Il Numero Negli Studi Etno-Antropologici." In *Numerare, Contare, Calcolare: Allo Studio Della Quantificazione*, ed. Claudio Pizzi, Serena Veggetti, Massimo Squillacciotti, and Aiban Wagwa, pp. 35–71. Roma: Cadmo Editore.

———. 1988. "La Dialettica del Contatto: Ecologia, Turismo, Ideologia." *Latinoamerica* 29:105–110.

———. 1992. *America: Cinque Secoli Dalla Conquista*. Siena, Italy: Saggi dal seminario Interdisciplinare della Facoltà di Lettere e Filosofia, Università di Siena.

———. 1998. *I Cuna di Panamá. Identità di Popolo Tra Storia Ed Antropologia*. Torino: L'Harmattan Italia.

Stavenhagen, Rodolfo. 1994. "Indigenous Rights: Some Conceptual Problems." In *Indigenous Peoples' Experience with Self-Government*, ed. Willem Assies and André Hoekma, pp. 9–29. Amsterdam, Copenhagen: IWGIA.

———. 2002. "Indigenous Peoples and the State in Latin America: An Ongoing Debate." In *Multiculturalism in Latin America: Indigenous Rights, Diversity, and Democracy*, ed. Rachel Sieder, pp. 24–44. New York: Palgrave MacMillan.

Stefanoni, Silvia. 1984. "Severità Dei Corpi, Ridondanza Delle Parole. Cinesica e Prossemica Tra i Cuna di Panama." Honors thesis, Università di Siena.

———. 1987. "Gli 'Habitus' Posturali Dei Cuna di Panamá." *Annali Della Facoltà di Lettere e Filosofia Dell'Università di Siena* 8:237–282.

———. 1988. "La Dialettica del Contatto: Il Caso Dei Cuna." *Latinoamerica* 29:110–112.

Steward, Julian. 1948. "The Circum-Caribbean Tribes: An Introduction." In *Handbook of South American Indians*, Vol. 4, *The Circum-Caribbean Tribes*, ed. Julian Steward, pp. 1–42. Washington, D.C.: Bureau of American Ethnology Bulletin 143.

———, ed. 1949. *Handbook of South American Indians*. Vol. 5, *The Comparative Ethnology of South American Indians*. Washington, D.C.: Bureau of American Ethnology Bulletin 143.

Steward, Julian, and Louis Faron. 1959. *Native Peoples of South America*. New York: McGraw-Hill.

Stier, Frances. 1979. "The Effect of Demographic Change on Agriculture in San Blas." Ph.D. diss., University of Arizona.

Stirling, Matthew. n.d. "'Description of a Trip to the Tule Villages of the San Blas Coast,' by M. W. Stirling. Copy of Diary, October 1931." 4451-b, CUNA & Tule, Manuscripts, National Archives of Anthropology, Smithsonian Institution, Washington, D.C.

Stoddard, Lothrop. 1920. *The Rising Tide of Color against White World-Supremacy*. New York: Scribner.

Stoler, Ann Laura. 1989. "Making Empire Respectable: The Politics of Race and Sexual Morality in 20th Century Colonial Cultures." *American Ethnologist* 16:634–660.

———. 1992. "Sexual Affronts and Racial Frontiers: European Identities and the Cultural Politics of Exclusion in Colonial Southeast Asia." *Comparative Studies in Society and History* 34:514–551.

———. 2002a. *Carnal Knowledge and Imperial Power: Race and the Intimate in Colonial Rule*. Berkeley: University of California Press.

———. 2002b. "Colonial Archives and the Arts of Governance." *Archival Science* 2:87–109.

Stoler, Ann Laura, and Frederick Cooper. 1997. "Between Metropole and Colony: Rethinking a Research Agenda." In *Tensions of Empire: Colonial Cultures in a Bourgeois World*, ed. Frederick Cooper and Ann Laura Stoler, pp. 1–56. Berkeley: University of California Press.

Stout, David. 1947. *San Blas Cuna Acculturation: An Introduction*. New York: Viking Fund Publications in Anthropology.

———. 1948. "The Cuna." In *Handbook of South American Indians*, Vol. 4, *The Circum-Caribbean Tribes*, ed. Julian Steward, pp. 257–268. Washington, D.C.: Bureau of American Ethnology Bulletin 143.

Street, Brian. 1984. *Literacy in Theory and Practice*. Cambridge: Cambridge University Press.

Sullivan, Paul. 1989. *Unfinished Conversations: Mayas and Foreigners between Two Wars*. Berkeley: University of California Press.

Swain, Margaret. 1977. "Cuna Women and Ethnic Tourism: A Way to Persist and an Avenue of Change." In *Hosts and Guests: The Anthropology of Tourism*, ed. Valene Smith, pp. 71–81. Philadelphia: University of Pennsylvania Press.

———. 1978. "Ailigandi Women: Continuity and Change in Cuna Female Identity." Ph.D. diss., University of Washington.

———. 1989. "Gender Roles in Indigenous Tourism: Kuna Mola, Kuna Yala, and Cultural Survival." In *Hosts and Guests: The Anthropology of Tourism*, 2nd ed., ed. Valene Smith, pp. 83–104. Philadelphia: University of Pennsylvania Press.

Swanson, Philip. 2004. *Latin American Fiction: A Short Introduction.* Malden, Mass.: Blackwell Publishers.

Sweig, Renée. 1987. "Molas as Elaborating Symbol: An Analysis of Images of Plants and Birds in the Cuna Aesthetic System." Ph.D. diss., University of California, Los Angeles.

Szasz, Margaret Connell, ed. 1994. *Between Indian and White Worlds: The Cultural Broker.* Norman: University of Oklahoma Press.

Szok, Peter A. 2001. *La Última Gaviota: Liberalism and Nostalgia in Early Twentieth-Century Panama.* Westport, Conn.: Greenwood Press.

———. 2004. "'Rey sin corona,' Belisario Porras y la formación de estado nacional: 1903–1931." In *Historia general de Panamá,* ed. Alfredo Castillero Calvo, vol. 3, book 1, *El siglo XX,* pp. 49–70. Panamá: Comité Nacional del Centenario de la República.

Taussig, Michael. 1993. *Mimesis and Alterity: A Particular History of the Senses.* New York: Routledge.

Teng, Emma. 2004. *Taiwan's Imagined Geography: Chinese Colonial Travel Writing and Pictures, 1683–1895.* Cambridge, Mass.: Harvard University Press.

Thomas, Nicholas. 1994. *Colonialism's Culture: Anthropology, Travel, and Government.* Princeton, N.J.: Princeton University Press.

———. 1997. "Anthropological Epistemologies." *International Social Science Journal* 49:333–343.

Tice, Karin. 1989. "Gender, Capitalism, and Egalitarian Forms of Social Organization in San Blas, Panama." Ph.D. diss., Columbia University.

———. 1995. *Kuna Crafts, Gender, and the Global Economy.* Austin: University of Texas Press.

Tinnin, J. V. 1940. *Roughing It in the San Blas Islands.* Panamá: Panama America Publishing.

Torres de Araúz (de Ianello), Reina. 1957. *La mujer cuna.* México: Instituto Indigenista Interamericano.

———. 1958. "La organización política cuna." *Revista Lotería* 30:81–96.

———. 1961. "El valor etnográfico de las cartas del misionero Jesuita Rev. Padre L. Gassó." *Revista Lotería* 6 (65): 69–74.

———. 1962a. "Fred McKim y los indios cuna." *Revista Lotería* 7 (77): 24–36.

———. 1962b. "El indigenismo: empresa científica impostergable en Panamá." *Revista Lotería* 7 (74): 51–59.

———. 1966. *La cultura chocó.* Panamá: Centro de Investigaciones Antropológicas, Universidad de Panamá.

———. 1967. *Human Ecology Studies, Panama, Phase 1: Final Report.* Columbus, Ohio: Battelle Memorial Institute.

———. 1967–1968. "Estudio etnológico e histórico de la cultura chocó." *Revista Lotería* 12 (145): 40–55; 13 (147): 49–84; 13 (151): 60–95; 13 (153): 81–87.

———. 1968. *Demographic Characteristics of Human Groups Inhabiting the Eastern Region of the Republic of Panama.* Columbus, Ohio: Battelle Memorial Institute.

———. 1970. *Human Ecology of Route 17 (Sasardi-Morti) Region, Darien, Panama.* Columbus, Ohio: Battelle Memorial Institute.

———. 1973. "La leyenda de los indios blancos del Darién y su influencia en la historia política nacional." *Hombre y Cultura* 4:5–67.

———. 1974. *Etnohistoria cuna*. Pamphlet. Panamá: Instituto Nacional de Cultura.

———. 1975. *Darién: etnoecología de una region histórica*. Panamá: Instituto Nacional de Cultura.

———. 1979. *Machiuita, muchachito*. Panamá: Ediciones Instituto Nacional de Cultura.

———. 1980. *Panamá indígena*. Panamá: Instituto Nacional de Cultura.

Turpana, Arysteides. 1968. *Archipiélago*. n.p.: n.p.

———. 1982. "La correspondencia del diablo." *Diálogo Social* 15 (146): 51–56.

———. 1983. *Mi hogar queda entre la infancia y el sueño*. Panamá: Ediciones Formato Dieciseis.

———. 1985. "Poder ejecutivo de la unión, decreta: y nos recortaron la patria." *Niskua Ginid*. Panamá.

———. 1987. *Narraciones populares del País Dule*. México: Editorial Factor.

———. 1991. "Los indios y la política indigenista." *La Prensa*, May 7.

———. 1995. "To Be or Not to Be." In *Plants and Animals in the Life of the Kuna*, ed. Jorge Ventocilla, Heraclio Herrera, and Valerio Núñez, pp. 111–114. Austin: University of Texas Press.

———. 1996. *Literatura dule: un esbozo*. Panamá: Instituto Cooperativo Interamericano.

Tylor, Edward. 1958. *Religion in Primitive Culture*. New York: Harper & Row.

United States Office of Indian Affairs. 1941. *Final Act of the First Inter-American Conference on Indian Life*. Washington, D.C.: U.S. Government Printing Office.

Uvin, Peter. 2002. "On Counting, Categorizing, and Violence in Burundi and Rwanda." In *Census and Identity: The Politics of Race, Ethnicity, and Language in National Censuses*, ed. David Kertzer and Dominique Arel, pp. 148–175. Cambridge: Cambridge University Press.

Valdés, Ramón. 1905. *Geografía de Panamá*. 2nd ed. Chicago: Appleton [1914 edition, Panamá: Andreve].

VandeCastle, Robert. 1975. *Dream and ESP Studies among Cuna Indians of Panama*. Videocassette. Psychiatric Grand Rounds. Charlottesville: University of Virginia.

Varese, Stefano. 2006. *Witness to Sovereignty: Essays on the Indian Movement in Latin America*. Copenhagen: IWGIA.

Vargas, Patricia. 1993. *Los emberá y los cuna: Impacto y reacción ante la ocupación española, siglos XVI y XVII*. Bogotá: CEREC.

Velarde, Aiban. 1996. "Lineas en honor a Rubén Pérez Kantule." *Onmaked* 2 (6): 19–20.

Velásquez Runk, Julie. 2005. "And the Creator Began to Carve Us of Cocobolo: Culture, History, Forest Ecology, and Conservation among Wounaan in Eastern Panama." Ph.D. diss., Yale University.

Ventocilla, Jorge. 1992. *Caceria y subsistencia en Cangandi*. Quito: Abya Yala.

———. 1997. "Ologuagdi, irreductible indio de acero inoxidable." *Revista Nacional de Cultura*, nueva época, 27:45–49.

Ventocilla, Jorge, Heraclio Herrera, and Valerio Núñez, eds. 1995. *Plants and Animals in the Life of the Kuna*. Translated by Elizabeth King. Austin: University of Texas Press.

———. 1997. *El espíritu de la tierra: Plantas y animales en la vida del pueblo kuna*. Barcelona: Icaria Editorial [second edition, 1999, Quito: Ediciones Abya-Yala].

Ventocilla, Jorge, Valerio Núñez, Francisco Herrera, Heraclio Herrera, and Mac Chapin. 1995. "Los indígenas kunas y la conservación ambiental." *Mesoamerica* 29:95–124.

Verner, Samuel. 1920. "The San Blas Indians of Panama." *Geographical Review* 10 (1): 23–30.

Verrill, A. Hyatt. 1921. *Panama, Past and Present*. New York: Dodd, Mead.

———. 1922. *The Boy Adventurers in the Forbidden Land*. New York: Putnam.

———. 1924. "Hunting the White Indians." *McClure's Magazine*, July, pp. 46–59.

Wafer, Lionel. 1970. *A New Voyage and Description of the Isthmus of America*, ed. George Parker Winship. New York: Burt Franklin. [1934 edition, edited by L. E. Elliott Joyce. Oxford: Hakluyt Society.]

Wali, Alaka. 1984. "Kilowatts and Crisis among the Kuna, Choco, and Colonos: The National and Regional Consequences of the Bayano Hydroelectric Complex in Eastern Panama." Ph.D. diss., Columbia University.

———. 1989. *Kilowatts and Crisis: Hydroelectric Power and Social Dislocation in Eastern Panama*. Boulder, Colo.: Westview Press.

———. 1995. "La política del desarrollo y las relaciones entre región y Estado: el caso del oriente de Panamá, 1972–1990." *Mesoamérica* 29:125–158.

Wallace, Anthony. 1993. *The Long, Bitter Trail: Andrew Jackson and the Indians*. New York: Hill and Wang.

Warren, Kay. 1998. *Indigenous Movements and Their Critics*. Princeton, N.J.: Princeton University Press.

Warren, Kay, and Jean Jackson, eds. 2002. *Indigenous Movements, Self-Representation, and the State in Latin America*. Austin: University of Texas Press.

Wassén, S. Henry. 1932a. "La misión científica de un indio de la 'República' de Tule en Europa." *La Prensa* (Argentina), September 10.

———. 1932b. "Le Musée Ethnographique de Göteborg, et l'Oeuvre d'Erland Nordenskiöld. *Revista del Instituto de Etnología de Tucumán* 2:233–262.

———. 1932c. "La Visite de l'Indien Cuna Rubén Pérez Kantule au Musée de Gothembourg en 1931." *Société de Américanistes de Paris*, n.s., 24:235–243.

———. 1934. "Mitos y cuentos de los indios cunas." *Journal de la Societé Des Americanistes* 26:1–35.

———. 1937. *Some Cuna Indian Animal Stories, with Original Texts*. Etnologiska Studier 4:12–34.

———. 1938a. Editorial Chapter. In *An Historical and Ethnological Survey of the Cuna Indians*, Erland Nordenskiöld, with R.P. Kantule, pp. xi–xxvii. Göteborg: Etnografiska Museum.

———. 1938b. *Original Documents from the Cuna Indians of San Blas, Panama*, *as Recorded by the Indians Guillermo Hayans and Rubén Pérez Kantule*. Etnologiska Studier 6. Göteborg: Etnografiska Museum.

———. 1949. *Contributions to Kuna Ethnography: Results of an Expedition to Panama and Colombia in 1947*. Etnologiska Studier 16. Göteborg: Etnografiska Museum.

———. 1952. *New Cuna Myths, According to Guillermo Hayans*. Etnologiska Studier 20:86–106. Göteborg: Etnografiska Museum.

———. 1959. "A Comparative Reconstruction of the Post-Columbian Change in Certain Religious Concepts among the Cuna Indians of Panama." *33d International Congress of Americanists* 2:502–509.

———. 1963a. "Fran Mexiko Och Centralamerika 1962 Samt Sr. Hayan Resa Tell Río Caimán, Colombia." *Göteborgs Musei Årstryck* 1959–1962:67–96.

———. 1963b. "Río Bayano, 'región de mañana'" (book review). *Hombre y Cultura* 1 (2): 89–93.

———. 1982. "Rubén Pérez Kantule, indio cuna en Gotemburgo, Suecia, en 1931, muerto en 1978." Årstryck 1979/80, Göteborgs Etnografiska Museum, 39–43.

———. 1987–1988. "Studies and Museum Work for Erland Nordenskiöld during the Years 1929 to 1932: His Last Student Looks Back over More Than Half a Century." Årstryck, Etnografiska Museum, 35–44.

———. 1989/90. "Cambios en algunos conceptos religiosos de los indios cuna después de la conquista." Årstryck, Etnografiska Museum, 18–27.

Weber, David. 2005. *Bárbaros: Spaniards and Their Savages in the Age of Enlightenment*. New Haven, Conn.: Yale University Press.

Weir, Hugh. 1909. *The Conquest of the Isthmus*. New York: Putnam.

Wellin, Christopher, and Gary Alan Fine. 2001. "Ethnography as Work: Career Socialization, Settings and Problems." In *Handbook of Ethnography*, ed. Paul Atkinson, Amanda Coffey, Sara Delamont, John Lofland, and Lyn Lofland, pp. 323–338. London: Sage Publications.

Werner, Roland. 1984. "Traditionelle Priesterärzte und Moderne Medizin. Das Öffentliche Gesundheitswesen der Cuna-Indianer auf dem San Blas–Archipel von Panama." *Curare* 7:3–32.

White, Richard. 1991. *The Middle Ground: Indians, Empires, and Republics in the Great Lakes Region, 1650–1800*. Cambridge: Cambridge University Press.

Whiteley, Peter. 1998. *Rethinking Hopi Ethnography*. Washington, D.C.: Smithsonian Institution Press.

Wickstrom, Stefanie. 2001. "The Political Ecology of Development and Indigenous Resistance in Panama and the United States: A Comparative Study of the Ngöbe, Kuna, Zuni, and Skokomish Societies." Ph.D. diss., University of Oregon, Eugene.

———. 2003. "The Politics of Development in Indigenous Panama." *Latin American Perspectives* 30 (4): 43–68.

Williams, Jerry Ray. 1967. "The Human Ecology of Mulatupu San Blas: Caribbean Gateway to a Proposed Sea-Level Canal." Master's thesis, University of Florida.

Williams, Raymond. 1977. *Marxism and Literature*. Oxford: Oxford University Press.

Williamson, Joel. 1984. *The Crucible of Race: Black-White Relations in the American South since Emancipation*. Oxford: Oxford University Press.

Wogan, Peter. 1994. "Perceptions of European Literacy in Early Contact Situations." *Ethnohistory* 41:407–429.

Zarate, Manuel. 1962. *Tambor y socavón*. Panamá: n.p.

Zydler, Nancy Schwalbe, and Tom Zydler. 1996. *The Panama Guide: A Cruising Guide to the Isthmus of Panama*. Brookfield, Wisc.: Seaworthy Publications.

INDEX

Page numbers in italics indicate images.

Abisua, Chief, 23, 254n4
absogedi (converser), 27, 83, 260n5, 269n18
Abya Yala (the Americas), 220, 275nn15–16
Abya Yala (journal), 221
acculturation, as theory of change, 187–188
Achutupu. *See* Kainora
actas (minutes), 50; importance to archives, 216, 274n4
Agnew, Louise, 201
agriculture, Kuna, 227, 269n14, 269n20
Affairs of Honor (Freeman), 61
Afro-Panamanians, 121, 239, 268n4. *See also* Blacks
Aiban Wagwa, 221, 224, 225, 229, 238; on Father's Way, 223
Ailigandi, 40, 109; Colman, home of, 30, 83, 109, 125; flag controversy, 207; Protestant mission on, 175; rebellion and, 103; schools and, 30, 41
Akkwanusatupu. *See* Nusatupu/Corazón de Jesus

Alba, Manuel María, 168; and Blacks, attitude towards, 167; on chiefs, 270n36; "Etnología y población histórica de Panamá," 166; on Father's Way, 270n37; *Geografía descriptiva de la República de Panamá*, 166–167; *Introducción al estudio de las lenguas indígenas de Panamá*, 186; on Kuna religion, 186, 270n37; "Urraca, Biographical Sketch of a National Hero," 167
Alemancia, Jesús, 221
Alfaro, Horatio, 109–110, *111*
Alfaro, Ricardo, 61–62, 78, 86, 87, 109–110
Alteraciones del Darien (De Páramo y Cepeda), 167, 257n2
alterity, 8, 20, 81; of the Kuna, 11, 17, 66, 111–112
Alvarado, Eligio, 221, 225; *El perfil de los pueblos indígenas de Panamá*, 226
Amador Guerrero, Miguel, 23
América Indígena (journal), 214, 219
Among the San Blas Indians of Panama (De Smidt), 181–182

Anderson, Benedict: *Imagined Communities*, 14, 240. *See also* "the imaginary"
Anglophone writers: and Kuna racial and sexual exclusion, 95–96, 261n8; and popular discourse, 103; representation of Kuna, 88, 90–99
Anmar igar: normas kunas, 226
Anthropological Romance of Bali (Boon), 19–20
anthropologists, 7, 17, 44; and activism, 190, 208, 209; amateur, 182–183; and collaborators, recognition of, 141; European, 202, 272–273nn32–35; and gender studies, 272n26; *indigenista*, 185; Kuna, 214, 220–224, 275–276n22; and Kuna language, 272n31; and Kuna, relationship with, xi, 19, 205–207, 273n45; and molas, 201; North American, 196, 272nn28–31; Panamanian, 196; professionalization of, 173, 190; and "Pueblo" Indians, 20; and salvage anthropology, 249, 250–251; in San Blas, 164, 190; Swedish, 21, 117, 173, 214, 218; and traditional society, perceived loss of, 250. *See also* ethnography, general; ethnography, Kuna
A-oba (Eoba, Oba), 103, 104, 160, 184
Apples of Immortality from the Cuna Tree of Life (Keeler), 198
Arango, Ricardo, 178
Araucana, La (Ercilla), 167
Araucanians, 167
Araúz, Amado, 194, 214
Araúz, Mateo: *El problema indígena en Panamá*, 165
Archibold, Guillermo, 221
Archibold, Juan Peréz, 238; "Historic Memory, Social Structure, and Theology of the Kuna Nation," 238. *See also* PEMASKY
archives, 274nn3–4; Kuna archivists, 215–217

Arel, Dominique: on censuses and identity formation, 80
argar (chief's spokesperson) 27, 51
Arguedas, José Maria, 185
Ariza, Andrés de, 65
Art of Being Kuna, The (Salvador), 208, 225
artifacts, Kuna, 103, 124, 131, 200, 237, 265n3, 273n39; and Nordenskiöld, 264n19
Asociación Panameña de Antropología, 196
Aspinwall. *See* Colón
Assies, Willem: on indigenous intellectuals, 234
auto-ethnography, Kuna: 21, 124, 214, 221; changes in, 243–244; importance of ritual knowledge to, 235–238; male-centered, 227; molas and, 227–228, 276nn25–26; omissions in, 227–228, 276n27. *See also* ethnography, Kuna
Axtell, James: *The Invasion Within*, 3
Aztec empire, 167; hieroglyphs, 267n30

Bab igar. *See* Father's Way
Bailey, F. G.: *Stratagems and Spoils*, 6
Balboa, Vasco Nuñez de, 168
Balburger (Walburger), Jacobo, 65, 66, 93, 265n13, 269n17
Balikwa (José Paulino), x
Baptist Church, 199
Battelle Institute, 194
Bayano Valley, 23, 35, 36, 182, 183, 239, 258n16, 272n31; and Torres de Araúz, 194
Bazerman, Charles, 46
Beidelman, Thomas, 254n11
Beltrán, Aguirre, 188
Berengueras, José Mariá, 173, 175, 177–178, 261n9, 268–269n13, 269nn14–16; and alleged conspirators, 174–175; and Kuna myth-history, 173–174; on Republic

of Tule, 174–175; on rebellion, 174–175; on rituals, 174
Between Worlds: Interpreters, Guides, and Survivors (Karttunen), 6
Beverley, John, 10
Bible, the, 24, 149, 173, 178, 237, 238, 277n40
Birket-Smith, Kai, 134
Blacks, 89, 97; Alba's view of, 167; Kuna attitudes toward, 98–99; Marsh's attitudes toward, 105–106; Nordenskiöld's view of, 119, 121, 122, 128, 263n6. *See also* Afro-Panamanians
Blommaert, Jan; on semiotic mobility 51, 256n13
Boas, Franz, 119, 120
Bogotá, Colombia, x, 67, 194, 237
Bolinder, Gustav, 118
Bolívar, Simón, 168, 237
Boon, James: *Anthropological Romance of Bali*, 19–20
Bourdieu, Pierre, 256n12
Bourgois, Philippe, 247
Brenes, Mateo, 35, 36, 43
Brown, McKenna: on pan-Mayanists, 228
Bruner, Edward, 165, 245
Brysk, Alison: on indigenous intellectuals, 234
burba (*purba*, soul), 136, 147, 155, 156
Bureau of American Ethnology, 181
Buzard, James, 133

cacique (high chief, Spanish name for chiefs), 90, 90–93, 164, 168, 223, 247. *See also* chiefs, Kuna
Cacao Way. *See* Sia Igar
Caledonia (Magemmulu), 36
camoturo. *See gandule*
"Can the Subaltern Speak?" (Spivak), 19
Canaday, John: on molas, 200
Canal Zone, 25, 89–90, 98, 99, 124; and amateur anthropology, 272n22; tourism in, 260n3, 261n1; tribes of, 260n2. *See also* Panama Canal; Zonians
Cantón, Alfredo: errors in work, 274n52; *Nalu-Nega*, 209–211, 274nn51–54; on rebellion, 274n53
Cardenal, Ernesto, 211–213, 274nn55–57; *El estrecho dudoso*, 211; and *exteriorismo*, 212; Ezra Pound, influenced by, 212; *Homage to the American Indians*, 211–212; *Homenaje a los indios americanos*, 211; "Los indios cunas, 'una nación soberana,'" 211; *Mayapán*, 211; *Ovnis de oro: Poemas indios*, 211–212; *Quetzalcoatl*, 211–212
Caribe-Kuna, 19, 80. *See also* Kuna
Carnival, 171, 172, 268n9
Carta Orgánica (1945 Kuna constitution), 164
Carti Suitupu, 30, 100, 107, 109, 180, 181, 187, 189, 199, 201, 255n21
Castillero, Efrain, 183, 184
Castillero Calvo, Alfredo, 197
Castillo, Bernal, 46, 243
Catholic Church: activism of, 223; and Anna Coope, 52; and the civilizing project, 33, 176; and ethnography, 173, 177, 178; and French colonists, 146; and inculturation, 223–224, 237; and Kuna rebellion, 208; missionaries, 24, 26, 175–176, 186, 191, 202; and schools, 24, 40, 41, 211, 255n16; and Spanish language, 30; and study abroad, promotion of, 41. *See also* missionaries; *and specific orders*
census, 157, 255nn21–22, 259n32–34, 267n31, 267n34; and identity formation, 79–80; Kuna appropriation of, 158
Central America, ix, 109, 146, 160
Centro de Investigaciones Antropológicas, 196, 204
Centro Investigaciones Kuna (CIK), 221

chants, Kuna, 28, 124, 192, 235–236; curing, 39, 179; and description, 159–160; Hayans and, 217–219; intelligibility of, 152, 266n14; inventory project, 225, 236–237; names in, 266n20; Nordenskiöld and, 148–149, 150–153, 266n22; and picture writing, 153–157; Reverte and, 192; tape recordings of, 224. *See also specific chants*
Chapin, Mac, 145, 152; on cultural loss, 248–249; on Kuna curing, 159–160, 203; "Losing the Way of the Great Father," 248; *Pab igala*, 204, 206, 273n42; and PEMASKY, 225, 248; on picture writing, 153–155; "Tad Ibe gi namaket," 204
Cherokee: syllabary, 157; writing and resistance, 4
Cherokee Renascence in the New Republic (McLoughlin), 4
chichas, 56, 82, 92, 236, 270n31, 272n27; Cantón on, 210; Garay and, 172; Gassó and, 174, opposition to, 236, 269n15, 270n31; Peréz Kantule on, 215; Robinson on, 181; videotape of, 225. *See also* puberty ceremonies
chiefs: letters of, 47–53, 59–62; and Colombia, loyalty to, 67, 70, 256n9; and customs, defense of, 82–85, 87; and languages, 256n15; and Panamanian government, 73–76; rivalry and antagonism between, 48–50, 52–54, 61; as tragic heroes, 96–97; and writing, 46. *See also* cacique
Chocó Indians, 56, 120, 121, 186, 191, 194, 195. *See also* Emberá Chocó; Wounan Chocó
Christian Brothers: and Normal School in Panama, 23
Christianity, 121; ethnography, 177; Kuna morality, supposed influence on, 146, 151; Kuna religion, supposed influence on, 238, 265–266n13; Protestant, 149
Chucunaque River, 102, 106, 194, 261n8; Kuna population, 95, 167
Circumscription of San Blas (Circunscripción de San Blas), 25, 45, 69
ciudad letrada, La (Rama), 5
Civilización de los indios Tules, x
Claretian order, 40, 255n16
Clifford, James: on salvage ethnography, 250–251; ethnographic allegory, 160, 246
Coast of San Blas, ix, 1, 13, 23, 35, 36, 38, 54, 65, 67, 70, 74, 78, 99, 100, 117, 129, 219, 275n14; and census, 79–80; confederacies, 25; isolation of, 53–59; literacy, 42; rebellion and, 39; schools, 25, 26, 40, 41, 255n16; tourism in, 199; travel writing about, 199–200; visitors to, 164. *See also* Gulf of San Blas; Kuna Yala
Colley, Linda, 12
Colman, Ceferino, 30
Colman, Cimral (Sam Colman, Sancurman, Inagindibipilele), 25, 27, 35, 36, 38–39, 41, 51, 52, 54–55, 60, 61, 72, 74, 75, 82–85, 100, 125, 133, 139, 168, 179, 224, 254n10, 255n2, 259n38, 259n42, 259n45, 259n47; and confederacy, 25, 30–31, 34, 50; cultural defense, 85–86, 255n38, 269n49; on Kuna customs, 53, 82–85, 250n49; letters, 48, 49, 50, 53, 82–84, 124, 256n11; and Peréz Kantule, 103, 109, 111, 117, 123; target of officials' invective, 74–75
Colman, Juan, 224
Colombia: 129, 211, 229, 238, 268n38; Kuna chiefs, allegiance of, 47, 51, 61, 74; letters to government from Kuna chiefs, 256n9; native intellectuals, 238–239; and Panamanian independence, 23; representations of Kuna, 65; treaty with the Kuna, x, 243

Colón, 35, 42, 53, 54, 65, 66, 72, 85, 88, 92, 121; schools, 42
colonial discourse, 11, 15, 68
"colonial nostalgia," 97, 249–250
Colonial Police, 33, 35. *See also* police
Columbus, Christopher, 88, 91, 147
Comarca de San Blas, 164
Comaroff, Jean and John: on hegemony, 8–9
Communist Party, 7
Complete Mu-Igala, The, 275n11
CONAPI (Coordinación Nacional de Pastoral Indigena), 224
Congreso General. *See* General Congress
Congreso General de la Cultura Kuna (Onmaked Dummad Namakaled), 223, 264n28
Congresos. *See* General Congress; onomaked
Con los indios cunas de Panamá (Gálvez), 183
"Consequences of Literacy, The" (Watt, Goody), 3
Coope, Anna, 24–25, 26, 31, 32, 40, 52, 54, 71–72, 76, 99, 114, 258n18; and English language, 25; and Kuna custom, 24, 67; and Protestantism, 24; and schools, establishment of on Nargana and Nusatupu, 24; and Zonian support, 100, 101, 261n13
Cooper, Frederick: *Tensions of Empire*, 14–15
Cooperativa de Molas, 225
Corazón de Jesús. *See* Nusatupu/Corazón
Costello, Richard, 202
Crehan, Kate: on Gramsci, 9
criados, 22, 24, 35, 38, 42, 254n2
Cuna. *See* Kuna
Cuna (Kelly), 199
Cuna-Cuna, 95. *See also* Kuna
"Cuna Folk of Darien," 187
curing, Kuna, 82–84, 149, 235–236, 265n4; Cantón on, 210; Chapin on, 153, 203; Nordenskiöld on, 159; Peréz Kantule and, 125. *See also* chants
Curtin, Philip: and "defensive modernization," 4

Dada Fransoa: supposed collaboration with French, 147
Dad Ibe (Machi Olowaibipiler, Ibelele), 145, 265n9
Dagargunyala, 139, 173–174, 275n15
Dalbyö, Sweden, 131, 133, 134, 135, 136
Danakwe Dupir. *See* Tupile
Darién, ethnoecología de una región histórica, El (Torres de Araúz), 195
Darién Isthmus, ix, 1, 56, 99, 102, 120, 121, 133, 175, 194, 230, 262n38, 270n40; whether Kuna descended from early Darién societies, 270n40; pirates in, ix, 98, 145–147, 160, 162, 232
Davies, Father Juan José (Ibelele), 220, 275n6
Declaration of Independence and Human Rights of the Tule People of San Blas and Darien (Marsh), 103–107, 187, 261n19, 262n20, 274n2; and rebellion, 107, 117; reception of, 107; as voice of the Kuna, 97–99. See also Kuna rebellion
De Gerdes, Marta, 197, 259n2
De James, Ana, 31
De la Ossa, Francisco, 37, 109
De la Rosa, José, 35, 54–55, 72, 78, 86, 100
De León, Cebaldo Iwinapi, 221, 222
Deloria, Philip: *Playing Indian*, 13
De Montaigne, Michel, 115
Denis, Guillermo, 33
De Páramo y Cepeda, Juan Francisco: *Alteraciones del Dariel*, 167
Department of Public Instruction, 26
De Smidt, Leon: *Among the San Blas Indians of Panama*, 181–182

"Developmental Change in San Blas" (Holloman), 202
Diálogo Social (journal), 207
Diario de Panamá, 68
difference or similarity: and oppression, 11–12, 25, 80, 81, 260n52
Diolele. *See* religion, Kuna
doctor as honorific, 83–84, 259n45
Dominican Order: missions, 147
dress, Kuna women's: defense of, 37, 82, 85; and difference, 68, 111–112; Garay on, 171, 173; and identity, 56, 101–102; in Kuna ethnology, 226–227, 276n26; Markham on, 101, 272n25; Marsh on, 104–105; Peréz Kantule on, 215; Reynolds on, 99; suppression of, 31, 236
drinking, by Indians: outsider's views on, 68, 82, 174. *See also* chichas
dule (Kuna language, *dulegaya*, mother tongue), 228. *See also* Kuna; Tule
Dunham, Jacob, ix
Duque family, 114
Durkheim, Emile, 149

Earle, Rebecca: on the "indianesque," 167
Ebensten, Hanns: *Volleyball with the Cuna Indians and Other Gay Travel Adventures*, 199
education: and conquest, 25–26; and nationalism, 25–26; and social mobility, 57
Ehrmann, Juan, 37
Elliot, J. H.: on hegemony, 9
El Porvenir, 25, 107, 109, 121
Emberá Chocó, 56, 120, 121, 122, 124, 127–128, 194, 207, 247
Encuentros de comunidades de base de Kuna Yala, 223
Encuentros nacionales de pastoral indígena, 224
endogamy. *See* Kuna separatism
England: British pirates in Darién, ix

England, Nora: on Guatemalan Indian languages, 228
English language: and accounts of the Kuna, 88, 93; and Coope, 25; and expatriates in Panama, 88–89; and Kuna language, 29; and Kuna secretaries, 46–47, 256n16; and Kuna self-representation, 56; and Kuna sympathizers, 99–100, 114, 232–233; and Peréz Kantule, 124, 129, 135; and Protestantism, 23; and Robinson, 23, 52; and schooling, 23, 25, 29–30
environmentalism: and indigenous ideology, 233–235, 240, 242
Eoba. *See* A-oba
Ercilla y Zuniga, Alonso de: *La Araucana*, 167
Erice, Jesús, 178, 269n24
Ernstson, Bo, 119, 266n17
Escuela de Artes y Oficios (Panama), 25, 40
essentialism, indigenous, 240–244
estrecho dudoso, El (Cardenal), 211
Estrella de Panamá, La, 85, 114, 115, 129. See also *Panama Star and Herald*
"Estudios sobre la vida de los indios de San Blas" (Peréz Kantule), 214–215, 274nn1–2
ethnocide: and cultural politics, 67–70, 257n12. *See also* Kuna culture: suppression of; Panama, Republic of
ethnography, general: 15–20; and advocacy, 12–13, 18–19, 90–93, 99–116, 182, 184–185, 207–209; and anthropology, 1; and authority, 19; context important in, 148–151; and exclusion, 17; and identification, 18–19; indigenous, 226–238; investigator/informant relationship, 16–17, 205–206; native, 178, 226; popular, 88; and representation, 17–19; as public relations or self-defense, 81–85, 122–125, 214–216; salvage, 249–251; text-based,

142–145, 148–149, 238; Southwestern, 20
ethnography, Kuna, 16–18, 122–127, 198; amateur, 198–202; Catholic, 173–178; Christian, 177; collaboration between Kuna and Swedish anthropologists, 21, 140–163; early period, 64–66, 182; Kuna mediators, 182; later period, 219–224; literary representations of Kuna, 209–213; native, 219, 227, 235–238, 277n40; by North Americans, 180–183; by Panamanians, 185–186, 197–198; positive representations of Kuna, 208; post-rebellion, 164; professional growth of, 203; tensions in, 245–247; texts, 142–143; by Zonians, 181. *See also* anthropologists; auto-ethnography, Kuna
"Etnología y población histórica de Panamá" (Alba), 166
etymology in cultural interpretation, 229–232

Fabian, Johannes, 193
Falla, Ricardo: *Historia kuna, historia rebelde*, 208; *El tesoro de San Blas*, 208
Faron, Louis, 189
Father's Way (Bab igar), 27, 28, 36, 125, 270n37, 275n15, 276–277n36; and Bible, 237–238, 277nn39–40; centrality of, 236–237, 266n14, 268n38; changes to, 237–238, 268n38; and inculturation, 237; variant traditions, 237–238, 277nn38–39; written interpretations, 238
First Inter-American Indigenist Congress, 185
Fischer, Edward, 226; on pan-Mayanists in Guatemala, 228, 241
Fortis, Paolo, 201
Foucault, Michel, 2, 10; on power and knowledge, 13

Frago, Manuela, 35
France: and albino Kuna, 265n13; anthropology, 203; and canal, early attempt, 89; colonization of Darién 99, 145–147, 172; colonization of North America, 73; identification with Kuna, 112; pirates in Darién, 98, 145–147, 160, 162, 232
Franciscan order, 40; mission work post rebellion, 173; and orthography, 4
fraternal organizations. *See* Improved Order of Red Men
Frazer Medal, 129
Freeman, Joanna: *Affairs of Honor*, 61
Fundacíon Dobo Yala, 223

gaburduled (pepper chanter), 83
galu (kalu, spirit stronghold), 155, 275n7
Gálvez, Maria Albertina, 183–184, 218; *Con los indios cunas de Panamá*, 183
Gamio, Manuel, 166, 188
gana (ritualist), 254n9. *See also* immar wisit
gandule (flute man), 27, 36, 83, 257n1, 269n18, 275n17
Garay, Narciso, 78, 191, 268nn6–10; attitude towards Indians, 171; on Carnival, 171, 172; and chichas, 236; on churches, 172; and Kuna collaborators, 170–171; and Panamanian anthropologists, 173; and Richard Marsh, 170; *Tradiciones y Cantares de Panamá*, 169–173
garda (*karta*), 26, 29, 254n5
Gassieu, Pierre, 206, 273n41
Gassó, Father Leonardo, 23–25, 26, 31, 36, 38, 86, 121, 131, 133, 149, 150, 151, 156, 160, 177, 179, 256n9, 257n6, 259n38, 261n9, 265n13; on Caribe-Kunas, 19, 80; and *criados*, 24; diary of, 65–66, 149, 254n8; on Indian customs, 67;

and Kuna language, 66; morality, focus on, 66; oral, privileging of, 24; on third party influences, 258n16
gathering, Kuna. See onomaked
gender: in representations of Kuna society, 194, 201, 227, 272nn25–26, 276nn25–26
General Congress, Kuna, 46, 216, 221, 223, 238, 244, 246, 273n45, 274n4
Geografía de Panamá (Valdés), 158, 257n4, 2
Geografía descriptiva de la República de Panamá (Alba), 166–167
Gerardi, Bishop Juan: Reverte on death of, 270n2
Gess, George. *See* Sequoyah
Gilbert, James, 90–93, 95, 99, 100, 127, 171, 260n4; on Kuna rituals, 92–93; "The Land of the Cacique," 90–91, 113; Panama Patchwork, 90, *90*; sources, 92
Goffman, Erving, 256n16; *The Preservation of Self in Everyday Life*, 56–57; *Stigma*, 57
González, Manuel, 35–36, 43
González, Nicanor, 242
Goody, Jack: "The Consequences of Literacy," 3; *Literacy in Traditional Societies*, 3
Gordón, Miguel, 39
Göteborg (Gothenburg), Sweden, 118; Boas in, 119; Peréz Kantule in, 131–137, 157–158; Stout in, 187
Göteborg Ethnographic Museum (Museum of World Cultures), 118, *132*, 182
Gothenburg. *See* Göteborg, Sweden
Graham, Laura: "How Should an Indian Speak?" 55–56
Gramsci, Antonio, 9; hegemony, 8; "organic intellectuals," 7, 9
Gran Chaco, 118
Grandmother's Way. *See* Muu igar
Green, Abadio, 229, 246; on Kuna counting system, 231; on writing, 246
Guatemala: pan-Mayanists in, 226, 228; and native intellectuals, 238–239
Guavia (Francisco), x
Guaymí (Ngöbe), 121, 168, 208
Gudeman, Steven, 208
"guerras de Ibelele contra los pony e reyes en este mundo, Las" (Hayans), 218
Guerrero, Samuel, 46
Guillén, Benito, 35, 38–40
Guisinde, Father, 134
Gulf of San Blas, 107. *See also* Coast of San Blas; Mandinga Bay
Gulf of Urabá, 161
gurgin (aptitude), 136, 138

Hale, Charles: on multiculturalism in Guatemala, 239
Hall, Robert: and Rubén Peréz Kantule, 124–125
Handbook of South American Indians, 189, 198
Handler, Richard, 240
Harding, Joe (Francisco Soo, Soowadin), 23; chief of Nusatupu, 37
Harris, Reginald, 156
Hartmann, Gunther, 201
Hartmann, Ursula, 201
Haya de la Torre, Victor, 185
Hayans (Haya), Guillermo, 124–125, 131, 137–138, 141, 144, 147, 149, 151, 179, 191, 214, 217–218, 263n14; in Ailigandi, 125; as archivist, 216; and census, 157–158; and Muu igar, 153–155; and Nordenskiöld, 127; and picture writing, 153–156; and *Popol Vuh*, 184
Heckadon Moreno, Stanley, 208
hegemony, 8–9, 253n5
Helms, Mary, 133, 201
Hereward the Wake, 96, 97
Hernandez, Manuel, 35
Herrera, Francisco, 209, 273n36; time

in the field, 271n16; on Torres de Araúz, 197, 271n9
Herrera, Rodolfo, 225
Herrera, Simón: on Inabaginya, 224
Herrera, Tomás, 275n22
hieroglyphics, 28
Hirschfeld, Lawrence, 201
"Historia de los Antíguas Ságuilas el tiempo cuando reinaban el Colombia" (Hayans), 217
Historia kuna, historia rebelde (Falla), 208
Historical and Ethnological Survey of the Cuna Indians, An (Nordenskiöld, et al., 1938), 142–143, 143–145, 154, 157, 265n3, 275n12. *See also* Nordenskiöld, Erland
"Historic Memory, Social Structure, and Theology of the Kuna Nation" (Archibold), 238
historiography and historical consciousness, native, 143–148, 235–238, 243–244, 266n14
"History of an Indian Tribe over a Period of 400 Years, The," 143–145
History of My Fathers, My Beloved History, (Aiban Wagwa), 238
Hobsbawm, Eric, 5, 162, 240, 256n12
Holloman, Regina, 42, 254n2, 255n21; "Developmental Change in San Blas," 202
Holmer, Nils, 140, 150, 151, 152, 155, 179
Homage to the American Indians (Cardenal), 211–212
Hombre y Cultura (journal), 196
Homenaje a los indios americanos (Cardenal), 211, 274n55
Hopi. *See* "Pueblo" Indians
"Horatio at the Bridge" (Macauley), 96, 97, 263n40
Hospice of Don Bosco, 31. *See also* Salesian order
Howe, James, 202–203, 225, 272n28; *A People Who Would Not Kneel*, 2, 226

Howe, June, 202
"How Should an Indian Speak?" (Graham), 55–56
Hrdlička, Aleš, 105
Huacoriso, Selimo: and Nordenskiöld, 120–122, 124
Huegenots, 146
Human Ecology of Route 17 (Torres de Araúz), 195
Human Relations Area Files, 198
Huron Indians: and Jesuits, 3; and writing, 3
Hurtado, Enrique: as intendente, 69–70
Hymes, Dell, 204

Ibelele. *See* Davies, Father Juan José; Dad Ibe
Ibelergan (great shamans), 238
Ibeorgun, 138, 144, 145, 156, 228, 232, 238, 265n7, 265n9, 268n9
IDIKY, 223
igar wisid (chant knower), 27. *See also* Masar igar wised; Muu igar wisid
Iglesias, Alcibiades, 40, 181, 187, 191
Iglesias, Alicio (Elisco), 31
Iglesias, Claudio, 31–32, 34, 37, 40, 46, 54, 71, 85, 122, 258n18; letters and petitions, 60; and suppression of Kuna culture, 31
Iglesias, Marvel, 181
Igwa-Yabiliginya, Chief, 211; and Kuna self-representation, 277n39
"imaginary, the," 14, 96–97; and discourse on the Kuna, 76–77. *See also* Anderson, Benedict
Imagined Communities (Anderson), 14
Imagining India (Inden), 14
immar wisid (knower of things; plural, *immar wisimalat*), 2, 27, 125, 254n9
imperialism: and difference, 11; role of official documentation, 158
imperial liberalism, 113–114
Improved Order of Red Men, 89, 260n2

Inabaginya, Chief, 42, 61, 92, 128, 179, 211, 216, 224, 237, 264n23, 269n13; and Colman, 51; and Colombia, allegiance to 30, 67, 70; and confederacy, 30, 34, 50; letters, 46, 47–48, 49–50, 51, 256n11; and Panama, allegiance to, 47, 51, 74, 117; and schools, 42; target of officials' invective, 74

inaduledi (medicine person), 27, 83, 260n5

Inagindibipilele. *See* Colman, Cimral

Inakeliginia. *See* López, Carlos

Inanaginya, Chief, 91–92

inculturation, 223–224; and Father's Way, 237

In Defense of Life and Its Harmony (Aiban Wagwa), 238

Inden, Ronald B.: *Imagining India*, 14

independence, Kuna, 93–99; North American support for, 93; official objections, 68–70, 73–76; postrebellion, 164

India, British colonialism of, 11. *See also* Raj, the

india dormida, La, (Sosa), 168

"indianesque, the," 167–169

Indian identity, 55–56; appropriated by writers, 89–90

Indian Life in the Chaco (Nordenskiöld), 118

"Indian Question," the, 166, 185

Indians and Whites in Northeast Bolivia (Nordenskiöld), 118

Indígena y proletario, 208

"indígenas kunas y la conservación ambiental, Los" (Ventocilla, et al.), 242

indigenism, 85–87, 167; and Kuna names, 220, 275n17; and New Age movement, 233; and place names, 219–220; rights movement, 219

Indigenist Congress, Panama (1956), 191

indigenous essentialism. *See* essentialism, indigenous

indigenous ethnography. *See* ethnography, indigenous

"indios cunas, 'una nación soberana,' Los" (Cardenal), 211

indios cunas de San Blas, Los (Puig), 176–177

indio y las clases sociales, El, 208

individuals in Kuna ethnography, 149–150, 204, 266n17

information: politics of, 51–55, 256n9, 256n11

Instituto Indigenista Interamericano, 194

Instituto Nacional (Panama), 25, 40, 41, 124, 261n9

Intendencia, 46, 216

intendentes, 31, 32–33, 45, 50, 77, 79, 85; on character of Kuna chiefs, 73–76; Hurtado as, 69–70; on Kuna, 77–78; and Kuna rebellion, 68, 70–73, 102, 114; and letters, 37, 38–39, 47, 48, 53, 54, 71–72, 73–74, 75–76, 78, 256n11, 256n17; Mojica as, 54, 55, 70, 75, 76, 102, 114; reports of, 68–69, 75; Vaglio as, 54–55, 86, 254n10

International Bolivarian Congress, 166

International Congress of Americanists, 119, 222

Into the American Woods (Merrell), 6

Introducción al estudio de las lenguas indígenas de Panamá (Alba), 186, 186–187

Invasion Within, The (Axtell), 3

Iroquois, 213

Islam, 12, 22

Isla Pino (Tuppak), 128

islikwagwa (spiritually dangerous), 124

Isthmian Anthropological Society, Canal Zone, 272n22

Izikowitz, Karl-Gustav, 131, 140, 179, 265n1

Jackson, Jean, 240, 241–242

Jeambrun, Pascale, 203

Jesuit order: and the Children's Association, 37; and the Huron, 3; missions, 147, 269n21
Jesus Christ, 237, 277n39
J. K. B. (columnist): defense of Kuna, 114–115
Joyce, Elliot, 198
Juventud Samblaseña (bulletin), 178

Kahler, Erich, 193
Kainora (Achutupu), 122, 263n12
Kalman, Judy, 58–59
kalu. See *galu*
Kantulbipi, 170
kantule. See *gandule*
Kantule, Nele. See Nele Kantule
Kantule, Rubén Pérez. See Pérez Kantule, Rubén
Karsten, Rafael, 118
karta. See *garda*
Karttunen, Frances: *Between Worlds: Interpreters, Guides, and Survivors*, 6
Keeler, Clyde (Kilobipi): *Apples of Immortality from the Cuna Tree of Life*, 198; *Land of the Moon-Children*, 198; *Secrets of the Cuna Earthmother*, 198
Keesing, Roger, 17, 259–260n48
Kelly, Joanne: *Cuna*, 199
Kertzer, David: on census, 80
Kikadiryai, 228
Kilobipi. See Keeler, Clyde
Kilu, 153
Kingsley, Charles, 96
kinship, in Kuna culture, 276n22; Howe on, 202; in native ethnography, 227; Nordenskiöld, 148;
Kipling, Rudyard, 90
knower of things. See *immar wisit*
knowledge: and control of spirit world, 157–160; distribution in society, 160–162
Koskun Kalu, 223, 264n28; foreign writings on Kuna culture, 225–226; chants and chanters, inventory of, 236; "Origen del puelo kuna desde la memoria historica," 242
Kroeber, Alfred, 119
Kuna, representations of, 21, 186–187, 270n38, 270–271n3; Anglophone, 80, 90–99; colonial-era accounts, 145–148, 257n2; early, ix–xi, 64–66; and self-presentation, x–xi, 55–62, 81–85, 111, 158–160, 164–165
Kuna culture: and modernism, 162–163; and morality, 50; official indifference to, 21, 56, 68; and social class, 112–113, 161; structure of, 51; suppression of, 25, 32, 33–34, 36, 39, 54, 67–70. See also ethnocide; *specific features of Kuna culture*
Kuna language, 27, 43, 59, 253n43, 258n20; and Anglophone influence, 29; counting system, 230–232, 276n30; linguistics, 131, 229; and nonnative speakers, 33; orthography, 59, 229, 256n15, 276n29; and Spanish influence, 29–30; and translation, 45, 56. See also etymology
Kuna rebellion (1925), 2, 26, 35, 36, 38, 39, 67–68, 107–114, 114–116, 123; influences on, 75–76; justification for, 111–114; Markham and, 108; mural commemorating, 233; and Panamanian government, agreement with, 109; rhetoric of, 110; representation of by Kuna, 232–233; suppression of, 262n38. See also resistance, Kuna; Revolucíon Tule
Kuna Ways of Speaking (Sherzer), 203–204, 226
Kuna Yala, 202, 255n22, 275n14. See also Coast of San Blas
Kuna Yargi, 223, 275n20
Kungiler, Iguaniginappi, 230
Kupperman, Karen, 12, 253n4
Kwaio, the: and ethnography, 17. See also Keesing, Roger
Kwebdi. See Río Azúcar

Lamont, Michèle, 256n12
"Land of the Cacique, The" (Gilbert), 90–91, 93, 95, 113
Land of the Moon-Children (Keeler), 198
Las Casas, Bartolemé de, 147, 253n4; Premio Las Casas, 246
Latin America: schooling in, 22, 27; "scriptural economy" in, 5–6, 58; Spanish Empire, 5, 22
Layan, Camilo, 224
LeClezio, J. M., 203
Lefevre, President Ernesto, 55, 87
"L'Efficacité Symbolique" (Lévi-Strauss), 152
leg binding, in Kuna culture, 39, 67, 262n21
Leis, Raúl, 197; *Machi: un kuna en la ciudad*, 209
lele. See nele
letrados, 5, 170; as indigenous intellectuals, 6–7; as mediators, 6
letters, 46, 47–53, 256n11, 262n34; class and self-presentation, 55–62, 256n12, 256n14; flaws in, 59–62; and orality, 46; and polemics, 54–55; and translation, 46–47. See also letters, Kuna, specific
letters, Kuna, specific: Colman to Porras (1913), 30, 48–49, 82–84, 216; Colman to Vaglio (1919), 53; Guillén to Vaglio (1919), 38–39; Iglesias et al. to secretary (1921), 60; Inabaginya to Garrido (1919), 48, 49–50; Inabaginya to Vaglio (1919), 47–48; Olopanique to president (1919), 39; Robinson to Porras (1913), 52–53; Vaglio to Coope (1919), 71–72
Lévi-Strauss, Claude: on Muu igar, 152, 159; *Structural Anthropology*, 152; "L'Efficacité Symbolique," 152
Lévy-Bruhl, Lucien, 119, 149, 192
Lewis, Chief Charles, 49, 255n7
Liebersohn, Harry, 133
Linares, Olga, 202, 271n19

Lindberg, Christer, 162, 267–268n37
Lindo, Anibal, 35
Linné, Sigvald, 120, 121
Linton, Ralph, 188
literacy, 1, 22, 23, 28–29, 43–44, 57–58, 125, 255n21; and mediation, 32–35; models of, 3; and orality, 3; politics of, 2–7; rates of, 40–43, 255nn21–22; and self-worth, 27; and social mobility, 58. See also writing
Literacy in Traditional Societies (Goody), 3
Literatura oral de los indios cunas (Reverte), 192
López, Chief Carlos (Inakeliginia), 221, 224; diary, 274n5, 276n23
López, Estanislao, 32; as archivist, 216–217
López de Iglesias, Hildaura, 274n5
"Losing the Way of the Great Father" (Chapin), 248
Lotería (journal), 211
Lowie, Robert, 119–120
Lutz, Otto, 261n9

machi. See machigua
Machi: un kuna en la ciudad (Leis), 209, 274nn50–51
machigua or machigwa (boy, deprecatory term for Kuna), 66, 261n7, 275n17
Machigwa (Rosendo), x
Machi Olowaibipiler. See Dad Ibe
Magemmulu. See Caledonia
Magnificent Molas (Perrin), 208
Malinowski, Bronislaw, 119; *The Sexual Life of Savages*, 119
Mandinga Bay, 25, 199, 201, 259n32, 262n38
Maradikyan, Levon, 225
Margaret Johnson (ship), 130
Mariátegui, José Carlos, 166, 185
Markham, William, 124, 127, 180, 199; advocacy of Kuna, 100–102; on Coope, 101; and Kuna rebels,

coaching of, 108; letter to Porras, 101, 102, 111; representation of Kuna difference and rebellion, 107–110; rhetorical strategy, 108, 109, 110; on San Blas, 19; and social class, 113; on women, 101
marriage, in Kuna culture, 65, 66, 93; Berengueras on, 174; Cantón on, 210; and Catholicism, 178; in native ethnography, 227; Nordenskiöld on, 264n21; Reverte on, 191, 192; Reynolds on, 99; Tinnin on, 269n28
Marsh, Richard, 38, 102–107, 124, 128, 156, 164, 184, 262n23, 262n38; Blacks, attitude towards, 105–106; Declaration of Independence and Human Rights of the Tule People of San Blas and Darien, 103–107, 111, 160, 187, 262n20; and elite knowledge, 161; on Kuna racial purity, 106, 127; and Kuna rebellion, 107–111, 196, 232; and social class, 113; and Social Darwinism, 106; and white (albino) Indians, search for, 102–103, 121
Marshall, Donald, 198, 271n17
Martínez, Atilio, 223, 238
Martínez Mauri, Mònica, 234, 254n13
Marxism, 9
Marx, Karl, 10
Masar Igar, 27; Masar Igar wisid (masurduled, death chanter), 83
Maya, 105, 106, 113; and Kuna, language, 228; Pan-Maya activism, 226–230, 238
Mayapán (Cardenal), 211
Mayer, Dora, 166
McAndrews, Anita: translation of Tomás Herrera, 276n22
McKim, Fred, 183, 184, 187, 269nn29–30; *San Blas, an Account of the Cuna Indians of Panama*, 182
McLoughlin, William: *Cherokee Renascence in the New Republic*, 4

Medellín, Colombia, 211
mediation: and literacy, 32–35
memoria ritual, La (Severi), 225
Memorias de Gobierno y Justicia, 68–69, 81–82
Méndez, Horatio, 221: "Tad Ibe gi namaket," 204
Méndez Pereira, Octavio, 185; *Nuñez de Balboa: el tesoro del Dabaibe*, 168
Mendoza, President Carlos, 67
merchants and Kuna, 2, 26, 71, 89, 95, 96, 258n17, 274n54
mergi (anthropologists), 205
Merrell, James, 3; *Into the American Woods*, 6
Merton, Thomas, 211
mestizaje, 97, 168, 268n4
Metacom, 97
Metcalf, Thomas, 11
Metraux, Alfred, 118, 140
Mimesis and Alterity (Taussig), 17
Ministry of Culture (Panama), 196
Ministry of Education (Panama), 41
Ministry of Government (Panama), 41
Miró, Ricardo, 268n1
Misionero, El (journal), 173
missionaries, 54, 65, 66, 164; Catholic, 40, 202, 223–224, 237, 255n16, 266n13; Colman on, 85–86; and ethnography, 173–178; Protestant, 26, 71–72, 89, 124. *See also specific religious orders*
modernity, 17, 20–21, 66, 99, 125, 276n22
Mojica, Andrés: as intendente, 54, 55, 70, 75, 76, 102; on Marsh, 114
molas, 124, 157, 170, 199–202, 227–228, 272nn23–24, 276nn25–26; scholars on, 201
"monumentos históricos del Río Tuile, Los" (Hayans), 217
Moore, Alexander, 203, 225
Moore, James, 183
Morley, Sebastian, 16

Morris, Samuel, 31, 128
Movimiento de la Juventud Kuna, 207
mujer cuna, La (Torres de Araúz), 194, 195
Mulatupu (Sasardi), 42, 194, 202, 212–213
multiculturalism, 196–197, 239
Murphy, Elizabeth, 19
Museo de Antropología Médica-Forense, Paleopatología y Criminalística Profesor Reverte Coma, 191
Museo del Hombre Panameño, 196, 197
Museo Nacional de Panamá, 196
Muu igar (Muu-Igala, Grandmother's Way), 27, 151–152, 266n24, 275n11; and picture writing, 153–155, 179
Muu Igar wisid (chanter for difficult births), 83

Nagel, Joane: "ethnosexual politics," 97
Nalu-Nega (Cantón), 209–211, 274nn51–54
names, in Kuna auto-ethnography, 51, 157–160, 216–217, 219, 220, 275n17. *See also* individuals in Kuna ethnography
namnega (earth-place), 83
Nan Dummad (Great Mother), 150, 234
Napguana (the earth), 223, 272n27
Nargana, 23–24, 28, 29, 31, 35, 50, 54, 68, 71, 79, 82, 85, 100, 122, 124, 139, 171; and civilization, 32, 33; and literacy, 255n21; schools, 23–25, 26, 30, 40–41, 42; and Zonian visitors, 99. *See also* Nusatupu/Corazón
Naroll, Raoul, 177
Natchez Indians, 97
National Assembly of Panama, 164
National Geographic, 257n4
National Guardsmen, 42
native intellectuals, 6–7, 9, 16, 62, 160–163

natukin (one's own doing), 248
Navas, Eduardo and Narcisco, 33, 111
Neal, Avon, 201
negotiations, 110–111
nele (seer), 27, 65, 122, 269n18
Nele Kantule, Chief (Nele Wardada), 30–31, 38, 41, 61, 73, 78, 111, 117, 122, 123–124, 125, *126*, 133, 136, 143–144, 149, 179, 185, 186, 191; and census, 157–158; and Colman conspiracy, 30; and ethnographic project, 124–125, 263n13; as intellectual, 126, 149–150, 160–162, 266n18; historical account, 145–148; and Nordenskiöld, 122–123, 126–127, 130, 160; and post-rebellion reforms, 139; and *sikkiwis*, 34; target of officials' invective, 73–74; as teacher, 161–162; and Zonians, sponsorship of, 181. *See also* Kuna rebellion
Nele Wardada. *See* Nele Kantule, Chief
Nelson, Charlie, 32, 122, 149, 155, 159, 266n25; and Garay, 170; and Nordenskiöld, 127–128; and picture writing, 267n27
New York Times, 200
NGO (nongovernmental organization), 235; indigenous, 223. *See also specific organizations*
Ngöbe people of Panama (Guaymí), 247
Niatupu (Tigantiki), 35, 37
niga (vital force), 136, 138
Niga Gardaduled. See Robinson, Charlie
Niiskuamer Ebised Dule (The Star Counter) (Kubiler, Cole-igar), 230
Nimuendajú, Curt, 118, 119
Noanama Chocó. *See* Wounan Chocó
Noga Kope, 181
Nordenskiöld, Erik, 119
Nordenskiöld, Baron Erland, 21, *123*, *126*, 198, 203; awards, 129; and Blacks, attitude towards,

119, 121, 122, 128, 263n6; and Colombia, 128; criticism of books, 129; and customs, preservation of, 121; distribution studies, 118, 263n3; and Emberá Choco, 120–121; expeditions, 118, 266n15; and French influence on Kuna, 265n13; and Garay, 170, 268n8; and the Göteborg Ethnographic Museum, 118; and Hayans, 127; influences, 119–120; and Kuna collaborators, recognition of, 141, 219; on Kuna ethnography, 122–127; on Kuna picture writing, 122, 127–128, 153–157, 264n19, 266–267n25, 267n30; on Kuna racial purity, 127–128, 264n21; on Kuna religion, 136, 148–151, 265n11, 266nn18–19, 266n22; on Kuna separatism, 121; on Kuna texts, 127–128; on Kuna traditions, 121–122; and modernist impulses, 162–163; and Muu igar, 151; and Nele Kantule, 122–123, 125–126, 126–127, 160; and Nelson, 122, 127; in Panama, 119–121; and Peréz Kantule, 130–138, 148; and popular education, 118; publications, 140; and Roberto Peréz, 122, 127; and Selimo, 120–122, 124; social character of, 119; sources about, 263n9; in Ustupu, 128, 143–144, 147, 264nn22–23. *See also* Nordenskiöld, Baron Erland, works of

Nordenskiöld, Baron Erland, works of: *An Historical and Ethnological Survey of the Cuna Indians,* 142–143, 143–145, 178–179; *Indian Life in the Chaco,* 118; *Indians and Whites in Northeast Bolivia,* 118; *Picture Writing and Other Documents by Néle, Paramount Chief of the Cuna Indians, and Rubén Peréz Kantule, His Secretary,* 129; *Picture Writing and Other Documents by Néle, Charles Slater, Charlie Nelson, and Other Cuna Indians,* 129; *Researches and Adventures in South America 1913–1914,* 118

Nordenskiöld, Olga, 119, 121
Noriega, President Manuel, 202
normal schools, 23, 167
North Americans: referred to as *iamar,* 207; support for Kuna independence, 93; support for Kuna resistance, 96–97
noserings, Kuna: defense of, 71, 85–86; and difference, 56, 68; Garay on, 171; in Kuna ethnography, 226–227; suppression of, 32, 39, 53, 82, 261n13
nuchu (*sualluchu,* carving of familiar spirit), 82, 176, 259n41
Nuñez de Balboa: el tesoro del Dabaibe (Méndez Pereira), 168
Nusatupu/Corazón de Jesús, 219; and Brenes, 36; confederacies and, 48; Coope and, 24, 71; Garay and, 172; Gassó and, 24; Iglesias and, 31, 33; Lewis and, 255–256n7; missionaries and, 173; police, 45, 48, 125; schools, 23, 24–25, 26, 30, 40, 42

Oba. See A-oba
Olga (boat), 120, 122, *123,* 128, 129
Olivares, Olivio, 72, 100
Oller, Felix, 191
Ologuagdi, 225
Olonibiginya, Chief, 100, 110, 184, 254n10; and collaboration with North Americans, 180–181; and Colman's confederacy, 30
Olopanique, 39
Olotebiliginya, 218
Olotule (Golden People), 205
Olson, David, 3
Ong, Walter, 3
onomaked, or *onmaket* (gathering), 2, 148–149, 266n16

Onmaked Dummad Namakaled. *See* Congreso General de la Cultura Kuna
Operación Panamá (Reverte), 192
orality, 83–84; and literacy, 3; and social mobility, 58; and translation, 83
Orán, Reuter, 229–230
"organic intellectuals," 7, 9. *See also* Gramsci, Antonio
orientalism, 8, 9, 10–11, 14, 68
Orientalism (Said), 8
Ortiz, Milciades, 62
othering, 10–12, 18
Ovnis de oro: Poemas indios, Los (Cardenal) 211–212, 274n55

Pab igala (Chapin), 204–205, 273n42
Pacific Ocean, 186, 194, 274n6
Palace of the Herons, 45
Panama, Republic of: assimilation of the Kuna, 12, 123–124; attitudes toward Kuna, 27, 56, 60–62, 66, 73, 247; education, government support of, 25; and ethnocide, 67–68, 257n12; fiftieth anniversary of, 190–191; government officials, 45; government schools, 26, 27; independence from Colombia, 2, 23, 70; indigenous culture, 56, 80, 238–239; and Kuna chiefs, indictment of, 73; Kuna rebellion against, 2, 38, 69 (*see also* Kuna rebellion); multiculturalism, 239; race problems, 268n4; Spanish colonial period, 22; tourism, 239; and U.S., 107, 207; and Zonians, suspicions against, 100. *See also specific officials and offices*
Panamá América (newspaper), 139, 183, 214
Panama Bay, 120
Panama Canal, 93; and expatriates, 89; Gatun locks, 115; sand incident, 95, 115, 261n9; and tourists, 89. *See also* Canal Zone
Panama City, 37, 40, 121; schools, 42

Panama Guide, 94
Panamá indígena (Torres de Araúz), 194, 197
Panamanian Academy of History, *138*
Panama Patchwork (Gilbert), 90, *90*
Panama Railroad, 59, 88–89, 100, 255n6
Panama Star and Herald, 89, 103, 114
Panamerican Highway, 221
pan-Indianism: ideology, 233–234; Kuna and, 247–248
Pan-Mayanists. *See* Maya
Panquiaco (chief), 168
Panquiaco (gunboat), 170
Parades de Léon, Herman: on Kuna counting system, 231
Parker, Ann, 201
Parque Urraca, 167, 268n1
Partido del Pueblo, 207
Patrimonio Histórico (government agency), 196
Patrimonio Histórico (journal), 196
Pátzcuaro, Mexico, 185, 215
Peace Corps, 145, 202, 204
Pels, Peter, 177
PEMASKY (Proyecto de Estudio para el Manejo de Areas Silvestres de Kuna Yala), 221–223, 225, 248, 276n34; posters, *234, 243*
Penn (or Bean), Charlie, 111
People Who Would Not Kneel, A (Howe), 2, 226
Pérez, Benito, 82, 113
Pérez, Juan, 31
Pérez, Roberto, 122
Pérez Kantule, Rubén, *41*, 124–125, *132, 135, 138*, 141, 142, 147, 149, 155, 160, 162, 182, 183, 185, 263n15; as archivist, 216–217; and census, 157–158; and Colman, 125; diary of, 131, 132, 137, 138–139, 264n28; as "Erland's Indian," 134; "Estudios sobre la vida de los indios San Blas," 214–215, 274n2; and Gálvez, 184; in Göteborg, 130–136, *132*,

264n28; and Hall, 124–125; and Kuna language, 265n5; and Kuna linguistics, 131; later troubles, 139; and Nordenskiöld, 125–126, 127, 128, 129–138; and picture writing, 157, 267n25, 267n27, 267n30; as scribe, 131

perfil de los pueblos indígenas de Panamá, El (Alvarado), 226

Perrin, Michel, 201, 203; *Magnificent Molas*, 208

Philips (Filos), Fred, 31

picture writing, Kuna, 122, 124, 127, 141, 153–157, 154, 266n25, 267nn27–30

Picture Writing and Other Documents by Néle, Paramount Chief of the Cuna Indians, and Rubén Peréz Kantule, His Secretary (Nordenskiöld), 129

Picture Writing and Other Documents by Néle, Charles Slater, Charlie Nelson, and Other Cuna Indians (Nordenskiöld), 129

Pioneering on the Congo (Bentley), 192

Pirya, 36

Plantas y animales en la vida del pueblo kuna (Ventocilla, Herrera, Nuñez), 225, 242

Playing Indian (Deloria), 13

Playón Chico (Ukkup Senni), 35, 36, 38, 39; establishment of schools on, 25; and rebellion, 40

police, 45, 55, 78, 107, 122, 125, 128, 146; and chiefs, 73–76; Colonial Police, 33, 35; Coope and, 26; documentation, use of, 79, 158; Iglesias as chief, 32, 37–38; indigenous police, 31, 38; literacy and, 28, 32–35; in Nargana, 25–26, 67; "negro" police, racism towards, 103–105, 109–112, 121; in Niatupu, 36; Panamanian, 107–108, 147; Peréz Kantule on, 215; and rebellion, police violence as justification for, 98, 101–102, 103, 108, 109, 121, 122

Popol Vuh, 184

Porras, Hernán, 191

Porras, President Belisario, 25, 30, 35, 36, 38, 45, 50, 51, 52–53, 54–55, 57, 61–62, 82–84, 87, 101; archives, 46; and Kuna culture, suppression of, 25–26, 31–32, 39, 67, 78, 84, 86; and Markham, response to, 102; and schools, establishment of, 25–26; on Urraca, 167–168

Portogandi, 30, 73. *See also* Ustupu

power, in social analysis, 12–13

prejudice, anti-Indian, 27, 30, 56, 61–62, 67–68, 75–76, 81–82, 87, 165–166, 171, 175–176, 186–187, 193, 237–238, 271n8

Premio Bartolomé de las Casas, 246

Preservation of Self in Everyday Life, The (Goffman), 56–57

Prestán, Arnulfo: *El uso de la chicha y la sociedad kuna*, 220, 236

Price, Kayla, 229

problema indígena en Panamá, El (Araíz), 165

Protestant Church: in Caribbean, 23; and English language, 23, 30; mission schools, 26, 31, 42, 79; stance on Kuna customs, 24. *See also* missionaries: Protestant

Providencia (San Andrés), 22–23

Proyecto Banaba, El, 276n24

puberty ceremonies, 31, 36, 83, 148, 155, 170, 172, 203, 210, 220, 232, 236, 267n29, 268n9, 270n31, 271n6; Gassó and, 67. *See also* chichas

public speech, Kuna, 145, 202–204. *See also* orality

"Pueblo" Indians: as archetypal primitives, 20

Pueblos indígenas de Panamá: Hacedores de cultura y de historia (Picón, Alemancia, Gólcher), 225

Puerto Obaldía, 33, 45, 128

Puig, Manuel Mariá: compared to Nordenskiöld, 176–177; on Kuna

agriculture, 269n20; on Kuna rituals, 269n18; on Kuna virtues, 269n17; *Los indios cunas de San Blas*, 176–177; material from Gassó, 177
Puls, Herta, 201
purba. See *burba*
Purdy, Martha, 24, 26, 36, 71

Quetzalcoatl (Cardenal), 211–212

racial purity, Kuna, 94–96, 98, 99, 103, 261nn8–10
Radin, Paul, 120
Raj, the, 11–12, 14. See also India, British colonialism of
Rama, Angel: *La ciudad letrada*, 5
Ramos, Alcida, 56
Reclus, Armand, 65, 257n3
Reconquista (Reconquest of Spain from the Moors), 22
Redfield, Robert, 188; on Tepoztlán, 162
religion, Kuna, 148–151: cosmology, 158–160; deities, 150–151, 266nn19–20; emphasis on texts, 238; mapping of spiritual realm, 158–160; place in daily life, 150–151, 266nn21–22
reports and reported speech in Kuna discourse, 48–50, 144–145
"Rereading Tzotzil Ethnography" (Rus), 20
Researches and Adventures in South America 1913–1914 (Nordenskiöld), 118
resistance, Kuna: approval of, 96–97; as ideology, 96–97; uses of, 167–169. See also Kuna rebellion
Restall, Matthew, 4
Restrepo, Vicente, 65
Restrepo Tirado, Ernesto, 257n3
Reverte Coma, José Manuel, 191–193, 198, 271n16; archaism and backwardness, 192–193; on Kuna character, 270–271nn1–4, 271n8; on Kuna language, 192–193, 271nn5–6; *Literatura oral de los indios cunas*, 192; *Operación Panamá*, 192; *Tormenta en el Darién*, 192; and translation, 193, 271n7
Revolucíon Tule, 168, 196. See also Declaration of Human Rights of the Tule People of San Blas and the Darien; Kuna rebellion
Reynolds, Rene, 99
Richmond Brown, Lady Lilian Mabel, 124, 272n25
rights: discourse on, 86, 260n50, 260n52
Río Azúcar (Kwebdi, Wargandi), 32, 85, 117, 122; Nordenskiöld in, 148; schools, 40
Río Bayano (Reverte), 191
Río Caimán Nuevo, Colombia, 128
Río Sambú, 120
Río Sidra, 101
Río Tigre (Digir), 181
ritual knowledge and prestige, in Kuna society, 27–28, 149–150, 161–162, 235–238. See also *immar wisid*
Robinson, Charlie (Charles J.), 22–24, 25, 31–32, 33, 37, 60, 66, 74, 75, 87, 99, 254n3; chief of Nargana, 23; Coope, 52–53, 59; and Kuna culture, suppression of, 31–32; letters and writing, 46–49, 51, 52–53; and rebellion, 71
Robinson, Charles J. (sea captain), 22
Robinson, William, 180–181
Rodriguez, Faustino, 224
Rosaldo, Renato: on colonial nostalgia, 249–250
Roughing It in the San Blas Islands (Tinnin), 181
Route 17 (for projected canal), 194–195
Rubio, Angel, 185–186, 191, 270n35
Rudolf, Gloria, 208
Rus, Jan, "Rereading Tzotzil Ethnography," 20

Sáenz, Moisés, 166, 188
sagla dummagan (great chiefs), 164. See also cacique
ságuila. See *sailas*
Sahlins, Marshall: on hegemony, 8–9; on power, 13
Said, Edward, 7, 10–11, 14; *Orientalism*, 8; on western power, 12. See also orientalism
sailas (chiefs), 27, 66, 73, 258nn20–21. See also chiefs
Sta. María la Antigua del Darién, 128
Salcedo, Gonzalo, 224
Salcedo, Laurentino, 224
Salesian order, 31
Salvador, Mari Lyn, 201, 205; *The Art of Being Kuna*, 208, 225; *Yer Dailege!*, 208
Samblaseños, Sanblasinos. See Kuna
San Andrés. See Providencia
San Blas, an Account of the Cuna Indians of Panama (McKim), 182
San Blas Cuna Acculturation: An Introduction (Stout), 187
San Blas Indians (Kuna), 89, 90, 90; and Westerners, early encounters with, ix–xi. See also Kuna; Tule
San Blas. See Coast of San Blas
Sancurman. See Colman, Cimral
sand, refusal to sell, 95–96, 115–116, 261n9. See also Panama Canal
San Ignacio de Tupile. See Tupile
Sanjek, Roger, 16
Santiago (town), 167
Sapir, Edward, 120
Sasardi (Mulatupu), 30, 65, 67, 74, 91, 92, 194
Sayre, Gordon, 97, 110, 249
Schmidt, Wilhelm, 119, 149
schooling: beginnings, 22–26; and Catholic Church, 41, 255n16; and conquest, 25–26; of females, 24; government, 41; and Kuna society, 4–5, 26–32, 43–44; in Latin America, 27; and literacy, 3, 5; and nationalism, 25–26; in Panama, 27, 41; and Protestant Church, 41; students, *41*; urban, 40, 41
Scotland: colony in San Blas, x, 147, 266n13
Scott, James: on domination and resistance, 8–9
scribes, Kuna, 5, 34, 44, 58–59, 111, 246; Maya, 4. See also secretaries; *sikkwi*
"scriptural economy," 5–6, 58
Secretariat of Government and Justice (Panama). See Secretary of Government and Justice
secretaries, Kuna, 5, 34, 50, 59–60, 110, 256n16; limited Spanish of, 59–62. See also scribes, *sikkwi*
Secretary of Government and Justice (Panama), 45, 54, 55, 69, 78, 260n52
Secrets of the Cuna Earthmother (Keeler), 198
separatism, Kuna, 115, 165, 261n8; and endogamy, 97–99
Sepúlveda-Las Casas debate, 253n4
Sequoyah, 4
Severi, Carlo, 153; *La memoria ritual*, 225
Severino de Santa Teresa, Padre, 146
sexuality in representations of indigenous culture, 95–99, 110, 127–128, 264n21. See also separatism
Sexual Life of Savages, The (Malinowski), 119
Sherzer, Dina, 202
Sherzer, Joel, 202–203, 225, 229, 236, 271n28; on Kuna speech, 202–203, 203–204, 205; *Kuna Ways of Speaking*, 203–204, 226; on molas, 201; Nordenskiöld, compared to, 204; picture writing, 155; on ritual knowledge, distribution of, 161
sia bibi (name), 262n31
Sia igar, Sia igar kialed (the Cacao Way), 36, 236, 276n35
sikkwi, 34, 35–40. See also scribes; secretaries

Smith, Lino: Kuna language, 219
Smith, Sherry, 13; on representation of indigenous people, 9
Smith, Victoriano. *See* Aiban Wagwa
social class, social mobility, 57–58, 88, 112–113
Society of Americanists, 138
Solis, José: picture writing, 267nn28–29
Sommers, Doris, 209
Soo, Francisco. *See* Harding, Joe
Soo, Manual Jesús, 254n3
Soowadin. *See* Harding, Joe
Sosa, Julio: *La india dormida*, 168
South, John Glover, 262n27, 262nn33–34; and rebellion, 107–111; and social class, 113
South America, 118, 119
Spain, 2, 5; colonists in San Blas, 147; conflict with Scots, x
Spanish language: and Catholicism, 30; and the Kuna, 29–30; orthography, 142; and Panamanian nationalism, 30
Spirit of the Earth, Our Spirit, 238
Spirit of Kuna Yala, 276n34
Spivak, Gayatri, 253n6; "Can the Subaltern Speak?" 10
Squillacciotti, Massimo, 203, 225
Steward, Julian, 120, 189
Stier, Frances, 203
Stigma (Goffman), 57
Stirling, Matthew: on chichas, 181, 236
Stoler, Ann: *Tensions of Empire*, 14–15
Stout, David, 198; on acculturation, 188–189; Nordenskiöld, comparison with, 188–189; on Panamanian Indians, 19; *San Blas Cuna Acculturation: An Introduction*, 187
Stratagems and Spoils (Bailey), 6
Ström, Carl, 130
Structural Anthropology (Lévi-Strauss), 152

sualibed (town constable), 28
subalterns, xi, 253n7; silencing of, 10; portrayals of, 12–13
Suitupu. *See* Carti Suitupu
Sullivan, Paul: *Unfinished Conversations*, 16
Summer Institute of Linguistics, 229
Supreme Court of Panama, 109
Sweig, Renée, 201
Szok, Peter, 169

"Tad Ibe gi namaket" (Chapin and Méndez), 204
Taussig, Michael, 98, 105–106, 160; *Mimesis and Alterity*, 17
Tecumseh, 97
Teng, Emma, 12
Tensions of Empire (Cooper, Stoler), 14–15
tesoro de San Blas, El (Falla), 208
third parties in discourse about Indians, 54, 70–73, 174–175, 258n16
Thomas, Nicholas, 10, 15, 18
Thompson, Pilip (Felipe Thompson, Tansen), 35, 37–38, 254n3
Thompson, Ricardo, 37, 254n3
Tice, Karin, 201, 203, 225
Tierra para el guaymí, 208
Tigantiki. *See* Niatupu
Tinnin, J. V.: *Roughing It in the San Blas Islands*, 181; on Kuna marriage, 269n30
Tiolele, Tiosaila. *See* religion, Kuna
Tocqueville, Alexis de, 97
Tormenta en el Darién (Reverte), 192
Torres de Araúz, Reina, 191, 193–198, 255n21, 269n30, 271n16; career, 196; *El Darién, etnoecología de una región histórica*, 195; ethnic integration and multiculturalism, 195–197; *Human Ecology of Route 17*, 195; on Marsh, 196–197; *La mujer cuna*, 194, 195; *Panamá indígena*, 194, 197; on Revolución Tule, 196–197; schooling, 193–

194; and Torrijos government, 196, 221
Torrijos, General Omar, 196, 221
tourism, 89, 199, 208–209, 239, 247–248, 260n1, 271n20. *See also* travel writing
trade, 29, 30, 56, 65, 66, 112–113
Tradiciones y Cantares de Panamá (Garay), 169–173
translation, 32–34, 46–47, 83, 110–111, 142, 193, 271n7
travel writing, 199–200. *See also* tourism
Tulan, 105, 107, 184
Tule (Kuna), x, xi; flag, 117. *See also* San Blas Indians
Tule Declaration. *See* Declaration of Human Rights and Independence of the Tule People of San Blas and Darien
Tulenega, x
Tule sunnat (true Kuna), 248
Tummba (spurious name for Kuna heaven), 186
Tupile (Danakwe Dupir), 24, 38, 39; schools, 25
Tuppak. *See* Isla Pino
Turpana, Arysteides, 207, 220, 243, 273n46
Twiren, 237

Uhle, Max, 118
Ukkup Senni. *See* Playón Chico
UNESCO, 225, 236
Unfinished Conversations (Sullivan), 16–17
Urabá, 148
"Urraca, Biographical Sketch of a National Hero" (Alba), 167
Urraca, Chief, 167, 168, 186, 191, 268n1, 268n3
U.S. Canal administration, 46
U.S. Information Service, 204
U.S. Legation (Panama), 25, 46, 232
U.S. Protectorate, 105, 107
U.S. State Department, 107

uso de la chicha y la sociedad kuna, El (Prestán), 220, 236
U.S.S. Cleveland, 107, 109, 111
Ustupu, 40, 103, 117, 122, 125, 128, 139; schools, 41, 73, 264n22. *See also* Portogandi

Vaglio, Humberto, Intendente, 38–39, 53, 55, 61, 86, 87, 254n10; on Kuna resistance, 70; and suppression of Kuna culture, 54, 71–72, 258n12
Valdés, Ramón: *Geografía de Panamá*, 158, 257n4, 267n32
Valery, Paul, 137, 264n31
VandeCastle, Robert: on Kuna seers, 198–199
Ventocilla, Jorge, 197, 225
Victoria, Queen, 54
Villa Rojas, Alfonso, 16
Volleyball with the Cuna Indians and Other Gay Travel Adentures (Ebensten), 199

Wagwa, Aiban. *See* Aiban Wagwa
Wafer, Lionel, ix, x, 65, 121, 187
Walburger, Jacobo. *See* Balburger
Wali, Alaka, 203, 272n31
Washington, D.C., 37
Wassén, S. Henry, 140, 141, 143, 145, 150, 151, 152, 155, 179, 182, 219, 265n1, 271n6
Watt, Ian: "Consequences of Literacy, The," 3
Wellin, Christopher: on ethnography, 17
Whorfian analysis, 229
Wiboet Ikala, 275n8
Williams, Raymond: on hegemony, 8
Wissler, Clark, 120
Wogan, Peter, 3
World War II, 173, 187, 201
Wounán Chocó, 194, 208, 247
writing, xi, 1; and evangelization, 3; and indigenous struggles, 3–5; and the Kuna, 26–32, 46; and

material gain, 28; and mediation, 6–7; uses of, 45–46. *See also* letters; literacy

Yabiliginya, Chief. *See* Igwa-Yabiliginya
Yaginyanilele, x
Yaviza, 102
Yer Dailege! (Salvador), 208

Yucatán, 188
Yucatec Maya: and writing, 4; and ethnography, 16–17

Zonians, 89, 97; advocacy of Kuna, 99–102; attitudes towards Indians, 89–90; fraternal organizations, 89
Zuni. *See* "Pueblo" Indians